EDEXCEL BIOLOGY 1

A-Level Year 1/AS Student Workbook

EDEXCEL BIOLOGY 1
A-Level Year 1/AS **Student Workbook**

Meet the Writing Team

Tracey
Senior Author

Tracey Greenwood
I have been writing resources for students since 1993.
I have a Ph.D in biology, specialising in lake ecology and I
have taught both graduate and undergraduate biology.

Lissa
Author

Lissa Bainbridge-Smith
I worked in industry in a research and development
capacity for 8 years before joining BIOZONE in 2006.
I have an M.Sc from Waikato University.

Kent
Author

Kent Pryor
I have a BSc from Massey University majoring in zoology
and ecology and taught secondary school biology and
chemistry for 9 years before joining BIOZONE as an
author in 2009.

Richard
Founder & CEO

Richard Allan
I have had 11 years experience teaching senior
secondary school biology. I have a Masters degree
in biology and founded BIOZONE in the 1980s after
developing resources for my own students.

Thanks to:

The staff at BIOZONE, including Gemma Conn and Julie Fairless for design and
graphics support, Paolo Curray for IT support, Debbie Antoniadis and Tim Lind
for office handling and logistics, and the BIOZONE sales team.

Cover Photograph

The leopard (*Panthera pardus*) is found mainly in
sub-Saharan Africa although it once inhabited
areas in the Middle East and West Asia. It
occupies a range of habitats including rainforests
and grasslands. Leopards are opportunistic
hunters, using their well camouflaged coat to
move close to prey and their strength and speed
to capture it. Leopards can sometimes be found
in melanistic forms, known as black panthers.

Photo: art9858/ www.dollarphotoclub.com

First edition 2015

ISBN 978-1-927309-25-4

Copyright © 2015 Richard Allan
Published by **BIOZONE** International Ltd

Printed by REPLIKA PRESS PVT LTD using paper produced
from renewable and waste materials

Purchases of this workbook may be
made direct from the publisher:

BIOZONE

BIOZONE Learning Media (UK) Ltd.

Telephone local: 01283 530 366
Telephone international: +44 1283 530 366

Fax local: 01283 831 900
Fax international: +44 1283 831 900

Email: sales@biozone.co.uk

www.**BIOZONE**.co.uk

Contents

Activity is marked: ⬜ to be done; ☑ when completed

Contents

Activity is marked: ● to be done; ✓ when completed

Using This Workbook

This first edition of Edexcel Biology 1 has been specifically written to meet the content and skills requirements of AS/A Level Edexcel Biology. Learning outcomes in the introduction to each chapter provide you with a concise guide to the knowledge and skills requirements for each section of work. Each learning outcome is matched to the activity or activities addressing it. The eight core practicals for AS are identified in the chapter introductions by a code (*CP-#*) and supported by activities designed to provide background and familiarity with apparatus, techniques, experimental design, and interpretation of results. A range of activities will help you to build on what you already know, explore new topics, work collaboratively, and practise your skills in data handling and interpretation. We hope that you find the workbook valuable and that you make full use of its features.

▶ The outline of the chapter structure below will help you to navigate through the material in each chapter.

Introduction
- A check list of understandings, applications, and skills for the chapter.
- A list of key terms.

Activities
- The KEY IDEA provides your focus for the activity.
- Annotated diagrams help you understand the content.
- Questions review the content of the page.

Review
- Create your own summary for review.
- Hints help you to focus on what is important.
- Your summary will consolidate your understanding of the content in the chapter.

Literacy
- Activities are based on, but not restricted to, the introductory key terms list.
- Several types of activities test your understanding of the concepts and biological terms in the chapter.

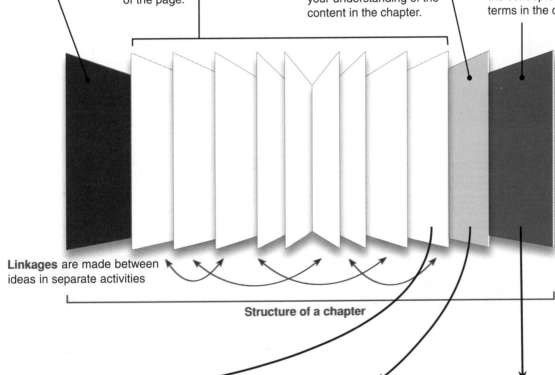

Linkages are made between ideas in separate activities

Structure of a chapter

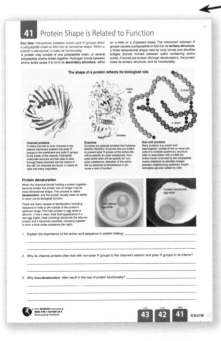

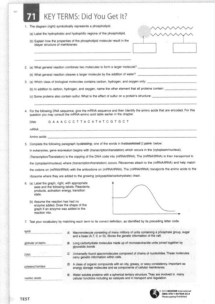

▶ Understanding the activity coding system and making use of the online material identified will enable you to get the most out of this resource. The chapter content is structured to build knowledge and skills but this structure does not necessarily represent a strict order of treatment. Be guided by your teacher, who will assign activities as part of a wider programme of independent and group-based work.

Look out for these features and know how to use them:

The **chapter introduction** provides you with a summary of the knowledge and skills requirements for the topic, phrased as a set of learning outcomes. Use the check boxes to identify and mark off the points as you complete them. The chapter introduction also provides you with a list of key terms for the chapter, from which you can construct your own glossary as you work through the activities.

The **activities** form most of this workbook. They are numbered sequentially and each has a task code identifying the skill emphasised. Each activity has a short introduction with a key idea identifying the main message of the page. Most of the information is associated with pictures and diagrams, and your understanding of the content is reviewed through the questions. Some of the activities involve modelling and group work.

Free response questions allow you to use the information provided to answer questions about the content of the activity, either directly or by applying the same principles to a new situation. In some cases, an activity will assume understanding of prior content.

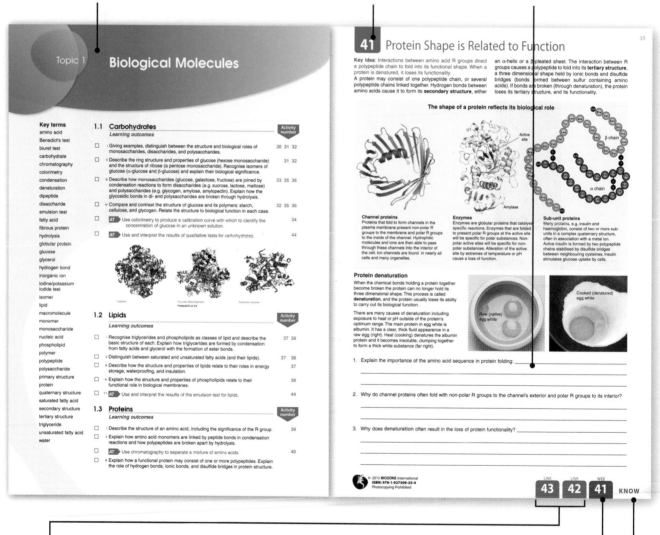

LINK tabs at the bottom of the activity page identify activities that are related in that they build on content or apply the same principles to a new situation.

WEB tabs at the bottom of the activity page alert the reader to the **Weblinks** resource, which provides external, online support material for the activity, usually in the form of an animation, video clip, photo library, or quiz. Bookmark the Weblinks page (see next page) and visit it frequently as you progress through the workbook.

A **TASK CODE** on the page tab identifies the type of activity. For example, is it primarily information-based (KNOW), or does it involve modelling or practical work (PRAC), or data handling (DATA)? A full list of codes is given on the following page but the codes themselves are relatively self-explanatory.

Using the Tab System

The tab system is a useful system for quickly identifying related content and online support. Links generally refer to activities that build on the information in the activity in depth or extent. In the example below, activity 41 provides information on how the shape of a protein is related to its functional role in an organism. Activities 42 and 43 cover protein folding and the structure of globular and fibrous proteins respectively, each examining the topic in more detail. Sometimes, a link will reflect on material that has been covered earlier as a reminder for important terms that have already been defined or for a formula that may be required to answer a question. The weblinks code is always the same as the activity number on which it is cited. On visiting the webink page (below), find the number and it will correspond to one or more external websites providing a video or animation of some aspect of the activity's content. Occasionally, the webiink may access a reference paper of provide a bank of photographs where images are provided in colour, e.g. for plant and animal histology.

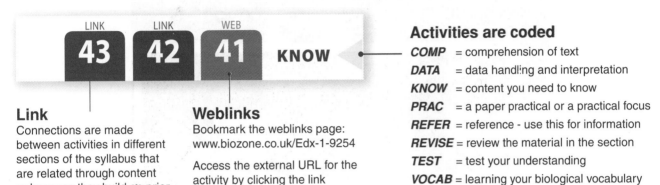

LINK	LINK	WEB	
43	**42**	**41**	KNOW

Activities are coded

COMP = comprehension of text
DATA = data handling and interpretation
KNOW = content you need to know
PRAC = a paper practical or a practical focus
REFER = reference - use this for information
REVISE = review the material in the section
TEST = test your understanding
VOCAB = learning your biological vocabulary

Link
Connections are made between activities in different sections of the syllabus that are related through content or because they build on prior knowledge.

Weblinks
Bookmark the weblinks page:
www.biozone.co.uk/Edx-1-9254

Access the external URL for the activity by clicking the link

www.biozone.co.uk/Edx-1-9254

This WEBLINKS page provides links to **external web sites** with supporting information for the activities. These sites are separate to those provided in the BIOLINKS area of BIOZONE's web site. Almost exclusively, they are narrowly focused animations and video clips directly relevant to the activity on which they are cited. They provide great support to aid student understanding of basic concepts, especially for visual learners.

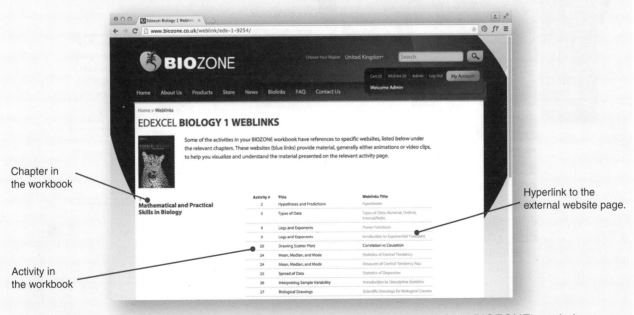

Chapter in the workbook

Hyperlink to the external website page.

Activity in the workbook

Bookmark weblinks by typing in the address: it is not accessible directly from BIOZONE's website
Corrections and clarifications to current editions are always posted on the weblinks page

Using BIOZONE's Website

Access the **BIOLINKS** database of web sites directly from the homepage of our website.

Contact us with questions, feedback, ideas, and critical commentary. We welcome your input.

Use Google to search for websites of interest. The more precise your search words are, the better the list of results. Be specific, e.g. "biotechnology medicine DNA uses", rather than "biotechnology".

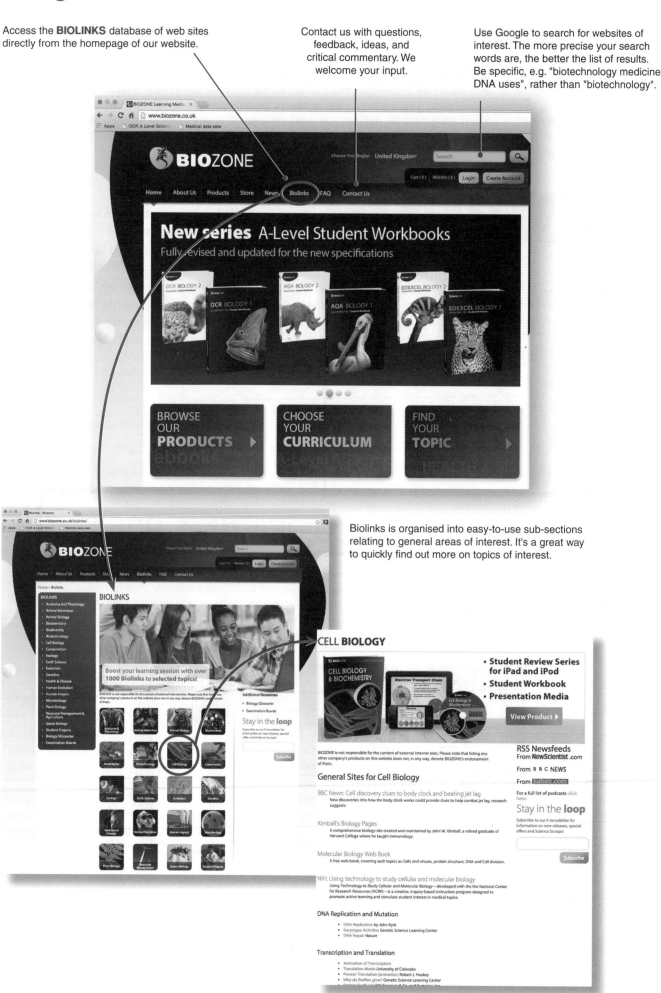

Biolinks is organised into easy-to-use sub-sections relating to general areas of interest. It's a great way to quickly find out more on topics of interest.

Practical & Mathematical
Skills in Biology
Also supported in Edexcel Biology 2

Key terms

accuracy

assumption

bar graph

chi-squared test

control

controlled variable

correlation

dependent variable

fair test

histogram

hypothesis

independent variable

line graph

mean

median

mode

observation

percentage error

precision

prediction

quantitative data

qualitative data

sample

scatter graph

standard deviation

statistical test

Student's *t* test

variable

CP AS core practical activities

Core practicals supported as indicated

		Activity number
☐	1 Investigate the effect of a named variable (e.g. temperature or substrate concentration) on the rate of an enzyme controlled reaction.	63
☐	2 Set up and use a light microscope, including simple stage micrometer and eyepiece graticule, to examine and measure specimen material. Draw cells from a specialised plant or animal tissue.	89 90 94
☐	3 Prepare stained squashes of cells from a plant root tip to show stages of mitosis in the meristem under a light microscope..	93 101
☐	4 Investigate the effect of sucrose concentrations on the growth of pollen tubes.	119
☐	5 Investigate the effect of temperature on the permeability of plasma membranes, e.g. in beetroot.	164
☐	6 Determine the water potential of plant tissue, e.g. by using a calibration curve based on a dilution series of a solute.	168 169
☐	7 Dissect an insect to show the structure of the gas exchange system.	182
☐	8 Use a potometer to investigate factors affecting water uptake (and loss) by shoots.	213

  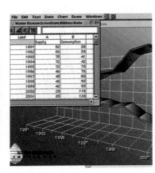

AT Use of apparatus and techniques

Supported as indicated but also throughout Edexcel Biology 1 & 2

		Activity number
☐	1 Use appropriate apparatus to record a range of quantitative data, including mass, time, volume, temperature, length, and pH.	12 90
☐	2 Use appropriate instrumentation, such as a colorimeter or potometer, to record quantitative data.	34 213
☐	3 Use laboratory glassware for a range of techniques, including serial dilution.	12 168
☐	4 Use a light microscope (including graticule) at high and low power.	89 90
☐	5 Make annotated scientific drawings from observations.	27 94
☐	6 Use qualitative reagents to identify biological molecules.	4 44
☐	7 Separate biological compounds, e.g. mixtures of monosaccharides, amino acids, or pigments, using thin layer or paper chromatography or gel electrophoresis.	40 126
☐	8 Record physiological functions and plant or animal responses safely and ethically.	180 197
☐	9 Use aseptic techniques in microbiological investigations.	78 Edx 2
☐	10 Use dissection equipment safely.	182 194
☐	11 Use sampling techniques e.g. quadrats, transects, in fieldwork.	151 Edx2
☐	12 Use ICT, e.g in computer modelling or to collect or process data.	13 23

Practical skills for assessment
Supported as indicated but also throughout Edexcel Biology 1 & 2

Activity number

☐ a Independent thinking
Solve problems in a practical context. Apply scientific knowledge to practical contexts. Apply investigative approaches and methods to practical work.

5 29

☐ b Use and application of scientific methods and practices
Evaluate experimental design and methods. Use practical equipment and materials, following written instructions, and making and recording observations and measurements. Collect, process, and present data appropriately. Evaluate results and draw conclusions with reference to measurement errors.

5 12-14
28 213

☐ c Research and referencing. Use of mathematics in a practical context
Plot and interpret graphs. Process and analyse data. Consider margins of error, and accuracy and precision of data. Use online and offline research skills. Correctly cite sources of information.

1 6 15-24

☐ d Instruments and equipment
Demonstrate an understanding of how a range of instruments, equipment, and techniques are used in experimental work.

65 92 93
168 213

Mathematical skills
Supported as indicated but also throughout Edexcel Biology 1 & 2

Activity number

A0: Arithmetic and numerical computation

☐ 1 Recognise and use appropriate units in calculations. | 6 7

☐ 2 Recognise and use expressions in both decimal and standard form. | 7 11

☐ 3 Carry out calculations involving fractions, percentages, and ratios. | 8 11

☐ 4 Estimate results to assess if calculated values are appropriate. | 7

☐ 5 Use a calculator to find and use power, exponential, and logarithmic functions (AL). | 9

A1: Handling data

☐ 1 Use an appropriate number of significant figures in reporting calculations. | 6

☐ 2 Find arithmetic means for a range of data. | 24 28

☐ 3 Represent and interpret frequency data in the form of bar graphs and histograms. | 16 17 26

☐ 4 Demonstrate an understanding of simple probability. | 150

☐ 5 Show understanding of the principles of sampling as applied to scientific data and analyse random data collected by an appropriate sampling method. | 150-153

☐ 6 Calculate or compare mean, mode, and median for sample data. | 24 26 28

☐ 7 Plot and interpret scatter graphs to identify correlation between two variables. | 19 20

☐ 8 Make order of magnitude calculations, e.g. in calculating magnification. | 91

☐ 9 Select and apply appropriate statistical tests to analyse and interpret data, e.g. the chi-squared test, the Student's t test, and Spearman's rank correlation. | 22 23 & Edx2

☐ 10 Understand and use measures of dispersion, e.g. standard deviation and range. | 25 26

☐ 11 Identify and determine uncertainties in measurements. | 12

A2: Algebra

☐ 1 Demonstrate understanding of the symbols =, <, <<, >>, >, ∝, ~ | 7

☐ 2 Manipulate equations to change the subject. | 84

☐ 3 Substitute numerical values into algebraic equations using appropriate units. | 21 152

☐ 4 Solve algebraic equations. | 8 196

☐ 5 Use logs in relation to quantities ranging over several orders of magnitude (AL). | 9

A3: Graphs

☐ 1 Translate information between graphical, numerical, and algebraic forms. | 21

☐ 2 Select an appropriate format to plot two variables from experimental or other data. | 15

☐ 3 Predict or sketch the shape of a graph with a linear relationship ($y = mx + c$). | 21

☐ 4 Determine the intercept of a graph (AL). | 21

☐ 5 Calculate rate of change from a graph showing a linear relationship. | 21 64

☐ 6 Draw and use the slope of a tangent to a curve as a measure of rate of change. | 64

A4: Geometry and trigonometry

☐ 1 Calculate the circumferences, surface areas, and volumes of regular shapes. | 10

1 How Do We Do Science?

Key Idea: The scientific method is a rigorous process of observation, measurement, and analysis that helps us to explain phenomena and predict changes in a system.
Scientific knowledge is gained through a non-linear, dynamic process called the **scientific method**. The scientific method is not a strict set of rules to be followed, but rather a way of approaching problems in a rigorous, but open-minded way. It involves inspiration and creativity, it is dynamic and context dependent, and usually involves collaboration. The model below is one interpretation of the scientific method.

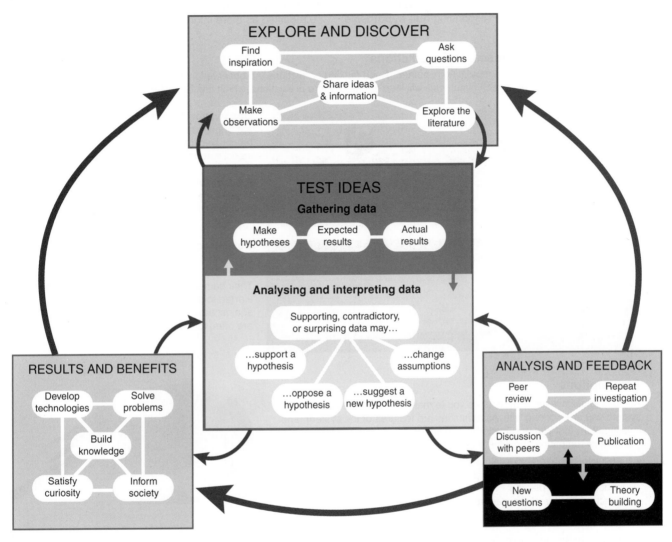

Citation and reference by numbers

Introduction

Hemoglobin is surely the most studied of all proteins. Indeed, the molecular analysis of hemoglobin has been the testing ground for many contemporary ideas and concepts in biology, particularly the understanding of the crystallographic structure and structure-function relationship of proteins, ligand binding, structural transitions between conformers, allosteric interactions, and others (1,2).

The ability of the aerobic metabolism of animals to satisfy the demands for... only possible thanks to the role... such as hemoglobins, contained i... or erythrocytes, which facilitate t... tion of large quantities of gas and...

References

1. Perutz MF. Species adaptation in a protein molecule. *Adv Protein Chem* 1984; 36: 213-244.
2. Berenbrink M. Evolution of vertebrate haemoglobins: Histidine side chains, specific buffer value and Bohr effect. *Respir Physiol Neurobiol* 2006; 154: 165-184.
3. Giardina B, Mosca D, De Rosa MC. The Bohr effect of haemoglobin

Citation and reference by authors

the long-term viability of a population. **Individual fitness, resistance to disease and parasites, and the ability of populations to respond to environmental changes may decrease as a con...** (Lacy 1997). Al...
"bottlenecks, ft...

Author

Keller, L. F., P. Arcese, J. N. M. Smith, W. M. Hochachka, and S. C. Stearns. 1994. Selection against inbred Song Sparrows during a natural population bottleneck. Nature 372:356-357.
Lacy, R. C. 1997. Importance of genetic variation to the viability of mammalian populations. Journal of Mammalogy 78:320-335.
Lande, R. 1999. Extinction risks from anthropogenic, ecological and genetic factors. Pages 1-22 in L. F. Landweber and A. P. Dobson,

Year Title Publication Volume and pages

The style you choose is not as important as being consistent, thorough, and honest about drawing on other people's work.
All the information needed to locate the reference should be included (above).

Citation and references

All scientific work acknowledges sources of information through citation and a list of references. Citations support the statements made in the text in context, and **all** citations are then listed alphabetically, or identified and referenced sequentially by number. Internet sites are dated and site author acknowledged.

Thorough and accurate citation and referencing shows you have explored the topic, have evidence to support your work, and you are not taking credit for work that is not your own. Each publication sets its own particular referencing style and these can vary widely. In your own work, it is most important to be consistent.

1. What is the role of citation and correct referencing when reporting on scientific investigations? _____

_____

2. Study the diagram and write a paragraph on the scientific process and the role of surprising results in the progression of science. Staple it to this page. At the end of your course, reexamine what you wrote. Have your ideas changed?

LINK **132**   LINK **55**   LINK **51**   LINK **47**   LINK **28**

KNOW

2 Hypotheses and Predictions

Key Idea: Observations are the basis for forming hypotheses and making predictions about systems. An assumption is something that is accepted as true but is not tested.

A **hypothesis** offers a tentative explanation to questions generated by observations and leads to one or more predictions about the way a biological system will behave. For every hypothesis, there is a corresponding **null hypothesis**:

a hypothesis of no difference or no effect. A null hypothesis allows a hypothesis to be tested using statistical tests. If the experimental results are statistically significant, the null hypothesis can be rejected. If a hypothesis is accepted, anyone should be able to test the predictions with the same methods and get a similar result. Scientific hypotheses may be modified as more information becomes available.

Observations, hypotheses, and predictions

Observation is the basis for formulating hypotheses and making predictions. An observation may generate a number of plausible hypotheses, and each hypothesis will lead to one or more predictions, which can be tested by further investigation.

Observation 1: Some caterpillar species are brightly coloured and appear to be conspicuous to predators such as insectivorous (insect-eating) birds.

Predators appear to avoid these species. These caterpillars are often found in groups, rather than as solitary animals.

Observation 2: Some caterpillar species are cryptic in their appearance or behaviour.

Their camouflage is so convincing that, when alerted to danger, they are difficult to see against their background. Such caterpillars are often found alone.

Assumptions

Any biological investigation requires you to make assumptions about the system you are working with. Assumptions are features of the system (and investigation) that you assume to be true but do not (or cannot) test. Possible assumptions about the biological system described above include:

- insectivorous birds have colour vision;
- caterpillars that look bright or cryptic to us, also appear that way to insectivorous birds; and
- insectivorous birds can learn about the palatability of prey by tasting them.

1. Study the example above illustrating the features of cryptic and conspicuous caterpillars, then answer the following:

   (a) Generate a hypothesis to explain the observation that some caterpillars are brightly coloured and conspicuous while others are cryptic and blend into their surroundings:

   Hypothesis: _____

   _____

   _____

   (b) State the null form of this hypothesis: _____

   _____

   (c) Describe one of the **assumptions** being made in your hypothesis:_____

   _____

   _____

   (d) Based on your hypothesis, generate a **prediction** about the behaviour of insectivorous birds towards caterpillars:

   _____

   _____

© 2015 **BIOZONE** International
ISBN: 978-1-927309-23-4
Photocopying Prohibited

3 Types of Data

Key Idea: Data is information collected during an investigation. Data may be quantitative, qualitative, or ranked.

Data is information collected during an investigation and it can be quantitative, qualitative, or ranked (below). When planning a biological investigation, it is important to consider the type of data that will be collected. It is best to collect quantitative data, because it is mathematically versatile and easier to analyse it objectively (without bias).

Types of data

Quantitative (interval or ratio)

Characteristics for which measurements or counts can be made, e.g. height, weight, number.
Summary measures: mean, median, standard deviation.

Qualitative (nominal)

Non-numerical and descriptive, e.g. sex, colour, viability (dead/alive), presence or absence of a specific feature.
Summary measures: frequencies and proportions

e.g. Sex of children in a family (male, female)

Ranked (ordinal)

Data are ranked on a scale that represents an order, although the intervals between the orders on the scale may not be equal, e.g. abundance (abundant, common, rare). Summary measures: frequencies and proportions

e.g. Birth order in a family (1, 2, 3)

Discontinuous (discrete)

e.g. Number of children in a family (3, 0, 4)

Continuous

e.g. Height of children in a family (1.5 m, 0.8 m)

Discontinuous or discrete data:
The unit of measurement cannot be split up (e.g. can't have half a child).

Continuous data:
The unit of measurement can be a part number (e.g. 5.25 kg).

1. For each of the photographic examples A-C below, classify the data as quantitative, ranked, or qualitative:

A: Skin colour

B: Eggs per nest

C: Tree trunk diameter

(a) Skin colour: _____

(b) Number of eggs per nest: _____

(c) Tree trunk diameter: _____

2. Why is it best to collect quantitative data where possible in biological studies? _____
_____
_____

3. Give an example of data that could not be collected quantitatively and explain your answer: _____
_____
_____

4. Students walked a grid on a football field and ranked plant species present as abundant, common, or rare. How might they have collected and expressed this information more usefully?
_____
_____

LINK 5   LINK 4   WEB 3   **KNOW**

4 Making A Qualitative Investigation

Key Idea: Qualitative data is non-numerical and descriptive. Qualitative data is more difficult to analyse and interpret objectively than quantitative data. It is also more likely to be biased. However, sometimes it is appropriate to collect qualitative data, e.g. when recording colour changes in simple tests for common components of foods. Two common tests for carbohydrates are the iodine/potassium iodide test for starch and the Benedict's test for reducing sugars, such as glucose. These tests indicate the presence of a substance with a colour change. All monosaccharides are reducing sugars as are the disaccharides, lactose and maltose. The monosaccharide fructose is a ketose, but it gives a positive test because it is converted to glucose in the reagent. When a starchy fruit ripens, the starch is converted to reducing sugars.

The aim
To investigate the effect of ripening on the relative content of starch and simple sugars in bananas.

The tests

Iodine-potassium iodide test for starch
The sample is covered with the iodine in potassium iodide solution. The sample turns blue-black if starch is present.

Benedict's test for reducing sugars
The sample is heated with the reagent in a boiling water bath. After 2 minutes, the sample is removed and stirred, and the colour recorded immediately after stirring. A change from a blue to a brick red colour indicates a reducing sugar.

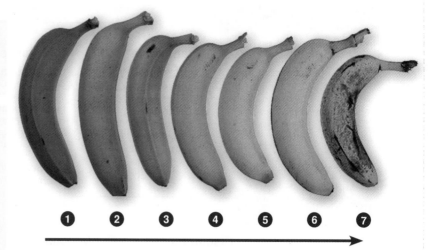

| Green unripe and hard | | | Bright yellow ripening but firm with green tip | | | Mottled yellow/brown ripe and soft |

Summary of the method

Two 1 cm thick slices of banana from each of seven stages of ripeness were cut and crushed to a paste. One slice from each stage was tested using the I/KI test for starch, and the other was tested using the Benedict's test.

The colour changes were recorded in a table. Signs (+/–) were used to indicate the intensity of the reaction relative to those in bananas that were either less or more ripe.

Stage of ripeness	Starch-iodine test		Benedict's test	
1	blue-black	+++++	blue clear	–
2	blue-black	++++	blue clear	–
3	blue-black	+++	green	+
4	blue-black	++	yellow cloudy	++
5	slight darkening	+	orange thick	+++
6	no change	–	orangey-red thick	++++
7	no change	–	brick-red thick	+++++

1. Explain why each of the following protocols was important:

   (a) All samples of banana in the Benedict's reagent were heated for 2 minutes: _____

   _____

   (b) The contents of the banana sample and Benedict's reagent were stirred after heating: _____

   _____

2. Explain what is happening to the relative levels of starch and glucose as bananas ripen: _____

   _____

   _____

3. Fructose is a ketose sugar (not an aldose with an aldehyde functional group like glucose).

   (a) Explain why fructose also gives a positive result in a Benedict's test: _____

   _____

   (b) What could this suggest to you about the results of this banana test? _____

   _____

© 2015 **BIOZONE** International
ISBN: 978-1-927309-25-4
Photocopying Prohibited

5 Making A Quantitative Investigation

Key Idea: Practical work carried out in a careful and methodical way makes analysis of the results much easier.

The next stage after planning an experiment is to collect the data. Practical work may be laboratory or field based. Typical laboratory based experiments involve investigating how a biological response is affected by manipulating a particular **variable**, e.g. temperature. The data collected for a quantitative practical task should be recorded systematically, with due attention to safe practical techniques, a suitable quantitative method, and accurate measurements to an appropriate degree of precision. If your quantitative practical task is executed well, and you have taken care throughout, your evaluation of the experimental results will be much more straightforward and less problematic.

Carrying out your practical work

Preparation

Familiarise yourself with the equipment and how to set it up. If necessary, calibrate equipment to give accurate measurements.

Read through the methodology and identify key stages and how long they will take.

Execution

Identify any **assumptions** you make about your set up. Assumptions are features of the system that you assume to be true but do not (or cannot) test. Know how you will take your measurements, how often, and to what degree of precision.

Recording

Record your results systematically, in a hand-written table or on a spreadsheet.

Record your results to the appropriate number of significant figures according to the precision of your measurement.

Identifying variables

A variable is any characteristic or property able to take any one of a range of values. Investigations often look at the effect of changing one variable on another. It is important to identify all variables in an investigation: independent, dependent, and controlled, although there may be nuisance factors of which you are unaware. In all fair tests, only one variable is changed by the investigator.

Dependent variable

- Measured during the investigation.
- Recorded on the y axis of the graph.

Controlled variables

- Factors that are kept the same or controlled.
- List these in the method, as appropriate to your own investigation.

Independent variable

- Set by the experimenter.
- Recorded on the graph's x axis.

Experimental controls

A control refers to standard or reference treatment or group in an experiment. It is the same as the experimental (test) group, except that it lacks the one variable being manipulated by the experimenter. Controls are used to demonstrate that the response in the test group is due a specific variable (e.g. temperature). The control undergoes the same preparation, experimental conditions, observations, measurements, and analysis as the test group. This helps to ensure that responses observed in the treatment groups can be reliably interpreted.

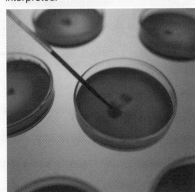

The experiment above tests the effect of a certain nutrient on microbial growth. All the agar plates are prepared in the same way, but the control plate does not have the test nutrient applied. Each plate is inoculated from the same stock solution, incubated under the same conditions, and examined at the same set periods. The control plate sets the baseline; any growth above that seen on the control plate is attributed to the presence of the nutrient.

Examples of investigations

Aim		Variables	
Investigating the effect of varying...	on the following...	Independent variable	Dependent variable
Temperature	Leaf width	Temperature	Leaf width
Light intensity	Activity of woodlice	Light intensity	Woodlice activity
Soil pH	Plant height at age 6 months	pH	Plant height

© 2015 **BIOZONE** International
ISBN: 978-1-927309-25-4
Photocopying Prohibited

LINK 213 LINK 65 LINK 28

KNOW

Investigation: catalase activity

Catalase is an enzyme that converts hydrogen peroxide (H_2O_2) to oxygen and water.

An experiment to investigate the effects of temperature on the rate of the catalase reaction is described below.

- 10 cm³ test tubes were used for the reactions, each tube contained 0.5 cm³ of catalase enzyme and 4 cm³ of H_2O_2.

- Reaction rates were measured at four temperatures (10°C, 20°C, 30°C, 60°C).

- For each temperature, there were two reaction tubes (e.g. tubes 1 and 2 were both kept at 10°C).

- The height of oxygen bubbles present after one minute of reaction was used as a measure of the reaction rate. A faster reaction rate produced more bubbles than a slower reaction rate.

- The entire experiment was repeated on two separate days.

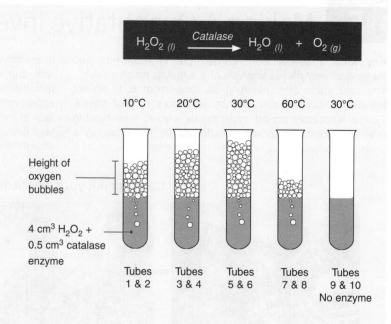

$$H_2O_2 \,_{(l)} \xrightarrow{\text{Catalase}} H_2O \,_{(l)} + O_2 \,_{(g)}$$

Height of oxygen bubbles

4 cm³ H_2O_2 + 0.5 cm³ catalase enzyme

| 10°C | 20°C | 30°C | 60°C | 30°C |
| Tubes 1 & 2 | Tubes 3 & 4 | Tubes 5 & 6 | Tubes 7 & 8 | Tubes 9 & 10 No enzyme |

1. Write a suitable aim for this experiment: _____

_____

2. Write an hypothesis for this experiment: _____

_____

3. (a) What is the independent variable in this experiment? _____

   (b) What is the range of values for the independent variable? _____

   (c) Name the unit for the independent variable: _____

   (d) List the equipment needed to set the independent variable, and describe how it was used: _____

   _____

   _____

   _____

4. (a) What is the dependent variable in this experiment? _____

   (b) Name the unit for the dependent variable: _____

   (c) List the equipment needed to measure the dependent variable, and describe how it was used: ____

   _____

5. (a) Each temperature represents a treatment/sample/trial (circle one):

   (b) How many tubes are at each temperature? _____

   (c) What is the sample size for each treatment? _____

   (d) How many times was the whole investigation repeated? _____

6. Which tubes are the control for this experiment? _____

7. Identify three variables that might have been controlled in this experiment, and how they could have been monitored:

   (a) _____

   (b) _____

   (c) _____

6 Accuracy and Precision

Key Idea: Accuracy refers to the correctness of a measurement (how true it is to the real value). Precision refers to how close the measurements are to each other.

Accuracy refers to how close a measured or derived value is to its true value. Simply put, it is the correctness of the measurement. Precision refers to the closeness of repeated measurements to each other, i.e. the ability to be exact. A balance with a fault in it could give very precise (repeatable) but inaccurate (untrue) results. Data can only be reported as accurately as the measurement of the apparatus allows and is often expressed as significant figures (the digits in a number that express meaning to a degree of accuracy).

The accuracy of a measurement refers to how close the measured (or derived) value is to the true value. The precision of a measurement relates to its repeatability. In most laboratory work, we usually have no reason to suspect a piece of equipment is giving inaccurate measurements (is biased), so making precise measures is usually the most important consideration. We can test the precision of our measurements by taking repeated measurements from individual samples.

Population studies present us with an additional problem. When a researcher makes measurements of some variable in a study (e.g. fish length), they are usually trying to obtain an estimate of the true value for a parameter of interest, e.g. the mean size (which is correlated with age) of fish. Populations are variable, so we can more accurately estimate a population parameter if we take a large number of random samples from the population.

Accurate but imprecise	**Inaccurate and imprecise**	**Precise but inaccurate**	**Accurate and precise**

The measurements are all close to the true value but quite spread apart.	The measurements are all far apart and not close to the true value.	The measurements are all clustered close together but not close to the true value.	The measurements are all close to the true value and also clustered close together.
Analogy: The arrows are all close to the bullseye.	**Analogy**: The arrows are spread around the target.	**Analogy**: The arrows are all clustered close together but not near the bullseye.	**Analogy**: The arrows are clustered close together near the bullseye.

Significant figures

Significant figures (sf) are the digits of a number that carry meaning contributing to its precision. They communicate how well you could actually measure the data.

For example, you might measure the height of 100 people to the nearest cm. When you calculate their mean height, the answer is 175.0215 cm. If you reported this number, it implies that your measurement technique was accurate to 4 decimal places. You would have to round the result to the number of significant figures you had accurately measured. In this instance the answer is 175 cm.

Non-zero numbers (1-9) are always **significant**.

All zeros between non-zero numbers are always **significant**.

$$0.005704510$$

Zeros to the left of the first non-zero digit after a decimal point are **not significant**.

Zeros at the end of number where there is a decimal place are **significant** (e.g. 4600.0 has five sf).
BUT
Zeros at the end of a number where there is no decimal point are **not significant** (e.g. 4600 has two sf).

1. Distinguish between accuracy and precision: _____

_____

_____

2. State the number of significant figures in the following examples:

(a) 3.15985 _____ (b) 0.0012 _____

(c) 1000 _____ (d) 1000.0 _____

(e) 42.3006 _____ (f) 120 _____

© 2015 **BIOZONE** International
ISBN: 978-1-927309-25-4
Photocopying Prohibited

LINK

7

DATA

7 Working with Numbers

Key Idea: Using correct mathematical notation and being able to carry out simple calculations and conversions are fundamental skills in biology.

Mathematics is used in biology to analyse, interpret, and compare data. It is important that you are familiar with mathematical notation (the language of mathematics) and can confidently apply some basic mathematical principles and calculations to your data.

Commonly used mathematical symbols

In mathematics, universal symbols are used to represent mathematical concepts. They save time and space when writing. Some commonly used symbols are shown below.

=   Equal to

<   The value on the left is **less than** the value on the right

<<   The value on the left is **much less than** the value on the right

>   The value on the left is **greater than** the value on the right

>>   The value on the left is **much greater than** the value on the right

∝   Proportional to. A ∝ B means that A = a constant X B

~   Approximately equal to

Conversion factors and expressing units

Measurements can be converted from one set of units to another by the use of a **conversion factor**.

A conversion factor is a numerical factor that multiplies or divides one unit to convert it into another. Conversion factors are commonly used to convert non-SI units to SI units (e.g. converting pounds to kilograms). Note that mL and cm^3 are equivalent, as are L and dm^3.

In the space below, convert 5.6 cm^3 to mm^3 (1 cm^3 = 1000 mm^3):

1. _____

The value of a variable must be written with its units where possible. SI units or their derivations should be used in recording measurements: volume in cm^3 or dm^3, mass in kilograms (kg) or grams (g), length in metres (m), time in seconds (s).

For example the rate of oxygen consumption would be expressed:

Oxygen consumption$/cm^3 g^{-1} s^{-1}$

cm^3/gs

Estimates

When carrying out mathematical calculations, typing the wrong number into your calculator can put your answer out by several orders of magnitude. An **estimate** is a way of roughly calculating what answer you should get, and helps you decide if your final calculation is correct.

Numbers are often rounded to help make estimation easier. The rounding rule is, if the next digit is 5 or more, round up. If the next digit is 4 or less, it stays as it is.

For example, to estimate 6.8 x 704 you would round the numbers to 7 x 700 = 4900. The actual answer is 4787, so the estimate tells us the answer (4787) is probably right.

Use the following examples to practise estimating:

2.   43.2 x 1044: _____

3.   3.4 x 72 ÷ 15: _____

4.   658 ÷ 22: _____

Decimal and standard form

Decimal form (also called ordinary form) is the longhand way of writing a number (e.g. 15 000 000). Very large or very small numbers can take up too much space if written in decimal form and are often expressed in a condensed **standard form**. For example, 15 000 000 is written as 1.5×10^7 in standard form.

In standard form a number is always written as $A \times 10^n$, where A is a number between 1 and 10, and n (the exponent) indicates how many places to move the decimal point. n can be positive or negative.

For the example above, A = 1.5 and n = 7 because the decimal point moved seven places (see below).

$$1.5\ 000\ 000 = 1.5 \times 10^7$$

Small numbers can also be written in standard form. The exponent (n) will be negative. For example, 0.00101 is written as 1.01×10^{-3}.

$$0.00101 = 1.01 \times 10^{-3}$$

Converting can make calculations easier. Work through the following example to solve $4.5 \times 10^4 + 6.45 \times 10^5$.

5.   Convert $4.5 \times 10^4 + 6.45 \times 10^5$ to decimal form:

_____

6.   Add the two numbers together: _____

7.   Convert to standard form: _____

Rates

Rates are expressed as a measure per unit of time and show how a variable changes over time. Rates are used to provide meaningful comparisons of data that may have been recorded over different time periods.

Often rates are expressed as a mean rate over the duration of the measurement period, but it is also useful to calculate the rate at various times to understand how rate changes over time. The table below shows the reaction rates for a gas produced during a chemical reaction. A worked example for the rate at 4 minutes is provided below the table.

Time / Minute	Cumulative gas produced / cm^3	Rate of reaction / $cm^3\ min^{-1}$
0	0	0
2	34	17
4	42	4*
6	48	3
8	50	1
10	50	0

* Gas produced between 2-4 min: 42 cm^3 − 34 cm^3 = 8 cm^3

Rate of reaction between 2-4 mins: 8 ÷ 2 minutes = 4 $cm^3\ min^{-1}$

© 2015 **BIOZONE** International
ISBN: 978-1-927309-25-4
Photocopying Prohibited

DATA

8 Fractions, Percentages, and Ratios

Key Idea: Percentages and ratios are alternative ways to express fractions. All forms are commonly used in biology. The data collected in the field or laboratory are called raw data. Data are often expressed in ways that make them easy to understand, visualise, and work with. Fractions, ratios, and percentages are widely used in biology and are often used to provide a meaningful comparison of sample data where the sample sizes are different.

Fractions

- Fractions express how many parts of a whole are present.

- Fractions are expressed as two numbers separated by a solidus (/) (e.g. 1/2).

- The top number is the numerator. The bottom number is the denominator. The denominator can not be zero.

- Fractions are often written in their simplest form (the top and bottom numbers cannot be any smaller, while still being whole numbers). Simplifying makes working with fractions easier.

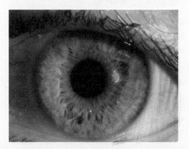

In a class of 20 students, five had blue eyes. This fraction is 5/20. To simplify this fraction, divide the numerator and denominator by a common factor (a number which both are divisible by). In this instance the lowest common factor is five (1/4). To add fractions with different denominators, obtain a common denominator, add numerators, then simplify.

Ratios

- Ratios give the relative amount of two or more quantities, and provide an easy way to identify patterns.

- Ratios do not require units.

- Ratios are usually expressed as a : b.

- Ratios are calculated by dividing all the values by the smallest number.

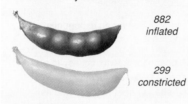

882 inflated

299 constricted

Pea pod shape:
Ratio = 2.95 : 1

495 round yellow

152 wrinkled yellow

158 round green

55 wrinkled green

Pea seed shape and colour:
Ratio = 9 : 2.8 : 2.9 : 1

Example: Calculating phenotype ratios in Mendelian genetics

Percentages

- Percentages are expressed as a fraction of 100 (e.g. 20/100 = 20%).

- Percentages provide a clear expression of what proportion of data fall into any particular category, e.g. for pie graphs.

- Allows meaningful comparison between different samples.

- Useful to monitor change (e.g. % increase from one year to the next).

Volume of food colouring / cm³	Volume of water / cm³	Concentration of solution / %
10	0	100
8	2	80
6	4	60
4	6	40
2	8	20
0	10	0

Example: Producing standards for a calibration curve.

---

1. (a) A student prepared a slide of the cells of an onion root tip and counted the cells at various stages in the cell cycle. The results are presented in the table (right). Calculate the ratio of cells in each stage (show your working):

    _____

    _____

    (b) Assuming the same ratio applies in all the slides examined in the class, calculate the number of cells in each phase for a cell total count of 4800.

Cell cycle stage	No. of cells counted	No. of cells calculated
Interphase	140	
Prophase	70	
Telophase	15	
Metaphase	10	
Anaphase	5	
Total	240	4800

2. Simplify the following fractions:

    (a) 3/9 : _____ (b) 84/90: _____ (c) 11/121: _____

3. In the fraction example pictured above 5/20 students had blue eyes. In another class, 5/12 students had blue eyes. What fraction of students had blue eyes in both classes combined?

    _____

4. The total body mass and lean body mass for women with different body types is presented in the table (right). Complete the table by calculating the % lean body mass column.

Women	Body mass / kg	Lean body mass / kg	% lean body mass
Athlete	50	38	
Lean	56	41	
Normal weight	65	46	
Overweight	80	48	
Obese	95	52	

DATA

9 Logs and Exponents

Key Idea: A function relates an input to an output. Functions are often defined through a formula that tells us how to compute the output for a given input. Logarithmic, power, and exponential functions are all common in biology.

A function is a rule that allows us to calculate an output for any given input. In biology, power functions are often observed in biological scaling, for example, heart beat slows with increasing size in mammals. Exponential growth is often seen in bacterial populations and also with the spread of viral diseases if intervention does not occur. The 2014 Ebola outbreak is one such example. The numbers associated with exponential growth can be very large and are often log transformed. Log transformations reduce skew in data and make data easier to analyse and interpret.

Power function

Power functions are a type of scaling function showing the relationship between two variables, one of which is usually size.

- In power functions, the base value is variable and the exponent (power number) is fixed (constant).

- The equation for an exponential function is $y = x^c$.

- Power functions are not linear, one variable changes more quickly relative to the other.

- Examples of power functions include metabolic rate versus body mass (below), or surface area to volume ratio.

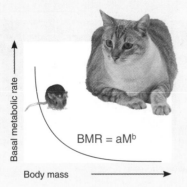

$$BMR = aM^b$$

Example: Relationship between body mass and metabolic rate.
M = mass and a and b are constants.

Exponential function

Exponential growth occurs at an increasingly rapid rate in proportion to the growing total number or size.

- In an exponential function, the base number is fixed (constant) and the exponent is variable.

- The equation for an exponential function is $y = c^x$.

- Exponential growth is easy to identify because the curve has a J-shape appearance due to its increasing steepness over time. It grows more rapidly than a power function

- Examples of exponential growth include the growth of microorganisms in an unlimiting growth environment.

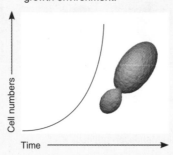

Example: Cell growth in a yeast culture in optimal growth conditions.

Log transformations

A log transformation has the effect of normalising data and making very large numbers easier to work with. Biological data often have a positive skew so log transformations can be very useful.

- The log of a number is the exponent to which a fixed value (the base) is raised to get that number. So $\log_{10}(1000) = 3$ because $10^3 = 1000$.

- Both $\log_{10}$ and $\log_e$ (natural logs or *ln*) are commonly used.

- Log transformations are useful for data where there is an exponential increase in numbers (e.g. cell growth).

- Log transformed data will plot as a straight line.

- To find the $\log_{10}$ of a number, e.g. 32, using a calculator, key in [log] [32] = . The answer should be 1.51.

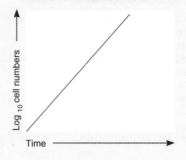

Example: Yeast cell growth plotted on logarithmic scale.

1. Describe the relationship between body mass and metabolic rate: _____
_____

2. Describe the difference between a power function and exponential growth: _____
_____
_____
_____

3. (a) On what type of data would you carry out a log transformation? _____
_____

(b) What is the purpose of a log transformation? _____
_____
_____

10 Properties of Geometric Shapes

Key Idea: Circumference, surface area, and volume are useful calculations that can be applied in biological situations. Biology often requires you to evaluate the effect of a physical property, such as cell volume, on function. For example, how does surface area to volume ratio influence the transport of materials into a cell? The cells of organisms, and sometimes the organisms themselves, are often rather regular shapes, so their physical properties (e.g. cell volume or surface area) can be calculated (or approximated) using the simple formulae applicable to standard geometric shapes.

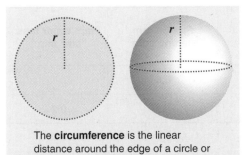   

The **circumference** is the linear distance around the edge of a circle or sphere and is given by the formula $2\pi r$

| r = radius | l = length | w = width | h = height | π = 3.14 |

	Sphere	Cube	Rectangular prism	Cylinder
Biological example	*Staphylococcus* bacterial cell	Kidney tubule cell	Intestinal epithelial cell	Axon of neuron
Surface area: The sum of all areas of all shapes covering an object's surface.	$4\pi r^2$	$6w^2$	$2(lh + lw + hw)$	$(2\pi r^2) + (2\pi rh)$
Volume: The amount that a 3-dimensional shape can hold.	$\frac{4}{3}\pi r^3$	w^3	lwh	$\pi r^2 h$

1. For a sphere with a radius of 2 cm, calculate the:

   (a) Circumference: _____

   (b) Surface area: _____

   (c) Volume: _____

2. For a rectangular prism with the dimensions l = 3 mm, w = 0.3 mm, and h = 2 mm calculate the:

   (a) Surface area: _____

   (b) Volume: _____

3. For a cylinder with a radius of 4.9 cm and height of 11 cm, calculate the:

   (a) Surface area: _____

   (b) Volume: _____

4. Find the height of a rectangular prism with a volume of 48 cm³, a length of 4 cm, and a width of 2.5 cm: _____

   _____

5. Find the radius of a cylinder with a volume of 27 cm³ and a height of 3 cm: _____

   _____

6. A spherical bacterium with a radius of 0.2 µm divides in two. Each new cell has a radius that is 80% of the original cell.

   (a) Calculate the surface area of the 'parent' bacterial cell: _____

   (b) Calculate the volume of the 'parent' bacterial cell: _____

   (c) Calculate the surface area of each new cell: _____

   (d) Calculate the volume of each new cell: _____

   (e) Which cell has the greatest surface area to volume ratio: _____

LINK 170 LINK 86 LINK 85 DATA

11 Practising with Data

Key Idea: This activity allows you to practise working with data and applying the skills you have learned in previous activities.

1. Complete the transformations for each of the tables below. The first value is provided in each case.

(a) Photosynthetic rate at different light intensities

Light intensity / %	Average time for leaf disc to float / min	Reciprocal of time* / min^{-1}
100	15	0.067
50	25	0.005
25	50	
11	93	
6	187	

Reciprocal of time gives a crude measure of rate.

(b) Plant water loss using a bubble potometer

Time / min	Pipette arm reading / cm^3	Plant water loss / cm^3 min^{-1}
0	9.0	–
5	8.0	0.2
10	7.2	
15	6.2	
20	4.9	

(c) Incidence of cyanogenic clover in different areas

Clover plant type	Frost free area		Frost prone area		Totals
	Number	%	Number	%	
Cyanogenic	124	78	26		
Acyanogenic	35		115		
Total	159				

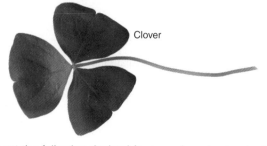

Clover

(d) Frequency of size classes in a sample of eels

Size class / mm	Frequency	Relative frequency / %
0-50	7	2.6
50-99	23	
100-149	59	
150-199	98	
200-249	50	
250-299	30	
300-349	3	
Total	270	

2. Convert the following decimal form numbers to standard form:

(a) 8970 _____   (b) 0.046 _____   (c) 1 467 851 _____

3. Convert the following standard form numbers to decimal form:

(a) 4.3×10^{-1} _____   (b) 0.0031×10^{-2} _____   (c) 6.2×10^4 _____

4. (a) The table on the right shows the nutritional label found on a can of chilli beans. Use the information provided to complete the table by calculating the percentage composition for each of the nutritional groups listed:

(b) How much of the total carbohydrates is made up of:

Dietary fibre? _____

Sugars? _____

(c) Manufacturers do not have to state the volume of water, which makes up the remainder of the serving size. What percentage of the can of beans is water?

_____

Chilli Beans Nutrition Facts Serving size 1 cup (253 g)	
Amount per serving	% Composition
Total Fat 8 g	
– Saturated Fat 3 g	
Total Carbohydrate 22 g	
– Dietary Fibre 9 g	
– Sugars 4 g	
Protein 25 g	

© 2015 **BIOZONE** International
ISBN: 978-1-927309-25-4
Photocopying Prohibited

12 Apparatus and Measurement

Key Idea: The apparatus used in experimental work must be appropriate for the experiment or analysis and it must be used correctly to eliminate experimental errors.
Using scientific equipment can generate experimental errors.

These can be reduced by selecting the right equipment for what you want to measure and by using it correctly. Some error is inevitable, but evaluating experimental error helps to interpret and assess the validity of the results.

Selecting the correct equipment

When measuring physical properties it is vital that you choose equipment that is appropriate for the type of measurement you want to take. For example, if you wanted to accurately weigh out 5.65 g of sucrose, you need a balance that accurately weighs to two decimal places. A balance that weighs to only one decimal place would not allow you to make an accurate enough measurement.

Study the glassware (right). Which would you use if you wanted to measure 225 mL? The graduated cylinder has graduations every 10 mL whereas the beaker has graduations every 50 mL. It would be more accurate to measure 225 mL in a graduated cylinder.

Recognising potential sources of error

It is important to know how to use equipment correctly to reduce errors. A spectrophotometer measures the amount of light absorbed by a solution at a certain wavelength. This information can be used to determine the concentration of the absorbing molecule (e.g. density of bacteria in a culture). The more concentrated the solution, the more light is absorbed. Incorrect use of the spectrophotometer can alter the results. Common mistakes include incorrect calibration, errors in sample preparation, and errors in sample measurement.

Percentage errors

Percentage error is a way of mathematically expressing how far out your result is from the ideal result. The equation for measuring percentage error is:

$$\frac{\text{experimental value - ideal value}}{\text{ideal value}} \times 100$$

For example, you want to know how accurate a 5 mL pipette is. You dispense 5 mL of water from a pipette and weigh the dispensed volume on a balance. The volume is 4.98 mL.

$$\frac{\text{experimental value (4.98) - ideal value (5.0)}}{\text{ideal value (5.0)}} \times 100$$

The percentage error = –0.4% (the negative sign tells you the pipette is dispensing **less** than it should).

A cuvette (left) is a small clear tube designed to hold spectrophotometer samples. Inaccurate readings occur when:

- The cuvette is dirty or scratched (light is absorbed giving a falsely high reading).

- Some cuvettes have a frosted side to aid alignment. If the cuvette is aligned incorrectly, the frosted side absorbs light, giving a false reading.

- Not enough sample is in the cuvette and the beam passes over, rather than through the sample, giving a lower absorbance reading.

---

1. Assume that you have the following measuring devices available: 50 mL beaker, 50 mL graduated cylinder, 25 mL graduated cylinder, 10 mL pipette, 10 mL beaker. What would you use to accurately measure:

   (a) 21 mL: _____   (b) 48 mL: _____   (c) 9 mL: _____

2. Calculate the percentage error for the following situations (show your working):

   (a) A 1 mL pipette delivers a measured volume of 0.98 mL: _____

   _____

   (b) A 10 mL pipette delivers a measured volume of 9.98 mL: _____

   _____

   (c) The pipettes used in (a) and (b) above both under-delivered 0.02 mL, yet the percentage errors are quite different. Use this data to describe the effect of volume on percentage error:

   _____

   _____

KNOW

13 Recording Results

Key Idea: Accurately recording results in a table makes it easier to understand and analyse your data later.

A table is a good way to record your results systematically, both during the course of your experiment and in presenting your results. A table can also be used to show calculated values, such as rates or means. An example of a table for recording results is shown below. It relates to an investigation of the net growth of plants at three pH levels, but it represents a relatively standardised layout. The labels on the columns and rows are chosen to represent the design features of the investigation. The first column shows the entire range of the independent variable. There are spaces for multiple sampling units, repeats (trials), and calculated mean values. A version of this table would be given in the write-up of the experiment.

Dependent variable and its units

Space for repeats of the experimental design (in this case, three trials).

All masses are in grams and to the nearest 0.1 g.

Space for three plants at each pH

The range of values for the independent variable are in this column

Recordings of the dependent variable

Space for calculated means

		Trial 1 / plant mass in grams						Trial 2 / plant mass in grams						Trial 3 / plant mass in grams					
		Day No.						Day No.						Day No.					
		0	2	4	6	8	10	0	2	4	6	8	10	0	2	4	6	8	10
pH 3	1	0.5	1.1																
	2	0.6	1.2																
	3	0.7	1.3																
	Mean	0.6	1.2																
pH 5	1	0.6	1.4																
	2	0.8	1.7																
	3	0.5	1.9																
	Mean	0.6	1.7																
pH 7	1	0.7	1.3																
	2	0.8	1.3																
	3	0.4	1.7																
	Mean	0.6	1.4																

1. In the box (below) design a table to collect data from the case study below. Include space for individual results and averages from the three set ups (use the table above as a guide).

CO$_2$ levels in a respiration chamber

A datalogger was used to monitor the concentrations of carbon dioxide (CO$_2$) in respiration chambers containing five green leaves from one plant species. The entire study was performed in conditions of full light (quantified) and involved three identical set-ups.

The CO$_2$ concentrations were measured every minute, over a period of 10 minutes, using a CO$_2$ sensor. A mean CO$_2$ concentration (for the three set-ups) was calculated. The study was carried out two more times, two days apart.

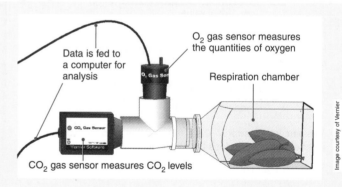

O$_2$ gas sensor measures the quantities of oxygen

Data is fed to a computer for analysis

Respiration chamber

CO$_2$ gas sensor measures CO$_2$ levels

Image courtesy of Vernier

2. Next, the effect of various light intensities (low light, half-light, and full light) on CO$_2$ concentration was investigated. How would the results table for this investigation differ from the one you have drawn above (for full light only):

_____

_____

LINK **26**   LINK **28**

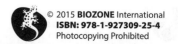
© 2015 **BIOZONE** International
ISBN: 978-1-927309-25-4
Photocopying Prohibited

14 Constructing Tables and Graphs

Key Idea: Tables and graphs provide a way to organise and visualise data in a way that helps to identify trends.

Tables and graphs are ways to present data and they have different purposes. **Tables** provide an accurate record of numerical values and allow you to organise your data so that relationships and trends are apparent. **Graphs** provide a visual image of trends in the data in a minimum of space.

It is useful to plot your data as soon as possible, even during your experiment, as this will help you to evaluate your results as you proceed and make adjustments as necessary (e.g. to the sampling interval). The choice between graphing or tabulation in the final report depends on the type and complexity of the data and the information that you are wanting to convey. Usually, both are appropriate.

Presenting data in tables

An accurate, descriptive title.

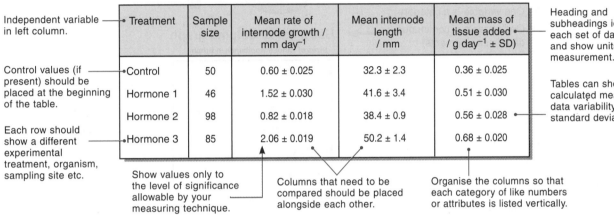

Table 1: Length and growth of the third internode of bean plants receiving three different hormone treatments (data are given ± standard deviation).

Independent variable in left column.

Control values (if present) should be placed at the beginning of the table.

Each row should show a different experimental treatment, organism, sampling site etc.

Treatment	Sample size	Mean rate of internode growth / mm day⁻¹	Mean internode length / mm	Mean mass of tissue added / g day⁻¹ ± SD)
Control	50	0.60 ± 0.025	32.3 ± 2.3	0.36 ± 0.025
Hormone 1	46	1.52 ± 0.030	41.6 ± 3.4	0.51 ± 0.030
Hormone 2	98	0.82 ± 0.018	38.4 ± 0.9	0.56 ± 0.028
Hormone 3	85	2.06 ± 0.019	50.2 ± 1.4	0.68 ± 0.020

Heading and subheadings identify each set of data and show units of measurement.

Tables can show a calculated measure of data variability (e.g. standard deviation).

Show values only to the level of significance allowable by your measuring technique.

Columns that need to be compared should be placed alongside each other.

Organise the columns so that each category of like numbers or attributes is listed vertically.

Presenting data in graph format

Plot points accurately. Different responses can be distinguished using different symbols, lines or bar colours.

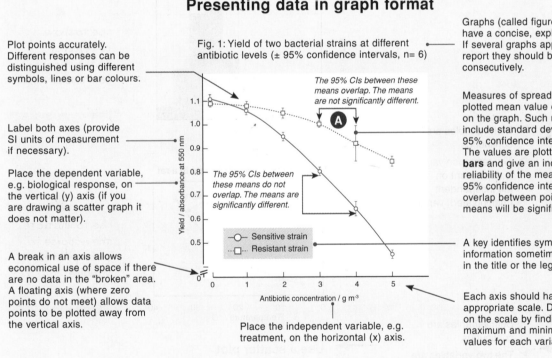

Fig. 1: Yield of two bacterial strains at different antibiotic levels (± 95% confidence intervals, n= 6)

Graphs (called figures) should have a concise, explanatory title. If several graphs appear in your report they should be numbered consecutively.

Label both axes (provide SI units of measurement if necessary).

Place the dependent variable, e.g. biological response, on the vertical (y) axis (if you are drawing a scatter graph it does not matter).

A break in an axis allows economical use of space if there are no data in the "broken" area. A floating axis (where zero points do not meet) allows data points to be plotted away from the vertical axis.

The 95% CIs between these means overlap. The means are not significantly different.

The 95% CIs between these means do not overlap. The means are significantly different.

Key (graph legend): Sensitive strain (○), Resistant strain (□)

Yield / absorbance at 550 nm (y-axis)
Antibiotic concentration / g m⁻³ (x-axis)

Measures of spread about the plotted mean value can be shown on the graph. Such measures include standard deviation and 95% confidence intervals (CI). The values are plotted as **error bars** and give an indication of the reliability of the mean value. If the 95% confidence intervals do not overlap between points, then these means will be significantly different.

A key identifies symbols. This information sometimes appears in the title or the legend.

Each axis should have an appropriate scale. Decide on the scale by finding the maximum and minimum values for each variable.

Place the independent variable, e.g. treatment, on the horizontal (x) axis.

1. What can you conclude about the difference (labelled A) between the two means plotted above? Explain your answer:

_____

2. Explain the reasons for including both graphs and tables in a final report: _____

_____

_____

_____

LINK
15

KNOW

15 Which Graph to Use?

Key Idea: The type of graph you choose to display your data depends on the type of data you have collected.

Before you graph your data, it is important to identify what type of data you have. Choosing the correct type of graph can highlight trends or reveal relationships between variables. Choosing the wrong type of graph can obscure information and make the data difficult to interpret. Examples of common types of graphs and when to use them are provided below.

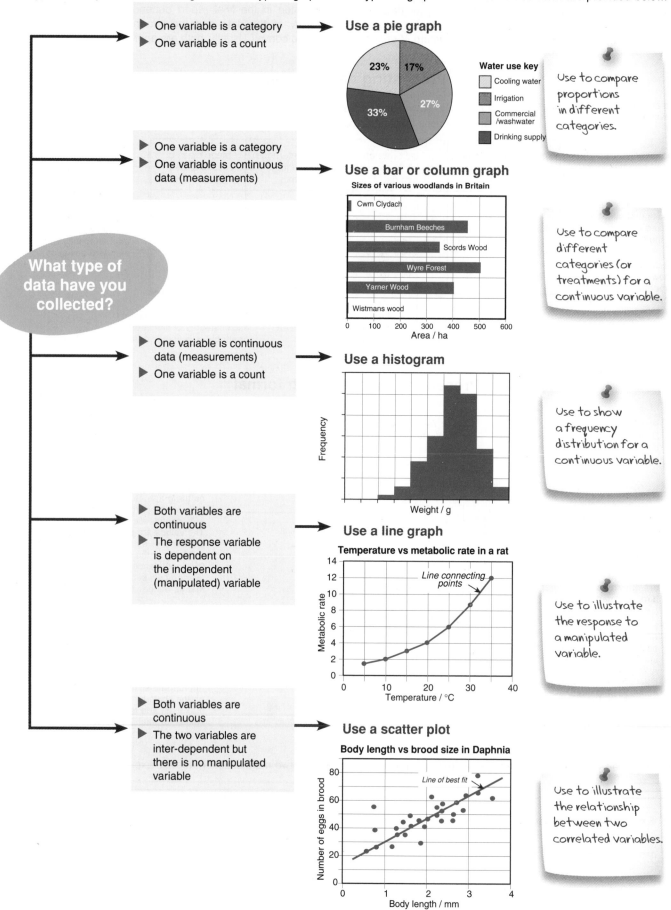

What type of data have you collected?

- One variable is a category
- One variable is a count

Use a pie graph

23% 17% 27% 33%

Water use key
- Cooling water
- Irrigation
- Commercial /washwater
- Drinking supply

Use to compare proportions in different categories.

- One variable is a category
- One variable is continuous data (measurements)

Use a bar or column graph

Sizes of various woodlands in Britain

Cwm Clydach
Burnham Beeches
Scords Wood
Wyre Forest
Yarner Wood
Wistmans wood

0 100 200 300 400 500 600
Area / ha

Use to compare different categories (or treatments) for a continuous variable.

- One variable is continuous data (measurements)
- One variable is a count

Use a histogram

Frequency

Weight / g

Use to show a frequency distribution for a continuous variable.

- Both variables are continuous
- The response variable is dependent on the independent (manipulated) variable

Use a line graph

Temperature vs metabolic rate in a rat

Line connecting points

Metabolic rate: 14, 12, 10, 8, 6, 4, 2, 0
Temperature / °C: 0 10 20 30 40

Use to illustrate the response to a manipulated variable.

- Both variables are continuous
- The two variables are inter-dependent but there is no manipulated variable

Use a scatter plot

Body length vs brood size in Daphnia

Line of best fit

Number of eggs in brood: 80, 60, 40, 20, 0
Body length / mm: 0 1 2 3 4

Use to illustrate the relationship between two correlated variables.

REFER LINK 16 LINK 17 LINK 18 LINK 20

16 Drawing Bar Graphs

Key Idea: Bar graphs are used to plot data that is non-numerical or discrete for at least one variable.

Guidelines for bar graphs

Bar graphs are appropriate for data that are non-numerical and **discrete** for at least one variable, i.e. they are grouped into categories. There are no dependent or independent variables. Important features of this type of graph include:

- Data are collected for discontinuous, non-numerical categories (e.g. colour, species), so the bars do not touch.

- Data values may be entered on or above the bars.

- Multiple sets of data can be displayed side by side for comparison (e.g. males and females).

- Axes may be reversed so that the categories are on the x axis, i.e. bars can be vertical or horizontal. When they are vertical, these graphs are called column graphs.

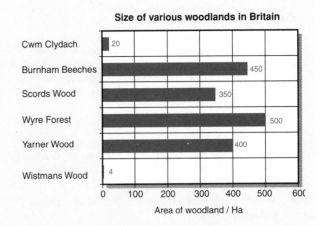

Size of various woodlands in Britain

1. Counts of eight mollusc species were made from a series of quadrat samples at two sites on a rocky shore. The summary data are presented here.

   (a) Tabulate the mean (**average**) numbers per square metre at each site in Table 1 (below left).

   (b) Plot a **bar graph** of the tabulated data on the grid below. For each species, plot the data from both sites side by side using different colours to distinguish the sites.

Mean abundance of 8 molluscan species from two sites along a rocky shore.

Species	Mean / no. m^{-2}	
	Site 1	Site 2

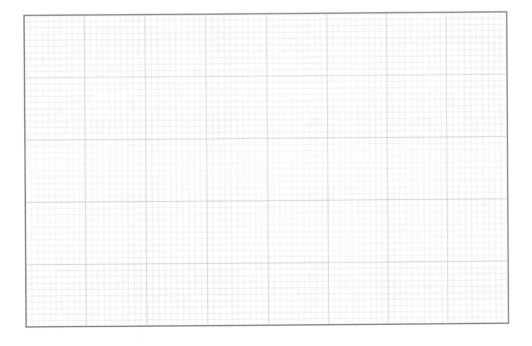

Field data notebook

Total counts at site 1 (11 quadrats) and site 2 (10 quadrats). Quadrats 1 sq m.

Species	Site 1 No m^{-2}		Site 2 No m^{-2}	
	Total	Mean	Total	Mean
Ornate limpet	232	21	299	30
Radiate limpet	68	6	344	34
Limpet sp. A	420	38	0	0
Cats-eye	68	6	16	2
Top shell	16	2	43	4
Limpet sp. B	628	57	389	39
Limpet sp. C	0	0	22	2
Chiton	12	1	30	3

DATA

17 Drawing Histograms

Key Idea: Histograms graphically show the frequency distribution of continuous data.

Guidelines for histograms

Histograms are plots of **continuous** data and are often used to represent frequency distributions, where the y-axis shows the number of times a particular measurement or value was obtained. For this reason, they are often called frequency histograms. Important features of this type of graph include:

- The data are numerical and continuous (e.g. height or weight), so the bars touch.

- The x-axis usually records the class interval. The y-axis usually records the number of individuals in each class interval (frequency).

- A neatly constructed tally chart doubles as a simple histogram.

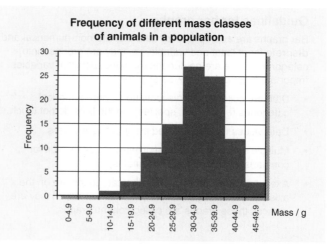

Frequency of different mass classes of animals in a population

1. The weight data provided below were recorded from 95 individuals (male and female), older than 17 years.

   (a) Create a tally chart (frequency table) in the frame provided, organising the weight data into a form suitable for plotting. An example of the tally for the weight grouping 55-59.9 kg has been completed for you as an example. Note that the raw data values are crossed off the data set in the notebook once they are recorded as counts on the tally chart. It is important to do this in order to prevent data entry errors.

   (b) Plot a **frequency histogram** of the tallied data on the grid provided below.

Weight / kg	Tally	Total
45~49.9		
50~54.9		
55~59.9	⑭ II	7
60~64.9		
65~69.9		
70~74.9		
75~79.9		
80~84.9		
85~89.9		
90~94.9		
95~99.9		
100~104.9		
105~109.9		

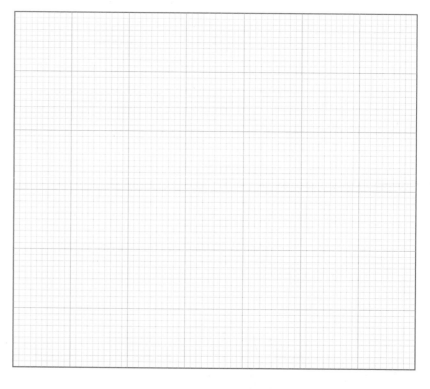

Lab notebook

Weight (in kg) of 95 individuals

63.4	81.2	65
56.5	83.3	75.6
84	95	76.8
81.5	105.5	67.8
73.4	82	68.3
56	73.5	63.5
60.4	75.2	58
83.5	63	58.5
82	70.4	50
61	82.2	92
55.2	87.8	91.5
48	86.5	88.3
53.5	85.5	81
63.8	87	72
69	98	66.5
82.8	71	61.5
68.5	76	66
67.2	72.5	65.5
82.5	61	67.4
83	60.5	73
78.4	67	67
76.5	86	71
83.4	85	70.5
77.5	93.5	65.5
77	62	68
87	62.5	90
89	63	83.5
93.4	60	73
83	71.5	66
80	73.8	57.5
76	77.5	76
56	74	

LINK

DATA 26

© 2015 **BIOZONE** International
ISBN: 978-1-927309-25-4
Photocopying Prohibited

18 Drawing Line Graphs

Key Idea: Line graphs are used to plot continuous data in which one variable (the independent variable) directly affects the other (dependent) variable. They are appropriate for data in which the independent variable is manipulated.

Guidelines for line graphs

Line graphs are used when one variable (the independent variable) affects another, the dependent variable. Line graphs can be drawn without a measure of spread (top figure, right) or with some calculated measure of data variability (bottom figure, right). Important features of line graphs include:

- The data must be continuous for both variables.

- The dependent variable is usually the biological response.

- The independent variable is often time or experimental treatment.

- In cases where there is an implied trend (e.g. one variable increases with the other), a line of best fit is usually plotted through the data points to show the relationship.

- If fluctuations in the data are likely to be important (e.g. with climate and other environmental data) the data points are usually connected directly (point to point).

- Line graphs may be drawn with measure of error. The data are presented as points (which are the calculated means), with bars above and below, indicating a measure of variability or spread in the data (e.g. standard error, standard deviation, or 95% confidence intervals).

- Where no error value has been calculated, the scatter can be shown by plotting the individual data points vertically above and below the mean. By convention, bars are not used to indicate the range of raw values in a data set.

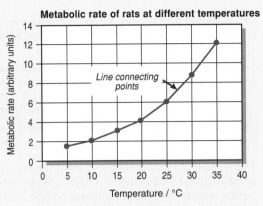

Metabolic rate of rats at different temperatures

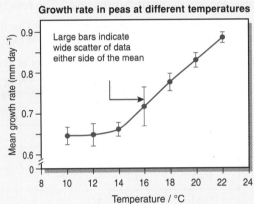

Growth rate in peas at different temperatures

1. The results (shown right) were collected in a study investigating the effect of temperature on the activity of an enzyme.

(a) Using the results provided (right), plot a line graph on the grid below:

(b) Estimate the rate of reaction at 15°C: _____

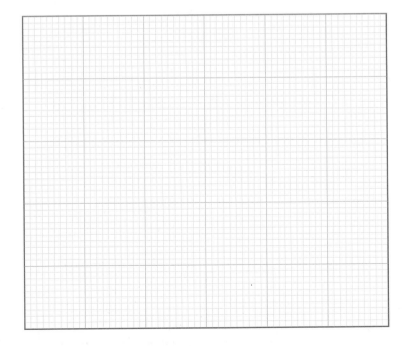

Lab Notebook

An enzyme's activity at different temperatures

Temperature / °C	Rate of reaction (mg of product formed per minute)
10	1.0
20	2.1
30	3.2
35	3.7
40	4.1
45	3.7
50	2.7
60	0

LINK **21** DATA

Plotting multiple data sets

A single figure can be used to show two or more data sets, i.e. more than one curve can be plotted per set of axes. This type of presentation is useful when comparing the trends for two or more treatments, or the response of one species against the response of another. Important points regarding this format are:

- If the two data sets use the same measurement units and a similar range of values for the independent variable, one scale on the y axis is used.

- If the two data sets use different units and/or have a very different range of values for the independent variable, two scales for the y axis are used (see example right). The scales can be adjusted if necessary to avoid overlapping plots

- The two curves must be distinguished with a key.

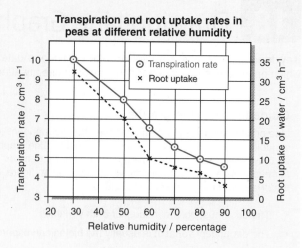

Transpiration and root uptake rates in peas at different relative humidity

2. The number of perch and trout in a hydro-electric reservoir were monitored over 19 years. A colony of black shag was also present. Shags feed on perch and (to a lesser extent) trout. In 1960-61, 424 shags were removed from the lake during the nesting season and nest counts were made every spring in subsequent years. In 1971, 60 shags were removed from the lake, and all existing nests dismantled. The results of the population survey are tabulated below.

(a) Plot a line graph (joining the data points) for the survey results. Use one scale (on the left) for numbers of perch and trout and another scale for the number of shag nests. Use different symbols to distinguish the lines and include a key.

(b) Use a vertical arrow to indicate the point at which shags and their nests were removed.

Year	Mean number of fish per haul		Shag nest numbers	Year (continued)	Mean number of fish per haul		Shag nest numbers
	Trout	Perch			Trout	Perch	
1960	–	–	16	1970	1.5	6	1.5
1961	–	–	4	1971	0.5	0.7	1.5
1962	1.5	11	5	1972	1	0.8	0
1963	0.8	9	10	1973	0.2	4	0
1964	0	5	22	1974	0.5	6.5	0
1965	1	1	25	1975	0.6	7.6	2
1966	1	2.9	35	1976	1	1.2	10
1967	2	5	40	1977	1.2	1.5	32
1968	1.5	4.6	26	1978	0.7	1.2	28
1969	1.5	6	32				

Source: Data adapted from 1987 Bursary Examination

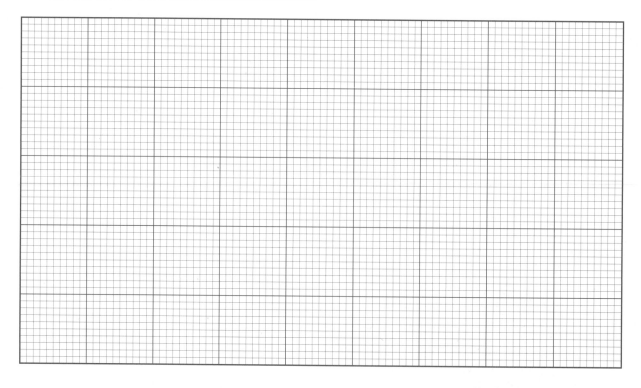

19 Correlation or Causation

Key Idea: A correlation is a mutual relationship or association between two or more variables. A correlation between two variables does not imply that one causes change in the other. Researchers often want to know if two variables have any **correlation** (relationship) to each other. This can be achieved by plotting the data as a scatter graph and drawing a line of best fit through the data, or by testing for correlation using a statistical test. The strength of a correlation is indicated by the correlation coefficient (r), which varies between 1 and -1. A value of 1 indicates a perfect (1:1) relationship between the variables. A value of -1 indicates a 1:1 negative relationship and 0 indicates no relationship between the variables.

Correlation does not imply causation

You may come across the phrase "correlation does not necessarily imply causation". This means that even when there is a strong correlation between variables (they vary together in a predictable way), you cannot assume that change in one variable caused change in the other.

Example: When data from the organic food association and the office of special education programmes is plotted (below), there is a strong correlation between the increase in organic food and rates of diagnosed autism. However it is unlikely that eating organic food causes autism, so we can not assume a causative effect here.

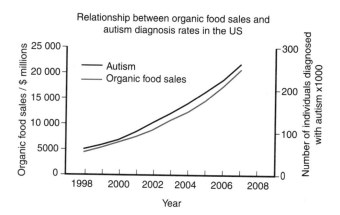

Relationship between organic food sales and autism diagnosis rates in the US

Drawing the line of best fit

Some simple guidelines need to be followed when drawing a line of best fit on your scatter plot.

▶ Your line should follow the trend of the data points.

▶ Roughly half of your data points should be above the line of best fit, and half below.

▶ The line of best fit does not necessarily pass through any particular point.

▶ The line of best fit should pivot around the point which represents the mean of the x and the mean of the y variables.

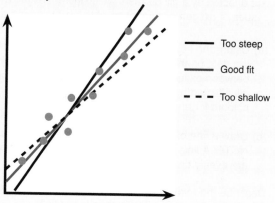

1. What does the phrase "correlation does not imply causation" mean? _____

_____

_____

2. A student measured the hand span and foot length measurements of 21 adults and plotted the data as a scatter graph (right).

   (a) Draw a line of best fit through the data:

   (b) Describe the results: _____

   _____

   _____

   _____

   _____

   (c) Using your line of best fit as a guide, comment on the correlation between handspan and foot length:

   _____

   _____

   _____

   _____

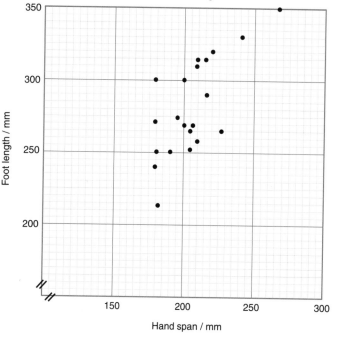

Hand span vs foot length in adults

20 Drawing Scatter Plots

Key Idea: Scatter graphs are used to plot continuous data where there is a relationship between two interdependent variables.

Guidelines for scatter graphs

A scatter graph is used to display continuous data where there is a relationship between two interdependent variables.

- The data must be continuous for both variables.

- There is no independent (manipulated) variable, but the variables are often correlated, i.e. they vary together in some predictable way.

- Scatter graphs are useful for determining the relationship (correlation) between two variables. A relationship does not imply that change in one variable causes change in the other variable.

- The points on the graph need not be connected, but a line of best fit is often drawn through the points to show the relationship between the variables (this may be drawn by eye or computer generated).

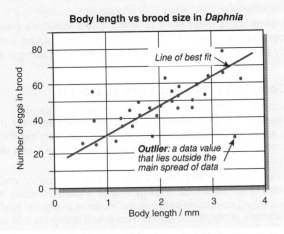

Body length vs brood size in *Daphnia*

Line of best fit

Outlier: a data value that lies outside the main spread of data

1. In the example below, metabolic measurements were taken from seven Antarctic fish *Pagothenia borchgrevinski*. The fish are affected by a gill disease, which increases the thickness of the gas exchange surfaces and affects oxygen uptake. The results of oxygen consumption of fish with varying amounts of affected gill (at rest and swimming) are tabulated below.

(a) Using **one** scale only for oxygen consumption, plot the data on the grid below to show the relationship between oxygen consumption and the amount of gill affected by disease. Use different symbols or colours for each set of data (at rest and swimming).

(b) Draw a line of best fit through each set of points. NOTE: A line of best fit is drawn so that the points are evenly distributed on either side of the line.

2. Describe the relationship between the amount of gill affected and oxygen consumption in the fish:

(a) For the **at rest** data set: _____

_____

_____

_____

_____

_____

(b) For the **swimming** data set: _____

_____

_____

_____

_____

_____

Oxygen consumption of fish with affected gills

Fish number	Percentage of gill affected	Oxygen consumption / cm³ g⁻¹ h⁻¹	
		At rest	Swimming
1	0	0.05	0.29
2	95	0.04	0.11
3	60	0.04	0.14
4	30	0.05	0.22
5	90	0.05	0.08
6	65	0.04	0.18
7	45	0.04	0.20

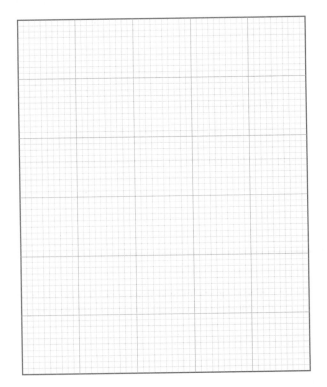

3. How does the gill disease affect oxygen uptake in resting fish? _____

_____

WEB LINK

DATA 20 21

© 2015 **BIOZONE** International
ISBN: 978-1-927309-25-4
Photocopying Prohibited

21 Interpreting Line Graphs

Key Idea: The equation for a straight line is y = mx + c. A line may have a positive, negative, or zero slope.

The equation for a linear (straight) line on a graph is y = mx + c. The equation can be used to calculate the gradient (slope) of a straight line and tells us about the relationship between x and y (how fast y is changing relative to x). For a straight line, the rate of change of y relative to x is always constant. A line may have a positive, negative, or zero slope.

Measuring gradients and intercepts

The equation for a straight line is written as:

y = mx + c

Where :

y = the y-axis value

m = the slope (or gradient)

x = the x-axis value

c = the y intercept (where the line cross the y-axis).

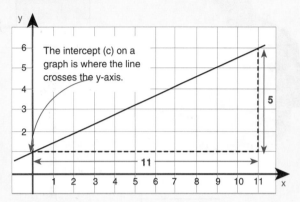

The intercept (c) on a graph is where the line crosses the y-axis.

Determining "m" and "c"

To find "c" just find where the line crosses the y-axis.

To find m:

1. Choose any two points on the line.

2. Draw a right-angled triangle between the two points on the line.

3. Use the scale on each axis to find the triangle's vertical length and horizontal length.

4. Calculate the gradient of the line using the following equation:

$$\frac{\text{change in y}}{\text{change in x}}$$

For the example above:

c = 1

m = 0.45 (5 ÷11)

Once c and m have been determined you can choose any value for x and find the corresponding value for y.

For example, when x = 9, the equation would be:

y = 9 x 0.45 + 1

y = 5.05

Interpreting gradients

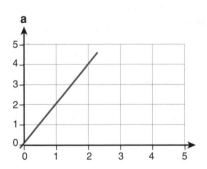

a

Positive gradients: the line slopes upward to the right (y is increasing as x increases).

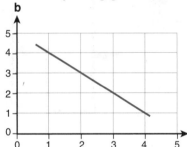

b

Negative gradients: the line slopes downward to the right (y is decreasing as x increases).

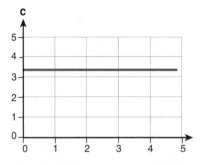

c

Zero gradients: the line is horizontal (y does not change as x increases).

1. State the gradient for graphs a, b, and c (above):   (a) _____   (b) _____   (c) _____

2. For a straight line y = 3x + 2,

   (a) Identify the value of c: _____   (b) Determine y if x = 4: _____

3. For the graph (right):

   (a) Identify the value of c: _____

   (b) Calculate the value of m: _____

   (c) Determine y if x = 2: _____

   _____

   (d) Describe the slope of the line: _____

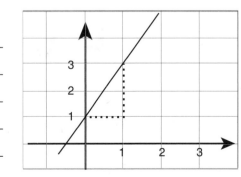

DATA

22 Which Test to Use?

Key Idea: How your data is analysed depends on the type of data you have collected. Plotting your initial data can help you to decide what statistical analysis to carry out.

Data analysis provides information on the biological significance of your investigation. Never under-estimate the value of plotting your data, even at a very early stage. This will help you decide on the best type of data analysis. Sometimes, statistical analysis may not be required.

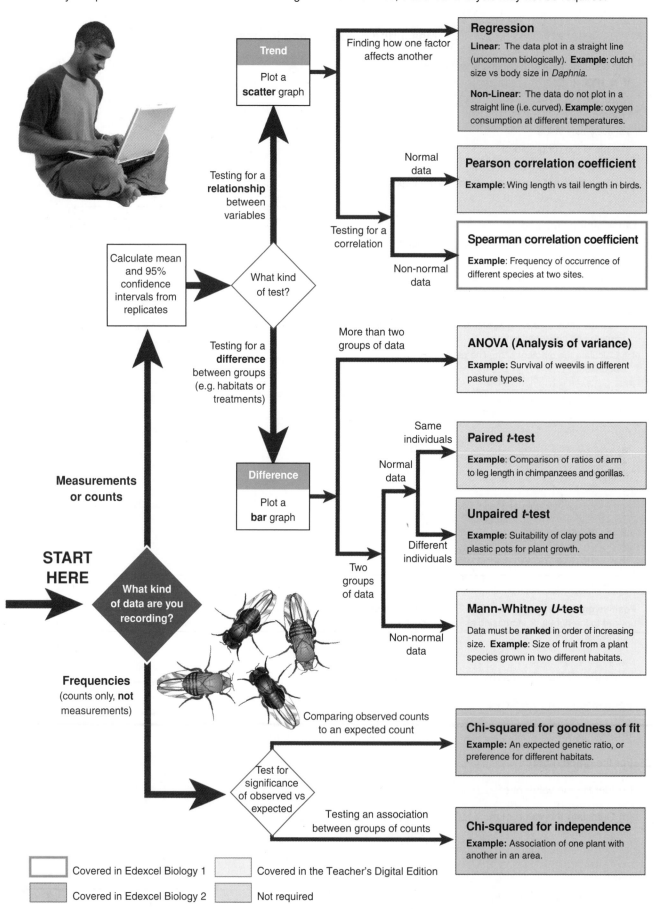

Trend
Plot a **scatter** graph

Finding how one factor affects another

Regression
Linear: The data plot in a straight line (uncommon biologically). **Example**: clutch size vs body size in *Daphnia*.

Non-Linear: The data do not plot in a straight line (i.e. curved). **Example**: oxygen consumption at different temperatures.

Testing for a **relationship** between variables

Normal data

Pearson correlation coefficient
Example: Wing length vs tail length in birds.

Testing for a correlation

Non-normal data

Spearman correlation coefficient
Example: Frequency of occurrence of different species at two sites.

Calculate mean and 95% confidence intervals from replicates

What kind of test?

Testing for a **difference** between groups (e.g. habitats or treatments)

More than two groups of data

ANOVA (Analysis of variance)
Example: Survival of weevils in different pasture types.

Same individuals

Paired *t*-test
Example: Comparison of ratios of arm to leg length in chimpanzees and gorillas.

Normal data

Measurements or counts

Difference
Plot a **bar** graph

Different individuals

Unpaired *t*-test
Example: Suitability of clay pots and plastic pots for plant growth.

Two groups of data

Non-normal data

Mann-Whitney *U*-test
Data must be **ranked** in order of increasing size. **Example**: Size of fruit from a plant species grown in two different habitats.

START HERE

What kind of data are you recording?

Frequencies
(counts only, **not** measurements)

Comparing observed counts to an expected count

Chi-squared for goodness of fit
Example: An expected genetic ratio, or preference for different habitats.

Test for significance of observed vs expected

Testing an association between groups of counts

Chi-squared for independence
Example: Association of one plant with another in an area.

☐ Covered in Edexcel Biology 1   ☐ Covered in the Teacher's Digital Edition

☐ Covered in Edexcel Biology 2   ☐ Not required

LINK
REFER 23

© 2015 **BIOZONE** International
ISBN: 978-1-927309-25-4
Photocopying Prohibited

23 Spearman Rank Correlation

Key Idea: The Spearman rank correlation is a test used to determine if there is a statistical dependence (correlation) between two variables.

The Spearman rank correlation is appropriate for data that have a non-normal distribution (or where the distribution is not known) and assesses the degree of association between the X and Y variables (if they are correlated). For the test to work, the values used must be monotonic i.e. the values must increase or decrease together or one increases while the other decreases. A value of 1 indicates a perfect correlation; a value of 0 indicates no correlation between the variables. The example below examines the relationship between the frequency of the drumming sound made by male frigatebirds (Y) and the volume of their throat pouch (X).

Spearman's rank data for frigate bird pouch volume and drumming frequency

Bird	Volume of pouch / cm³	Rank (R₁)	Frequency of drumming sound (Hz)	Rank (R₂)	Difference (D) (R₁-R₂)	D²
1	2550		461			
2	2440	I	473	6	-5	25
3	2740		532			
4	2730		465			
5	3010		485			
6	3370		488			
7	3080		527			
8	4910		478			
9	3740		485			
10	5090		434			
11	5090		468			
12	5380		449			
			Σ(Sum)			

Based on Madsen et al 2004

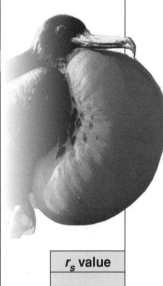

rₛ value

Analysing the data

Step one: Rank the data for each variable. For each variable, the numbers are ranked in descending order, e.g. for the variable, volume, the highest value 5380 cm³ is given the rank of 12 while its corresponding frequency value is given the rank of 2. Fill in the rank columns in the table above in the same way. If two numbers have the same rank value, then use the mean rank of the two values (e.g. 1+2 = 3. 3/2= 1.5).

Step two: Calculate the difference (D) between each pair of ranks (R₁-R₂) and enter the value in the table (as a check, the sum of all differences should be 0).

Step three: Square the differences and enter them into the table above (this removes any negative values).

Step four: Sum all the D² values and enter the total into the table.

Step five: Use the formula below to calculate the Spearman Rank Correlation Coefficient (rₛ). Enter the rₛ value in the box above.

$$r_s = 1 - \left(\frac{6\Sigma D^2}{n(n^2-1)} \right)$$

Spearman rank correlation coefficient

Step six: Compare the rₛ value to the table of critical values (right) for the appropriate number of pairs. If the rₛ value (ignoring sign) is greater than or equal to the critical value then there is a significant correlation. If rₛ is positive then there is a positive correlation. If rₛ is negative then there is a negative value correlation.

Number of pairs of measurements	Critical value
5	1.00
6	0.89
7	0.79
8	0.74
9	0.68
10	0.65
12	0.59
14	0.54
16	0.51
18	0.48
20	0.45

1. State the null hypothesis for the data set. _____

2. (a) Identify the critical value for the frigate bird data: _____

   (b) State if the correlation is positive of negative: _____

   (c) State whether the correlation is significant: _____

3. In your class, gather data on heart rate (beats per minute measured by carotid or radial pulse) and breathing rate (breaths per minute). Use the Spearman rank coefficient to determine if there is a relationship between these variables. Complete your analysis and staple it to this page.

LINK **19** DATA

24 Mean, Median, and Mode

Key Idea: Mean, median, and mode are measures of the central tendency of data. The distribution of the data will determine which measurement of central tendency you use. Measures of a biological response are usually made from more than one sampling unit. In lab-based investigations, the sample size (the number of sampling units) may be as small as three or four (e.g. three test-tubes in each of four treatments). In field studies, each individual may be a sampling unit, and the sample size can be very large (e.g. 100 individuals). It is useful to summarise data using **descriptive statistics.** Descriptive statistics, such as mean, median, and mode, can identify the central tendency of a data set. Each of these statistics is appropriate to certain types of data or distribution (as indicated by a frequency distribution).

Variation in data

Whether they are obtained from observation or experiments, most biological data show variability. In a set of data values, it is useful to know the value about which most of the data are grouped, i.e. the centre value. This value can be the mean, median, or mode depending on the type of variable involved (see below). The main purpose of these statistics is to summarise important features of your data and to provide the basis for statistical analyses.

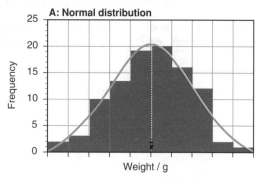

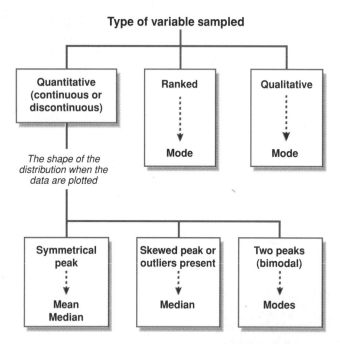

The shape of the distribution will determine which statistic (mean, median, or mode) best describes the central tendency of the sample data.

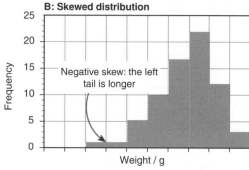

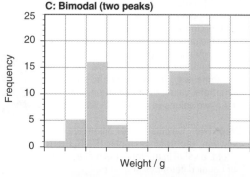

Statistic	Definition and use	Method of calculation
Mean	• The average of all data entries. • Measure of central tendency for normally distributed data.	• Add up all the data entries. • Divide by the total number of data entries.
Median	• The middle value when data entries are placed in rank order. • A good measure of central tendency for skewed distributions.	• Arrange the data in increasing rank order. • Identify the middle value. • For an even number of entries, find the mid point of the two middle values.
Mode	• The most common data value. • Suitable for bimodal distributions and qualitative data.	• Identify the category with the highest number of data entries using a tally chart or a bar graph.
Range	• The difference between the smallest and largest data values. • Provides a crude indication of data spread.	• Identify the smallest and largest values and find the difference between them.

When NOT to calculate a mean:

In some situations, calculation of a simple arithmetic mean is not appropriate.

Remember:

• *DO NOT* calculate a mean from values that are already means (averages) themselves.

• *DO NOT* calculate a mean of ratios (e.g. percentages) for several groups of different sizes. Go back to the raw values and recalculate.

• *DO NOT* calculate a mean when the measurement scale is not linear, e.g. pH units are not measured on a linear scale.

 © 2015 **BIOZONE** International
ISBN: 978-1-927309-25-4
Photocopying Prohibited

$$\frac{\text{Total of data entries}}{\text{Number of entries}} = \frac{5221}{29} = \boxed{180} \text{ cm}$$

Mean

Height of swimmers (in rank order)		
174	177	185
175	177	185
175	178	185
175	178	186
176	178	186
176	178	186
176	180	188
176	180	188
176	180	189
177	181	

Mode → 176
Median → 178

Height (cm)	Tally	Total
174	✔	1
175	✔✔✔	3
176	✔✔✔✔✔	5
177	✔✔✔	3
178	✔✔✔✔	4
179		0
180	✔✔✔	3
181	✔	1
182		0
183		0
184		0
185	✔✔✔	3
186	✔✔✔	3
187		0
188	✔✔	2
189	✔	1

Case study: height of swimmers

Data (below) and descriptive statistics (left) from a survey of the height of 29 members of a male swim squad.

Raw data: Height / cm					
178	177	188	176	186	175
180	181	178	178	176	175
180	185	185	175	189	174
178	186	176	185	177	176
176	188	180	186	177	

1. Give a reason for the difference between the mean, median, and mode for the swimmers' height data:

_____

_____

_____

Case study: fern reproduction

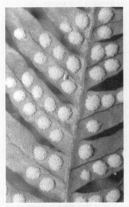

Fern spores

Raw data (below) and descriptive statistics (right) from a survey of the number of sori found on the fronds of a fern plant.

Raw data: Number of sori per frond							
64	60	64	62	68	66	66	63
69	70	63	70	70	63	63	62
71	69	59	70	66	61	61	70
67	64	63	64				

$$\frac{\text{Total of data entries}}{\text{Number of entries}} = \frac{1641}{25} = \boxed{66} \text{ sori}$$

Mean

Number of sori per frond (in rank order)	
59	66
60	66
61	67
62	68
62	69
63	69
63	70
63	70
63	70
63	70
64	70
64	70
64	71
64	

Median → 64

Sori per frond	Tally	Total
59	✔	1
60	✔	1
61	✔	1
62	✔✔	2
63	✔✔✔✔	4
64	✔✔✔✔	4
65		0
66	✔✔	2
67	✔	1
68	✔	1
69	✔✔	2
70	✔✔✔✔✔	5
71	✔	1

Mode → 70

2. Give a reason for the difference between the mean, median, and mode for the fern sori data:

_____

_____

_____

_____

3. Calculate the mean, median, and mode for the data on ladybird masses below. Draw up a tally chart and show all calculations:

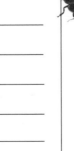

Ladybird mass / mg		
10.1	8.2	7.7
8.0	8.8	7.8
6.7	7.7	8.8
9.8	8.8	8.9
6.2	8.8	8.4

25 Spread of Data

Key Idea: Standard deviation is used to quantify the variability around the central value and evaluate the reliability of estimates of the true mean.

While it is important to know the central tendency (e.g. mean) of a data set, it is also important to know how well the mean represents the data set. This is determined by measuring the spread of data around the central measure. The variance (s^2) or its square root, standard deviation (s) are often used to give a simple measure of the spread or dispersion in data. In general, if the spread of values in a data set around the mean is small, the mean will more accurately represent the data than if the spread of data is large.

Standard deviation

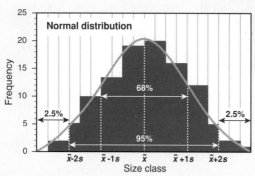

The **standard deviation** is a frequently used measure of the variability (spread) in a set of data. It is usually presented in the form $\bar{x} \pm s$. In a normally distributed set of data, 68% of all data values will lie within one standard deviation (s) of the mean ($\bar{x}$) and 95% of all data values will lie within two standard deviations of the mean (left).

Two different sets of data can have the same mean and range, yet the distribution of data within the range can be quite different. In both the data sets pictured in the histograms below, 68% of the values lie within the range $\bar{x} \pm 1s$ and 95% of the values lie within $\bar{x} \pm 2s$. However, in B, the data values are more tightly clustered around the mean.

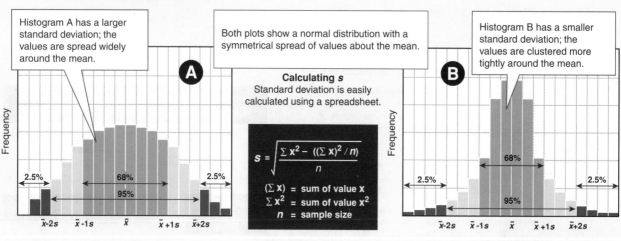

Histogram A has a larger standard deviation; the values are spread widely around the mean.

Both plots show a normal distribution with a symmetrical spread of values about the mean.

Histogram B has a smaller standard deviation; the values are clustered more tightly around the mean.

Calculating s
Standard deviation is easily calculated using a spreadsheet.

$$s = \sqrt{\frac{\sum x^2 - ((\sum x)^2 / n)}{n}}$$

$(\sum x)$ = sum of value x
$\sum x^2$ = sum of value x^2
n = sample size

NOTE: you may sometimes see the standard deviation equation written as

$$s = \sqrt{\frac{\sum(x - \bar{x})^2}{n}}$$

This equation will give you the same answer as the first equation (above), but the first equation is often used because it is easier to calculate.

Birth weights / kg

3.740	3.810	3.220
3.830	2.640	3.135
3.530	2.980	3.090
3.095	3.350	3.830
1.560	3.780	3.840
3.910	3.260	4.710
4.180	3.800	4.050
3.570	4.170	4.560
3.150	4.400	3.380
3.400	3.770	3.690
3.380	3.825	1.495
2.660	3.130	3.260
3.840	3.400	
3.630	3.260	

1. Two data sets have the same mean. The standard deviation of the first data set is much larger than the standard deviation of the second data set. What does this tell you about the spread of data around the central measure for each set?

_____

_____

_____

2. The data on the left are the birth weights of 40 newborn babies.

   (a) Calculate the mean for the data: _____

   _____

   (b) Calculate the standard deviation (s) for the data: _____

   (c) State the mean ± 1s: _____

   (d) What percentage of values are within 1s of the mean? _____

   (e) What does this tell you about the spread of the data? _____

   _____

© 2015 **BIOZONE** International
ISBN: 978-1-927309-25-4
Photocopying Prohibited

26 Interpreting Sample Variability

Key Idea: The sampling method can affect the results of the study, especially if it has an unknown bias.

The **standard deviation** (s) gives a simple measure of the spread or **dispersion** in data. It is usually preferred over the **variance** (s^2) because it is expressed in the original units. Two data sets could have the same mean, but very different values of dispersion. If we simply used the mean to compare these data sets, the results would (incorrectly) suggest that they were alike. The assumptions we make about a population will be affected by what the sample data tell us. This is why it is important that sample data are unbiased (e.g. collected by **random sampling**) and that the sample set is as large as practicable. This exercise will help to illustrate this principle.

Random sampling, sample size, and dispersion in data

Sample size and sampling bias can both affect the information we obtain when we sample a population. In this exercise you will calculate some descriptive statistics for some sample data. The complete set of sample data we are working with comprises 689 length measurements of year zero (young of the year) perch (column left). Basic descriptive statistics for the data have been calculated for you below and the frequency histogram has also been plotted.

Look at this data set and then complete the exercise to calculate the same statistics from each of two smaller data sets (tabulated right) drawn from the same population. This exercise shows how random sampling, large sample size, and sampling bias affect our statistical assessment of variation in a population.

Complete sample set
n = 689 (random)

Length in mm	Freq
25	1
26	0
27	0
28	0
29	0
30	0
31	0
32	2
33	3
34	3
35	4
36	5
37	10
38	23
39	22
40	33
41	39
42	41
43	41
44	36
45	49
46	32
47	14
48	32
49	27
50	25
51	24
52	17
53	18
54	27
55	21
56	20
57	11
58	18
59	16
60	22
61	13
62	8
63	10
64	5
65	7
66	2
67	3
68	3
69	1
70	0
71	1
	689

Small sample set
n = 30 (random)

Length in mm	Freq
25	1
26	0
27	0
28	0
29	0
30	0
31	0
32	0
33	0
34	0
35	2
36	0
37	0
38	3
39	2
40	1
41	3
42	0
43	0
44	0
45	0
46	1
47	0
48	2
49	0
50	0
51	1
52	3
53	0
54	0
55	0
56	0
57	1
58	0
59	3
60	2
61	2
62	0
63	0
64	0
65	0
66	0
67	2
68	1
	30

Small sample set
n = 50 (bias)

Length in mm	Freq
46	1
47	0
48	0
49	1
50	0
51	0
52	1
53	1
54	1
55	1
56	0
57	2
58	2
59	4
60	1
61	0
62	8
63	10
64	13
65	2
66	0
67	2
	50

The person gathering this set of data was biased towards selecting larger fish because the mesh size on the net was too large to retain small fish

This population was sampled randomly to obtain this data set

This column records the number of fish of each size

Number of fish in the sample

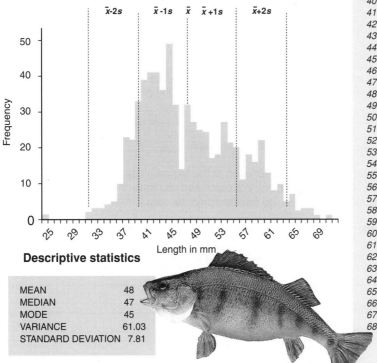

Length of year zero perch

$\bar{x}-2s$ $\bar{x}-1s$ $\bar{x}$ $\bar{x}+1s$ $\bar{x}+2s$

Length in mm

Descriptive statistics

MEAN	48
MEDIAN	47
MODE	45
VARIANCE	61.03
STANDARD DEVIATION	7.81

1. For the complete data set ($n = 689$) calculate the percentage of data falling within:

   (a) ± one standard deviation of the mean: _____

   (b) ± two standard deviations of the mean: _____

   (c) Explain what this information tells you about the distribution of year zero perch from this site: _____

   _____

2. Give another reason why you might reach the same conclusion about the distribution: _____

   _____

LINK 25   LINK 24   WEB 26   **DATA**

Calculating descriptive statistics using Excel®

You can use Microsoft Excel® or other similar spreadsheet programme to easily calculate descriptive statistics for sample data.

In this first example, the smaller data set ($n = 30$) is shown as it would appear on an Excel® spreadsheet, ready for the calculations to be made. Use this guide to enter your data into a spreadsheet and calculate the descriptive statistics as described.

When using formulae in Excel®, = indicates that a formula follows. The cursor will become active and you will be able to select the cells containing the data you are interested in, or you can type the location of the data using the format shown. The data in this case are located in the cells B2 through to B31 (B2:B31).

Karori age zero perch 12-15 F

	A	B	C	D
		LENGTH	WEIGHT	
		25	0.15	
		35	0.44	
		35	0.44	
		38	0.57	
		38	0.57	
		38	0.57	
		39	0.61	
		39	0.61	
		40	0.67	
11		41	0.72	
12		41	0.72	
13		41	0.72	
14		46	1.03	
15		48	1.18	
16		48	1.18	
17		51	1.43	
18		52	1.52	
			1.52	
			1.52	
			2.04	
			2.27	
			2.27	
			2.27	
25		60	2.39	
26		60	2.39	
27		61	2.52	
28		61	2.52	
29		67	3.39	
30		67	3.39	
31		68	3.56	
32				
33				
34	N	=COUNT(B2:B31)		
35	MEAN	=AVERAGE(B2:B31)		
36	MEDIAN	=MEDIAN(B2:B31)		
37	MODE	=MODE(B2:B31)		
38	VARIANCE	=VAR(B2:B31)		
39	STANDARD DEVIATION	=STDEV(B2:B31)		
40				
41				

Callout boxes:

The variables being measured. Both length and weight were measured, but here we are working with only the length data.

Enter the data values in separate cells under an appropriate descriptor

Ignore this WEIGHT column. Sometimes the data we are interested in is part of larger data set.

The cells for the calculations below are B2 to B31

Type in the name of the statistic Excel® will calculate. This gives you a reference for the row of values.

Type the formula into the cell beside its label. When you press return, the cell will contain the calculated value.

3. For this set of data, use a spreadsheet to calculate:

(a) Mean: _____

(b) Median: _____

(c) Mode: _____

(d) Sample variance: _____

(e) Standard deviation: _____

Staple the spreadsheet into your workbook.

4. Repeat the calculations for the second small set of sample data ($n = 50$) on the previous page. Again, calculate the statistics as indicated below and staple the spreadsheet into your workbook:

(a) Mean: _____ (b) Median: _____ (c) Mode: _____

(d) Variance: _____ (e) Standard deviation: _____

5. On a separate sheet, plot **frequency histograms** for each of the two small data sets. Label them $n = 30$ and $n = 50$. Staple them into your workbook. If you are proficient in Excel® and you have the "Data Analysis" plug in loaded, you can use Excel® to plot the histograms for you once you have entered the data.

6. Compare the descriptive statistics you calculated for each data set with reference to the following:

(a) How close the median and mean to each other in each sample set: _____

_____

(b) The size of the standard deviation in each case: _____

_____

(c) How close each small of the sample sets resembles the large sample set of 689 values: _____

_____

_____

7. (a) Compare the two frequency histograms you have plotted for the two smaller sample data sets: _____

_____

_____

(b) Why do you think two histograms look so different? _____

_____

_____

27 Biological Drawings

Key Idea: Good biological drawings provide an accurate record of the specimen you are studying and enable you to make a record of its important features.

Drawing is a very important skill to have in biology. Drawings record what a specimen looks like and give you an opportunity to record its important features. Often drawing something will help you remember its features at a later date (e.g. in a test). Annotated drawings provide explanatory notes about the labelled structures, while plan diagrams label the main structures observed, but provide no additional detail.

▶ Biological drawings require you to pay attention to detail. It is very important that you draw what you actually see, and not what you think you should see.

▶ Biological drawings should include as much detail as you need to distinguish different structures and types of tissue, but avoid unnecessary detail which can make your drawing confusing.

▶ Attention should be given to the symmetry and proportions of your specimen. Accurate labeling, a statement of magnification or scale, the view (section type), and type of stain used (if applicable) should all be noted on your drawing.

▶ Some key points for making good biological drawing are described on the example below. The drawing of *Drosophila* (right) is well executed but lacks the information required to make it a good biological drawing.

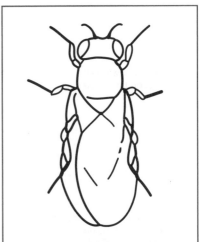

This drawing of *Drosophila* is a fair representation of the animal, but has no labels, title, or scale.

All drawings must include a title. Underline the title if it is a scientific name. ⟶ **Copepod**

Centre your drawing on the page, not in a corner. This will leave room to place labels around the drawing.

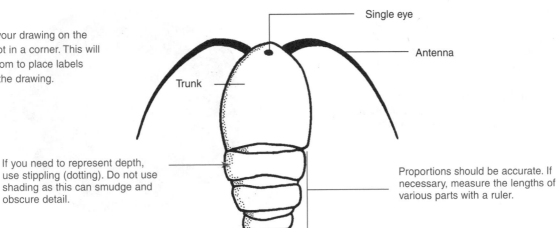

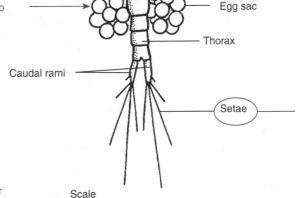

If you need to represent depth, use stippling (dotting). Do not use shading as this can smudge and obscure detail.

Proportions should be accurate. If necessary, measure the lengths of various parts with a ruler.

Use simple, narrow lines to make your drawings.

Single eye

Antenna

Trunk

Egg sac

Thorax

Use a sharp pencil to draw with. Make your drawing on plain white paper.

Caudal rami

Setae

All parts of your drawing must be labelled accurately.

Labeling lines should be drawn with a ruler and should not cross over other label lines. Try to use only vertical or horizontal lines.

Your drawing must include a scale or magnification to indicate the size of your subject. ⟶ Scale

0.2 mm

Annotated diagrams

An annotated diagram is a diagram that includes a series of explanatory notes. These provide important or useful information about your subject.

Transverse section through collenchyma of *Helianthus* stem. Magnification x 450

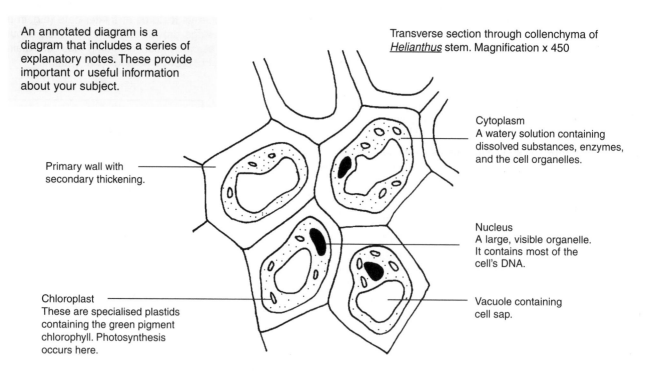

Primary wall with secondary thickening.

Cytoplasm
A watery solution containing dissolved substances, enzymes, and the cell organelles.

Nucleus
A large, visible organelle. It contains most of the cell's DNA.

Chloroplast
These are specialised plastids containing the green pigment chlorophyll. Photosynthesis occurs here.

Vacuole containing cell sap.

Plan diagrams

Plan diagrams are drawings made of samples viewed under a microscope at low or medium power. They are used to show the distribution of the different tissue types in a sample without any cellular detail. The tissues are identified, but no detail about the cells within them is included.

The example here shows a plan diagram produced after viewing a light micrograph of a transverse section through a dicot stem.

Light micrograph of a transverse section through a dicot stem.

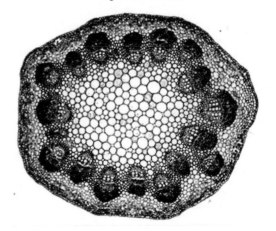

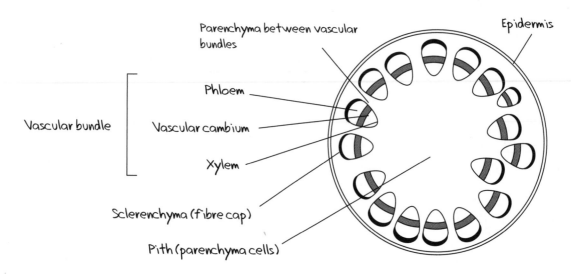

Parenchyma between vascular bundles

Epidermis

Phloem

Vascular bundle

Vascular cambium

Xylem

Sclerenchyma (fibre cap)

Pith (parenchyma cells)

28 Test Your Understanding

Key Idea: Systematic recording and analysis of results can help identify trends and draw conclusions about a biological response in an experiment.

Using the information below, analyse results and draw conclusions about the effect of a nitrogen fertiliser on the growth of radish plants.

Radishes

Experimental method

This experiment was designed to test the effect of nitrogen fertiliser on plant growth. Radish seeds were planted in separate identical pots (5 cm x 5 cm wide x 10 cm deep) and grown together in normal room temperature (22°C) conditions.

The radishes were watered every day at 10 am and 3 pm with 1.25 L per treatment. Water soluble fertiliser was mixed and added with the first watering on the 1st, 11th and 21st days. The fertiliser concentrations used were: 0.00, 0.06, 0.12, 0.18, 0.24, and 0.30 gL⁻¹ with each treatment receiving a different concentration. The plants were grown for 30 days before being removed, washed, and the root (radish) weighed. Results were tabulated below:

The Aim

To investigate the effect of a nitrogen fertiliser on the growth of radish plants.

Hypothesis

Radish growth will increase with increasing nitrogen concentration.

Background

Inorganic fertilisers revolutionised crop farming when they were introduced during the late 19th and early 20th century. Crop yields soared and today it is estimated around 50% of crop yield is attributable to the use of fertiliser. Nitrogen is a very important element for plant growth and several types of purely nitrogen fertiliser are manufactured to supply it, e.g. urea.

To investigate the effect of nitrogen on plant growth, a group of students set up an experiment using different concentrations of nitrogen fertiliser. Radish seeds were planted into a standard soil mixture and divided into six groups, each with five sample plants (30 plants in total).

Table 1: Mass (g) of radish plant roots under six different fertiliser concentrations (data given to 1dp).

Fertiliser concentration / gL⁻¹	Mass of radish root / g†					Total mass	Mean mass
	Sample / n						
	1	2	3	4	5		
0	80.1	83.2	82.0	79.1	84.1	408.5	81.7
0.06	109.2	110.3	108.2	107.9	110.7		
0.12	117.9	118.9	118.3	119.1	117.2		
0.18	128.3	127.3	127.7	126.8	DNG*		
0.24	23.6	140.3	139.6	137.9	141.1		
0.30	122.3	121.1	122.6	121.3	123.1		

† Based on data from M S Jilani, *et al* Journal Agricultural Research

* DNG: Did not germinate

1. Identify the independent variable for the experiment and its range: _____

_____

2. What is the sample size for each concentration of fertiliser? _____

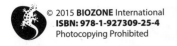

LINK 25 LINK 24 LINK 18 LINK 14 DATA

3. One of the radishes recorded in Table 1 did not grow as expected and produced an extreme value. Record the **outlying value** here and decide whether or not you should include it in future calculations:

_____

_____

_____

4. Complete the table on the previous page by calculating the **total mass** and **mean mass** of the radish roots:

5. Use the grid below to draw a **line graph** of the experimental results. Use your calculated means and remember to include a title and correctly labelled axes.

6. The students recorded the wet mass of the root (the root still containing water) in their table. What mass should they have actually recorded to get a better representation of the effect of the fertiliser on root mass?

_____

_____

_____

7. Why would measuring just root mass not be a totally accurate way of measuring the effect of fertiliser on radish growth?

_____

_____

8. Describe some other measurements the students could have taken to make their experiment more complete:

_____

_____

© 2015 **BIOZONE** International
ISBN: 978-1-927309-25-4
Photocopying Prohibited

9. Complete Table 2 by calculating the mean, median and mode for each concentration of fertiliser:

The students decided to further their experiment by recording the number of leaves on each radish plant:

Table 2: Number of leaves on radish plant under six different fertiliser concentrations.

| Fertiliser concentration / g L^{-1} | Number of leaves | | | | | Mean | Median | Mode |
| | Sample / n | | | | | | | |
	1	2	3	4	5			
0	9	9	10	8	7			
0.06	15	16	15	16	16			
0.12	16	17	17	17	16			
0.18	18	18	19	18	DNG*			
0.24	6	19	19	18	18			
0.30	18	17	18	19	19			

* DNG: Did not germinate

10. (a) Identify the outlier in the table above: _____

   (b) Recalculate the mean if the outlier was included: _____

   (c) Calculate the standard deviation for the fertiliser concentration affected by an outlier:

   With the outlier included: _____

   Without the outlier included: _____

   (d) Compare the results in (c). What can you conclude about how accurately the mean reflects the data set when the outlier is included?

   _____

   _____

11. Which concentration of fertiliser appeared to produce the best growth results? _____

12. Describe some sources of error for the experiment: _____

   _____

   _____

   _____

13. Write a conclusion for the experiment with reference to the aim, hypothesis, and results: _____

   _____

   _____

   _____

   _____

14. The students decided to replicate the experiment (carry it out again). How might this improve the experiment's results?

   _____

   _____

   _____

© 2015 **BIOZONE** International
ISBN: 978-1-927309-25-4
Photocopying Prohibited

29 KEY TERMS: Did You Get It?

1. For the graph (right) use the equation y = mx + c to answer the following questions:

   (a) What is the value of c?: _____

   (b) Using the two reference points marked on the graph, calculate m: _____

   (c) Describe the slope and the relationship between the variables: _____

   (d) What is the value of y when x=5? _____

2. A balance has a calibration error of +0.04 g. A student weighs out 11.71 g of sodium hydroxide. Calculate the percentage error (show your working):

   _____

   _____

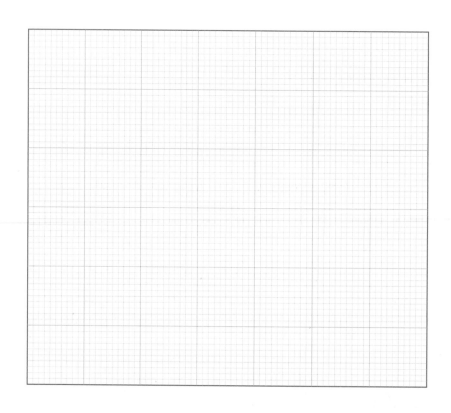

3. The table (below right) shows the rate of sweat production in an athlete on a stationary cycle. Complete the table to:

   (a) Convert the cumulative sweat loss to cm^3:

   (b) Determine the rate of sweat loss $(cm^3 min^{-1})$:

   (c) Plot a double axis graph on the grid below to show cumulative sweat loss in cm^3 and rate of sweat loss against time.

   (d) Describe how the rate of sweat loss changes over time:

   _____

Time / minutes	Cumulative sweat loss / mm^3	Cumulative sweat loss / cm^3	Rate of sweat loss / $cm^3 min^{-1}$
0	0		
10	50 000		
20	130 000		
30	220 000		
60	560 000		

_____

_____

_____

TEST

Biological Molecules

Key terms

amino acid

Benedict's test

biuret test

carbohydrate

chromatography

colorimetry

condensation

denaturation

dipeptide

disaccharide

emulsion test

fatty acid

fibrous protein

hydrolysis

globular protein

glucose

glycerol

hydrogen bond

inorganic ion

iodine/potassium iodide test

isomer

lipid

macromolecule

monomer

monosaccharide

nucleic acid

phospholipid

polymer

polypeptide

polysaccharide

primary structure

protein

quaternary structure

saturated fatty acid

secondary structure

tertiary structure

triglyceride

unsaturated fatty acid

water

1.1 Carbohydrates

Learning outcomes

		Activity number
☐	i Giving examples, distinguish between the structure and biological roles of monosaccharides, disaccharides, and polysaccharides.	30 31 32
☐	ii Describe the ring structure and properties of glucose (hexose monosaccharide) and the structure of ribose (a pentose monosaccharide). Recognise isomers of glucose (α-glucose and β-glucose) and explain their biological significance.	31 32
☐	iii Describe how monosaccharides (glucose, galactose, fructose) are joined by condensation reactions to form disaccharides (e.g. sucrose, lactose, maltose) and polysaccharides (e.g. glycogen, amylose, amylopectin). Explain how the glycosidic bonds in di- and polysaccharides are broken through hydrolysis.	33 35 36
☐	iv Compare and contrast the structure of glucose and its polymers: starch, cellulose, and glycogen. Relate the structure to biological function in each case.	32 35 36
☐	**AT** Use colorimetry to produce a calibration curve with which to identify the concentration of glucose in an unknown solution.	34
☐	**AT** Use and interpret the results of qualitative tests for carbohydrates.	44

Catalase

Pyruvate dehydrogenase
FontanaCG cc 3.0

Restriction enzyme

1.2 Lipids

Learning outcomes

		Activity number
☐	i Recognise triglycerides and phospholipids as classes of lipid and describe the basic structure of each. Explain how triglycerides are formed by condensation from fatty acids and glycerol with the formation of ester bonds.	37 38
☐	ii Distinguish between saturated and unsaturated fatty acids (and their lipids).	37 38
☐	iii Describe how the structure and properties of lipids relate to their roles in energy storage, waterproofing, and insulation.	37
☐	iv Explain how the structure and properties of phospholipids relate to their functional role in biological membranes.	38
☐	11 **AT** Use and interpret the results of the emulsion test for lipids.	44

1.3 Proteins

Learning outcomes

		Activity number
☐	i Describe the structure of an amino acid, including the significance of the R group.	39
☐	ii Explain how amino acid monomers are linked by peptide bonds in condensation reactions and how polypeptides are broken apart by hydrolysis.	
☐	**AT** Use chromatography to separate a mixture of amino acids.	40
☐	iii Explain how a functional protein may consist of one or more polypeptides. Explain the role of hydrogen bonds, ionic bonds, and disulfide bridges in protein structure.	

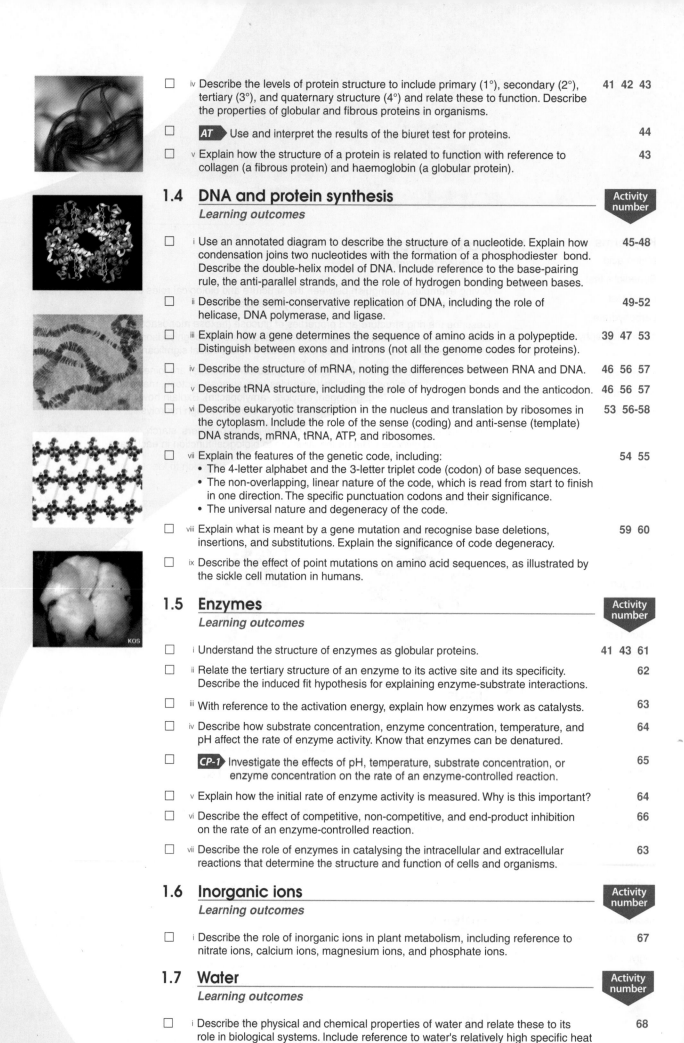

□ iv Describe the levels of protein structure to include primary (1°), secondary (2°), tertiary (3°), and quaternary structure (4°) and relate these to function. Describe the properties of globular and fibrous proteins in organisms. — 41 42 43

□ **AT** Use and interpret the results of the biuret test for proteins. — 44

□ v Explain how the structure of a protein is related to function with reference to collagen (a fibrous protein) and haemoglobin (a globular protein). — 43

1.4 DNA and protein synthesis

Learning outcomes

Activity number

□ i Use an annotated diagram to describe the structure of a nucleotide. Explain how condensation joins two nucleotides with the formation of a phosphodiester bond. Describe the double-helix model of DNA. Include reference to the base-pairing rule, the anti-parallel strands, and the role of hydrogen bonding between bases. — 45-48

□ ii Describe the semi-conservative replication of DNA, including the role of helicase, DNA polymerase, and ligase. — 49-52

□ iii Explain how a gene determines the sequence of amino acids in a polypeptide. Distinguish between exons and introns (not all the genome codes for proteins). — 39 47 53

□ iv Describe the structure of mRNA, noting the differences between RNA and DNA. — 46 56 57

□ v Describe tRNA structure, including the role of hydrogen bonds and the anticodon. — 46 56 57

□ vi Describe eukaryotic transcription in the nucleus and translation by ribosomes in the cytoplasm. Include the role of the sense (coding) and anti-sense (template) DNA strands, mRNA, tRNA, ATP, and ribosomes. — 53 56-58

□ vii Explain the features of the genetic code, including: — 54 55
  • The 4-letter alphabet and the 3-letter triplet code (codon) of base sequences.
  • The non-overlapping, linear nature of the code, which is read from start to finish in one direction. The specific punctuation codons and their significance.
  • The universal nature and degeneracy of the code.

□ viii Explain what is meant by a gene mutation and recognise base deletions, insertions, and substitutions. Explain the significance of code degeneracy. — 59 60

□ ix Describe the effect of point mutations on amino acid sequences, as illustrated by the sickle cell mutation in humans.

1.5 Enzymes

Learning outcomes

Activity number

□ i Understand the structure of enzymes as globular proteins. — 41 43 61

□ ii Relate the tertiary structure of an enzyme to its active site and its specificity. Describe the induced fit hypothesis for explaining enzyme-substrate interactions. — 62

□ iii With reference to the activation energy, explain how enzymes work as catalysts. — 63

□ iv Describe how substrate concentration, enzyme concentration, temperature, and pH affect the rate of enzyme activity. Know that enzymes can be denatured. — 64

□ **CP-1** Investigate the effects of pH, temperature, substrate concentration, or enzyme concentration on the rate of an enzyme-controlled reaction. — 65

□ v Explain how the initial rate of enzyme activity is measured. Why is this important? — 64

□ vi Describe the effect of competitive, non-competitive, and end-product inhibition on the rate of an enzyme-controlled reaction. — 66

□ vii Describe the role of enzymes in catalysing the intracellular and extracellular reactions that determine the structure and function of cells and organisms. — 63

1.6 Inorganic ions

Learning outcomes

Activity number

□ i Describe the role of inorganic ions in plant metabolism, including reference to nitrate ions, calcium ions, magnesium ions, and phosphate ions. — 67

1.7 Water

Learning outcomes

Activity number

□ i Describe the physical and chemical properties of water and relate these to its role in biological systems. Include reference to water's relatively high specific heat capacity, its role as a solvent, its cohesive properties (responsible for surface tension), its incompressibility, and its maximum density at 4°C. — 68

30 The Biochemical Nature of Cells

Key Idea: The main components of cells are water and organic compounds of carbon, hydrogen, nitrogen and oxygen. Monomers can join together to form larger polymers. About 70% or more of a cell's mass is water. The remainder comprises molecules made up mainly of carbon, hydrogen, oxygen, and nitrogen. The combination of carbon with other elements provides a wide variety of molecular structures, called organic molecules. The organic molecules that make up living things can be grouped into four broad classes: carbohydrates, lipids, proteins, and nucleic acids. Organic molecules consist of small molecules (**monomers**) joined together to form larger, more complex molecules (**polymers**).

Carbohydrates form the structural components of cells, e.g. cellulose cell walls (arrowed). They are important in energy storage, and they are involved in cellular recognition. Carbohydrate monomers include glucose and fructose. Carbohydrate polymers are called polysaccharides, and include starch, cellulose, and glycogen.

Nucleotides and nucleic acids
Nucleic acids encode information for the construction and functioning of an organism. The nucleotide ATP is the energy currency of the cell. Nucleotides are the monomers from which nucleic acid polymers (DNA and RNA) are formed.

Chromosome

Water is a major component of cells: many substances dissolve in it, metabolic reactions occur in it, and it provides support and turgor.

Lipids provide a concentrated source of energy. Phospholipids are a major component of cellular membranes, including the membranes of organelles such as chloroplasts (below). Fatty acids are the building blocks of more complex lipids.

A small number of inorganic ions are also components of larger molecules.

Proteins may be structural (e.g. collagen in skin, proteins in ribosomes), catalytic (enzymes), or they may be involved in movement, signalling, internal defence and transport, or storage. Proteins are polymers made up of amino acid monomers. This micrograph (above) shows ribosomes synthesising proteins.

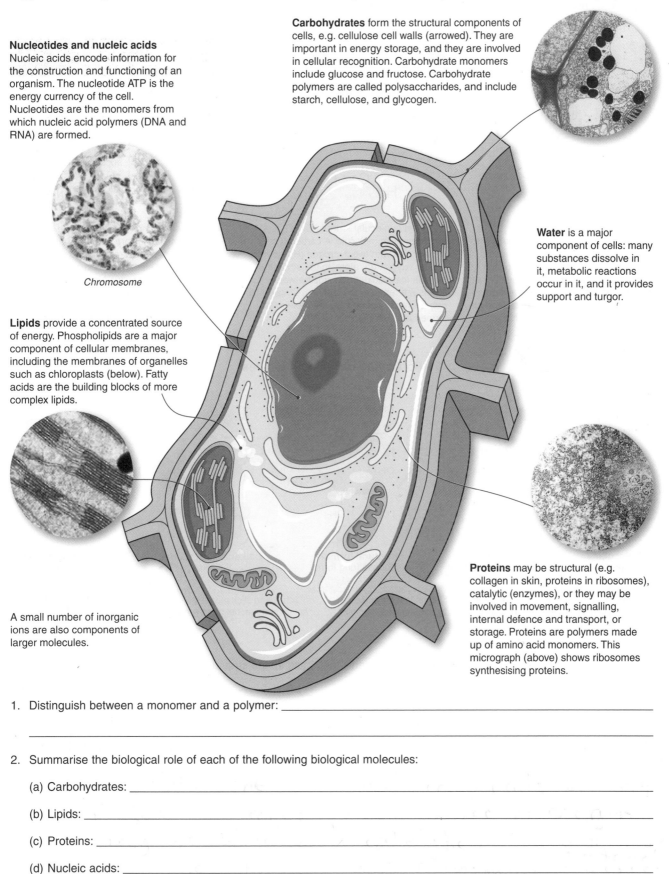

1. Distinguish between a monomer and a polymer: _____

_____

2. Summarise the biological role of each of the following biological molecules:

   (a) Carbohydrates: _____

   (b) Lipids: _____

   (c) Proteins: _____

   (d) Nucleic acids: _____

© 2015 **BIOZONE** International
ISBN: 978-1-927309-25-4
Photocopying Prohibited

31 Organic Molecules

Key Idea: Organic molecules are those with carbon-hydrogen bonds. They make up most of the chemicals found in living organisms and can be portrayed as formulae or models.

Molecular biology is a branch of science that studies the molecular basis of biological activity. All life is based around carbon, which is able to combine with many other elements to form a large number of carbon-based (or organic) molecules.

Specific groups of atoms, called functional groups, attach to a C-H core and determine the specific chemical properties of the molecule. The organic macromolecules that make up living things can be grouped into four classes: carbohydrates, lipids, proteins, and nucleic acids. The diagram (bottom) illustrates some of the common ways in which organic molecules are portrayed.

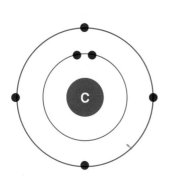

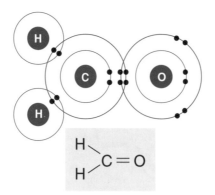

$$\begin{array}{c} H \\ \diagdown \\ C=O \\ \diagup \\ H \end{array}$$

Organic macromolecule	Structural unit	Elements
Carbohydrates	Sugar monomer	C, H, O
Proteins	Amino acid	C, H, O, N, S
Lipids	Not applicable	C, H, O
Nucleic acids	Nucleotide	C, H, O, N, P

A carbon atom (above) has four electrons that are available to form up to four **covalent bonds** with other atoms. A covalent bond forms when two atoms share a pair of electrons. The number of covalent bonds formed between atoms in a molecule determines the shape and chemical properties of the molecule.

Methanal (molecular formula CH_2O) is a simple organic molecule. A carbon (C) atom bonds with two hydrogen (H) atoms and an oxygen (O) atom. In the structural formula (blue box), the bonds between atoms are represented by lines. Covalent bonds are very strong, so the molecules formed are very stable.

The most common elements found in organic molecules are carbon, hydrogen, and oxygen, but organic molecules may also contain other elements, such as nitrogen, phosphorus, and sulfur. Most organic macromolecules are built up of one type of repeating unit or 'building block', except lipids, which are quite diverse in structure.

Portraying organic molecules

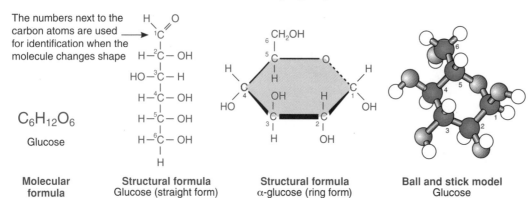

The numbers next to the carbon atoms are used for identification when the molecule changes shape

$C_6H_{12}O_6$

Glucose

| Molecular formula | Structural formula Glucose (straight form) | Structural formula α-glucose (ring form) | Ball and stick model Glucose | Space filling model β-D-glucose |

The molecular formula expresses the number of atoms in a molecule, but does not convey its structure. This is indicated by the structural formula.

A ball and stick model shows the arrangement of bonds while a space filling model gives a more realistic appearance of a molecule.

1. Study the table above and state the three main elements that make up the structure of organic molecules: _____

_____

2. Name two other elements that are also frequently part of organic molecules: _____

3. (a) On the diagram of the carbon atom top left, mark with arrows the electrons that are available to form covalent bonds with other atoms.

(b) State how many covalent bonds a carbon atom can form with neighbouring atoms: _____

4. Distinguish between molecular and structural formulae for a given molecule: _____

_____

_____

© 2015 **BIOZONE** International
ISBN: 978-1-927309-25-4
Photocopying Prohibited

32 Sugars

Key Idea: Monosaccharides are the building blocks for larger carbohydrates. They can exist as isomers.

Sugars (monosaccharides and disaccharides) play a central role in cells, providing energy and joining together to form carbohydrate macromolecules, such as starch and glycogen.

Monosaccharide polymers form the major component of most plants (as cellulose). Monosaccharides are important as a primary energy source for cellular metabolism. Carbohydrates have the general formula $C_x(H_2O)_y$, where x and y are variable numbers (often but not always the same).

Monosaccharides

Monosaccharides are single-sugar molecules and include glucose (grape sugar and blood sugar) and fructose (honey and fruit juices). They are used as a primary energy source for fuelling cell metabolism. They can be joined together to form disaccharides (two monomers) and polysaccharides (many monomers).

Monosaccharides can be classified by the number of carbon atoms they contain. Some important monosaccharides are the hexoses (6 carbons) and the pentoses (5 carbons). The most common arrangements found in sugars are hexose (6 sided) or pentose (5 sided) rings (below).

The commonly occurring monosaccharides contain between three and seven carbon atoms in their carbon chains and, of these, the 6C hexose sugars occur most frequently. All monosaccharides are reducing sugars (they can participate in reduction reactions).

Examples of monosaccharide structures

Triose	Pentose	Hexose
e.g. glyceraldehyde	e.g. ribose, deoxyribose	e.g. glucose, fructose, galactose

Ribose: a pentose monosaccharide

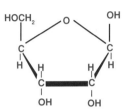

Ribose is a pentose (5 carbon) monosaccharide which can form a ring structure (left). Ribose is a component of the nucleic acid ribonucleic acid (RNA).

Glucose isomers

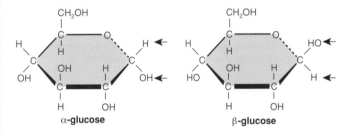

α-glucose   β-glucose

Isomers are compounds with the same chemical formula (same types and numbers of atoms) but different arrangements of atoms. The different arrangement of the atoms means that each isomer has different properties.

Molecules such as glucose can have many different isomers (e.g. α and β glucose, above) including straight and ring forms.

Glucose is a versatile molecule. It provides energy to power cellular reactions, can form energy storage molecules such as glycogen, or it can be used to build structural molecules.

Plants make their glucose via the process of photosynthesis. Animals and other heterotrophic organisms obtain their glucose by consuming plants or other organisms.

Fructose, often called fruit sugar, is a simple monosaccharide. It is often derived from sugar cane (above). Both fructose and glucose can be directly absorbed into the bloodstream.

1. Describe the two major functions of monosaccharides:

   (a) _____

   (b) _____

2. Describe the structural differences between the ring forms of glucose and ribose: _____

   _____

   _____

3. Using glucose as an example, define the term **isomer** and state its importance: _____

   _____

   _____

33 Condensation and Hydrolysis of Sugars

Key Idea: Condensation reactions join monosaccharides together to form disaccharides and polysaccharides. Hydrolysis reactions split disaccharides and polysaccharides into smaller molecules.

Monosaccharide monomers can be linked together by **condensation reactions** to produce larger molecules (disaccharides and polysaccharides). The reverse reaction, **hydrolysis**, breaks compound sugars down into their constituent monosaccharides. Disaccharides (double-sugars) are produced when two monosaccharides are joined together. Different disaccharides are formed by joining together different combinations of monosaccharides (below).

Condensation and hydrolysis reactions

Monosaccharides can combine to form compound sugars in what is called a condensation reaction. Compound sugars can be broken down by hydrolysis to simple monosaccharides.

Two mono-saccharides

Condensation reaction

Two monosaccharides are joined together to form a disaccharide with the release of a water molecule (hence its name). A net energy input is required for the reaction to proceed.

Hydrolysis reaction

When a disaccharide is split, as in digestion, a water molecule is used as a source of hydrogen and a hydroxyl group. The reaction is catalysed by specific enzymes.

$+$

H_2O Glycosidic bond

Disaccharide + water

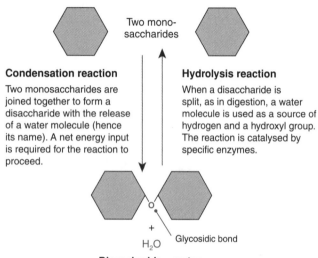

α-glucose   α-glucose

A   **B**

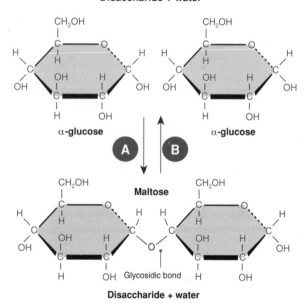

Maltose

Glycosidic bond

Disaccharide + water

Disaccharides

Disaccharides (below) are double-sugar molecules and are used as energy sources and as building blocks for larger molecules. They are important in human nutrition and are found in milk (lactose), table sugar (sucrose), and malt (maltose).

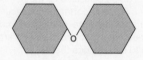

The type of disaccharide formed depends on the monomers involved and whether they are in their α- or β- form. Only a few disaccharides (e.g. lactose) are classified as reducing sugars. Some common disaccharides are described below.

Lactose, a milk sugar, is made up of β-glucose + β-galactose. Milk contains 2-8% lactose by weight. It is the primary carbohydrate source for suckling mammalian infants.

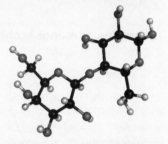

Maltose is composed of two α-glucose molecules. Germinating seeds contain maltose because the plant breaks down their starch stores to use it for food.

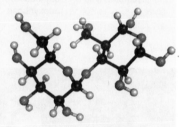

Sucrose (table sugar) is a simple sugar derived from plants such as sugar cane, sugar beet, or maple sap. It is composed of an α-glucose molecule and a β-fructose molecule.

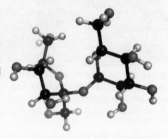

1. Explain briefly how disaccharide sugars are formed and broken down: _____

_____

_____

_____

2. On the diagram above, name the reaction occurring at points **A** and **B** and name the product that is formed:

_____

_____

3. On the lactose, maltose, and sucrose molecules (above right), circle the two monomers on each molecule.

© 2015 **BIOZONE** International
ISBN: 978-1-927309-25-4
Photocopying Prohibited

34 Colorimetry

Key Idea: Colorimetric analysis can be used to determine the concentration of a substance in a solution.

Colorimetric analysis is a simple quantitative technique used to determine the concentration of a specific substance in a solution. A specific reagent is added to the test solution where it reacts with the substance of interest to produce a colour. The samples are placed in a colorimeter, which measures the solution's absorbance at a specific wavelength. A dilution series can be used to produce a calibration curve, which can then be used to quantify that substance in samples of unknown concentration. This is illustrated for glucose in the example below.

1 **Prepare glucose standards**

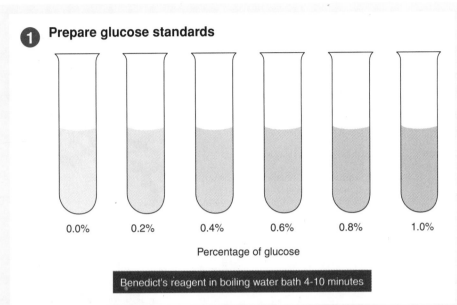

| 0.0% | 0.2% | 0.4% | 0.6% | 0.8% | 1.0% |

Percentage of glucose

Benedict's reagent in boiling water bath 4-10 minutes

Solutions containing a range of known glucose concentrations are prepared in test tubes. Benedict's reagent (used to detect the presence of a reducing sugar) is added and the test tubes are heated in a boiling waterbath for 4-10 minutes.

At the end of the reaction time, samples containing glucose will have undergone a colour change. The samples are cooled, then filtered or centrifuged to remove suspended particles.

2 **Produce a calibration curve**

The absorbance of each standard is measured in a colorimeter (or sometimes a spectrophotometer) at 735 nm. These values are used to produce a calibration curve for glucose. The calibration curve can then be used to determine the glucose concentration of any 'unknown' based on its absorbance. For the best results, a new calibration curve should be generated for each new analysis. This accounts for any possible changes in the conditions of the reactants.

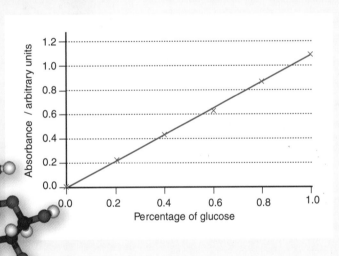

Glucose

1. (a) A sample has an absorbance of 0.5. Use the calibration curve above to estimate how much glucose it contains.

   _____

   (b) What would you do if the absorbance values you obtained for most of your 'unknowns' were outside the range of your calibration curve?

   _____

   _____

2. How could you quantify the amount of glucose in a range of commercially available glucose drinks? _____

   _____

   _____

3. Why is it important to remove suspended solids from a sample before measuring its absorbance? _____

   _____

LINK LINK
168 **32** **KNOW**

35 Polysaccharides

Key Idea: Polysaccharides consist of many monosaccharides joined by condensation. Their functional properties depend on composition and monosaccharide isomer involved.

Polysaccharides are macromolecules consisting of straight or branched chains of many monosaccharides. They can consist of one or more types of monosaccharides. The most common polysaccharides (cellulose, starch, and glycogen) contain only glucose, but their properties are very different. These differences are a function of the glucose isomer involved and the types of linkages joining the monomers. Different polysaccharides can thus be a source of readily available glucose or a structural material that resists digestion.

Cellulose

Cellulose is a structural material found in the cell walls of plants. It is made up of unbranched chains of β-glucose molecules held together by β-1,4 glycosidic links. As many as 10 000 glucose molecules may be linked together to form a straight chain. Parallel chains become cross-linked with hydrogen bonds and form bundles of 60-70 molecules called **microfibrils**. Cellulose microfibrils are very strong and are a major structural component of plants, e.g. as the cell wall. Few organisms can break the β-linkages so cellulose is an ideal structural material.

Starch

Starch is also a polymer of glucose, but it is made up of long chains of α-glucose molecules linked together. It contains a mixture of 25-30% amylose (unbranched chains linked by α-1,4 glycosidic bonds) and 70-75% amylopectin (branched chains with α-1, 6 glycosidic bonds every 24-30 glucose units). Starch is an energy storage molecule in plants and is found concentrated in insoluble starch granules within specialised plastids called amyloplasts in plant cells (see photo, right). Starch can be easily hydrolysed by enzymes to soluble sugars when required.

Glycogen

Glycogen, like starch, is a branched polysaccharide. It is chemically similar to amylopectin, being composed of α-glucose molecules, but there are more α-1,6 glycosidic links mixed with α-1,4 links. This makes it more highly branched and more water-soluble than starch. Glycogen is a storage compound in animal tissues and is found mainly in liver and muscle cells (photo, right). It is readily hydrolysed by enzymes to form glucose making it an ideal energy storage molecule for active animals.

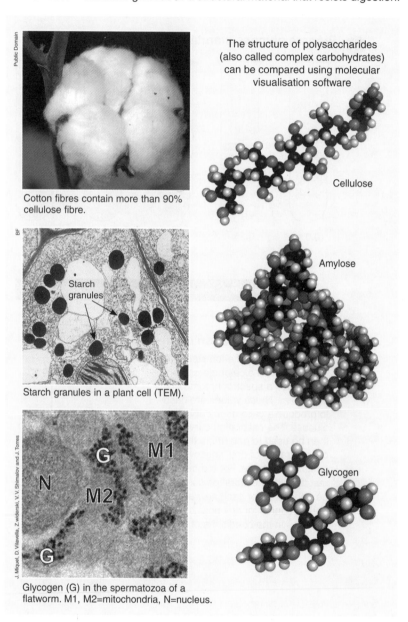

Cotton fibres contain more than 90% cellulose fibre.

Starch granules in a plant cell (TEM).

Glycogen (G) in the spermatozoa of a flatworm. M1, M2=mitochondria, N=nucleus.

The structure of polysaccharides (also called complex carbohydrates) can be compared using molecular visualisation software

Cellulose

Amylose

Glycogen

1. (a) Why are polysaccharides such a good source of energy? _____

_____

(b) How is the energy stored in polysaccharides mobilised? _____

_____

2. Contrast the properties of the polysaccharides starch, cellulose, and glycogen and relate these to their roles in the cell:

_____

_____

_____

_____

_____

© 2015 **BIOZONE** International
ISBN: 978-1-927309-25-4
Photocopying Prohibited

36 Starch and Cellulose

Key Idea: Starch and cellulose are important polysaccharides in plants. Starch is a storage carbohydrate made up of two α-glucose polymers, amylose and amylopectin. Cellulose is a β-glucose polymer which forms the plant cell wall.

Glucose monomers can be linked in condensation reactions to form large structural and energy storage polysaccharides. The glucose isomer involved and the type of glycosidic linkage determines the properties of the molecule.

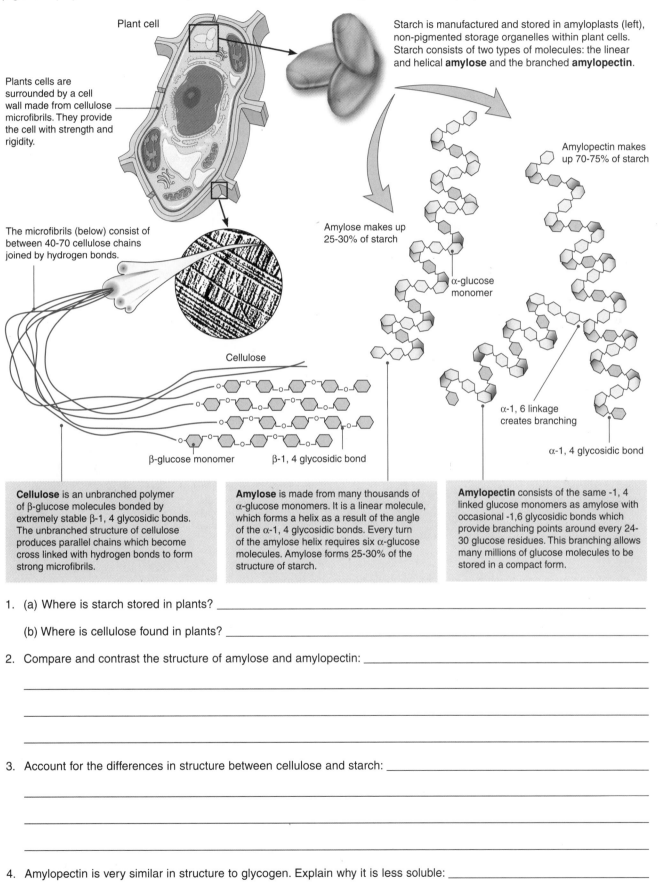

Plant cell

Plants cells are surrounded by a cell wall made from cellulose microfibrils. They provide the cell with strength and rigidity.

The microfibrils (below) consist of between 40-70 cellulose chains joined by hydrogen bonds.

Cellulose

β-glucose monomer   β-1, 4 glycosidic bond

Starch is manufactured and stored in amyloplasts (left), non-pigmented storage organelles within plant cells. Starch consists of two types of molecules: the linear and helical **amylose** and the branched **amylopectin**.

Amylopectin makes up 70-75% of starch

Amylose makes up 25-30% of starch

α-glucose monomer

α-1, 6 linkage creates branching

α-1, 4 glycosidic bond

Cellulose is an unbranched polymer of β-glucose molecules bonded by extremely stable β-1, 4 glycosidic bonds. The unbranched structure of cellulose produces parallel chains which become cross linked with hydrogen bonds to form strong microfibrils.

Amylose is made from many thousands of α-glucose monomers. It is a linear molecule, which forms a helix as a result of the angle of the α-1, 4 glycosidic bonds. Every turn of the amylose helix requires six α-glucose molecules. Amylose forms 25-30% of the structure of starch.

Amylopectin consists of the same -1, 4 linked glucose monomers as amylose with occasional -1,6 glycosidic bonds which provide branching points around every 24-30 glucose residues. This branching allows many millions of glucose molecules to be stored in a compact form.

1. (a) Where is starch stored in plants? _____

   (b) Where is cellulose found in plants? _____

2. Compare and contrast the structure of amylose and amylopectin: _____

   _____

   _____

   _____

3. Account for the differences in structure between cellulose and starch: _____

   _____

   _____

   _____

4. Amylopectin is very similar in structure to glycogen. Explain why it is less soluble: _____

   _____

© 2015 **BIOZONE** International
ISBN: 978-1-927309-25-4
Photocopying Prohibited

LINK
84

LINK
32

KNOW

37 Lipids

Key Idea: Lipids are non-polar, hydrophobic organic molecules, which have many important biological functions. Fatty acids are the building blocks of more complex lipids.
Lipids are organic compounds which are mostly nonpolar (have no overall charge) and hydrophobic, so they do not readily dissolve in water. Lipids include fats, waxes, sterols, and phospholipids. Fatty acids are a major component of neutral fats and phospholipids. Most fatty acids consist of an even number of carbon atoms, with hydrogen bound along the length of the chain. The carboxyl group (–COOH) at one end makes them an acid. They are generally classified as saturated or unsaturated fatty acids (below).

Triglycerides

Glycerol Ester bond Fatty acids

Triglyceride: an example of a neutral fat

Neutral fats and oils are the most abundant lipids in living things. They make up the fats and oils found in plants and animals. They consist of a glycerol attached to one (mono-), two (di-) or three (tri-) fatty acids by **ester bonds**. Lipids have a high proportion of hydrogen present in the fatty acid chains. When the molecule is metabolised, the chemical energy is released. Being so reduced and anhydrous, they are an economical way to store fuel reserves, and provide more than twice as much energy as the same quantity of carbohydrate.

Lipids containing a high proportion of saturated fatty acids tend to be solids at room temperature (e.g. butter). Lipids with a high proportion of unsaturated fatty acids are oils and tend to be liquid at room temperature (e.g. olive oil). This is because the unsaturation causes kinks in the straight chains so that the fatty acid chains do not pack closely together.

Saturated and unsaturated fatty acids

Fatty acids are carboxylic acids with long hydrocarbon chains. They are classed as either saturated or unsaturated. **Saturated fatty acids** contain the maximum number of hydrogen atoms. **Unsaturated fatty acids** contain some double-bonds between carbon atoms and are not fully saturated with hydrogens. A chain with only one double bond is called monounsaturated, whereas a chain with two or more double bonds is called polyunsaturated.

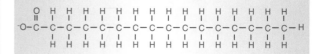

Formula (above) and molecular model (below) for a saturated fatty acid (palmitic acid).

Formula (above) and molecular model (right) for an unsaturated fatty acid (linoleic acid). The arrows indicate double bonded carbon atoms that are not fully saturated with hydrogens.

1. Identify the main components (a-c) of the symbolic triglyceride below:

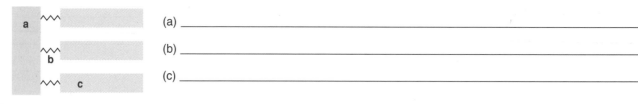

(a) _____

(b) _____

(c) _____

2. Why do lipids have such a high energy content? _____

_____

_____

3. (a) Distinguish between saturated and unsaturated fatty acids: _____

_____

(b) Relate the properties of a neutral fat to the type of fatty acid present: _____

_____

_____

© 2015 **BIOZONE** International
ISBN: 978-1-927309-25-4
Photocopying Prohibited

Triglycerides are formed by condensation reactions

Triglycerides form when glycerol bonds with three fatty acids. Glycerol is an alcohol containing three carbons. Each of these carbons is bonded to a hydroxyl (-OH) group.

When glycerol bonds with the fatty acid, an **ester bond** is formed and water is released. Three separate condensation reactions are involved in producing a triglyceride.

> **Esterification**: A condensation reaction of an alcohol (e.g. glycerol) with an acid (e.g. fatty acid) to produce an ester and water. In the diagram right, the ester bonds are indicated by blue lines.
>
> **Lipolysis:** The breakdown of lipids. It involves hydrolysis of triglycerides into glycerol molecules and free fatty acids.

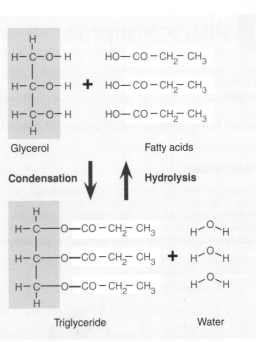

Glycerol   Fatty acids

Condensation ↓   ↑ **Hydrolysis**

Triglyceride   Water

Biological functions of lipids

Lipids are concentrated sources of energy and provide fuel for aerobic respiration.

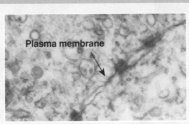

Phospholipids form the structure of cellular membranes in eukaryotes and prokaryotes.

Waxes and oils secreted onto surfaces provide waterproofing in plants and animals.

Fat absorbs shocks. Organs that are prone to bumps and shocks (e.g. kidneys) are cushioned with a relatively thick layer of fat.

Lipids are a source of metabolic water. During respiration stored lipids are metabolised for energy, producing water and carbon dioxide.

Stored lipids provide insulation. Increased body fat levels in winter reduce heat losses to the environment.

---

4. (a) Describe what happens during the esterification (condensation) process to produce a triglyceride:

_____

_____

(b) Describe what happens when a triglyceride is hydrolysed: _____

_____

_____

5. Discuss the biological role of lipids: _____

_____

_____

_____

_____

_____

38 Phospholipids

Key Idea: Phospholipids are modified triglycerides. They are important components of cellular membranes.

Phospholipids are similar in structure to a triglyceride except that a phosphate group replaces one of the fatty acids attached to the glycerol. Phospholipids naturally form bilayers in aqueous solutions and are the main component of all cellular membranes. The fatty acid tails can be saturated (forming straight chains) or unsaturated (kinked chains). The level of phospholipids with saturated or unsaturated tails affects the fluidity of the phospholipid bilayer.

Phospholipids

Phospholipids consist of a glycerol attached to two fatty acid chains and a phosphate (PO_4^{3-}) group. The phosphate end of the molecule is attracted to water (it is hydrophilic) while the fatty acid end is repelled (hydrophobic). The hydrophobic ends turn inwards in the membrane to form a **phospholipid bilayer**.

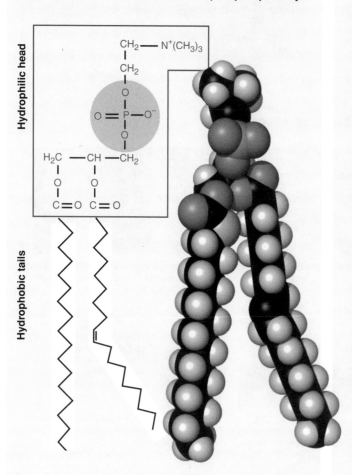

Phospholipids and membranes

The amphipathic (having hydrophobic and hydrophilic ends) nature of phospholipids means that when in water they spontaneously form bilayers. This bilayer structure forms the outer boundary of cells or organelles. Modifications to the different hydrophobic ends of the phospholipids cause the bilayer to change its behaviour. The greater the number of double bonds in the hydrophobic tails, the greater the fluidity of the membrane.

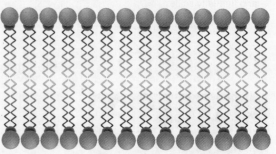

Membrane containing only phospholipids with saturated fatty acid tails.

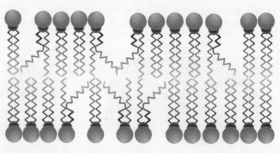

Membrane containing phospholipids with unsaturated fatty acid tails. The fact that the phospholipids do not stack neatly together produces a more fluid membrane.

1. (a) Relate the structure of phospholipids to their chemical properties and their functional role in cellular membranes:

_____

_____

_____

(b) Suggest how the cell membrane structure of an Arctic fish might differ from that of tropical fish species: _____

_____

_____

2. Explain why phospholipid bilayers containing many phospholipids with unsaturated tails are particularly fluid:

_____

_____

_____

© 2015 **BIOZONE** International
ISBN: 978-1-927309-25-4
Photocopying Prohibited

39 Amino Acids

Key Idea: Amino acids join together in a linear chain by condensation reactions to form polypeptides. The sequence of amino acids in a protein is defined by a gene and encoded in the genetic code. In the presence of water, they can be broken apart by hydrolysis into their constituent amino acids.

Amino acids are the basic units from which proteins are made. Twenty amino acids commonly occur in proteins and they can be linked in many different ways by peptide bonds to form a huge variety of polypeptides. Proteins are made up of one or more polypeptide molecules.

The structure and properties of amino acids

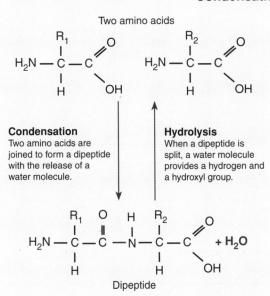

Chemically variable 'R' group

Amine group — NH₂

Carboxyl group

Carbon atom

Hydrogen atom

All amino acids have a common structure (above), but the R group is different in each kind of amino acid (right). The property of the R group determines how it will interact with other amino acids and ultimately determines how the amino acid chain folds up into a functional protein. For example, the hydrophobic R groups of soluble proteins are folded into the protein's interior, while the hydrophilic groups are arranged on the outside.

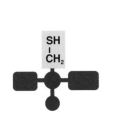

Cysteine

This 'R' group can form **disulfide bridges** with other cysteines to create cross linkages in a polypeptide chain.

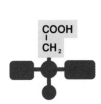

Lysine

This 'R' group gives the amino acid an **alkaline** property.

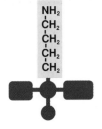

Aspartic acid

This 'R' group gives the amino acid an **acidic** property.

Condensation and hydrolysis reactions

Two amino acids

Condensation
Two amino acids are joined to form a dipeptide with the release of a water molecule.

Hydrolysis
When a dipeptide is split, a water molecule provides a hydrogen and a hydroxyl group.

Dipeptide

Amino acids are linked by **peptide bonds** to form long **polypeptide chains** of up to several thousand amino acids. Peptide bonds form between the carboxyl group of one amino acid and the amine group of another (left). Water is formed as a result of this bond formation.

The sequence of amino acids in a polypeptide is called the **primary structure** and is determined by the order of nucleotides in DNA and mRNA (the gene sequence). The linking of amino acids to form a polypeptide occurs on ribosomes. Once released from the ribosome, a polypeptide will fold into a secondary structure determined by the composition and position of the amino acids making up the chain.

A polypeptide chain

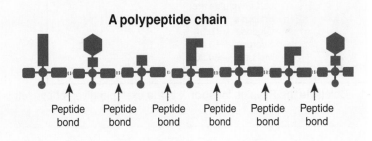

Peptide bond   Peptide bond   Peptide bond   Peptide bond   Peptide bond   Peptide bond

1. (a) What makes each of the amino acids in proteins unique? _____

   (b) What is the primary structure of a protein? _____

   (c) What determines the primary structure? _____

   _____

   (d) How do the sequence and composition of amino acids in a protein influence how a protein folds up? _____

   _____

   _____

2. (a) What type of bond joins neighbouring amino acids together? _____

   (b) How is this bond formed? _____

   (c) Circle this bond in the dipeptide above: _____

   (d) How are di- and polypeptides broken down? _____

LINK 53   LINK 41   LINK 40   WEB 39   **KNOW**

40 Chromatography

Key Idea: Paper chromatography is used to separate substances in a sample solution.

Chromatography is a technique used to separate a mixture of molecules. Chromatography involves passing a mixture dissolved in a mobile phase (a solvent) through a stationary phase, which separates the molecules according to their specific characteristics (e.g. size or charge). Paper chromatography is a simple technique in which porous paper serves as the stationary phase, and a solvent, either water or ethanol, serves as the mobile phase.

Paper chromatography

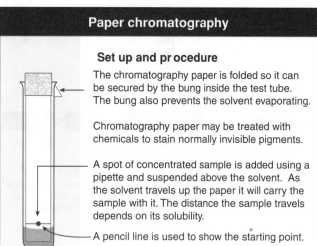

Set up and procedure

The chromatography paper is folded so it can be secured by the bung inside the test tube. The bung also prevents the solvent evaporating.

Chromatography paper may be treated with chemicals to stain normally invisible pigments.

A spot of concentrated sample is added using a pipette and suspended above the solvent. As the solvent travels up the paper it will carry the sample with it. The distance the sample travels depends on its solubility.

A pencil line is used to show the starting point.

Solvent

Determining Rf values

To identify the substances in a mixture an Rf value is calculated using the equation:

$$R_f = \frac{\text{Distance travelled by the spot (x)}}{\text{Distance travelled by the solvent (y)}}$$

These Rf values can then be compared with Rf values from known samples or standards, for example Rf values for the the following carbohydrates are:

Fructose = 0.68
Glucose = 0.64
Sucrose = 0.62
Maltose = 0.50
Lactose = 0.46

Using chromatography to separate amino acids

Mixtures of amino acids can be separated by paper chromatography. The R_f values for amino acids separated using paper chromatography are given below:

Glycine: 0.50
Alanine: 0.70
Arginine: 0.72
Leucine: 0.91

A student was given a solution containing two unknown amino acids. They separated them by paper chromatography and obtained the results below.

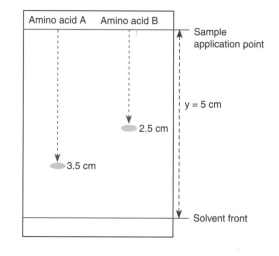

1. Calculate the R_f value for **spot X** in the example given above left (show your working): _____

_____

2. Why is the R_f value of a substance always less than 1? _____

_____

3. Predict what would happen if a sample was immersed in the chromatography solvent, instead of suspended above it:

_____

_____

4. (a) Calculate the R_f values for the two unknown amino acid samples (above right): _____

_____

(b) Based on the R_f values calculated in (a), identify the two amino acids:

Amino acid A: _____   Amino acid B: _____

5. (a) Which two amino acids could be difficult to separate by chromatography?_____

(b) Explain your reasoning: _____

_____

© 2015 **BIOZONE** International
ISBN: 978-1-927309-25-4
Photocopying Prohibited

41 Protein Shape is Related to Function

Key idea: Interactions between amino acid R groups direct a polypeptide chain to fold into its functional shape. When a protein is denatured, it loses its functionality.

A protein may consist of one polypeptide chain, or several polypeptide chains linked together. Hydrogen bonds between amino acids cause it to form its **secondary structure**, either an α-helix or a β-pleated sheet. The interaction between R groups causes a polypeptide to fold into its **tertiary structure**, a three dimensional shape held by ionic bonds and disulfide bridges (bonds formed between sulfur containing amino acids). If bonds are broken (through denaturation), the protein loses its tertiary structure, and its functionality.

The shape of a protein reflects its biological role

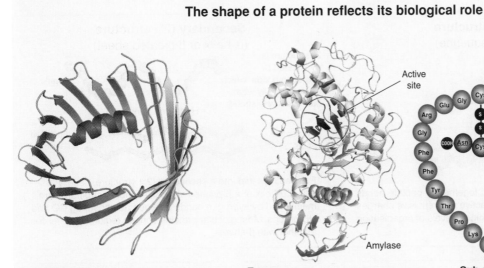

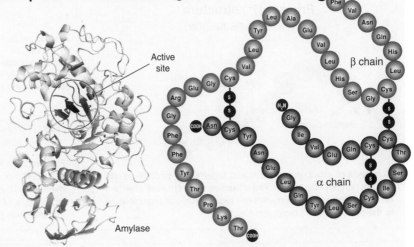

Channel proteins
Proteins that fold to form channels in the plasma membrane present non-polar R groups to the membrane and polar R groups to the inside of the channel. Hydrophilic molecules and ions are then able to pass through these channels into the interior of the cell. Ion channels are found in nearly all cells and many organelles.

Enzymes
Enzymes are globular proteins that catalyse specific reactions. Enzymes that are folded to present polar R groups at the active site will be specific for polar substances. Non-polar active sites will be specific for non-polar substances. Alteration of the active site by extremes of temperature or pH cause a loss of function.

Sub-unit proteins
Many proteins, e.g. insulin and haemoglobin, consist of two or more sub-units in a complex quaternary structure, often in association with a metal ion. Active insulin is formed by two polypeptide chains stabilised by disulfide bridges between neighbouring cysteines. Insulin stimulates glucose uptake by cells.

Protein denaturation

When the chemical bonds holding a protein together become broken the protein can no longer hold its three dimensional shape. This process is called **denaturation**, and the protein usually loses its ability to carry out its biological function.

There are many causes of denaturation including exposure to heat or pH outside of the protein's optimum range. The main protein in egg white is albumin. It has a clear, thick fluid appearance in a raw egg (right). Heat (cooking) denatures the albumin protein and it becomes insoluble, clumping together to form a thick white substance (far right).

Raw (native) egg white

Cooked (denatured) egg white

1. Explain the importance of the amino acid sequence in protein folding: _____

2. Why do channel proteins often fold with non-polar R groups to the channel's exterior and polar R groups to its interior?

3. Why does **denaturation** often result in the loss of protein functionality? _____

© 2015 **BIOZONE** International
ISBN: 978-1-927309-25-4
Photocopying Prohibited

LINK 43 LINK 42 WEB 41 **KNOW**

42 Protein Structure

Key Idea: The sequence and type of amino acids in a protein determines the protein's three-dimensional shape and function.

Proteins are large, complex **macromolecules**, built up from a linear sequence of repeating units called **amino acids**. Proteins are molecules of central importance in the chemistry of life. They account for more than 50% of the dry weight of most cells, and they are important in virtually every cellular process. The folding of a protein into its functional form creates a three dimensional arrangement of the active 'R' groups. It is this **tertiary structure** that gives a protein its unique chemical properties. If a protein loses this precise structure (through **denaturation**), it is usually unable to carry out its biological function.

Primary (1°) structure
(amino acid sequence)

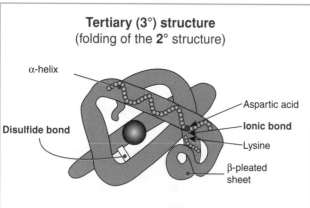

Hundreds of amino acids are linked together by peptide bonds to form polypeptide chains. The attractive and repulsive charges on the amino acids determines the higher levels of organisation in the protein and its biological function.

Secondary (2°) structure
(α-helix or β pleated sheet)

2° structure is maintained by hydrogen bonds, which are individually weak but collectively strong

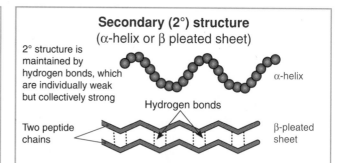

α-helix

Hydrogen bonds

Two peptide chains

β-pleated sheet

Polypeptides fold into a secondary (2°) structure, usually a coiled α-helix or a β-pleated sheet. Secondary structures are maintained by hydrogen bonds between neighbouring CO and NH groups. Most globular proteins contain regions of α-helices together with β-sheets.

Tertiary (3°) structure
(folding of the 2° structure)

α-helix

Disulfide bond

Aspartic acid

Ionic bond

Lysine

β-pleated sheet

A protein's tertiary structure is the three-dimensional shape it forms when the secondary structure folds up. Chemical bonds such as **disulfide bridges** between cysteine amino acids, ionic bonds, hydrogen bonds, and hydrophobic interactions result in protein folding. These bonds can be destroyed by heavy metals or some solvents, and extremes of pH and temperature.

Quaternary (4°) structure

In haemoglobin, each polypeptide chain encloses an iron-containing prosthetic group (haem group).

Alpha chain

Beta chain

Many complex proteins exist as groups of polypeptide chains. The arrangement of the polypeptide chains into a functional protein is termed the quaternary structure. The example (above) shows haemoglobin, which has a quaternary structure comprising two alpha and two beta polypeptide chains, each enclosing a complex iron-containing prosthetic group.

---

1. Describe the main features that aid the formation of each part of a protein's structure:

   (a) Primary structure: _____

   (b) Secondary structure: _____

   _____

   (c) Tertiary structure: _____

   _____

   (d) Quaternary structure: _____

   _____

2. How are proteins built up into a functional structure? _____

   _____

   _____

43 Comparing Globular and Fibrous Proteins

Key Idea: Protein structure is related to its biological function. Proteins can be classified according to their structure or their function. **Globular proteins** are spherical and soluble in water (e.g. enzymes). **Fibrous proteins** have an elongated structure and are not water soluble. They are often made up of repeating units and provide stiffness and rigidity to the more fluid components of cells and tissues. They have important structural and contractile roles.

Globular proteins

Properties
- Easily water soluble
- Tertiary structure critical to function
- Polypeptide chains folded into a spherical shape

Function
- Catalytic, *e.g. enzymes*
- Regulatory, *e.g. hormones (insulin)*
- Transport, *e.g. haemoglobin*
- Protective, *e.g. immunoglobulins (antibodies)*

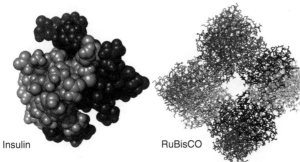

Insulin

RuBisCO

Insulin is a peptide hormone involved in the regulation of blood glucose. Insulin is composed of two peptide chains (the A chain and the B chain) linked together by two disulfide bonds.

RuBisCo is a large multi-unit enzyme found in green plants and catalyses the first step of carbon fixation in the Calvin cycle. It consists of 8 large (L) and 8 small (S) subunits arranged as 4 dimers. RuBisCO is the most abundant protein on Earth.

Haemoglobin is an oxygen-transporting protein found in vertebrate red blood cells. One haemoglobin molecule consists of four polypeptide chains (two identical alpha chains and two identical beta chains). Each polypeptide subunit contains a non-protein prosthetic group, an iron-containing haem group, which binds oxygen.

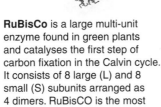

Haemoglobin

Fibrous proteins

Properties
- Water insoluble
- Very tough physically; may be supple or stretchy
- Parallel polypeptide chains in long fibres or sheets

Function
- Structural role in cells and organisms e.g. *collagen found in connective tissue, cartilage, bones, tendons, and blood vessel walls.*
- Contractile e.g. *myosin, actin*

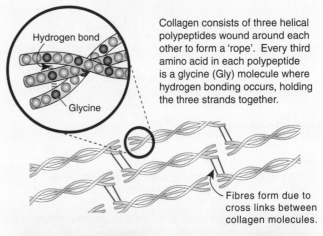

Hydrogen bond

Glycine

Collagen consists of three helical polypeptides wound around each other to form a 'rope'. Every third amino acid in each polypeptide is a glycine (Gly) molecule where hydrogen bonding occurs, holding the three strands together.

Fibres form due to cross links between collagen molecules.

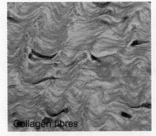

Collagen fibres

This rhinoceros' horn is keratin

Collagen is the main component of connective tissue, and is mostly found in fibrous tissues (e.g. tendons, ligaments, and skin). The elastic properties of **elastin** allows tissues to resume their shape after stretching. Skin, arteries, lungs, and bladder all contain elastin. **Keratin** is found in hair, nails, horn, hooves, wool, feathers, and the outer layers of the skin. The polypeptide chains of keratin are arranged in parallel sheets held together by hydrogen bonding.

1. How are proteins involved in the following roles? Give examples to help illustrate your answer:

   (a) Structural tissues of the body: _____

   _____

   _____

   (b) Catalysing metabolic reactions in cells: _____

   _____

   _____

2. How does the shape of a fibrous protein relate to its functional role? _____

   _____

3. How does the shape of a catalytic protein (enzyme) relate to its functional role? _____

   _____

44 Biochemical Tests

Key Idea: Qualitative biochemical tests detect the presence of a specific molecule in food.

Qualitative biochemical tests can be used to detect the presence of molecules such as lipids, proteins, or carbohydrates (sugars and starch). However, they cannot be used directly to determine absolute concentrations or distinguish between different molecules of the same type (e.g. different sugars in a mixed solution).

Simple food tests

Proteins: The Biuret Test

Reagent:	Biuret solution.
Procedure:	A sample is added to biuret solution and gently heated.
Positive result:	Solution turns from blue to lilac.

Starch: The Iodine Test

Reagent:	Iodine.
Procedure:	Iodine solution is added to the sample.
Positive result:	Blue-black staining occurs.

Lipids: The Emulsion Test

Reagent:	Ethanol.
Procedure:	The sample is shaken with ethanol. After settling, the liquid portion is distilled and mixed with water.
Positive result:	The solution turns into a cloudy-white emulsion of suspended lipid molecules.

Sugars: The Benedict's Test

Reagent:	Benedict's solution.
Procedure:	Non reducing sugars: The sample is boiled with dilute hydrochloric acid (acid hydrolysis), then cooled and neutralised. A test for reducing sugars is then performed.
	Reducing sugar: Benedict's solution is added, and the sample is placed in a water bath.
Positive result:	Solution turns from blue to orange to red-brown.

A Qualitative test for reducing sugar

To determine whether this muffin contains any reducing sugars (e.g. glucose), the Benedict's test for reducing sugar is carried out.

The muffin is placed in a blender with some water and mixed until it forms an homogenous (uniform) mixture.

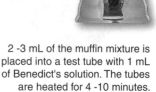

2 -3 mL of the muffin mixture is placed into a test tube with 1 mL of Benedict's solution. The tubes are heated for 4 -10 minutes.

The intensity of the colour depends on the concentration of glucose present in the sample. The darker the colour, the more glucose is present. A **colorimetric analysis** enables the amount of glucose present to be quantified (see the following activity).

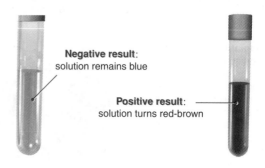

Negative result: solution remains blue

Positive result: solution turns red-brown

1. Explain why lipids must be mixed in ethanol before they will form an emulsion in water: _____

_____

_____

2. Explain why the emulsion of lipids, ethanol, and water appears cloudy: _____

_____

_____

3. What is the purpose of the acid hydrolysis step when testing for non-reducing sugars with Benedict's reagent?

_____

_____

4. What are the limitations of qualitative tests such as those described above? _____

_____

_____

© 2015 **BIOZONE** International
ISBN: 978-1-927309-25-4
Photocopying Prohibited

45 Nucleotides

Key Idea: Nucleotides make up nucleic acids. A nucleotide is made up of a base, a sugar, and a phosphate group. Nucleotides are the building blocks of the nucleic acids DNA and RNA, which are involved in the transmission of inherited information. Nucleotide derivatives, such as ATP and GTP, are involved in energy transfers in cells. A nucleotide has three components: a base, a sugar, and a phosphate group. Nucleotides may contain one of five bases. The combination of bases in the nucleotides making up DNA or RNA stores the information controlling the cell's activity. The bases in DNA are the same as RNA except that thymine (T) in DNA is replaced with uracil (U) in RNA.

Pyrimidines

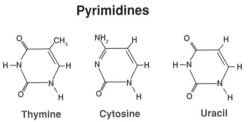

Thymine   **Cytosine**   **Uracil**

Pyrimidines are single ringed bases. DNA contains the pyrimidines cytosine (C) and thymine (T). RNA contains the pyrimidines cytosine and uracil (U).

Purines

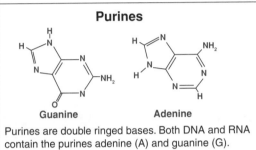

Guanine   **Adenine**

Purines are double ringed bases. Both DNA and RNA contain the purines adenine (A) and guanine (G).

Phosphate

Phosphate groups are represented by circles. Along with the pentose sugar they form the "backbone" of the DNA or RNA molecule.

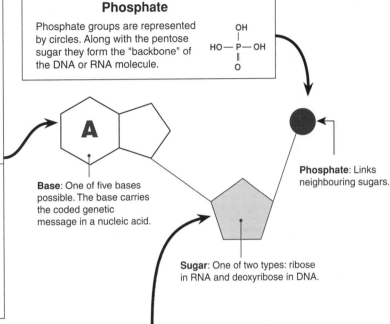

Phosphate: Links neighbouring sugars.

Base: One of five bases possible. The base carries the coded genetic message in a nucleic acid.

Sugar: One of two types: ribose in RNA and deoxyribose in DNA.

Nucleotide derivatives

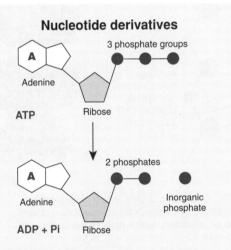

ATP   Ribose

ADP + Pi   Ribose

Adenine

Inorganic phosphate

ATP is a nucleotide derivative used to provide chemical energy for metabolism. It consists of an adenine linked to a ribose sugar and 3 phosphate groups. Energy is made available when a phosphate group is transferred to a target molecule. Other nucleoside triphosphates (NTPs) have similar roles.

Sugars

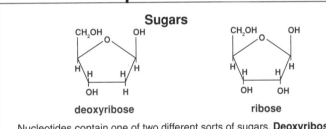

deoxyribose   **ribose**

Nucleotides contain one of two different sorts of sugars. **Deoxyribose** sugar is only found in DNA. **Ribose** sugar is found in RNA.

Nucleotide formation

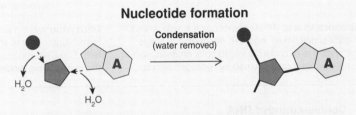

Condensation (water removed)

Phosphoric acid and a base are chemically bonded to a sugar molecule by a **condensation** reaction in which water is given off. The reverse reaction is **hydrolysis**.

1. List the nucleotide bases present:

   (a) In DNA: _____

   (b) In RNA: _____

2. Name the sugar present: (a) In DNA: _____ (b) In RNA: _____

3. How can simple nucleotide units combine to store genetic information? _____

   _____

   _____

LINK   WEB

46   **45**   **KNOW**

46 Nucleic Acids

Key Idea: Nucleic acids are macromolecules made up of long chains of nucleotides, which store and transmit genetic information. DNA and RNA are nucleic acids.

DNA and RNA are nucleic acids involved in the transmission of inherited information. Nucleic acids have the capacity to store the information that controls cellular activity. The central nucleic acid is called **deoxyribonucleic acid** (DNA). **Ribonucleic acids** (RNA) are involved in the 'reading' of the DNA information. All nucleic acids are made up of nucleotides linked together to form chains or strands. The strands vary in the sequence of the bases found on each nucleotide. It is this sequence which provides the 'genetic code' for the cell.

Joining nucleotides

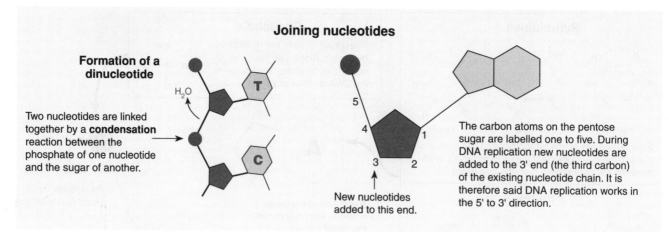

Formation of a dinucleotide

Two nucleotides are linked together by a **condensation** reaction between the phosphate of one nucleotide and the sugar of another.

H_2O

New nucleotides added to this end.

The carbon atoms on the pentose sugar are labelled one to five. During DNA replication new nucleotides are added to the 3' end (the third carbon) of the existing nucleotide chain. It is therefore said DNA replication works in the 5' to 3' direction.

RNA molecule

In RNA, uracil replaces thymine in the code.

Ribose sugar

Ribonucleic acid (RNA) comprises a single strand of nucleotides linked together. Although it is single stranded, it is often found folded back on itself, with complementary bases joined by hydrogen bonds.

DNA molecule

Deoxyribose sugar

Hydrogen bonds hold the two strands together. Only certain bases can pair.

Symbolic representation

Space filling model

Deoxyribonucleic acid (DNA) comprises a double strand of nucleotides linked together. It is shown unwound in the symbolic representation (above left). The DNA molecule takes on a twisted, double helix shape as shown in the space filling model above right.

Double-stranded DNA

The double-helix structure of DNA is like a ladder twisted into a corkscrew shape around its longitudinal axis. It is 'unwound' here to show the relationships between the bases.

▸ The DNA backbone is made up of alternating phosphate and sugar molecules, giving the DNA molecule an asymmetrical structure.

▸ The asymmetrical structure gives a DNA strand **direction**. Each strand runs in the opposite direction to the other.

▸ The ends of a DNA strand are labelled the 5' (five prime) and 3' (three prime) ends. The **5'** end has a terminal phosphate group (off carbon 5), the **3'** end has a terminal hydroxyl group (off carbon 3).

▸ The way the pairs of bases come together to form hydrogen bonds is determined by the number of bonds they can form and the configuration of the bases.

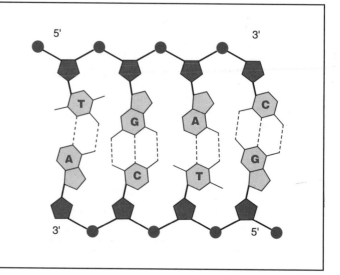

© 2015 **BIOZONE** International
ISBN: 978-1-927309-25-4
Photocopying Prohibited

RNAs are involved in decoding the genetic information in DNA, as messenger RNA (mRNA), transfer RNA (tRNA), and ribosomal RNA (rRNA). RNA is also involved in modifying mRNA after transcription and in regulating translation.

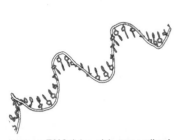

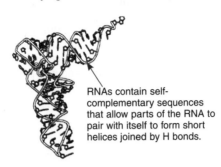

RNAs contain self-complementary sequences that allow parts of the RNA to pair with itself to form short helices joined by H bonds.

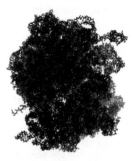

Messenger RNA (above) is transcribed (written) from DNA. It carries a copy of the genetic instructions from the DNA to ribosomes in the cytoplasm, where it is translated into a polypeptide chain.

Transfer RNA (above) carries amino acids to the growing polypeptide chain. One end of the tRNA carries the genetic code in a three-nucleotide sequence called the **anticodon**. The amino acid links to the 3' end of the tRNA.

Ribosomal RNA (above) forms ribosomes from two separate ribosomal components (the large and small subunits) and assembles amino acids into a polypeptide chain.

1. Label the following parts on the diagram of the double-stranded DNA molecule at the bottom of page 60:
   (a) Deoxyribose   (b) Phosphate   (c) Hydrogen bonds   (d) Purine bases   (e) Pyrimidine bases

2. (a) Explain the **base-pairing rule** that applies in double-stranded DNA: _____

   _____

   _____

   (b) How is the base-pairing rule for mRNA different? _____

   (c) What is the purpose of the hydrogen bonds in double-stranded DNA? _____

   _____

3. Briefly describe the roles of RNA: _____

   _____

4. (a) If you wanted to use a radioactive or fluorescent tag to label only the RNA in a cell and not the DNA, what molecule(s) would you label?

   _____

   (b) If you wanted to use a radioactive or fluorescent tag to label only the DNA in a cell and not the RNA, what molecule(s) would you label?

   _____

5. (a) Why do the DNA strands have an asymmetrical structure? _____

   _____

   (b) What are the differences between the 5' and 3' ends of a DNA strand? _____

   _____

6. Complete the following table summarising the differences between DNA and RNA molecules:

	DNA	RNA
Sugar present		
Bases present		
Number of strands		
Relative length		

47 Determining the Structure of DNA

Key Idea: Once the structure of DNA was known, it immediately suggested a mechanism for its replication.
DNA is easily extracted and isolated from cells (see below). This was first done in 1869, but it took the work of many scientists working in different areas many years to determine DNA's structure. The final pieces of evidence came from a photographic technique called X-ray crystallography in which X-rays are shone through crystallised molecules to produce a pattern on a film. The pattern can be used to understand the structure of the molecule. The focus of much subsequent research on DNA has been on DNA products, i.e. proteins and non-protein regulatory molecules (regulatory RNAs).

Discovering the structure of DNA

Although James Watson and Francis Crick are often credited with the discovery of the structure of DNA, at least two other scientists were instrumental in acquiring the images on which Watson and Crick based their discovery.

Maurice Wilkins and Rosalind Franklin produced X-ray diffraction patterns of the DNA molecule. The patterns provided measurements of different parts of the molecule and the position of different groups of atoms. Wilkins showed Franklin's X-ray image (photo 51) to Watson and Crick who then correctly interpreted the image and produced a model of the DNA molecule.

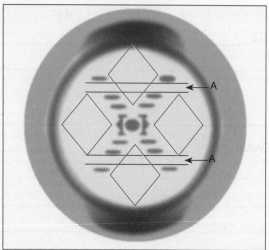

Diagram representing the image produced by Rosalind Franklin

Numerous distinct parts of the X-ray image indicate specific qualities of the DNA. The distinct X pattern indicates a helix structure, but Watson and Crick realised that the apparent gaps in the X (labelled **A**) were due to the repeating pattern of a *double* helix. The diamond shapes (in blue) indicate the helix is continuous and of constant dimensions and that the sugar-phosphate backbone is on the outside of the helix. The distance between the dark horizontal bands allows the calculation of the length of one full turn of the helix.

Structure and replication

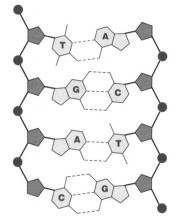

The realisation that DNA was a double helix consisting of antiparallel strands made of bases that followed a strict base pairing rule suggested a mechanism for its replication.

Watson and Crick hypothesised that each strand served as a template and that DNA replication was semi-conservative, producing two daughter strands consisting of half new and half parent material. This was confirmed by Meselson and Stahl.

Non protein-coding regions

Only about 2% of the DNA in humans codes for proteins. Much of the rest codes for RNA (e.g. tRNA) or has a regulatory function, e.g. the centromere or telomeres. In general, the genomes of more complex organisms contain much more of this so-called "non protein-coding" DNA. Even within protein coding sequences, parts of the DNA are excised from the primary transcript to create the mRNA that codes for the protein to be translated. The protein-coding regions (**exons**) are interrupted by non-protein-coding regions called **introns**. Introns are edited out of the protein-coding sequence prior to translation (protein synthesis). After processing, the introns may go on to serve a regulatory function.

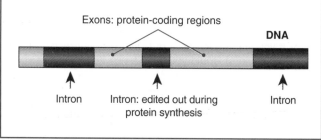

Exons: protein-coding regions

DNA

Intron   Intron: edited out during   Intron
                protein synthesis

1. What made Watson and Crick realise that DNA was a double helix? _____

_____

_____

2. How did the structure of DNA suggest a mechanism for its self replication? _____

_____

_____

3. (a) Describe the organisation of protein-coding regions in eukaryotic DNA: _____

_____

   (b) What might be the purpose of the introns? _____

_____

© 2015 **BIOZONE** International
ISBN: 978-1-927309-25-4
Photocopying Prohibited

48 Constructing a DNA Model

Key Idea: Nucleotides pair together in a specific way called the base pairing rule. In DNA, adenine always pairs with thymine, and cytosine always pairs with guanine. DNA molecules are double stranded. Each strand is made up of nucleotides. The chemical properties of each nucleotide mean it can only bind with one other type of nucleotide. This is called the **base pairing rule** and is explained in the table below. This exercise will help you to learn this rule.

DNA base pairing rule			
Adenine	is always attracted to	**Thymine**	A ◄──► T
Thymine	is always attracted to	**Adenine**	T ◄──► A
Cytosine	is always attracted to	**Guanine**	C ◄──► G
Guanine	is always attracted to	**Cytosine**	G ◄──► C

1. Cut around the nucleotides on page 65 and separate each of the 24 nucleotides by cutting along the columns and rows (see arrows indicating two such cutting points). Although drawn as geometric shapes, these symbols represent chemical structures.

2. Place one of each of the four kinds of nucleotide on their correct spaces below:

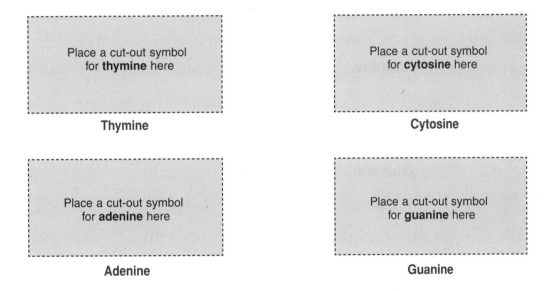

Place a cut-out symbol for **thymine** here

Thymine

Place a cut-out symbol for **cytosine** here

Cytosine

Place a cut-out symbol for **adenine** here

Adenine

Place a cut-out symbol for **guanine** here

Guanine

3. Identify and **label** each of the following features on the adenine nucleotide immediately above:
   phosphate, sugar, base, hydrogen bonds

4. Create one strand of the DNA molecule by placing the 9 correct 'cut out' nucleotides in the labelled spaces on the following page (DNA molecule). Make sure these are the right way up (with the **P** on the left) and are aligned with the left hand edge of each box. Begin with thymine and end with guanine.

5. Create the complementary strand of DNA by using the base pairing rule above. Note that the nucleotides have to be arranged upside down.

6. Under normal circumstances, it is not possible for adenine to pair up with guanine or cytosine, nor for any other mismatches to occur. Describe the **two factors** that prevent a mismatch from occurring:

Factor 1: _____

_____

Factor 2: _____

_____

7. Once you have checked that the arrangement is correct, you may glue, paste or tape these nucleotides in place.

> **NOTE:** There may be some value in keeping these pieces loose in order to practise the base pairing rule. For this purpose, *removable tape* would be best.

 © 2015 **BIOZONE** International
ISBN: 978-1-927309-25-4
Photocopying Prohibited

PRAC

64

DNA molecule

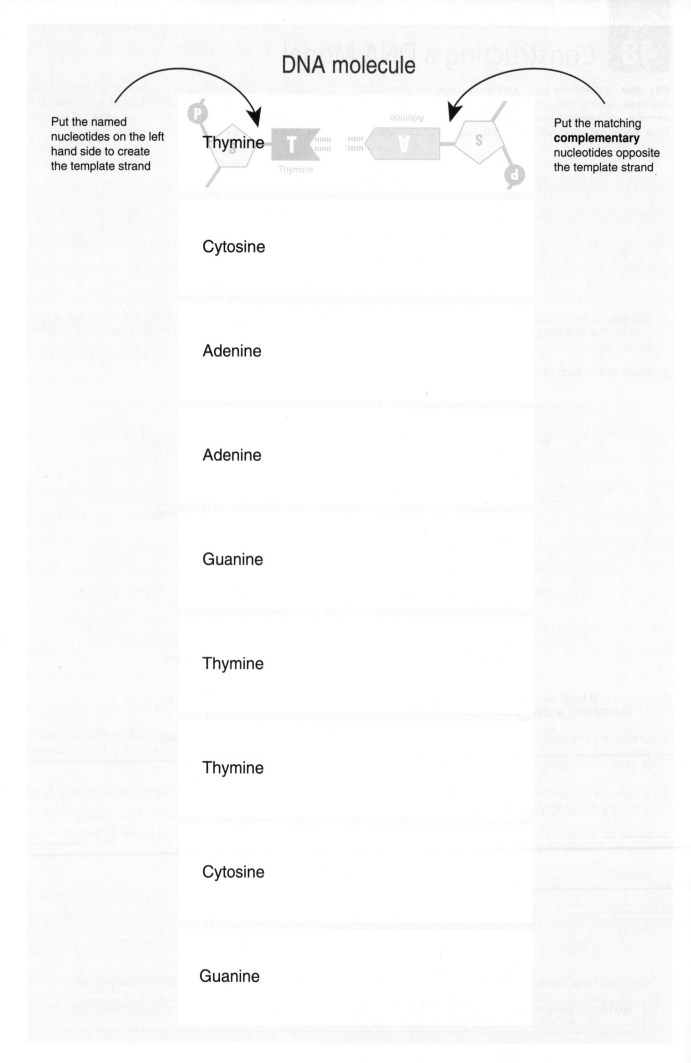

Put the named nucleotides on the left hand side to create the template strand

Put the matching **complementary** nucleotides opposite the template strand

Thymine

Thymine

Adenine

Cytosine

Adenine

Adenine

Guanine

Thymine

Thymine

Cytosine

Guanine

Nucleotides

Tear out this page along the perforation and separate each of the 24 nucleotides by cutting along the columns and rows (see arrows indicating the cutting points).

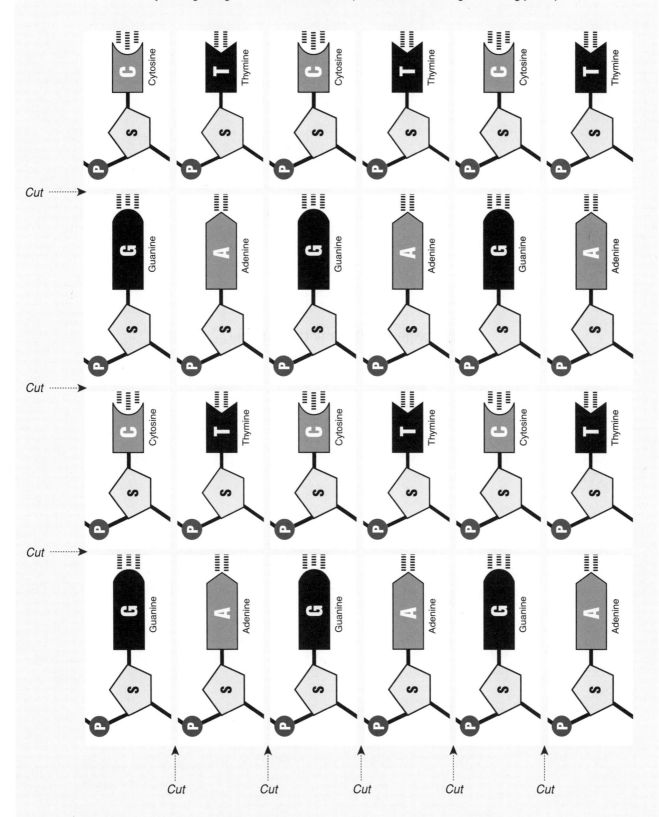

This page is left blank deliberately

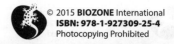

49 | DNA Replication

Key Idea: Semi conservative DNA replication produces two identical copies of DNA, each containing half original material and half new material.

Before a cell can divide, it must double its DNA. It does this by a process called DNA replication. This process ensures that each resulting cell receives a complete set of genes from the original cell. After the DNA has replicated, each chromosome is made up of two chromatids, joined at the centromere. The two chromatids will become separated during cell division to form two separate chromosomes. During DNA replication, nucleotides are added at the replication fork. Enzymes are responsible for all of the key events.

Step 1
Unwinding the DNA molecule

A normal chromosome consists of an unreplicated DNA molecule. Before cell division, this long molecule of double stranded DNA must be replicated.

For this to happen, it is first untwisted and separated (unzipped) at high speed at its replication fork by an enzyme called helicase. Another enzyme relieves the strain that this generates by cutting, winding and rejoining the DNA strands.

Step 2
Making new DNA strands

The formation of new DNA is carried out mostly by an enzyme complex called **DNA polymerase**.

DNA polymerase works in a 5' to 3' direction so nucleotides are assembled in a continuous fashion on one strand but in short fragments on the other strand. These fragments are later joined by an enzyme to form one continuous length.

Step 3
Rewinding the DNA molecule

Each of the two new double-helix DNA molecules has one strand of the original DNA (dark grey and white) and one strand that is newly synthesised (blue). The two DNA molecules rewind into their double-helix shape again.

DNA replication is semi-conservative, with each new double helix containing one old (parent) strand and one newly synthesised (daughter) strand. The new chromosome has twice as much DNA as a non-replicated chromosome. The two chromatids will become separated in the cell division process to form two separate chromosomes.

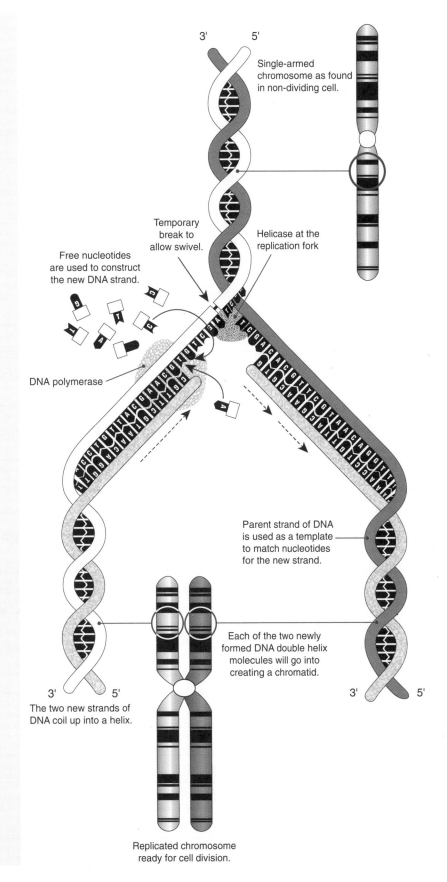

Single-armed chromosome as found in non-dividing cell.

Temporary break to allow swivel.

Helicase at the replication fork

Free nucleotides are used to construct the new DNA strand.

DNA polymerase

Parent strand of DNA is used as a template to match nucleotides for the new strand.

Each of the two newly formed DNA double helix molecules will go into creating a chromatid.

The two new strands of DNA coil up into a helix.

Replicated chromosome ready for cell division.

LINK **51**   LINK **50**   WEB **49**   KNOW

1. What is the purpose of DNA replication? _____

   _____

2. Summarise the three main steps involved in DNA replication:

   (a) _____

   _____

   (b) _____

   _____

   (c) _____

   _____

3. For a cell with 22 chromosomes, state how many chromatids would exist following DNA replication: _____

4. State the percentage of DNA in each daughter cell that is new and the percentage that is original: _____

   _____

5. What does it mean when we say DNA replication is semi-conservative? _____

   _____

   _____

6. How are the new strands of DNA lengthened during replication: _____

   _____

   _____

7. What rule ensures that the two new DNA strands are identical to the original strand? _____

   _____

8. Why does one strand of DNA need to be copied in short fragments? _____

   _____

   _____

   _____

9. Match the statements in the table below to form complete sentences, then put the sentences in order to make a
   coherent paragraph about DNA replication and its role:

The enzymes also proofread the DNA during replication...	...is required before mitosis or meiosis can occur.
DNA replication is the process by which the DNA molecule...	...by enzymes.
Replication is tightly controlled...	...to correct any mistakes.
After replication, the chromosome...	...and half new DNA.
DNA replication...	...during mitosis.
The chromatids separate...	...is copied to produce two identical DNA strands.
A chromatid contains half original ...	...is made up of two chromatids.

   Write the complete paragraph here: _____

   _____

   _____

   _____

   _____

   _____

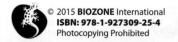 © 2015 **BIOZONE** International
ISBN: 978-1-927309-25-4
Photocopying Prohibited

50 Enzyme Control of DNA Replication

Key Idea: DNA replication is a directional process controlled by several different enzymes.

DNA replication involves many enzyme-controlled steps. They are shown below as separate, but many of the enzymes are clustered together as enzyme complexes. As the DNA is replicated, enzymes 'proof-read' it and correct mistakes. The polymerase enzyme can only work in one direction, so that one new strand is constructed as a continuous length (the leading strand) while the other new strand (the lagging strand) is made in short segments to be later joined together.

DNA replication occurs during interphase of the cell cycle at an astounding rate. As many as 4000 nucleotides per second are replicated. This explains how bacterial cells, with as many as 4 million nucleotides, can complete a cell cycle in about 20 minutes. Note that the nucleotides are present as deoxynucleoside triphosphates. When hydrolysed, these provide the energy for incorporating the nucleotide into the strand.

During the replication of the DNA, a mistake is made about once every 100 000 nucleotides replicated. These mistakes are corrected in two ways. A process called proof-reading occurs during replication. A second process called mis-match repair occurs after replication.

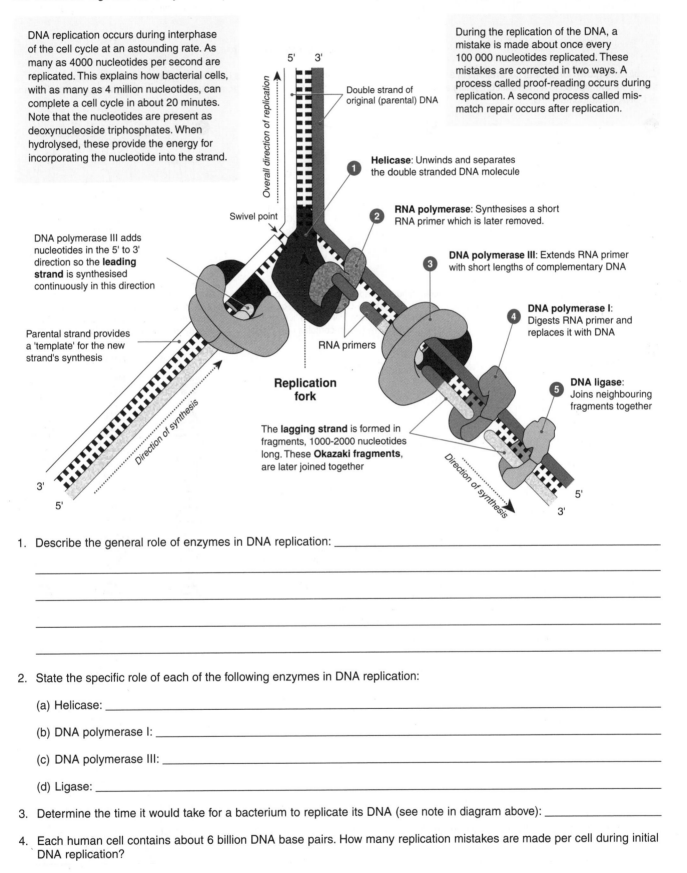

5'   3'

Double strand of original (parental) DNA

Overall direction of replication

Swivel point

Helicase: Unwinds and separates the double stranded DNA molecule ①

RNA polymerase: Synthesises a short RNA primer which is later removed. ②

DNA polymerase III: Extends RNA primer with short lengths of complementary DNA ③

DNA polymerase I: Digests RNA primer and replaces it with DNA ④

DNA ligase: Joins neighbouring fragments together ⑤

DNA polymerase III adds nucleotides in the 5' to 3' direction so the **leading strand** is synthesised continuously in this direction

Parental strand provides a 'template' for the new strand's synthesis

RNA primers

Replication fork

Direction of synthesis

The **lagging strand** is formed in fragments, 1000-2000 nucleotides long. These **Okazaki fragments**, are later joined together

Direction of synthesis

3'

5'

5'

3'

1. Describe the general role of enzymes in DNA replication: _____

_____

_____

_____

_____

2. State the specific role of each of the following enzymes in DNA replication:

   (a) Helicase: _____

   (b) DNA polymerase I: _____

   (c) DNA polymerase III: _____

   (d) Ligase: _____

3. Determine the time it would take for a bacterium to replicate its DNA (see note in diagram above): _____

4. Each human cell contains about 6 billion DNA base pairs. How many replication mistakes are made per cell during initial DNA replication?

_____

LINK   WEB
49   50   KNOW

51 Meselson and Stahl's Experiment

Key Idea: Meselson and Stahl devised an experiment that showed DNA replication is semi-conservative. The anti-parallel, complementary structure of DNA suggested three possible mechanisms for its replication. The **semi-conservative model** proposed that each strand served as a template, forming new DNA molecules that were half old and half new DNA. The **conservative model** proposed that the original DNA served as a complete template so that the new DNA comprised two new strands. The **dispersive model** proposed that the two new DNA molecules had new and old DNA mixed throughout them. **Meselson and Stahl** devised a simple experiment to determine which model was correct.

Meselson and Stahl's experiment

E. coli were grown for several generations in a medium containing a **heavy nitrogen isotope** (^{15}N). Once all the bacterial DNA contained ^{15}N, they were transferred to a medium containing a **light nitrogen isotope** (^{14}N). After the transfer, newly synthesised DNA would contain ^{14}N and old DNA would contain ^{15}N.

1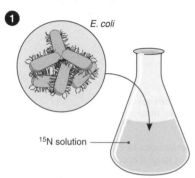

E. coli

^{15}N solution

E. coli were grown in a nutrient solution containing ^{15}N. After 14 generations, all the bacterial DNA contained ^{15}N. A sample is removed. This is **generation 0**.

2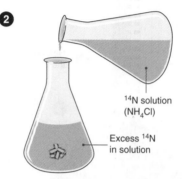

^{14}N solution (NH₄Cl)

Excess ^{14}N in solution

Generation 0 is added to a solution containing excess ^{14}N (as NH₄Cl). During replication, new DNA will incorporate ^{14}N and be 'lighter' than the original DNA (which contains only ^{15}N).

3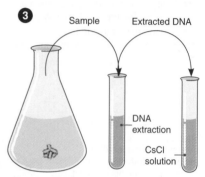

Sample   Extracted DNA

DNA extraction

CsCl solution

Every generation (~ 20 minutes), a sample is taken and treated to release the DNA. The DNA is placed in a CsCl solution which provides a density gradient for separation of the DNA.

4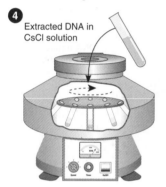

Extracted DNA in CsCl solution

Samples are spun in a high speed ultracentrifuge at 140,000 *g* for 20 hours. Heavier ^{15}N DNA moves closer to the bottom of the test tube than light ^{14}N DNA or intermediate $^{14}N/^{15}N$ DNA.

5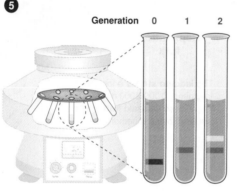

Generation   0   1   2

All the DNA in the generation 0 sample moved to the bottom of the test tube. All the DNA in the generation 1 sample moved to an intermediate position. At generation 2 half the DNA was at the intermediate position and half was near the top of the test tube. In subsequent generations, more DNA was near the top and less was in the intermediate position.

Models for DNA replication

Conservative   Semi-conservative   Dispersive

1. Describe each of the DNA replication models:

   (a) Conservative: _____

   _____

   (b) Semi-conservative: _____

   _____

   (c) Dispersive: _____

   _____

2. Explain why the *E. coli* were grown in an ^{15}N solution before being transferred to an ^{14}N solution: _____

   _____

   _____

© 2015 **BIOZONE** International
ISBN: 978-1-927309-25-4
Photocopying Prohibited

52 Modelling DNA Replication

Key Idea: Meselson and Stahl's experiment to determine the nature of DNA replication can be modelled.

There were three possible models proposed to explain how DNA replicated. Meselson and Stahl's experiment was able to determine which method was used by starting with parent DNA that was heavier than would normally be expected. They were then able to analyse the relative weight of the replicated DNA to work out the correct replication method.

Instructions:

1. Cut out the DNA shapes provided on this page.

2. Intertwine the first pair (labelled 0) of heavy ^{15}N (black) DNA. This forms Generation 0 (parental DNA).

3. Use the descriptions of the three possible models for DNA replication on the previous page to model DNA replication in semi-conservative, conservative, and dispersive DNA replication.

4. For each replication method, record in the spaces provided on page 105 the percentage of **heavy** ^{15}N-^{15}N (black-black), **intermediate** ^{15}N-^{14}N (black-grey), **light** ^{14}N-^{14}N (grey-grey), or other DNA molecules formed.

5. For the dispersive model you will need to cut the DNA along the dotted lines and then stick them back together in the dispersed sequence with tape. **Construct the dispersive model LAST.**

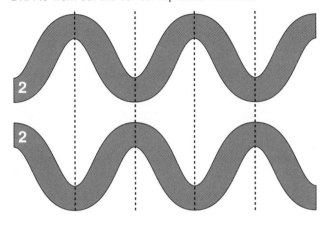

PRAC

This page is left blank deliberately

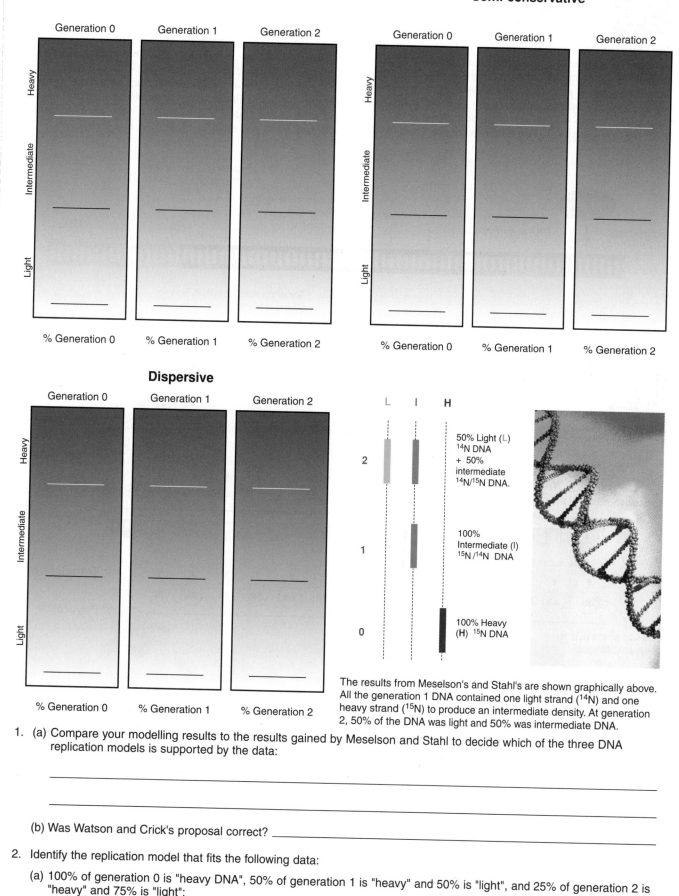

Conservative

Generation 0 | Generation 1 | Generation 2

Heavy — Intermediate — Light

% Generation 0 | % Generation 1 | % Generation 2

Semi-conservative

Generation 0 | Generation 1 | Generation 2

Heavy — Intermediate — Light

% Generation 0 | % Generation 1 | % Generation 2

Dispersive

Generation 0 | Generation 1 | Generation 2

Heavy — Intermediate — Light

% Generation 0 | % Generation 1 | % Generation 2

L   I   H

2 — 50% Light (L) ^{14}N DNA + 50% intermediate $^{14}N/^{15}N$ DNA.

1 — 100% Intermediate (I) $^{15}N/^{14}N$ DNA

0 — 100% Heavy (H) ^{15}N DNA

The results from Meselson's and Stahl's are shown graphically above. All the generation 1 DNA contained one light strand (^{14}N) and one heavy strand (^{15}N) to produce an intermediate density. At generation 2, 50% of the DNA was light and 50% was intermediate DNA.

1. (a) Compare your modelling results to the results gained by Meselson and Stahl to decide which of the three DNA replication models is supported by the data:

_____

_____

(b) Was Watson and Crick's proposal correct? _____

2. Identify the replication model that fits the following data:

(a) 100% of generation 0 is "heavy DNA", 50% of generation 1 is "heavy" and 50% is "light", and 25% of generation 2 is "heavy" and 75% is "light":

_____

(b) 100% of generation 0 is "heavy DNA", 100% of generation 1 is "intermediate DNA", and 100% generation 2 lies between the "intermediate" and "light" DNA regions:

_____

53 Genes to Proteins

Key Idea: Genes are sections of DNA that code for proteins. Genes are expressed when they are transcribed into messenger RNA (mRNA) and then translated into a protein. **Gene expression** is the process of rewriting a gene into a protein. It involves **transcription** of the DNA into mRNA and **translation** of the mRNA into protein. A gene is bounded by a start (promoter) region, upstream of the gene, and a terminator region, downstream of the gene. These regions control transcription by telling RNA polymerase where to start and stop transcription of the gene. The information flow for gene to protein is shown below. Nucleotides are read in groups of three called triplets. The equivalent on the mRNA molecule is the codon. Some codons have special control functions (start and stop) in the making of a protein.

Coding strand of DNA. This strand is not transcribed.

Protein coding sequence is transcribed into mRNA by RNA polymerase

RNA polymerase

RNAP

Promoter region RNA polymerase binds

Terminator region RNA polymerase dissociates

5'
3'

Template strand of DNA. This strand is transcribed.

RNAP

5'
ATGCCGTGGATATTTCTTTTTATATCAGCCAGGTAAAGTTCCGTGA
3' Coding strand

DNA

TACGGCACCTATAAAGAAAATATAGTCGGTCCATTTTCAAGGCACT
Template strand
5'

3. The code is read in groups of three nucleotides, called **triplets**

Transcription

Translation begins at the **start codon**

Translation stops at the **stop codon**

5'
AUGCCGUGGAUAUUUCUUUUUAUAUCAGCCAGGUAAAGUUCCGUGA
3' mRNA

Three nucleotides in mRNA make a **codon**

Translation

aa aa aa aa aa aa aa aa aa aa aa aa aa

Polypeptide

The first amino acid is always methionine

One codon codes for one amino acid

1. (a) The three base code on DNA is called: _____

   (b) The three base code on mRNA is called: _____

2. (a) What is a **gene**? _____

   _____

   (b) What molecule transcribes the gene? _____

   (c) What is the role of the promoter and terminator regions? _____

   _____

3. What does the term **gene expression** mean? _____

   _____

4. Recall the anti-parallel nature of DNA, with the strands orientated in opposite directions. Explain its significance:

   _____

   _____

© 2015 **BIOZONE** International
ISBN: 978-1-927309-25-4
Photocopying Prohibited

54 The Genetic Code

Key Idea: The genetic code is the set of rules by which the genetic information in DNA or mRNA is translated into proteins. The genetic information for the assembly of amino acids is stored as three-base sequence. These three letter codes on mRNA are called **codons**. Each codon represents one of 20 amino acids used to make proteins. The code is effectively universal, being the same in all living things (with a few minor exceptions). The genetic code is summarised in a mRNA-amino acid table, which identifies the amino acid encoded by each mRNA codon. The code is degenerate, meaning there may be more than one codon for each amino acid. Most of this degeneracy is in the third nucleotide of a codon.

Amino acid		Codons that code for this amino acid	No.	Amino acid		Codons that code for this amino acid	No.
Ala	Alanine	GCU, GCC, GCA, GCG	4	**Leu**	Leucine		
Arg	Arginine			**Lys**	Lysine		
Asn	Asparagine			**Met**	Methionine		
Asp	Aspartic acid			**Phe**	Phenylalanine		
Cys	Cysteine			**Pro**	Proline		
Gln	Glutamine			**Ser**	Serine		
Glu	Glutamic acid			**Thr**	Threonine		
Gly	Glycine			**Try**	Tryptophan		
His	Histidine			**Tyr**	Tyrosine		
Iso	Isoleucine			**Val**	Valine		

1. Use the **mRNA-amino acid table** (below) to list in the table above all the **codons** that code for each of the amino acids and the number of different codons that can code for each amino acid (the first amino acid has been done for you).

2. (a) How many amino acids could be coded for if a codon consisted of just two bases?_____

   (b) Why is this number of bases inadequate to code for the 20 amino acids required to make proteins?

   _____

   _____

3. Describe the consequence of the degeneracy of the genetic code to the likely effect of a change to one base in a triplet:

   _____

   _____

mRNA-amino acid table

How to read the table: The table on the right is used to 'decode' the genetic code as a sequence of amino acids in a polypeptide chain, from a given mRNA sequence. To work out which amino acid is coded for by a codon (triplet of bases) look for the first letter of the codon in the row label on the left hand side. Then look for the column that intersects the same row from above that matches the second base. Finally, locate the third base in the codon by looking along the row from the right hand end that matches your codon.

Example: Determine **CAG**

    C on the left row,
    A on the top column,
    G on the right row
    CAG is Gln (**glutamine**)

Read second letter here
Read first letter here
Read third letter here

First letter		Second letter				Third letter
		U	**C**	**A**	**G**	
U		UUU Phe	UCU Ser	UAU Tyr	UGU Cys	U
		UUC Phe	UCC Ser	UAC Tyr	UGC Cys	C
		UUA Leu	UCA Ser	UAA STOP	UGA STOP	A
		UUG Leu	UCG Ser	UAG STOP	UGG Trp	G
C		CUU Leu	CCU Pro	CAU His	CGU Arg	U
		CUC Leu	CCC Pro	CAC His	CGC Arg	C
		CUA Leu	CCA Pro	CAA Gln	CGA Arg	A
		CUG Leu	CCG Pro	CAG Gln	CGG Arg	G
A		AUU Ile	ACU Thr	AAU Asn	AGU Ser	U
		AUC Ile	ACC Thr	AAC Asn	AGC Ser	C
		AUA Ile	ACA Thr	AAA Lys	AGA Arg	A
		AUG Met	ACG Thr	AAG Lys	AGG Arg	G
G		GUU Val	GCU Ala	GAU Asp	GGU Gly	U
		GUC Val	GCC Ala	GAC Asp	GGC Gly	C
		GUA Val	GCA Ala	GAA Glu	GGA Gly	A
		GUG Val	GCG Ala	GAG Glu	GGG Gly	G

LINK 55   WEB 54 **KNOW**

55 Cracking the Genetic Code

Key Idea: Scientists used mathematics and experiments to unlock the genetic code. A series of three nucleotides, called a triplet, codes for a single amino acid.

In the 1960s, two scientists, Marshall Nirenberg and Heinrich Matthaei, developed an experiment to crack the genetic code. Their experiment, which is sometimes called the poly-U experiment because it used a synthetic mRNA containing only uracil, is shown below.

The genetic code

Once it was discovered that DNA carries the genetic code needed to produce proteins, the race was on to "crack the code" and find out how it worked.

The first step was to find out how many nucleotide bases code for an amino acid. Scientists knew that there were four nucleotide bases in mRNA, and that there are 20 amino acids. Simple mathematics (below) showed that a one or two base code did not produce enough amino acids, but a triplet code produced more amino acids than existed.

The triplet code was accepted once scientists confirmed that some amino acids have multiple codes.

Number of bases in the code	Working	Number of amino acids produced
Single (4^1)	4	4 amino acids
Double (4^2)	4 x 4	16 amino acids
Triple (4^3)	4 x 4 x 4	64 amino acids

A triplet (three nucleotide bases) codes for a single amino acid. The triplet code on mRNA is called a codon.

How was the genetic code cracked?

Once the triplet code was discovered, the next step was to find out which amino acid each codon produced. Two scientists, Marshall Nirenberg and Heinrich Matthaei, developed an experiment (below) to crack the code.

A cell free *E. coli* extract was produced for their experiment by rupturing the bacterial cells to release the cytoplasm. The extract had all the components needed to make proteins (except mRNA).

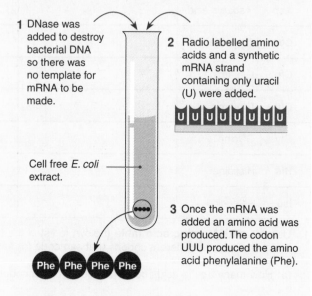

1 DNase was added to destroy bacterial DNA so there was no template for mRNA to be made.

2 Radio labelled amino acids and a synthetic mRNA strand containing only uracil (U) were added.

Cell free *E. coli* extract.

3 Once the mRNA was added an amino acid was produced. The codon UUU produced the amino acid phenylalanine (Phe).

4 Over the next few years, similar experiments were carried out using different combinations of nucleotides until all of the codes were known.

1. (a) How many types of nucleotide bases are there in mRNA? _____

   (b) How many types of amino acids are there? _____

   (c) Why did scientists reject a one or two base code when trying to work out the genetic code? _____
   _____
   _____

2. A triplet code could potentially produce 64 amino acids. Why are only 20 amino acids produced? _____
   _____

3. (a) Why was DNase added to the cell free *E. coli* extract? _____
   _____
   _____

   (b) What would it have been difficult to crack the code if no DNase was added?_____
   _____
   _____

© 2015 **BIOZONE** International
ISBN: 978-1-927309-25-4
Photocopying Prohibited

56 Transcription in Eukaryotes

Key Idea: Transcription is the first step of gene expression. A segment of DNA is transcribed (rewritten) into mRNA. In eukaryotes, transcription takes place in the nucleus.

The enzyme that directly controls transcription is RNA polymerase, which makes a strand of mRNA using the single strand of DNA (the **template strand**) as a template. The enzyme transcribes a gene length of DNA at a time and recognises start and stop signals (codes) at the beginning and end of the gene. Only RNA polymerase is involved in mRNA synthesis as it unwinds the DNA as well. It is common to find several RNA polymerase enzyme molecules on the same gene at any one time, allowing a high rate of mRNA synthesis to occur. In eukaryotes, non-coding sections called **introns** must first be removed and the remaining **exons** spliced together to form mature mRNA before the mRNA can be translated into a protein.

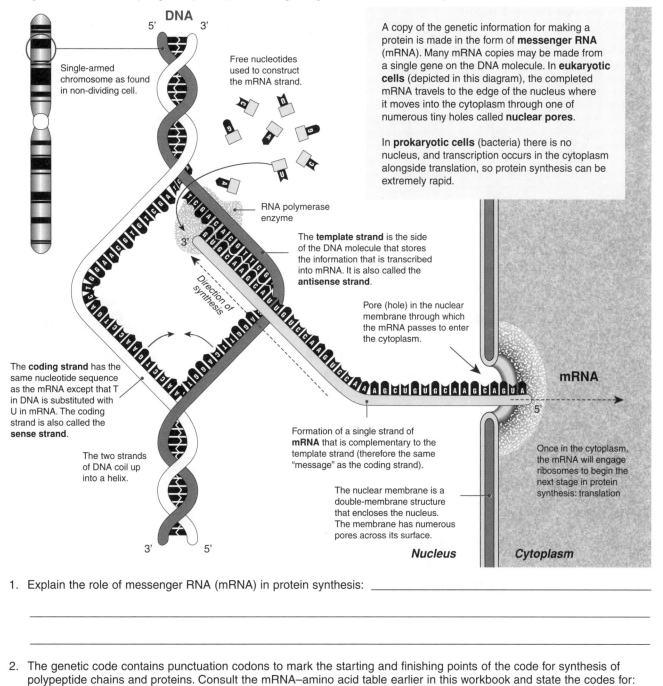

DNA

Single-armed chromosome as found in non-dividing cell.

Free nucleotides used to construct the mRNA strand.

RNA polymerase enzyme

The **template strand** is the side of the DNA molecule that stores the information that is transcribed into mRNA. It is also called the **antisense strand**.

Direction of synthesis

The **coding strand** has the same nucleotide sequence as the mRNA except that T in DNA is substituted with U in mRNA. The coding strand is also called the **sense strand**.

The two strands of DNA coil up into a helix.

Formation of a single strand of **mRNA** that is complementary to the template strand (therefore the same "message" as the coding strand).

The nuclear membrane is a double-membrane structure that encloses the nucleus. The membrane has numerous pores across its surface.

A copy of the genetic information for making a protein is made in the form of **messenger RNA** (mRNA). Many mRNA copies may be made from a single gene on the DNA molecule. In **eukaryotic cells** (depicted in this diagram), the completed mRNA travels to the edge of the nucleus where it moves into the cytoplasm through one of numerous tiny holes called **nuclear pores**.

In **prokaryotic cells** (bacteria) there is no nucleus, and transcription occurs in the cytoplasm alongside translation, so protein synthesis can be extremely rapid.

Pore (hole) in the nuclear membrane through which the mRNA passes to enter the cytoplasm.

mRNA

Once in the cytoplasm, the mRNA will engage ribosomes to begin the next stage in protein synthesis: translation

Nucleus   *Cytoplasm*

1. Explain the role of messenger RNA (mRNA) in protein synthesis: _____

_____

_____

2. The genetic code contains punctuation codons to mark the starting and finishing points of the code for synthesis of polypeptide chains and proteins. Consult the mRNA–amino acid table earlier in this workbook and state the codes for:

   (a) Start codon: _____ (b) Stop (termination) codons: _____

3. For the following triplets on the DNA, determine the **codon** sequence for the mRNA that would be synthesised:

   (a) Triplets on the DNA: T A C   T A G   C C G   C G A   T T T

   Codons on the mRNA: _____

   (b) Triplets on the DNA: T A C   A A G   C C T   A T A   A A A

   Codons on the mRNA: _____

LINK 58   WEB 56   **KNOW**

57 Translation

Key Idea: Translation is the second step of gene expression. It occurs in the cytoplasm, where ribosomes read the mRNA code and decode it to synthesise protein.

In eukaryotes, translation occurs in the cytoplasm associated with free ribosomes or ribosomes on the rough endoplasmic reticulum. The diagram below shows how a mRNA molecule can be 'serviced' by many ribosomes at the same time. The role of the tRNA molecules is to bring in the individual amino acids. The anticodon of each tRNA must make a perfect complementary match with the mRNA codon before the amino acid is released. Once released, the amino acid is added to the growing polypeptide chain by enzymes.

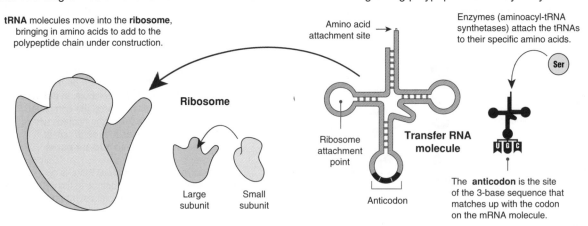

tRNA molecules move into the **ribosome**, bringing in amino acids to add to the polypeptide chain under construction.

Ribosome

Large subunit   Small subunit

Amino acid attachment site

Enzymes (aminoacyl-tRNA synthetases) attach the tRNAs to their specific amino acids.

Ser

Transfer RNA molecule

Ribosome attachment point

Anticodon

The **anticodon** is the site of the 3-base sequence that matches up with the codon on the mRNA molecule.

Ribosomes are made up of a complex of ribosomal RNA (rRNA) and proteins. They exist as two separate sub-units (above) until they are attracted to a binding site on the mRNA molecule, when they join together. Ribosomes have binding sites that attract transfer RNA (**tRNA**) molecules loaded with amino acids. The tRNA molecules are about 80 nucleotides in length and are made under the direction of genes in the chromosomes. There is a different tRNA molecule for each of the different possible anticodons (see the diagram below) and, because of the degeneracy of the genetic code, there may be up to six different tRNAs carrying the same amino acid.

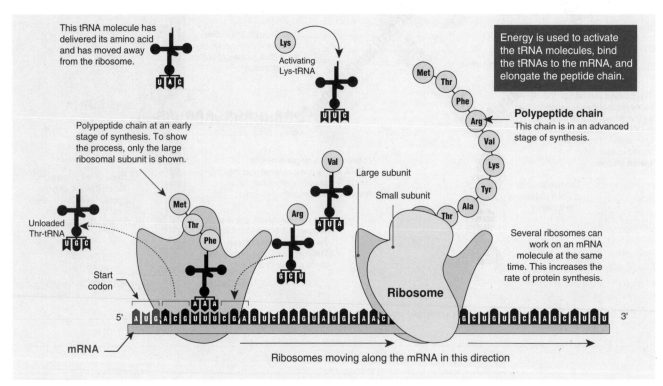

This tRNA molecule has delivered its amino acid and has moved away from the ribosome.

Lys

Activating Lys-tRNA

Energy is used to activate the tRNA molecules, bind the tRNAs to the mRNA, and elongate the peptide chain.

Met
Thr
Phe
Arg

Polypeptide chain
This chain is in an advanced stage of synthesis.

Val
Lys
Tyr
Ala

Polypeptide chain at an early stage of synthesis. To show the process, only the large ribosomal subunit is shown.

Val

Large subunit

Small subunit

Met
Thr
Phe

Arg
AUA

Unloaded Thr-tRNA
UGC

GCU

Thr

Several ribosomes can work on an mRNA molecule at the same time. This increases the rate of protein synthesis.

Start codon

AAA

Ribosome

5' AUGACGUUUCGAGUCAAGUAUGCAAC   GCUGUGCAAGCAUGU 3'

mRNA

Ribosomes moving along the mRNA in this direction

1. For the following codons on the mRNA, determine the **anticodons** for each tRNA that would deliver the amino acids:

   Codons on the mRNA: U A C   U A G   C C G   C G A   U U U

   Anticodons on the tRNAs: _____

2. There are many different types of tRNA molecules, each with a different anticodon (HINT: see the mRNA table).

   (a) How many different tRNA types are there, each with a unique anticodon? _____

   (b) Explain your answer: _____

   _____

© 2015 **BIOZONE** International
ISBN: 978-1-927309-25-4
Photocopying Prohibited

58 Protein Synthesis Summary

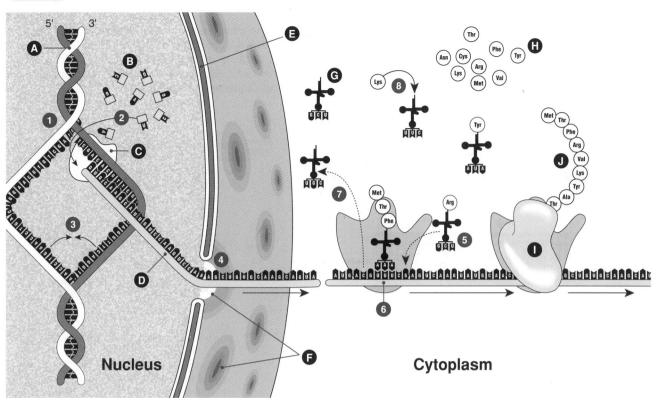

The diagram above shows an overview of the process of protein synthesis. It is a combination of the diagrams from the previous two pages. Each of the major steps in the process are numbered, while structures are labelled with letters.

1. Briefly describe each of the numbered processes in the diagram above:

   (a) Process 1: _____

   (b) Process 2: _____

   (c) Process 3: _____

   (d) Process 4: _____

   (e) Process 5: _____

   (f) Process 6: _____

   (g) Process 7: _____

   (h) Process 8: _____

2. Identify each of the structures marked with a letter and write their names below in the spaces provided:

   (a) Structure A: _____   (f) Structure F: _____

   (b) Structure B: _____   (g) Structure G: _____

   (c) Structure C: _____   (h) Structure H: _____

   (d) Structure D: _____   (i) Structure I: _____

   (e) Structure E: _____   (j) Structure J: _____

3. Describe two factors that would determine whether or not a particular protein is produced in the cell:

   (a) _____

   _____

   (b) _____

   _____

LINK 57   LINK 56   WEB 58   REVISE

59 The Nature of Mutations

Key Idea: Gene mutations are localised changes to the DNA base sequence.

Gene mutations are small, localised changes in the base sequence of a DNA strand caused by a mutagen or an error during DNA replication. The changes may involve a single nucleotide (a **point mutation**) or a change to a triplet. Point

mutations can occur by substitution, insertion, or deletion of bases. These changes alter the mRNA transcribed from the mutated DNA. A point mutation may not alter the amino acid sequence because more than one codon can code for the same amino acid. Mutations that result in a change in the amino acid sequence will most often be harmful.

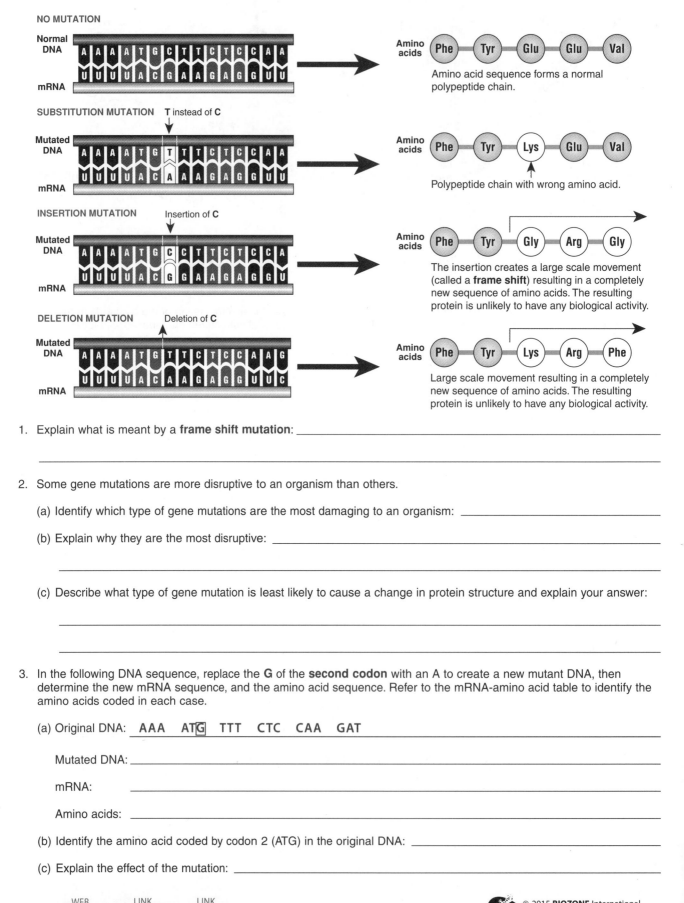

1. Explain what is meant by a **frame shift mutation**: _____

   _____

2. Some gene mutations are more disruptive to an organism than others.

   (a) Identify which type of gene mutations are the most damaging to an organism: _____

   (b) Explain why they are the most disruptive: _____

   _____

   (c) Describe what type of gene mutation is least likely to cause a change in protein structure and explain your answer:

   _____

   _____

3. In the following DNA sequence, replace the **G** of the **second codon** with an A to create a new mutant DNA, then determine the new mRNA sequence, and the amino acid sequence. Refer to the mRNA-amino acid table to identify the amino acids coded in each case.

   (a) Original DNA: AAA AT[G] TTT CTC CAA GAT _____

   Mutated DNA: _____

   mRNA: _____

   Amino acids: _____

   (b) Identify the amino acid coded by codon 2 (ATG) in the original DNA: _____

   (c) Explain the effect of the mutation: _____

© 2015 **BIOZONE** International
ISBN: 978-1-927309-25-4
Photocopying Prohibited

60 Sickle Cell Mutation

Key Idea: The substitution of one nucleotide from T to A results in sickle cell disease. The mutation is codominant. Sickle cell disease is an inherited blood disorder caused by a gene mutation (Hb^S), which produces a faulty beta (β) chain haemoglobin (Hb) protein. This in turn produces red blood cells with a deformed sickle appearance and a reduced capacity to carry oxygen. Many aspects of metabolism are also affected. The mutation is codominant (both alleles equally expressed), and people heterozygous for the mutation (carriers) have enough functional haemoglobin and suffer only minor effects.

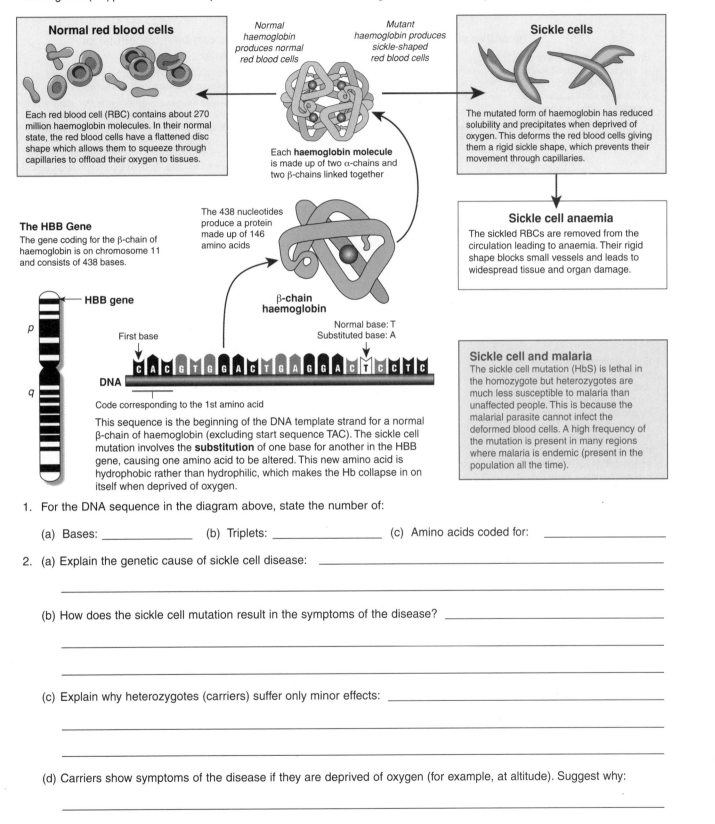

Normal red blood cells

Each red blood cell (RBC) contains about 270 million haemoglobin molecules. In their normal state, the red blood cells have a flattened disc shape which allows them to squeeze through capillaries to offload their oxygen to tissues.

Normal haemoglobin produces normal red blood cells

Each **haemoglobin molecule** is made up of two α-chains and two β-chains linked together

Mutant haemoglobin produces sickle-shaped red blood cells

Sickle cells

The mutated form of haemoglobin has reduced solubility and precipitates when deprived of oxygen. This deforms the red blood cells giving them a rigid sickle shape, which prevents their movement through capillaries.

Sickle cell anaemia

The sickled RBCs are removed from the circulation leading to anaemia. Their rigid shape blocks small vessels and leads to widespread tissue and organ damage.

The 438 nucleotides produce a protein made up of 146 amino acids

The HBB Gene

The gene coding for the β-chain of haemoglobin is on chromosome 11 and consists of 438 bases.

HBB gene

p

q

First base

β-chain haemoglobin

Normal base: T
Substituted base: A

C A C G T G G A C T G A G G A C T C C T C

DNA

Code corresponding to the 1st amino acid

This sequence is the beginning of the DNA template strand for a normal β-chain of haemoglobin (excluding start sequence TAC). The sickle cell mutation involves the **substitution** of one base for another in the HBB gene, causing one amino acid to be altered. This new amino acid is hydrophobic rather than hydrophilic, which makes the Hb collapse in on itself when deprived of oxygen.

Sickle cell and malaria

The sickle cell mutation (HbS) is lethal in the homozygote but heterozygotes are much less susceptible to malaria than unaffected people. This is because the malarial parasite cannot infect the deformed blood cells. A high frequency of the mutation is present in many regions where malaria is endemic (present in the population all the time).

1. For the DNA sequence in the diagram above, state the number of:

   (a) Bases: _____ (b) Triplets: _____ (c) Amino acids coded for: _____

2. (a) Explain the genetic cause of sickle cell disease: _____
   _____

   (b) How does the sickle cell mutation result in the symptoms of the disease? _____
   _____
   _____

   (c) Explain why heterozygotes (carriers) suffer only minor effects: _____
   _____
   _____

   (d) Carriers show symptoms of the disease if they are deprived of oxygen (for example, at altitude). Suggest why:
   _____
   _____

3. Briefly explain why there is a high frequency of the sickle cell mutation in populations where malaria is endemic:
   _____

LINK 204 WEB 60 **KNOW**

61 Enzymes

Key Idea: Enzymes are biological catalysts. The active site is critical to this functional role.

Most enzymes are globular proteins. Enzymes are biological catalysts because they speed up biochemical reactions, but the enzyme itself remains unchanged. The substrate in a reaction binds to a region of the enzyme called the active site, which is formed by the precise folding of the enzyme's amino acid chain. Enzymes control metabolic pathways. One enzyme will act on a substance to produce the next reactant in a pathway, which will be acted on by a different enzyme.

The active site

Enzymes have an **active site** to which specific substrates bind. The shape and chemistry of the active site is specific to an enzyme, and is a function of the polypeptide's complex tertiary structure.

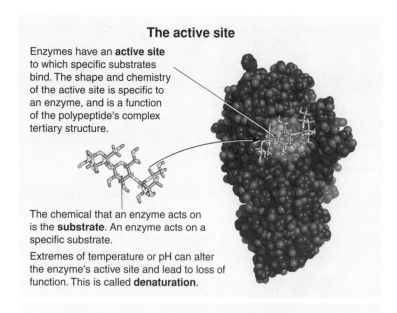

The chemical that an enzyme acts on is the **substrate**. An enzyme acts on a specific substrate.

Extremes of temperature or pH can alter the enzyme's active site and lead to loss of function. This is called **denaturation**.

Substrates collide with an enzyme's active site

For a reaction to occur reactants must collide with sufficient speed and with the correct orientation. Enzymes enhance reaction rates by providing a site for reactants to come together in such a way that a reaction will occur. They do this by orientating the reactants so that the reactive regions are brought together. They may also destabilise the bonds within the reactants making it easier for a reaction to occur.

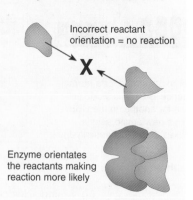

Incorrect reactant orientation = no reaction

X

Enzyme orientates the reactants making reaction more likely

Enzymes can be intracellular or extracellular

Enzymes can be defined based on where they are produced relative to where they are active.

An **intracellular enzyme** is an enzyme that performs its function within the cell that produces it. Most enzymes are intracellular enzymes, e.g. respiratory enzymes.
Example: Catalase.
Many metabolic processes produce hydrogen peroxide, which is harmful to cells. Catalase converts hydrogen peroxide into water and oxygen (below) to prevent damage to cells and tissues.

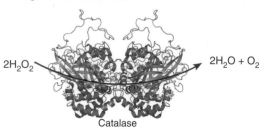

$2H_2O_2$ $2H_2O + O_2$

Catalase

An **extracellular enzyme** is an enzyme that functions outside the cell from which it originates (i.e. it is produced in one location but active in another).
Examples: Amylase and trypsin.
Amylase is a digestive enzyme produced in the salivary glands and pancreas in humans. However, it acts in the mouth and small intestine respectively to hydrolyse starch into sugars.

Trypsin is a protein-digesting enzyme and hydrolyses the peptide bond immediately after a basic residue (e.g. arginine). It is produced in an inactive form (called trypsinogen) and secreted into the small intestine by the pancreas. It is activated in the intestine by the enzyme enteropeptidase to form trypsin. Active trypsin can convert more trypsinogen to trypsin.

1. (a) What is meant by the **active site** of an enzyme and relate it to the enzyme's tertiary structure: _____

_____

_____

_____

  (b) Why are enzymes specific to one substrate (or group of closely related substrates)? _____

_____

_____

2. How do substrate molecules come into contact with an enzyme's active site? _____

_____

3. (a) Suggest why digestion (the breakdown of large macromolecules) is largely performed by extracellular enzymes:

_____

  (b) Why would an extracellular enzyme be produced and secreted in an inactive form? _____

_____

© 2015 **BIOZONE** International
ISBN: 978-1-927309-25-4
Photocopying Prohibited

62 Models of Enzyme Activity

Key Idea: Enzymes catalyse reactions by providing a reaction site for a substrate. The model that describes the behaviour of enzymes the best is the induced fit model.

The initial model of enzyme activity was the lock and key model proposed by Emil Fischer in the 1890s. Fischer proposed enzymes were rigid structures, similar to a lock, and the substrate was the key. While some aspects of

Fischer's model were correct, for example, substrates align with enzymes in a way that is likely to make a reaction more likely, the model has been adapted as techniques to study molecular structures have developed. The current 'induced-fit' model of enzyme function is supported by studies of enzyme inhibitors, which show that enzymes are flexible and change shape when interacting with the substrate.

The lock and key model of enzyme function

1 The substrate molecule is drawn into site of the enzyme. The enzyme's active site does not change shape.

2 The enzyme-substrate (ES) complex is formed.

3 The enzyme reaction takes place to form the enzyme-product (EP) complex.

4 The products are released from the enzyme. Note there has been no change in the shape of the active site throughout the reaction.

The **lock and key model** proposed earlier last century suggested that the (perfectly fitting) substrate was simply drawn into a matching site on the enzyme molecule. if the substrate did not perfectly fit the active site, the reaction did not proceed. This model was supported by early X-ray crystallography studies but has since been modified to recognise the flexibility of enzymes (the induced fit model).

The current induced fit model

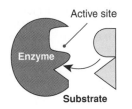

1 A substrate molecule is drawn into the enzyme's active site, which is like a cleft into which the substrate molecule(s) fit.

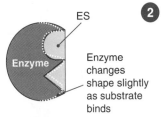

2 The enzyme changes shape as the substrate binds an enzyme-substrate (ES) complex. The shape change makes the substrate more amenable to alteration. In this way, the enzyme's interaction with its substrate is best regarded as an induced fit.

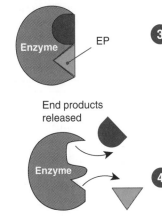

3 The ES interaction results in an intermediate enzyme-product (EP) complex. The substrate becomes bound to the enzyme by weak chemical bonds, straining bonds in the substrate and allowing the reaction to proceed more readily.

4 The end products are released and the enzyme returns to its previous shape.

Once the substrate enters the active site, the shape of the active site changes to form an active complex. The formation of an ES complex strains substrate bonds and lowers the energy required to reach the transition state. The induced-fit model is supported by X-ray crystallography, chemical analysis, and studies of enzyme inhibitors, which show that enzymes are flexible and change shape when interacting with the substrate.

1. Describe the key features of the '**lock and key**' model of enzyme action and explain its deficiencies as a working model:

_____

_____

_____

2. How does the current '**induced fit**' model of enzyme action differ from the lock and key model?

_____

_____

_____

63 How Enzymes Work

Key Idea: Enzymes increase the rate of biological reactions by lowering the reaction's activation energy.

Chemical reactions in cells are accompanied by energy changes. The amount of energy released or taken up is directly related to the tendency of a reaction to run to completion (for all the reactants to form products). Any reaction needs to raise the energy of the substrate to an unstable transition state before the reaction will proceed (below). The amount of energy needed to do this is the **activation energy** (*Ea*). Enzymes lower the *Ea* by destabilising bonds in the substrate so that it is more reactive. Enzyme reactions can break down a single substrate molecule into simpler substances (catabolic reactions), or join two or more substrate molecules together (anabolic reactions).

Lowering the activation energy

The presence of an enzyme simply makes it easier for a reaction to take place. All catalysts speed up reactions by influencing the stability of bonds in the reactants. They may also provide an alternative reaction pathway, thus lowering the activation energy (Ea) needed for a reaction to take place (see the graph below).

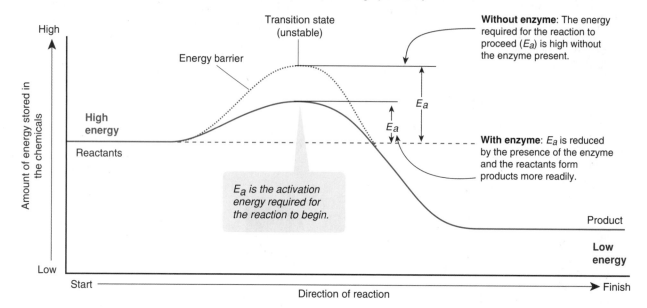

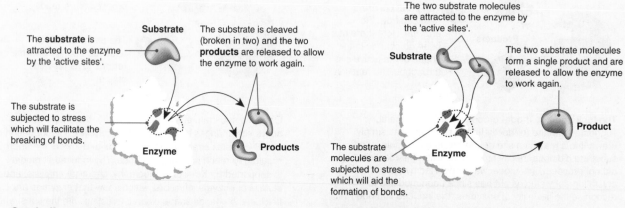

Catabolic reactions

Some enzymes can cause a single substrate molecule to be drawn into the active site. Chemical bonds are broken, causing the substrate molecule to break apart to become two separate molecules. Catabolic reactions break down complex molecules into simpler ones and involve a net release of energy, so they are called exergonic.
Examples: *hydrolysis, cellular respiration.*

Anabolic reactions

Some enzymes can cause two substrate molecules to be drawn into the active site. Chemical bonds are formed, causing the two substrate molecules to form bonds and become a single molecule. Anabolic reactions involve a net use of energy (they are endergonic) and build more complex molecules and structures from simpler ones.
Examples: *protein synthesis, photosynthesis.*

1. How do enzymes lower the activation energy for a reaction? _____

_____

_____

2. Describe the difference between a catabolic and anabolic reaction: _____

_____

© 2015 **BIOZONE** International
ISBN: 978-1-927309-25-4
Photocopying Prohibited

64 Enzyme Kinetics

Key Idea: Enzymes operate most effectively within a narrow range of conditions. The rate of enzyme-catalysed reactions is influenced by both enzyme and substrate concentration. Enzymes usually have an optimum set of conditions (e.g. of pH and temperature) under which their activity is greatest. Many plant and animal enzymes show little activity at low temperatures. Enzyme activity increases with increasing temperature, but falls off after the optimum temperature is exceeded and the enzyme is denatured. Extremes in pH can also cause denaturation. Within their normal operating conditions, enzyme reaction rates are influenced by enzyme and substrate concentration in a predictable way.

Graph 1

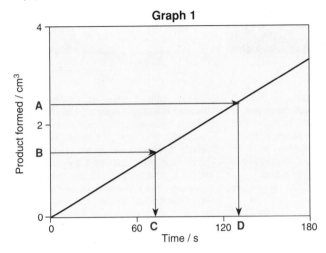

Graph 2

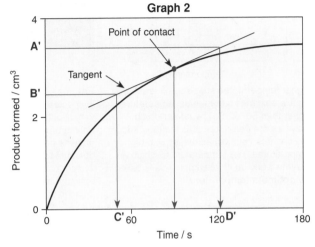

The rate of a reaction can be calculated from the amount of product produced during a given time period. For a reaction in which the rate does not vary (graph 1) the reaction rate calculated at any one point in time will be the same. For example: B/C = A/D = A-B/D-C = (Δp/Δt) (the change in product divided by the change in time).

In a reaction in which the rate varies (graph 2) a reaction rate can be calculated for any instantaneous moment in time by using a tangent. The tangent must touch the curve at only one point. The gradient of the tangent can then be used to calculate the rate of reaction at that point in time (A'-B'/D'-C').

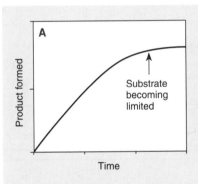

In a reaction where there is a limited amount of substrate, the reaction rate will slow down over time as the substrate is used up (graph A).

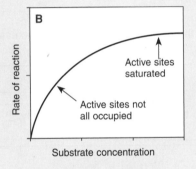

If there is unlimited substrate but the enzyme is limited, the reaction rate will increase until the enzyme is saturated, at which point the rate will remain static (graph B).

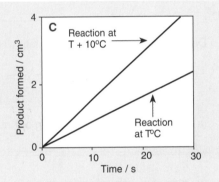

The effect of temperature on a reaction rate is expressed as the temperature coefficient, usually given as the Q_{10}. Q_{10} expresses the increase in the rate of reaction for every rise of 10°C. Q_{10} = **rate of reaction at (T + 10°C)/ rate of reaction at T**, where T is the temperature in °C (graph C).

1. Calculate the reaction rate in graph 1: _____

2. For graph 2, A Level students calculate:

   (a) The reaction rate at 90 seconds: _____

   (b) The reaction rate at 30 seconds: _____

3. (a) What would need to be happening to the reaction mix in graph 1 to produce a straight line (constant reaction rate)?

   (b) Explain why the reaction rate in graph 2 changes over time: _____

LINK 66 LINK 65 WEB 64 DATA

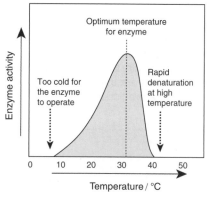

Antarctic icefish

Professor Dr. habil. Uwe Kils CC3.0

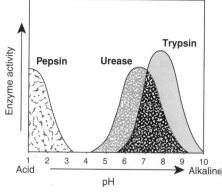

Higher temperatures speed up all reactions, but few enzymes can tolerate temperatures higher than 50–60°C. The rate at which enzymes are denatured (change their shape and become inactive) increases with higher temperatures. The temperature at which an enzyme works at its maximum rate is called the **optimum temperature**.

Enzymes performing the same function in species in different environments are very slightly different in order to maintain optimum performance. For example, the enzyme acetylcholinesterase has an optimum temperature of -2°C in the nervous system of an Antarctic icefish but an optimum temperature of 25°C in grey mullet found in the Mediterranean.

Like all proteins, enzymes are denatured by extremes of pH (very acid or alkaline). Within these extremes, most enzymes have a specific pH range for optimum activity. For example, digestive enzymes are specific to the region of the gut where they act: pepsin in the acid of the stomach and trypsin in the alkaline small intestine. Urease catalyses the hydrolysis of urea at a pH near neutral.

4. (a) Describe the change in reaction rate when the enzyme concentration is increased and the substrate is not limiting:

_____

_____

(b) Suggest how a cell may vary the amount of enzyme present: _____

_____

_____

5. Describe the change in reaction rate when the substrate concentration is increased (with a fixed amount of enzyme):

_____

_____

6. (a) Describe what is meant by an **optimum temperature** for enzyme activity: _____

_____

_____

(b) Explain why most enzymes perform poorly at low temperatures: _____

_____

_____

(c) For graph C opposite, calculate the Q_{10} for the reaction: _____

_____

_____

_____

7. (a) State the optimum pH for each of the enzymes:

Pepsin: _____   Trypsin: _____   Urease: _____

(b) Explain how the pH optima of each of these enzymes is suited to its working environment: _____

_____

_____

_____

65 Investigating Catalase Activity

Key Idea: Catalase activity can be measured in germinating seeds. Activity changes with stage of germination.

Enzyme activity can be measured easily in simple experiments. This activity describes an experiment in which germinating seeds of different ages were tested for their level of **catalase** activity using hydrogen peroxide solution as the substrate and a simple apparatus to measure oxygen production (see background). Completing this activity, which involves a critical evaluation of the second-hand data provided, will help to prepare you for making your own similar investigations.

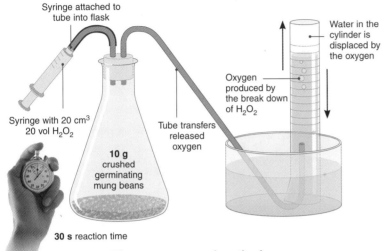

Syringe attached to tube into flask

Syringe with 20 cm³ 20 vol H₂O₂

10 g crushed germinating mung beans

Tube transfers released oxygen

30 s reaction time

Water in the cylinder is displaced by the oxygen

Oxygen produced by the break down of H₂O₂

The apparatus and method

In this experiment, 10 g germinating mung bean seeds (0.5, 2, 4, 6, or 10 days old) were ground by hand with a mortar and pestle and placed in a conical flask as above. There were six trials at each of the five seedling ages. With each trial, 20 cm³ of 20 vol H_2O_2 was added to the flask at time 0 and the reaction was allowed to run for 30 seconds. The oxygen released by the decomposition of the H_2O_2 by catalase in the seedlings was collected via a tube into an inverted measuring cylinder. The volume of oxygen produced is measured by the amount of water displaced from the cylinder. The results from all trials are tabulated below:

The aim and hypothesis

To investigate the effect of germination age on the level of catalase activity in mung beans. The students hypothesised that catalase activity would increase with germination age.

Background

Germinating seeds are metabolically very active and this metabolism inevitably produces reactive oxygen species, including hydrogen peroxide (H_2O_2). H_2O_2 helps germination by breaking dormancy, but it is also toxic. To counter the toxic effects of H_2O_2 and prevent cellular damage, germinating seeds also produce **catalase**, an enzyme that catalyses the breakdown of H_2O_2 to water and oxygen.

A class was divided into six groups with each group testing the seedlings of each age. Each group's set of results (for 0.5, 2, 4, 6, and 10 days) therefore represents one trial.

Stage of germination / days	Group (trial) #								Mean rate / $cm^3\ s^{-1}\ g^{-1}$
	Volume of oxygen collected after 30 s / cm^3						Mean	Standard deviation	
	1	2	3	4	5	6			
0.5	9.5	10	10.7	9.5	10.2	10.5			
2	36.2	30	31.5	37.5	34	40			
4	59	66	69	60.5	66.5	72			
6	39	31.5	32.5	41	40.3	36			
10	20	18.6	24.3	23.2	23.5	25.5			

1. Write the equation for the catalase reaction with hydrogen peroxide: _____

2. Complete the table above to summarise the data from the six trials:

   (a) Calculate the mean volume of oxygen for each stage of germination and enter the values in the table.

   (b) Calculate the standard deviation for each mean and enter the values in the table (you may use a spreadsheet).

   (c) Calculate the mean rate of oxygen production in cm³ per second per gram. For the purposes of this exercise, assume that the weight of germinating seed in every case was 10.0 g.

3. In another scenario, group (trial) #2 obtained the following measurements for volume of oxygen produced: 0.5 d: 4.8 cm³, 2 d: 29.0 cm³, 4 d: 70 cm³, 6 d: 30.0 cm³, 10 d: 8.8 cm³ (pencil these values in beside the other group 2 data set).

   (a) Describe how group 2's new data compares with the measurements obtained from the other group: _____

   _____

   (b) Describe how you would approach a reanalysis of the data set incorporating group 2's new data: _____

   _____

   _____

LINK WEB
5 65 DATA

(c) Explain the rationale for your approach _____

_____

4. Use the tabulated data to plot an appropriate graph of the results on the grid provided below:

5. (a) Describe the trend in the data: _____

_____

_____

(b) Explain the relationship between stage of germination and catalase activity shown in the data: _____

_____

_____

(c) Do the results support the students' hypothesis? _____

_____

6. Describe any potential sources of errors in the apparatus or the procedure: _____

_____

_____

_____

7. Describe two things that might affect the validity of findings in this experimental design: _____

_____

_____

_____

66 Enzyme Inhibition

Key Idea: Enzymes activity can be reduced or stopped by inhibitors. These may be competitive or non-competitive. Enzyme activity can be stopped, temporarily or permanently, by chemicals called enzyme inhibitors. **Irreversible inhibitors** bind tightly to the enzyme and are not easily displaced. **Reversible inhibitors** can be displaced from the enzyme and have a role as enzyme regulators in metabolic pathways.

Competitive inhibitors compete directly with the substrate for the active site and their effect can be overcome by increasing the concentration of available substrate. A **non-competitive inhibitor** does not occupy the active site, but distorts it so that the substrate and enzyme can no longer interact. Both competitive and non-competitive inhibition may be irreversible, in which case the inhibitors act as poisons.

Enzyme regulation by allostery

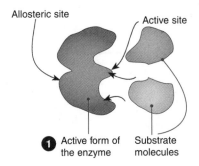

Allosteric site
Active site

1 Active form of the enzyme
Substrate molecules

Enzyme catalyses the reaction between the substrates producing a new molecule.

2 Enzyme-substrate complex

The new molecule (e.g. end product) attaches to the allosteric site of the enzyme, inhibiting the enzyme's activity.

3 Inactive form of the enzyme

Metabolic pathways can be controlled by their end products through **allosteric regulation.** When concentrations of the end product are high, it will bind to the **allosteric site** of the first enzyme in the pathway, inhibiting the enzyme and shutting down the pathway. When the concentration of the end product is reduced, it is released from the allosteric site and the pathway is reactivated.

Competitive inhibition

Competitive inhibitors compete with the normal substrate for the enzyme's active site.

Competitive inhibitors compete directly with the substrate for the active site, and their effect can be overcome by increasing the substrate concentration.

Enzyme
Substrate
Active site
Inhibitor
Substrate

1 Inhibitor is present in the cell (or solution) with the substrate

2 Inhibitor temporarily binds to the active site, blocking it so that the substrate cannot bind

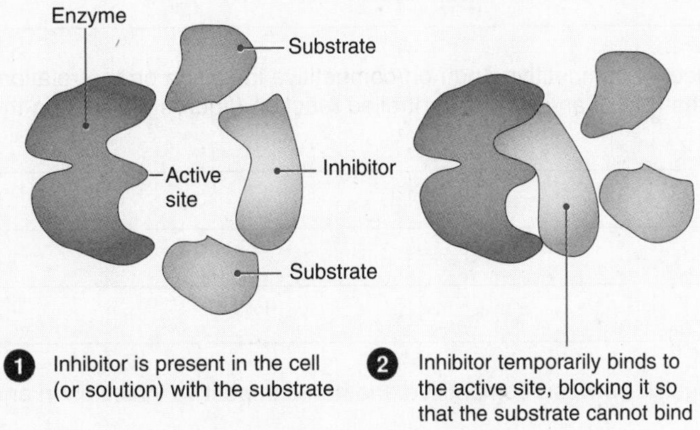

Fig.1 Effect of competitive inhibition on enzyme reaction rate at different substrate concentration

Maximum rate
no inhibitor
competitive inhibitor

Rate of reaction
Substrate concentration →

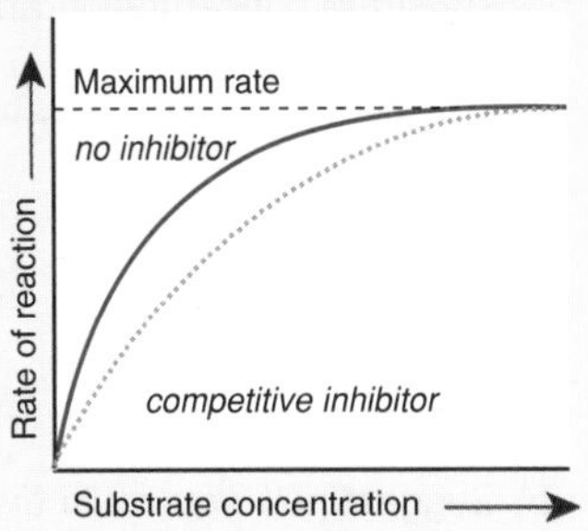

Non-competitive inhibition

Non-competitive inhibitors bind with the enzyme at a site other than the active site.

They inactivate the enzyme by altering its shape so that the substrate and enzyme can no longer interact.

Non-competitive inhibition cannot be overcome by increasing the substrate concentration.

Substrate
Inhibitor
Enzyme
Substrate

Active site cannot bind the substrates

1 Without the inhibitor bound, the enzyme can bind the substrate

2 When the inhibitor binds, the enzyme changes shape.

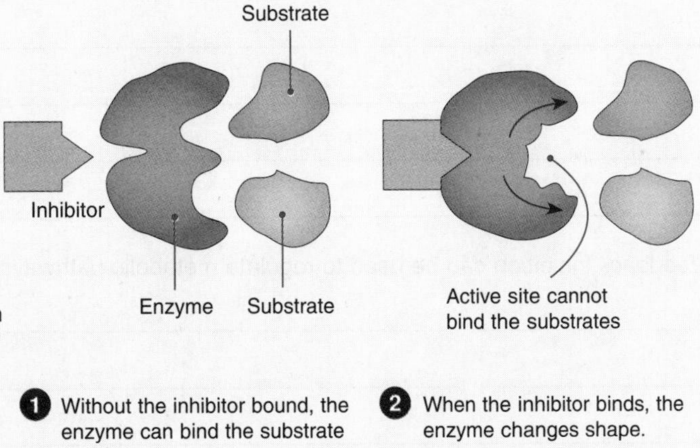

Fig.2 Effect of non-competitive inhibition on enzyme reaction rate at different substrate concentration

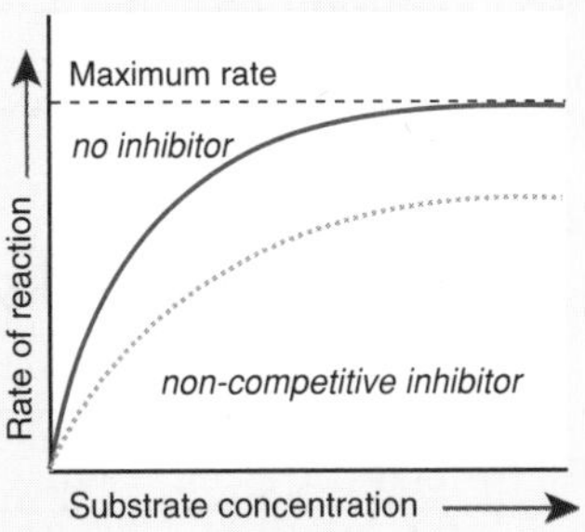

Maximum rate
no inhibitor
non-competitive inhibitor

Rate of reaction
Substrate concentration →

LINK
64
WEB
66

KNOW

End product inhibition

Many metabolic pathways are controlled by **end product inhibition** (a negative feedback loop). The pathway is stopped when a build-up of end product (or certain intermediate products) occurs (below). The build-up stops the enzymes in the pathway from working and allows cells to shut down a pathway when it is not needed. This conserves the cell's energy, so it is not manufacturing products it does not need.

Both linear pathways (e.g. glycolysis) and cyclic pathways (e.g. the Krebs cycle) can be regulated in this way (right).

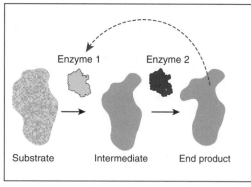

Substrate   Intermediate   End product

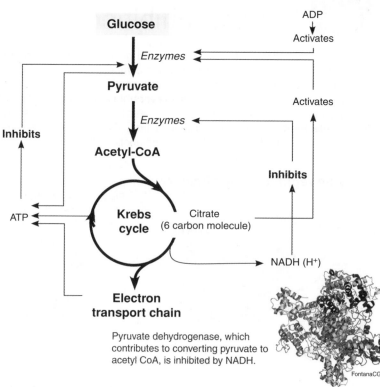

Pyruvate dehydrogenase, which contributes to converting pyruvate to acetyl CoA, is inhibited by NADH.

1. Distinguish between **competitive** and **non-competitive** inhibition: _____

_____

_____

_____

_____

2. (a) Compare and contrast the effect of competitive and non-competitive inhibition on the relationship between the substrate concentration and the rate of an enzyme controlled reaction (figures 1 and 2 on the previous page):

_____

_____

_____

_____

(b) Suggest how you could distinguish between competitive and non-competitive inhibition in an isolated system:

_____

_____

3. Describe how an **allosteric regulator** can regulate enzyme activity: _____

_____

_____

_____

_____

4. Using an example, explain how feedback inhibition can be used to regulate metabolic pathways: _____

_____

_____

_____

67 Inorganic Ions

Key Idea: Inorganic ions are charged molecules that do not contain carbon-hydrogen bonds. They are central to many biological structures and processes.

Inorganic compounds do not contain C-H bonds. An **inorganic ion** is an inorganic atom (or group of atoms) that has gained or lost one or more electrons and therefore has a positive or negative charge. Inorganic ions are central to the structure and metabolism of all living organisms, participating in metabolic reactions and combining with organic molecules to form complex molecules (e.g. magnesium and chlorophyll).

Cation: A positive ion; an atom or group of atoms that has lost one or more electrons.

Anion: A negative ion; an atom or group of atoms that has gained one or more electrons.

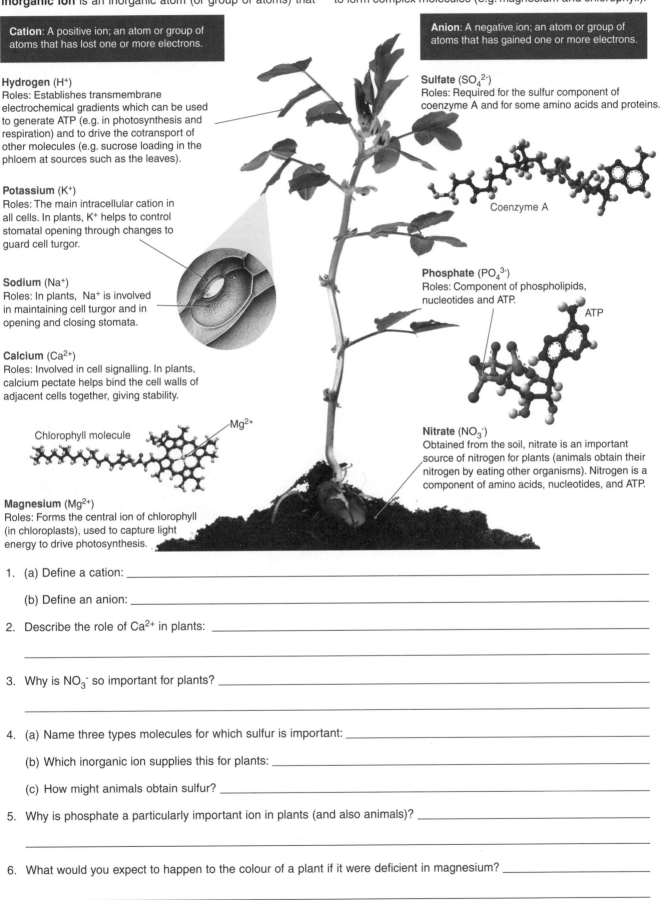

Hydrogen (H^+)
Roles: Establishes transmembrane electrochemical gradients which can be used to generate ATP (e.g. in photosynthesis and respiration) and to drive the cotransport of other molecules (e.g. sucrose loading in the phloem at sources such as the leaves).

Potassium (K^+)
Roles: The main intracellular cation in all cells. In plants, K^+ helps to control stomatal opening through changes to guard cell turgor.

Sodium (Na^+)
Roles: In plants, Na^+ is involved in maintaining cell turgor and in opening and closing stomata.

Calcium (Ca^{2+})
Roles: Involved in cell signalling. In plants, calcium pectate helps bind the cell walls of adjacent cells together, giving stability.

Chlorophyll molecule — Mg^{2+}

Magnesium (Mg^{2+})
Roles: Forms the central ion of chlorophyll (in chloroplasts), used to capture light energy to drive photosynthesis.

Sulfate (SO_4^{2-})
Roles: Required for the sulfur component of coenzyme A and for some amino acids and proteins.

Coenzyme A

Phosphate (PO_4^{3-})
Roles: Component of phospholipids, nucleotides and ATP.

ATP

Nitrate (NO_3^-)
Obtained from the soil, nitrate is an important source of nitrogen for plants (animals obtain their nitrogen by eating other organisms). Nitrogen is a component of amino acids, nucleotides, and ATP.

1. (a) Define a cation: _____

    (b) Define an anion: _____

2. Describe the role of Ca^{2+} in plants: _____

    _____

3. Why is NO_3^- so important for plants? _____

    _____

4. (a) Name three types molecules for which sulfur is important: _____

    (b) Which inorganic ion supplies this for plants: _____

    (c) How might animals obtain sulfur? _____

5. Why is phosphate a particularly important ion in plants (and also animals)? _____

    _____

6. What would you expect to happen to the colour of a plant if it were deficient in magnesium? _____

    _____

LINK   LINK   LINK   WEB
214 204 184 67   KNOW

68 Water

Key Idea: Water forms bonds between other water molecules and also with ions allowing water to act as a medium for transporting molecules and the biological reactions of life.
Water (H_2O) is the main component of living things, and typically makes up about 70% of any organism. Water is important in cell chemistry as it takes part in, and is a common product of, many reactions. Water can form bonds with other water molecules, and also with other ions (charged molecules). Because of this chemical ability, water is regarded as the universal solvent.

Water forms hydrogen bonds

A water molecule is polar, meaning it has a positively and a negatively charged region. In water, oxygen has a slight negative charge and each of the hydrogens have a slight positive charge. Water molecules have a weak attraction for each other, forming large numbers of weak hydrogen bonds with other water molecules (far right).

Intermolecular bonds between water and other polar molecules or ions are important for biological systems. Inorganic ions may have a positive or negative charge (e.g sodium ion is positive, chloride ion is negative). The charged water molecule is attracted to the charged ion and surrounds it (right). This formation of intermolecular bonds between water and the ions is what keeps the ions dissolved in water. Polar molecules such as amino acids and carbohydrates also dissolve readily in water.

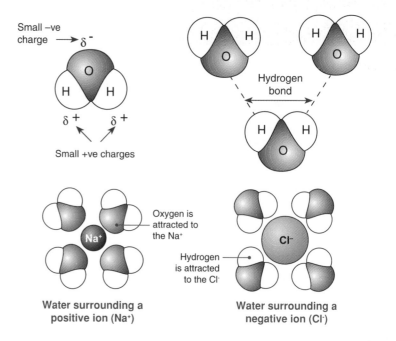

Small −ve charge → δ⁻
Small +ve charges δ⁺ δ⁺
Hydrogen bond

Oxygen is attracted to the Na⁺
Hydrogen is attracted to the Cl⁻

Water surrounding a positive ion (Na⁺)

Water surrounding a negative ion (Cl⁻)

The importance of water

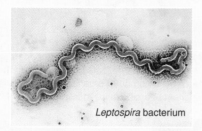

Leptospira bacterium

The metabolic reactions carried out by all organisms depend on dissolved reactants (solutes) coming into contact. Water provides the medium for metabolic reactions. Water can also act as an acid (donating H⁺) or a base (receiving H⁺) in chemical reactions.

Water provides an aquatic environment for organisms to live in. Ice is less dense than water and floats (water reaches maximum density at 4°C). A lot of energy is needed for water to change state, so water has an important buffering effect on climate.

Water is colourless, with a high transmission of visible light. Light penetrates aquatic environments, allowing photosynthesis to continue at depth. Water is also incompressible, so it transports materials by mass flow (e.g. blood flows through vessels, sap moves through phloem).

1. The diagram at the top of the page shows a positive sodium ion and a negative chloride ion surrounded by water molecules. On the diagram, draw on the charge of the water molecules.

2. Explain the formation of hydrogen bonds between water and other polar molecules: _____

_____

_____

_____

3. Explain the central role of water in metabolic processes: _____

_____

_____

_____

© 2015 **BIOZONE** International
ISBN: 978-1-927309-25-4
Photocopying Prohibited

69 The Properties of Water

Key Idea: Water's chemical properties influence its physical properties and its ability to transport molecules in solution. Water's cohesive, adhesive, thermal, and solvent properties come about because of its polarity and ability to form hydrogen bonds with other polar molecules. These physical properties allow water, and water based substances (such as blood), to transport polar molecules in solution. The ability of substances to dissolve in water varies. **Hydrophilic** (water-loving) substances dissolve readily in water (e.g. salts, sugars). **Hydrophobic** (water-hating) substances (e.g. oil) do not dissolve in water. Blood must transport many different substances, including hydrophobic ones.

Cohesive properties

Water molecules are cohesive, they stick together because hydrogen bonds form between water molecules. Cohesion allows water to form drops and allows the development of surface tension. **Example**: The cohesive and adhesive properties of water allow it to be transported as an unbroken column through the xylem of plants.

Adhesive properties

Water is attracted to other molecules because it forms hydrogen bonds with other polar molecules. **Example**: The adhesion of water molecules to the sides of a capillary tube is responsible for a meniscus (the curved upper surface of a liquid in a tube).

Solvent properties

Other substances dissolve in water because water's dipolar nature allows it to surround other charged molecules and prevent them from clumping together. **Example**: Mineral transport through a plant.

Thermal properties

▶ Water has the highest heat capacity of all liquids, so it takes a lot of energy before it will change temperature. As a result, water heats up and cools down slowly, so large bodies of water maintain a relatively stable temperature.

▶ Water is liquid at room temperature and has a high boiling point because a lot of energy is needed to break the hydrogen bonds. The liquid environment supports life and metabolic processes.

▶ Water has a high latent heat of vaporisation, meaning it takes a lot of energy to transform it from the liquid to the gas phase. In sweating, the energy is provided by the body, so sweat has a cooling effect.

Transporting substances in blood

Cholesterol — Protein — Phospholipid — Triglyceride

Sodium chloride	Glucose	Amino acids	Oxygen	Fats and cholesterol
Sodium chloride (NaCl) is highly soluble. NaCl dissolves in blood plasma into the ions Na⁺ and Cl⁻.	Glucose is a polar molecule so readily dissolves into blood plasma for transport around the body.	All amino acids have both a positive or negative charge, and are highly soluble in blood. However, their variable R-chain can alter the solubility of amino acids slightly.	Oxygen has low solubility in water. In blood, it is bound to the protein haemoglobin in red blood cells so it can be transported around the body.	Fats are non-polar substances and are insoluble in water. Cholesterol has a slight charge, but is also water insoluble. Both are transported in blood within lipoprotein complexes, spheres of phospholipids arranged with the hydrophilic heads and proteins facing out and hydrophobic tails facing inside.

1. (a) Describe the difference between a **hydrophilic** and **hydrophobic** molecule: _____

_____

_____

(b) Use an example to describe how a hydrophilic and a hydrophobic molecule are transported in blood: _____

_____

_____

_____

2. How does water act as a coolant during sweating? _____

_____

_____

LINK 212   LINK 211   LINK 199   WEB 69   KNOW

70 Chapter Review

Summarise what you know about this topic under the headings provided. You can draw diagrams or mind maps, or write short notes. Use the images and hints to help you and refer back to the introduction to check the points covered:

Carbohydrates:
HINT: Relate carbohydrate structure to function.

Proteins:
HINT: Describe the structure and function of proteins. Include reference to 1°, 2°, 3°, and 4° structure.

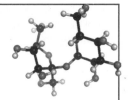

Lipids:
HINT: Compare the structure, properties, and biological roles of different lipids.

© 2015 BIOZONE International
ISBN: 978-1-927309-25-4
Photocopying Prohibited

DNA and protein synthesis:
HINT: Describe key features of DNA replication, transcription, and translation including the role of enzymes.

Enzymes:
HINT: Describe the induced fit model of enzyme activity and how enzyme activity is regulated.

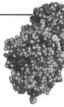

Inorganic ions and water:
HINT: What roles do inorganic ions pay in metabolism? Describe how water can form bonds with other molecules, and why this is important.

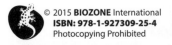

71 KEY TERMS: Did You Get It?

1. The diagram (right) symbolically represents a phospholipid.

   (a) Label the hydrophobic and hydrophilic regions of the phospholipid.

   (b) Explain how the properties of the phospholipid molecule result in the bilayer structure of membranes:

   _____

   _____

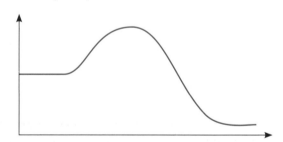

2. (a) What general reaction combines two molecules to form a larger molecule? _____

   (b) What general reaction cleaves a larger molecule by the addition of water? _____

3. (a) Which class of biological molecules contains carbon, hydrogen, and oxygen only: _____

   (b) In addition to carbon, hydrogen, and oxygen, name the other element that all proteins contain: _____

   (c) Some proteins also contain sulfur. What is the effect of sulfur on a protein's structure: _____

   _____

4. For the following DNA sequence, give the mRNA sequence and then Identify the amino acids that are encoded. For this question you may consult the mRNA-amino acid table earlier in the chapter.

   DNA: G A A A C C C T T A C A T A T C G T G C T

   mRNA: _____

   Amino acids: _____

5. Complete the following paragraph by **deleting** one of the words in the **bracketed () pairs** below:

   In eukaryotes, gene expression begins with (transcription/translation) which occurs in the (cytoplasm/nucleus).

   (Transcription/Translation) is the copying of the DNA code into (mRNA/tRNA). The (mRNA/tRNA) is then transported to

   the (cytoplasm/nucleus) where (transcription/translation) occurs. Ribosomes attach to the (mRNA/tRNA) and help match

   the codons on (mRNA/tRNA) with the anticodons on (mRNA/tRNA). The (mRNA/tRNA) transports the animo acids to the

   ribosome where they are added to the growing (polypeptide/carbohydrate) chain.

6. (a) Label the graph, right, with appropriate axes and the following labels: Reactants, products, activation energy, transition state.

   (b) Assume the reaction has had no enzyme added. Draw the shape of the graph if an enzyme was added to the reaction mix.

7. Test your vocabulary by matching each term to its correct definition, as identified by its preceding letter code.

   lipids _____

   globular proteins _____

   DNA _____

   polysaccharides _____

   nucleic acids _____

   A Macromolecule consisting of many millions of units containing a phosphate group, sugar and a base (A,T, C or G). Stores the genetic information of the cell.

   B Long carbohydrate molecules made up of monosaccharide units joined together by glycosidic bonds

   C Universally found macromolecules composed of chains of nucleotides. These molecules carry genetic information within cells.

   D A class of organic compounds with an oily, greasy, or waxy consistency. Important as energy storage molecules and as components of cellular membranes.

   E Water soluble proteins with a spherical tertiary structure. They are involved in many cellular functions including as catalysts and in transport and regulation.

© 2015 **BIOZONE** International
ISBN: 978-1-927309-25-4
Photocopying Prohibited

TEST

Topic 2

Cells, Viruses, and Reproduction

2.1 Eukaryotic and prokaryotic cells

Learning outcomes

Activity number

☐ i Appreciate that all life on Earth exists as cells. Appreciate the range of cell types and cell sizes. Outline the cell theory and the evidence supporting it. — 72 73 75

☐ ii Describe the hierarchy of organisation in multicellular organisms, using examples to show how specialised cells are organised into tissues, tissues into organs, and organs into organ systems. — 74 85-88

☐ iii Describe the ultrastructure and specific features of prokaryotic cells, including the cell wall, 70S ribosomes, nucleoid, bacterial chromosome, and plasmids. — 76

☐ iv Distinguish between gram positive and gram negative bacterial cell walls and relate these differences to different responses to antibiotics. — 77

☐ **AT** Use aseptic techniques, e.g. in measuring antibiotic sensitivity. — 78

☐ v Describe the ultrastructure of eukaryotic cells and the functions of the organelles found in plant and animal cells. Include the nucleus, nucleolus, 80S ribosomes, rough and smooth endoplasmic reticulum, mitochondria, centrioles, lysosomes, Golgi apparatus, cell wall, chloroplasts, vacuole, and tonoplast. — 79-84

☐ vi Describe the principles and limitations of optical (light) microscopes, transmission electron microscopes, and scanning electron microscopes. Include reference to magnification, resolution, and features of the images produced. — 89 95

☐ **AT** Calculate the magnification of drawings and the size of cell structures seen with a light microscope. — 91

☐ vii Explain the importance of staining specimens in microscopy. — 92 93

☐ **CP-2** Use a light microscope, including a stage micrometer and eyepiece graticule to view and draw cells from a specialised tissue. — 89 90 94

2.2 Viruses

Learning outcomes

Activity number

☐ i Describe how viruses are classified according to structure and type of nucleic acid, as illustrated by lambda phage, tobacco mosaic virus, Ebola, and human immunodeficiency virus. — 96

☐ ii Describe the lytic cycle of a virus (e.g. lambda phage). Describe the phenomenon of latency (e.g. in lambda phage and in a retrovirus, such as HIV) and explain its implications to the host cell. — 97 98

☐ iii Explain the action of antiviral drugs with reference to the key features of viral replication. Contrast their activity with drugs used to control cellular pathogens. — 99

☐ iv Explain why viral diseases can be difficult to treat and how they are most effectively controlled, as exemplified by the 2014 Ebola epidemic. — 100

☐ v Using a specific example, such as Ebola, evaluate the ethical implications of using untested drugs during epidemics. — 100

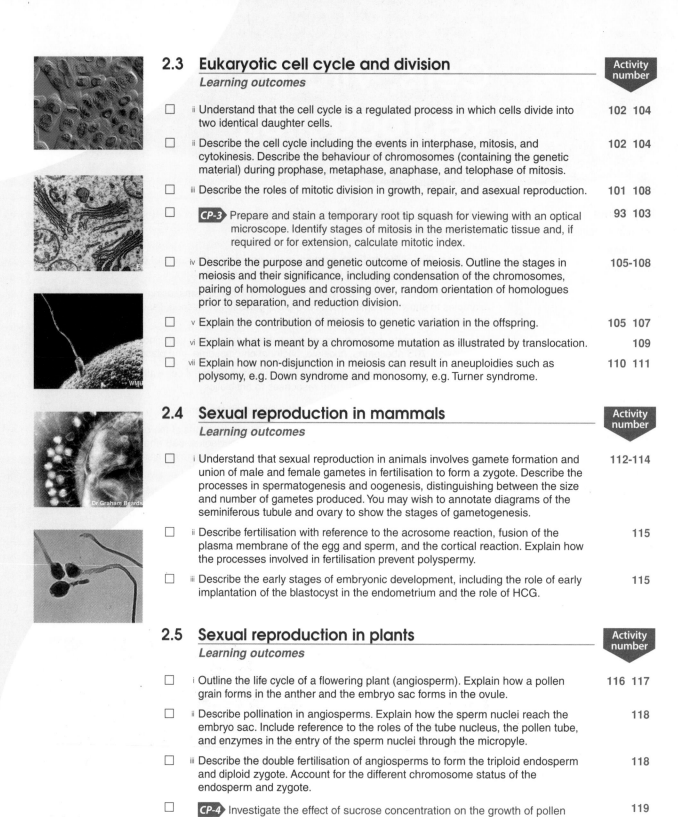

2.3 Eukaryotic cell cycle and division
Learning outcomes

2.4 Sexual reproduction in mammals
Learning outcomes

2.5 Sexual reproduction in plants
Learning outcomes

72 The Cell Theory

Key Idea: All living organisms are composed of cells. The cell is the basic unit of life.

The cell theory is a fundamental idea of biology. This idea, that all living things are composed of cells, developed over many years and is strongly linked to the invention and refinement of the microscope in the 1600s. The term cell was coined by Robert Hooke after observing a thin piece of cork under a microscope in which he saw cell-like walled compartments.

The cell theory

The idea that cells are fundamental units of life is part of the cell theory. The basic principles of the theory (as developed by early biologists) are:

▶ All living things are composed of cells and cell products.

▶ New cells are formed only by the division of pre-existing cells.

▶ The cell contains inherited information (genes) that are used as instructions for growth, functioning, and development.

▶ The cell is the functioning unit of life; all chemical reactions of life take place within cells.

Homeostasis: Cells maintain a stable internal environment by carrying out a continuous series of chemical reactions.

Metabolism: Life is a continual series of chemical reactions. Cells sustain these reactions by using the energy in food molecules (e.g. glucose).

Response: All cells respond to their environment. Receptors in the plasma membrane detect molecules in the environment and send signals to the internal machinery of the cell.

Amoeba cell

Life functions

All cells show the functions of life. They use food (e.g. glucose) to maintain a stable internal environment, grow, reproduce, and produce wastes.

Nutrition: All cells require food to provide energy to power chemical reactions and nutrients to build cell components.

Growth: Cells grow bigger over time. When they get big enough and acquire enough materials they may divide.

Reproduction: Cells divide to produce new cells. Some cells may copy their DNA and produce a genetically identical daughter cell. Other specialised cells divide their DNA to produce gametes.

Exceptions to the cell theory

The alga *Caulerpa* consists of one multi-nucleated cell, yet it grows to the size of a large plant. Its shape is maintained by the cell wall and microtubules, but there are no separate cells.

Muscle fibres form from the fusion of many myoblasts (individual muscle stem cells), producing a large multi-nucleated fibre. These fibres can be 20 cm or more long.

Mucor sp. hyphae

Some **fungi** produce hyphae that lack cross walls dividing the hyphae into cells. They are known as aseptate hyphae (as opposed to septate hyphae that do contain cross walls).

1. Cells are the fundamental unit of life. Explain what this means: _____

_____

_____

2. To what extent is an organism such as *Caulerpa* an exception to the cell theory?_____

_____

_____

_____

73 Types of Living Things

Key Idea: There are two broad types of cells, prokaryotic (or bacterial) cells and eukaryotic cells.

Living things (organisms) are made up of one or more cells. They are divided into two broad groups, **prokaryotic (bacterial) cells** and the more complex **eukaryotic cells**. Plant cells, animals cells, fungal cells, and protists are all eukaryotic cells. Viruses are classed as non-cellular as they have no cellular machinery of their own. All cells need energy to carry out their metabolic processes. **Autotrophs** are able to meet their energy requirements using light or chemical energy from the physical environment. **Heterotrophs** obtain their energy from the consumption of other organisms.

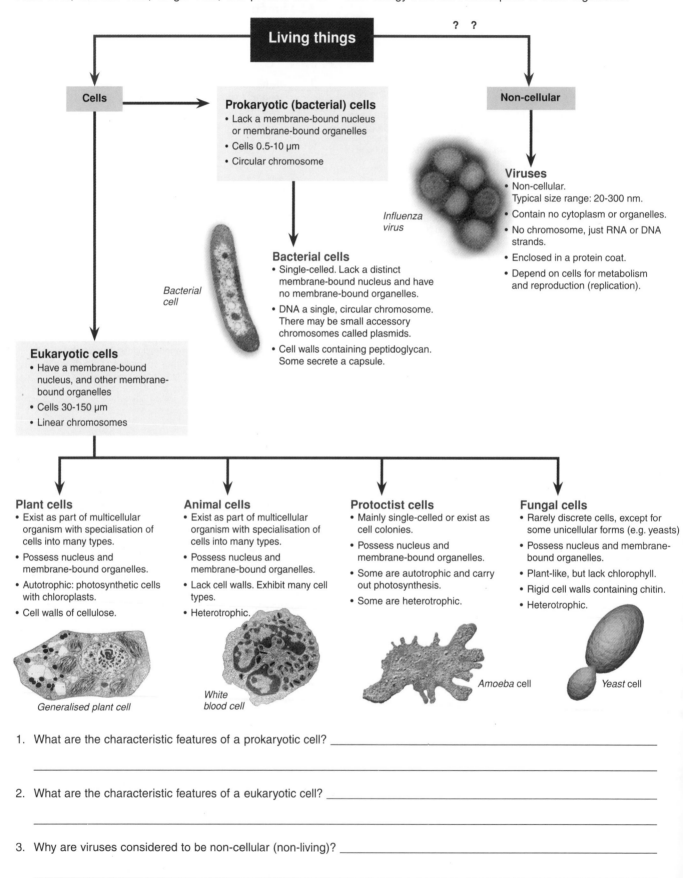

Living things

? ?

Cells

Prokaryotic (bacterial) cells
• Lack a membrane-bound nucleus or membrane-bound organelles
• Cells 0.5-10 µm
• Circular chromosome

Non-cellular

Influenza virus

Viruses
• Non-cellular. Typical size range: 20-300 nm.
• Contain no cytoplasm or organelles.
• No chromosome, just RNA or DNA strands.
• Enclosed in a protein coat.
• Depend on cells for metabolism and reproduction (replication).

Bacterial cell

Bacterial cells
• Single-celled. Lack a distinct membrane-bound nucleus and have no membrane-bound organelles.
• DNA a single, circular chromosome. There may be small accessory chromosomes called plasmids.
• Cell walls containing peptidoglycan. Some secrete a capsule.

Eukaryotic cells
• Have a membrane-bound nucleus, and other membrane-bound organelles
• Cells 30-150 µm
• Linear chromosomes

Plant cells
• Exist as part of multicellular organism with specialisation of cells into many types.
• Possess nucleus and membrane-bound organelles.
• Autotrophic: photosynthetic cells with chloroplasts.
• Cell walls of cellulose.

Generalised plant cell

Animal cells
• Exist as part of multicellular organism with specialisation of cells into many types.
• Possess nucleus and membrane-bound organelles.
• Lack cell walls. Exhibit many cell types.
• Heterotrophic.

White blood cell

Protoctist cells
• Mainly single-celled or exist as cell colonies.
• Possess nucleus and membrane-bound organelles.
• Some are autotrophic and carry out photosynthesis.
• Some are heterotrophic.

Amoeba cell

Fungal cells
• Rarely discrete cells, except for some unicellular forms (e.g. yeasts)
• Possess nucleus and membrane-bound organelles.
• Plant-like, but lack chlorophyll.
• Rigid cell walls containing chitin.
• Heterotrophic.

Yeast cell

1. What are the characteristic features of a prokaryotic cell? _____

_____

2. What are the characteristic features of a eukaryotic cell? _____

_____

3. Why are viruses considered to be non-cellular (non-living)? _____

_____

LINK 76   LINK 79   LINK 81   LINK 96

KNOW

© 2015 **BIOZONE** International
ISBN:978-1-927309-25-4
Photocopying Prohibited

74 Levels of Organisation

Key Idea: Structural organisation in multicellular organisms is hierarchical, with new properties arising at each level. Organisation and the emergence of novel properties in complex systems are two of the defining features of living organisms. Organisms are organised according to a hierarchy of structural levels, each level building on the one before it. At each level, new properties arise that were absent at the simpler level. Hierarchical organisation allows specialised cells to group together into tissues and organs to perform a specific function. This improves efficiency in the organism.

All multicellular organisms are organised in a hierarchy of structural levels, where each level builds on the one below it. It is traditional to start with the simplest components (parts) and build from there. Higher levels of organisation are more complex than lower levels.

Hierarchical organisation enables **specialisation** so that individual components perform a specific function or set of related functions. Specialisation enables organisms to function more efficiently.

The diagram below explains this hierarchical organisation for a human.

1. Assign each of the following emergent properties to the level at which it first appears:

(a) Metabolism: _____

(b) Behaviour: _____

(c) Replication: _____

3 **The cellular level**
Cells are the basic structural and functional units of an organism. Cells are specialised to carry out specific functions, e.g. cardiac (heart) muscle cells (below).

2 **The organelle level**
Molecules associate together to form the organelles and structural components of cells, e.g. the nucleus (above).

DNA

1

Atoms and molecules

The chemical level
All the chemicals essential for maintaining life, e.g. water, ions, fats, carbohydrates, amino acids, proteins, and nucleic acids.

6 **The system level**
Groups of organs with a common function form an organ system, e.g. cardiovascular system (left).

The tissue level **4**
Groups of cells with related functions form tissues, e.g. cardiac (heart) muscle (above). The cells of a tissue often have a similar origin.

7 **The organism**
The cooperating organ systems make up the organism, e.g. a human.

5 **The organ level**
An organ is made up of two or more types of tissues to carry out a particular function. Organs have a definite form and structure, e.g. heart (left).

LINK **87** LINK **86** LINK **81** WEB **74** **KNOW**

75 Cell Sizes

Key Idea: Cells vary in size (2-100 µm), with prokaryotic cells being approximately 10 times smaller than eukaryotic cells. Cells can only be seen properly when viewed through the magnifying lenses of a microscope. The images below show a variety of cell types, including a multicellular microscopic animal and a virus (non-cellular) for comparison. For each of these images, note the scale and relate this to the type of microscopy used.

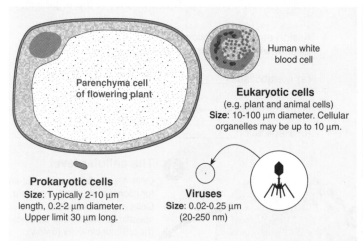

Parenchyma cell of flowering plant

Human white blood cell

Eukaryotic cells
(e.g. plant and animal cells)
Size: 10-100 µm diameter. Cellular organelles may be up to 10 µm.

Prokaryotic cells
Size: Typically 2-10 µm length, 0.2-2 µm diameter. Upper limit 30 µm long.

Viruses
Size: 0.02-0.25 µm (20-250 nm)

Unit of length (international system)

Unit	Metres	Equivalent
1 metre (m)	1 m	= 1000 millimetres
1 millimetre (mm)	10^{-3} m	= 1000 micrometres
1 micrometre (µm)	10^{-6} m	= 1000 nanometres
1 nanometre (nm)	10^{-9} m	= 1000 picometres

Micrometres are sometime referred to as microns. Smaller structures are usually measured in nanometres (nm) e.g. molecules (1 nm) and plasma membrane thickness (10 nm).

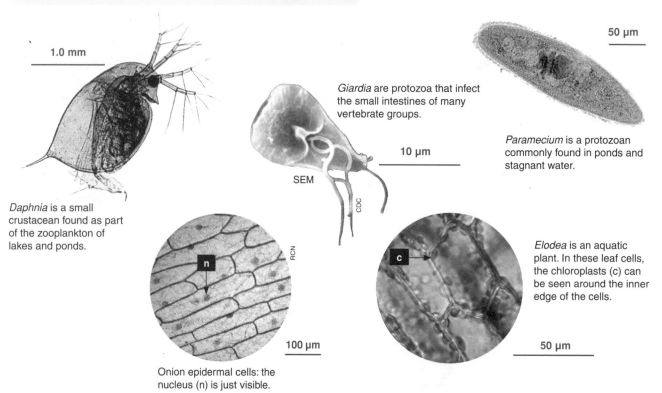

1.0 mm

50 µm

Giardia are protozoa that infect the small intestines of many vertebrate groups.

10 µm

SEM

CDC

Paramecium is a protozoan commonly found in ponds and stagnant water.

Daphnia is a small crustacean found as part of the zooplankton of lakes and ponds.

n

RCN

c

Elodea is an aquatic plant. In these leaf cells, the chloroplasts (c) can be seen around the inner edge of the cells.

100 µm

50 µm

Onion epidermal cells: the nucleus (n) is just visible.

1. Using the measurement scales provided on each of the photographs above, determine the longest dimension (length or diameter) of the cell/animal/organelle indicated in µm and mm. Attach your working:

   (a) *Daphnia*: _____ µm _____ mm   (d) *Elodea* leaf cell: _____ µm _____ mm

   (b) *Giardia*: _____ µm _____ mm   (e) Chloroplast: _____ µm _____ mm

   (c) Nucleus _____ µm _____ mm   (f) *Paramecium*: _____ µm _____ mm

2. (a) List a-f in question 1 in order of size, from the smallest to the largest:

   _____

   (b) Study your ruler. Which one of the above could you see with your unaided eye? _____

3. Calculate the equivalent length in millimetres (mm) of the following measurements:

   (a) 0.25 µm: _____   (b) 450 µm: _____   (c) 200 nm: _____

© 2015 **BIOZONE** International
ISBN: 978-1-927309-25-4
Photocopying Prohibited

76 Prokaryotic Cells

Key Idea: Prokaryotic cells lack many of the features of eukaryotic cells, including membrane-bound organelles. Bacterial (prokaryotic) cells are much smaller than eukaryotic cells and lack many eukaryotic features, such as a distinct nucleus and membrane-bound cellular organelles. The cell wall is an important feature. It is a complex, multi-layered structure and has a role in the organism's ability to cause disease. A generalised prokaryote, *E. coli*, is shown below.

E. coli structure

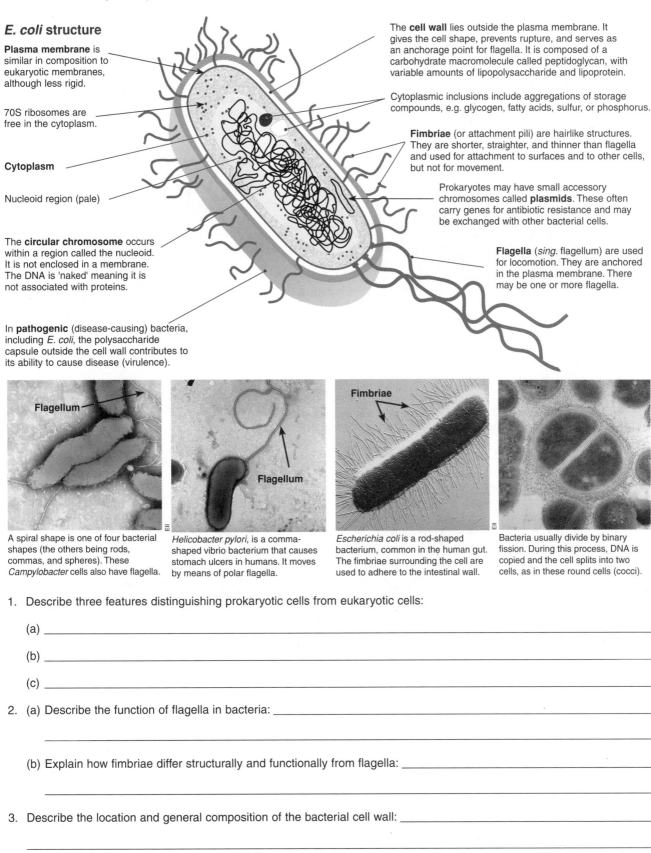

Plasma membrane is similar in composition to eukaryotic membranes, although less rigid.

70S ribosomes are free in the cytoplasm.

Cytoplasm

Nucleoid region (pale)

The **circular chromosome** occurs within a region called the nucleoid. It is not enclosed in a membrane. The DNA is 'naked' meaning it is not associated with proteins.

In **pathogenic** (disease-causing) bacteria, including *E. coli*, the polysaccharide capsule outside the cell wall contributes to its ability to cause disease (virulence).

The **cell wall** lies outside the plasma membrane. It gives the cell shape, prevents rupture, and serves as an anchorage point for flagella. It is composed of a carbohydrate macromolecule called peptidoglycan, with variable amounts of lipopolysaccharide and lipoprotein.

Cytoplasmic inclusions include aggregations of storage compounds, e.g. glycogen, fatty acids, sulfur, or phosphorus.

Fimbriae (or attachment pili) are hairlike structures. They are shorter, straighter, and thinner than flagella and used for attachment to surfaces and to other cells, but not for movement.

Prokaryotes may have small accessory chromosomes called **plasmids**. These often carry genes for antibiotic resistance and may be exchanged with other bacterial cells.

Flagella (*sing*. flagellum) are used for locomotion. They are anchored in the plasma membrane. There may be one or more flagella.

Flagellum

A spiral shape is one of four bacterial shapes (the others being rods, commas, and spheres). These *Campylobacter* cells also have flagella.

Flagellum

Helicobacter pylori, is a comma-shaped vibrio bacterium that causes stomach ulcers in humans. It moves by means of polar flagella.

Fimbriae

Escherichia coli is a rod-shaped bacterium, common in the human gut. The fimbriae surrounding the cell are used to adhere to the intestinal wall.

Bacteria usually divide by binary fission. During this process, DNA is copied and the cell splits into two cells, as in these round cells (cocci).

1. Describe three features distinguishing prokaryotic cells from eukaryotic cells:

   (a) _____

   (b) _____

   (c) _____

2. (a) Describe the function of flagella in bacteria: _____

   _____

   (b) Explain how fimbriae differ structurally and functionally from flagella: _____

   _____

3. Describe the location and general composition of the bacterial cell wall: _____

   _____

   _____

4. What is the purpose of binary fission in prokaryotes: _____

LINK 145   LINK 77   WEB 76 **KNOW**

77 | The Gram Stain and Antibiotic Sensitivity

Key Idea: The Gram-stain distinguishes between two major bacterial cell types on the basis of their cell wall structure.

Gram staining is a bacteriological technique used diagnostically to differentiate bacteria into two broad groups (Gram-positive or Gram-negative) on the basis of their cell walls. The technique is named after Hans Christian Gram

who invented it in 1884. Although not all bacteria fall into one of the two groups, the test is important because the two groups have different antibiotic sensitivities. Gram-positive bacterial cell walls contain large amounts of peptidoglycan and retain a crystal violet stain. The relationship between the stain and the cell wall structure is explained below.

Bacterial cell wall structure and the Gram stain

The **Gram stain** is the basis for distinguishing two broad groups of prokaryotes: the Gram-negatives and the Gram-positives. The test is based on the proportion of peptidoglycan in the cell wall. The stain is easily washed from the thin peptidoglycan layer of Gram-negative walls but is retained by the thick peptidoglycan layer of gram positive cells, which stain dark violet.

Gram-positive bacteria

The walls of gram positive bacteria consist of many layers of peptidoglycan forming a thick, simple structure that retains the Gram stain.

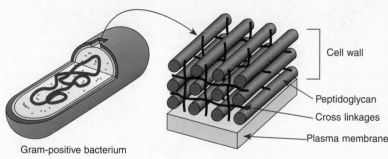

Gram-positive bacterium

- Cell wall
- Peptidoglycan
- Cross linkages
- Plasma membrane

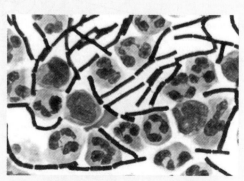

Bacillus anthracis: a Gram-positive rod. Note how the cells appear as dark rods against the white blood cells in the sample. In colour, they appear dark purple.

Gram-negative bacteria

The cell walls of gram negative bacteria contain only a small proportion of peptidoglycan, so the dark violet stain is not retained by the cell wall.

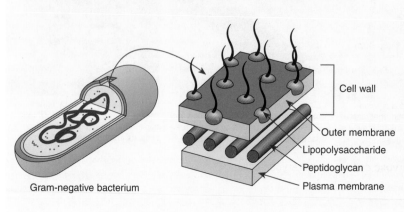

Gram-negative bacterium

- Cell wall
- Outer membrane
- Lipopolysaccharide
- Peptidoglycan
- Plasma membrane

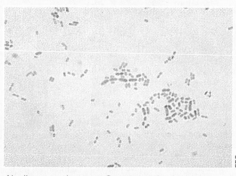

Alcaligenes odorans: a Gram-negative bacterium. Note how the cells appear pale. In colour, they appear pink because of the safranin counterstain.

1. What is the purpose of the Gram stain? _____

_____

_____

2. Describe the differences in the properties and structure of Gram-positive and Gram-negative cell walls: _____

_____

_____

_____

_____

_____

© 2015 **BIOZONE** International
ISBN:978-1-927309-25-4
Photocopying Prohibited

Gram staining

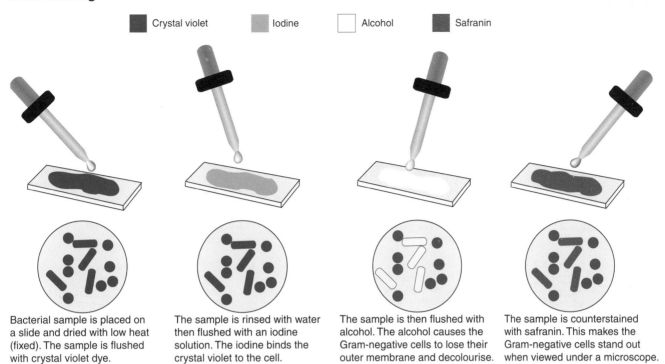

| Crystal violet | Iodine | Alcohol | Safranin |

Bacterial sample is placed on a slide and dried with low heat (fixed). The sample is flushed with crystal violet dye.

The sample is rinsed with water then flushed with an iodine solution. The iodine binds the crystal violet to the cell.

The sample is then flushed with alcohol. The alcohol causes the Gram-negative cells to lose their outer membrane and decolourise.

The sample is counterstained with safranin. This makes the Gram-negative cells stand out when viewed under a microscope.

Antibiotics and Gram-negative and Gram-positive bacteria

An important group of antibiotics includes those that attack the bacterial cell wall (e.g. penicillin). However, the differences between the cell walls of Gram-positive and Gram-negative bacteria mean that penicillins are only effective against Gram-positive bacteria.

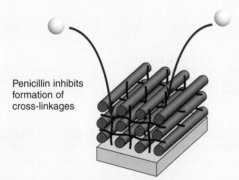

Penicillin inhibits formation of cross-linkages

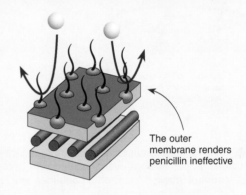

The outer membrane renders penicillin ineffective

The enzyme that makes the cross linkages between peptidoglycan layers of the cell wall of Gram-positive bacteria is inhibited by penicillin. This means that new cell walls cannot be synthesised or maintained so the bacteria cannot reproduce.

The thin peptidoglycan layer of Gram-negative bacteria is protected under the outer membrane of lipopolysaccharide. Penicillin cannot penetrate the outer membrane and is therefore ineffective against Gram-negative bacteria.

3. How does cell wall structure relate to the Gram-stain response? _____
_____
_____

4. Why are Gram-negative bacteria less susceptible to penicillin-type antibiotics: _____
_____
_____

5. Explain why the Gram-stain is an important test diagnostically in the treatment of disease: _____
_____
_____
_____

78 Measuring Antibiotic Sensitivity

Key Idea: Aseptic technique is required to reduce chances of contamination and ensure the effectiveness of an antibiotic is properly tested and quantified.

The effectiveness of antibiotics against a microbe can be tested by spreading agar plates with the microbe in question and placing discs impregnated with antibiotic on the agar.

The type of nutrient agar (growth medium) used depends on the particular microbe involved. Samples from patients with a bacterial infection are often tested to identify the most appropriate antibiotic and the most effective dose rate. This reduces the time they will need to be on the drug and reduces the chance of antibiotic resistance arising and spreading.

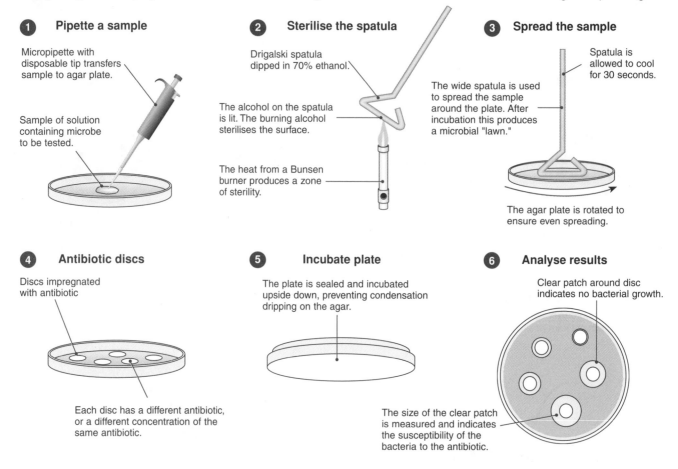

1 **Pipette a sample**

Micropipette with disposable tip transfers sample to agar plate.

Sample of solution containing microbe to be tested.

2 **Sterilise the spatula**

Drigalski spatula dipped in 70% ethanol.

The alcohol on the spatula is lit. The burning alcohol sterilises the surface.

The heat from a Bunsen burner produces a zone of sterility.

3 **Spread the sample**

Spatula is allowed to cool for 30 seconds.

The wide spatula is used to spread the sample around the plate. After incubation this produces a microbial "lawn."

The agar plate is rotated to ensure even spreading.

4 **Antibiotic discs**

Discs impregnated with antibiotic

Each disc has a different antibiotic, or a different concentration of the same antibiotic.

5 **Incubate plate**

The plate is sealed and incubated upside down, preventing condensation dripping on the agar.

6 **Analyse results**

Clear patch around disc indicates no bacterial growth.

The size of the clear patch is measured and indicates the susceptibility of the bacteria to the antibiotic.

1. Two students carried out an experiment to determine the effect of antibiotics on bacteria. They placed discs saturated with antibiotic on petri dishes evenly coated with bacterial colonies. Dish 1 contained four different antibiotics labelled A to D and a control labelled CL. Dish 2 contained four different concentrations of a single antibiotic and a control labelled CL.

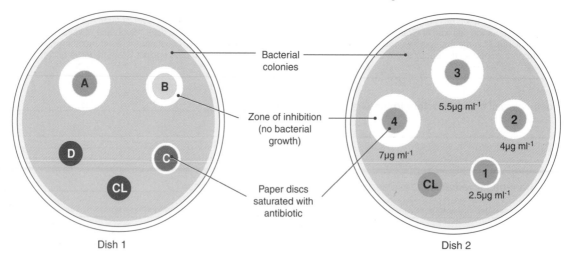

Bacterial colonies

Zone of inhibition (no bacterial growth)

Paper discs saturated with antibiotic

5.5µg ml⁻¹

7µg ml⁻¹

4µg ml⁻¹

2.5µg ml⁻¹

Dish 1

Dish 2

(a) Which was the most effective antibiotic on Dish 1? _____

(b) Which was the most effective concentration on Dish 2? _____

(c) Explain your choice in question 1(b): _____

_____

LINK

KNOW 145

© 2015 **BIOZONE** International
ISBN:978-1-927309-25-4
Photocopying Prohibited

79 Plant Cells

Key Idea: Plant cells are eukaryotic cells. They have features in common with animal cells, but also several unique features. Eukaryotic cells have a similar basic structure, although they may vary tremendously in size, shape, and function. Certain features are common to almost all eukaryotic cells, including their three main regions: a **nucleus**, surrounded by a watery **cytoplasm**, which is itself enclosed by the **plasma membrane**. Plant cells are enclosed in a cellulose cell wall, which gives them a regular, uniform appearance. The cell wall protects the cell, maintains its shape, and prevents excessive water uptake. It provides rigidity to plant structures but permits the free passage of materials into and out of the cell.

Generalised plant cell

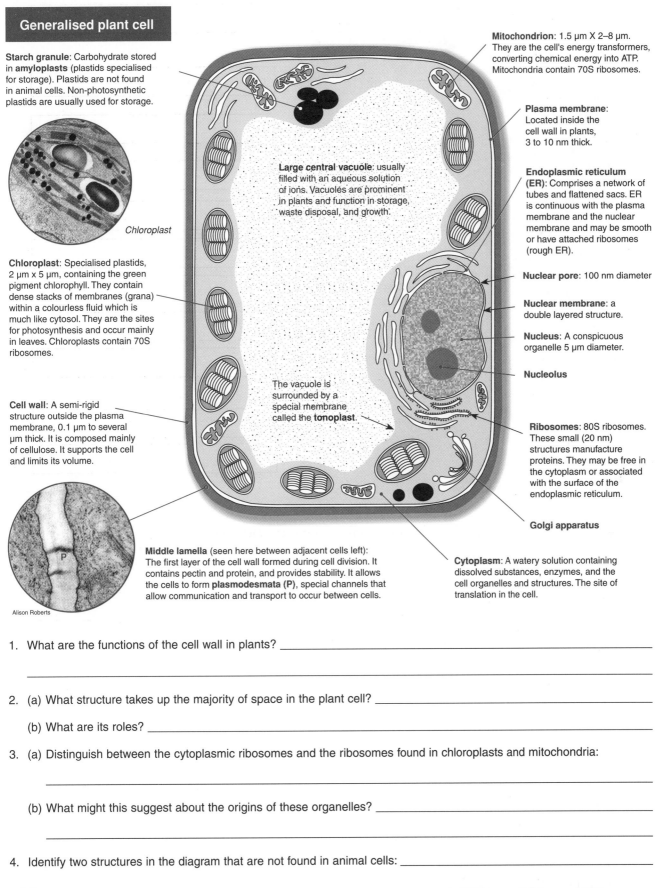

Starch granule: Carbohydrate stored in **amyloplasts** (plastids specialised for storage). Plastids are not found in animal cells. Non-photosynthetic plastids are usually used for storage.

Chloroplast

Chloroplast: Specialised plastids, 2 µm x 5 µm, containing the green pigment chlorophyll. They contain dense stacks of membranes (grana) within a colourless fluid which is much like cytosol. They are the sites for photosynthesis and occur mainly in leaves. Chloroplasts contain 70S ribosomes.

Cell wall: A semi-rigid structure outside the plasma membrane, 0.1 µm to several µm thick. It is composed mainly of cellulose. It supports the cell and limits its volume.

Alison Roberts

Mitochondrion: 1.5 µm X 2–8 µm. They are the cell's energy transformers, converting chemical energy into ATP. Mitochondria contain 70S ribosomes.

Plasma membrane: Located inside the cell wall in plants, 3 to 10 nm thick.

Endoplasmic reticulum (ER): Comprises a network of tubes and flattened sacs. ER is continuous with the plasma membrane and the nuclear membrane and may be smooth or have attached ribosomes (rough ER).

Nuclear pore: 100 nm diameter

Nuclear membrane: a double layered structure.

Nucleus: A conspicuous organelle 5 µm diameter.

Nucleolus

Large central vacuole: usually filled with an aqueous solution of ions. Vacuoles are prominent in plants and function in storage, waste disposal, and growth.

The vacuole is surrounded by a special membrane called the **tonoplast**.

Ribosomes: 80S ribosomes. These small (20 nm) structures manufacture proteins. They may be free in the cytoplasm or associated with the surface of the endoplasmic reticulum.

Golgi apparatus

Middle lamella (seen here between adjacent cells left): The first layer of the cell wall formed during cell division. It contains pectin and protein, and provides stability. It allows the cells to form **plasmodesmata (P)**, special channels that allow communication and transport to occur between cells.

Cytoplasm: A watery solution containing dissolved substances, enzymes, and the cell organelles and structures. The site of translation in the cell.

1. What are the functions of the cell wall in plants? _____

_____

2. (a) What structure takes up the majority of space in the plant cell? _____

   (b) What are its roles? _____

3. (a) Distinguish between the cytoplasmic ribosomes and the ribosomes found in chloroplasts and mitochondria:

   _____

   (b) What might this suggest about the origins of these organelles? _____

   _____

4. Identify two structures in the diagram that are not found in animal cells: _____

LINK **85** LINK **80** WEB **79** **KNOW**

80 Identifying Structures in a Plant Cell

Key Idea: Organelles can be identified in an electron micrograph by their size, position, and appearance.

1. Study the diagrams on the other pages in this chapter to familiarise yourself with the structures found in eukaryotic cells. Identify the 11 structures in the cell below using the following word list: *cytoplasm, smooth endoplasmic reticulum, mitochondrion, starch granule, chromosome, nucleus, vacuole, plasma membrane, cell wall, chloroplast, nuclear membrane*

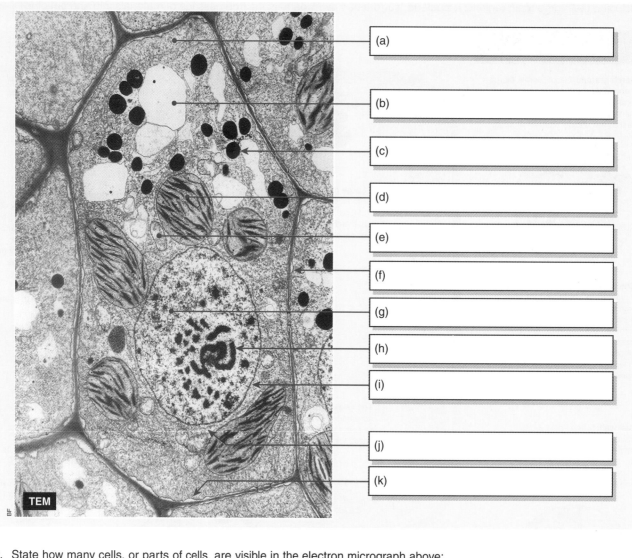

(a)

(b)

(c)

(d)

(e)

(f)

(g)

(h)

(i)

(j)

(k)

TEM

2. State how many cells, or parts of cells, are visible in the electron micrograph above: _____

3. Describe the features that identify this cell as a plant cell: _____

_____

_____

4. (a) Explain where cytoplasm is found in the cell: _____

_____

   (b) Describe what cytoplasm is made up of: _____

_____

5. Describe two structures, pictured in the cell above, that are associated with storage:

   (a) _____

_____

   (b) _____

_____

© 2015 **BIOZONE** International
ISBN:978-1-927309-25-4
Photocopying Prohibited

81 Animal Cells

Key Idea: Animal cells are eukaryotic cells. They have many features in common with plant cells, but also have a number of unique features.

Animal cells, unlike plant cells, do not have a regular shape. In fact, some animal cells (such as phagocytes) are able to alter their shape for various purposes (e.g. engulfing foreign material). The diagram below shows the structure and organelles of a liver cell. It contains organelles common to most relatively unspecialised human cells. Note the differences between this cell and the generalised plant cell. The plant cells activity provides further information on the organelles listed here but not described.

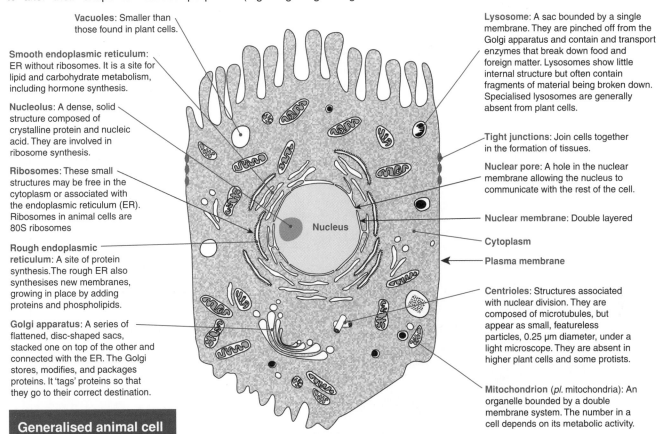

Vacuoles: Smaller than those found in plant cells.

Smooth endoplasmic reticulum: ER without ribosomes. It is a site for lipid and carbohydrate metabolism, including hormone synthesis.

Nucleolus: A dense, solid structure composed of crystalline protein and nucleic acid. They are involved in ribosome synthesis.

Ribosomes: These small structures may be free in the cytoplasm or associated with the endoplasmic reticulum (ER). Ribosomes in animal cells are 80S ribosomes

Rough endoplasmic reticulum: A site of protein synthesis. The rough ER also synthesises new membranes, growing in place by adding proteins and phospholipids.

Golgi apparatus: A series of flattened, disc-shaped sacs, stacked one on top of the other and connected with the ER. The Golgi stores, modifies, and packages proteins. It 'tags' proteins so that they go to their correct destination.

Lysosome: A sac bounded by a single membrane. They are pinched off from the Golgi apparatus and contain and transport enzymes that break down food and foreign matter. Lysosomes show little internal structure but often contain fragments of material being broken down. Specialised lysosomes are generally absent from plant cells.

Tight junctions: Join cells together in the formation of tissues.

Nuclear pore: A hole in the nuclear membrane allowing the nucleus to communicate with the rest of the cell.

Nuclear membrane: Double layered

Cytoplasm

Plasma membrane

Centrioles: Structures associated with nuclear division. They are composed of microtubules, but appear as small, featureless particles, 0.25 µm diameter, under a light microscope. They are absent in higher plant cells and some protists.

Mitochondrion (*pl.* mitochondria): An organelle bounded by a double membrane system. The number in a cell depends on its metabolic activity.

Nucleus

Generalised animal cell

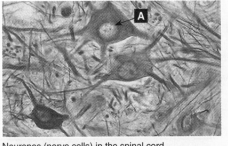

Neurones (nerve cells) in the spinal cord

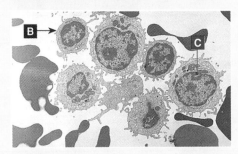

White blood cells and red blood cells (blood smear)

Photos: EII

1. The two photomicrographs (left) show several types of animal cells. Identify the features indicated by the letters **A-C**:

   A: _____

   B: _____

   C: _____

2. White blood cells are mobile, phagocytic cells, whereas red blood cells are smaller than white blood cells and, in humans, lack a nucleus.

   (a) In the photomicrograph (lower, left), circle a white blood cell and a red blood cell:

   (b) With respect to the features that you can see, explain how you made your decision.

   _____

   _____

   _____

   _____

3. Name one structure or organelle present in generalised animal cells but absent from plant cells and describe its function:

   _____

   _____

82 Identifying Structures in an Animal Cell

Key Idea: The position and angle of organelles in an electron micrograph can result in variations in their appearance. Transmission electron microscopy (TEM) is commonly used to view cellular organelles in detail. When interpreting TEMs, it is useful to remember that cellular organelles may have quite different appearances depending on how they have been sectioned and whether they are in transverse or longitudinal section.

1. Identify and label the structures in the animal cell below using the following list of terms: *cytoplasm, plasma membrane, rough endoplasmic reticulum, mitochondrion, nucleus, centriole, Golgi apparatus, lysosome*

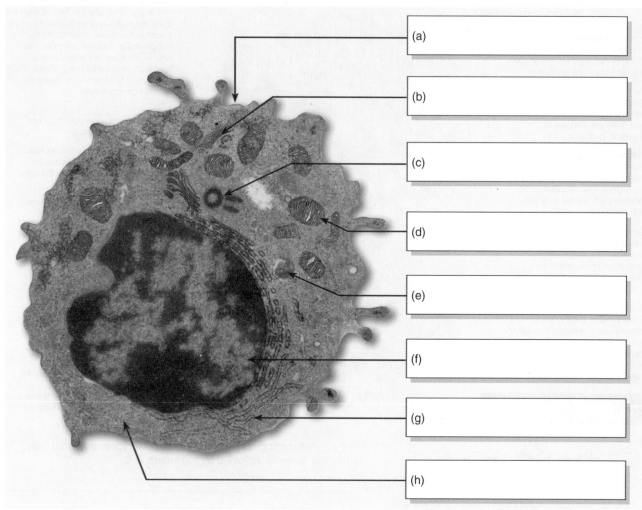

(a)

(b)

(c)

(d)

(e)

(f)

(g)

(h)

2. Which of the organelles in the EM above are obviously shown in both transverse and longitudinal section?

_____

3. Why do plants lack any of the mobile phagocytic cells typical of animal cells? _____

_____

_____

4. The animal cell pictured above is a lymphocyte. Describe the features that suggest to you that:

   (a) It has a role in producing and secreting proteins: _____

   _____

   (b) It is metabolically very active: _____

   _____

5. What features of the lymphocyte cell above identify it as eukaryotic? _____

   _____

   _____

WEB
82

LINK
83

© 2015 **BIOZONE** International
ISBN:978-1-927309-25-4
Photocopying Prohibited

83 Identifying Organelles

Key Idea: Cellular organelles can be identified in electron micrographs by their specific features.
Electron microscopes produce a magnified image at high resolution (distinguish between close together but separate objects). The transmission electron microscope (TEM) images below show the ultrastructure of some organelles.

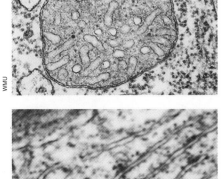

1. (a) Name the circled organelle: _____

   (b) Which kind of cell(s) would this organelle be found in?

   _____

   (c) Describe the function of this organelle: _____

   _____

   _____

   _____

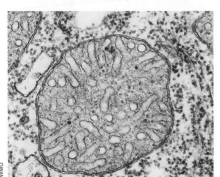

2. (a) Name this organelle (arrowed): _____

   (b) State which kind of cell(s) this organelle would be found in:

   _____

   (c) Describe the function of this organelle: _____

   _____

   _____

3. (a) Name the large, circular organelle: _____

   (b) State which kind of cell(s) this organelle would be found in:

   _____

   (c) Describe the function of this organelle: _____

   _____

   _____

   (d) Label **two** regions that can be seen **inside** this organelle.

4. (a) Name and label the ribbon-like organelle in this photograph (arrowed):

   _____

   (b) State which kind of cell(s) this organelle is found in:

   _____

   (c) Describe the function of this organelle: _____

   _____

   (d) Name the dark 'blobs' attached to the organelle you have labelled:

   _____

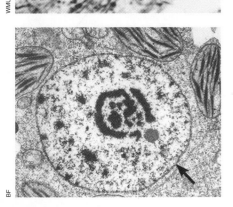

5. (a) Name this large circular organelle (arrowed): _____

   (b) State which kind of cell(s) this organelle would be found in: _____

   _____

   (c) Describe the function of this organelle: _____

   _____

   (d) Label three features relating to this organelle in the photograph.

TEST

84 Cell Structures and Organelles

Key Idea: Each type of organelle in a cell has a specific role. Not all cell types contain every type of organelle. The diagram below provides spaces for you to summarise information about the organelles found in eukaryotic cells. The log scale of measurements (top of next page) illustrates the relative sizes of some cellular structures.

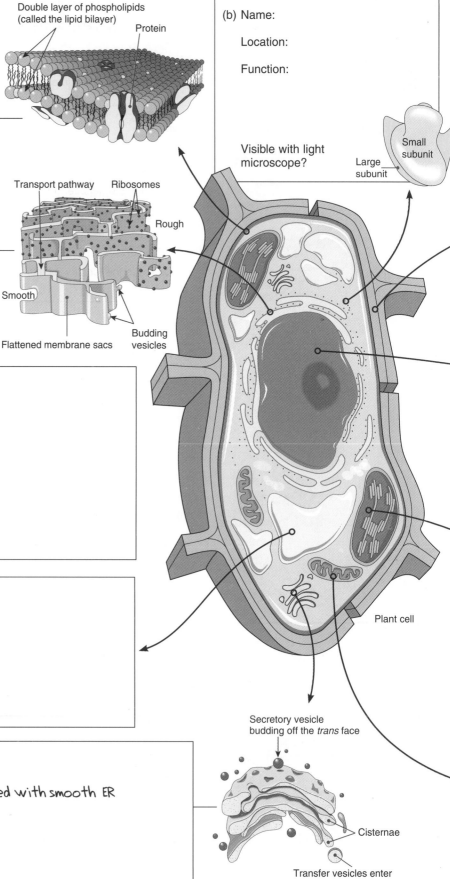

(a) Name: Plasma membrane
Location: Surrounds the cell
Function: Encloses cell contents and regulates movement of substances into and out of cell.

Visible with light microscope?
Yes (but no detail)

Double layer of phospholipids (called the lipid bilayer)
Protein

(b) Name:

Location:

Function:

Visible with light microscope?

Large subunit
Small subunit

(c) Name: Smooth and rough endoplasmic reticulum

Location: Penetrates the whole cytoplasm

Function or smooth ER:

Function of rough ER:

Visible with light microscope?

Transport pathway   Ribosomes
Rough
Smooth
Flattened membrane sacs
Budding vesicles

(d) Name:

Location:

Function:

Visible with light microscope?

Plant cell

(e) Name: Golgi apparatus

Location: Cytoplasm associated with smooth ER

Function:

Visible with light microscope?

Secretory vesicle budding off the *trans* face

Cisternae

Transfer vesicles enter from the smooth endoplasmic reticulum

© 2015 **BIOZONE** International
ISBN: 978-1-927309-25-4
Photocopying Prohibited

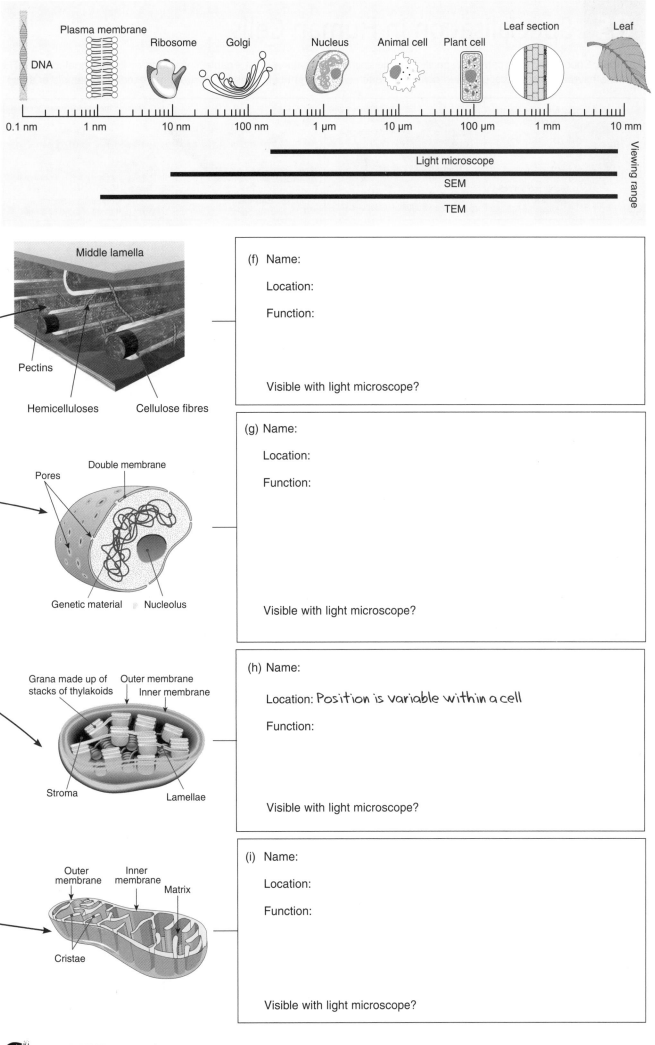

Plasma membrane

Ribosome

Golgi

Nucleus

Animal cell

Plant cell

Leaf section

Leaf

DNA

0.1 nm   1 nm   10 nm   100 nm   1 µm   10 µm   100 µm   1 mm   10 mm

Light microscope

SEM

TEM

Viewing range

Middle lamella

Pectins

Hemicelluloses   Cellulose fibres

(f) Name:

Location:

Function:

Visible with light microscope?

Pores   Double membrane

Genetic material   Nucleolus

(g) Name:

Location:

Function:

Visible with light microscope?

Grana made up of stacks of thylakoids   Outer membrane   Inner membrane

Stroma   Lamellae

(h) Name:

Location: Position is variable within a cell

Function:

Visible with light microscope?

Outer membrane   Inner membrane   Matrix

Cristae

(i) Name:

Location:

Function:

Visible with light microscope?

85 Specialisation in Human Cells

Key Idea: Specialised cells carry out specific roles in animals. Humans have at least 230 specialised cell types, each with features that enable it to perform its designated role. The eight cell types below are a representative sample of these.

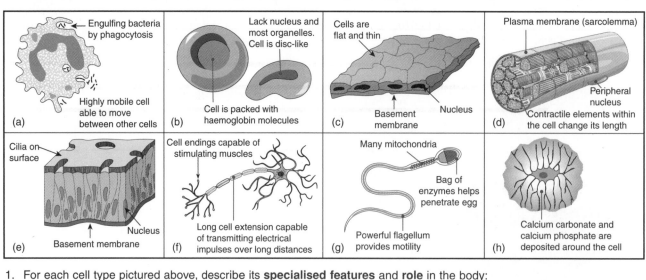

(a) Engulfing bacteria by phagocytosis. Highly mobile cell able to move between other cells

(b) Lack nucleus and most organelles. Cell is disc-like. Cell is packed with haemoglobin molecules

(c) Cells are flat and thin. Basement membrane. Nucleus

(d) Plasma membrane (sarcolemma). Peripheral nucleus. Contractile elements within the cell change its length

(e) Cilia on surface. Nucleus. Basement membrane

(f) Cell endings capable of stimulating muscles. Long cell extension capable of transmitting electrical impulses over long distances

(g) Many mitochondria. Bag of enzymes helps penetrate egg. Powerful flagellum provides motility

(h) Calcium carbonate and calcium phosphate are deposited around the cell

1. For each cell type pictured above, describe its **specialised features** and **role** in the body:

   (a) **Phagocytic white blood cell (neutrophil)**. Specialised features: _____

   Role of cell within body: _____

   (b) **Red blood cell (erythrocyte)**. Specialised features: _____

   Role of cell within body: _____

   (c) **Squamous epithelial cell**. Specialised features: _____

   Role of cell within body: _____

   (d) **Skeletal muscle cell**. Specialised features: _____

   Role of cell within body: _____

   (e) **Ciliated epithelial cell**. Specialised features: _____

   Role of cell within body: _____

   (f) **Motor neurone**. Specialised features: _____

   Role of cell within body: _____

   (g) **Sperm cell**. Specialised features: _____

   Role of cell within body: _____

   (h) **Bone cell (osteocyte)**. Specialised features: _____

   Role of cell within body: _____

 © 2015 **BIOZONE** International
ISBN:978-1-927309-25-4
Photocopying Prohibited

86 Specialisation in Plant Cells

Key Idea: The specialised cells in a plant have specific features associated with their particular roles.
The differentiation of cells gives rise to specialised cell types that fulfil specific roles in the plant, e.g. support, transport, or photosynthesis. Each of the cell types illustrated below has features that set it apart from other cell types.

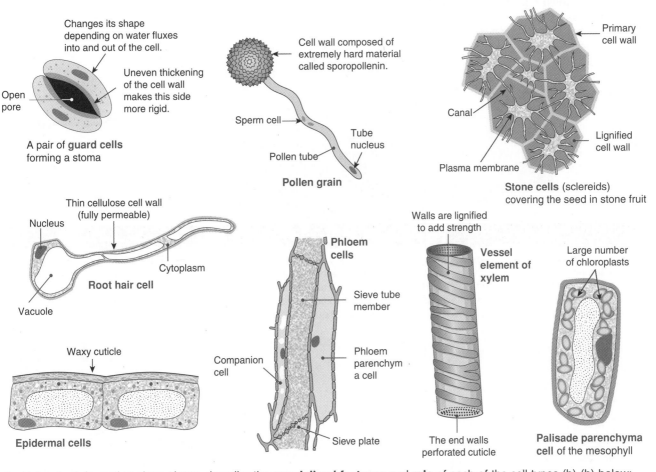

Changes its shape depending on water fluxes into and out of the cell.

Open pore

Uneven thickening of the cell wall makes this side more rigid.

A pair of **guard cells** forming a stoma

Cell wall composed of extremely hard material called sporopollenin.

Sperm cell

Pollen tube

Tube nucleus

Pollen grain

Primary cell wall

Canal

Plasma membrane

Lignified cell wall

Stone cells (sclereids) covering the seed in stone fruit

Nucleus

Thin cellulose cell wall (fully permeable)

Cytoplasm

Root hair cell

Vacuole

Waxy cuticle

Epidermal cells

Phloem cells

Sieve tube member

Companion cell

Phloem parenchyma cell

Sieve plate

Walls are lignified to add strength

Vessel element of xylem

The end walls perforated cuticle

Large number of chloroplasts

Palisade parenchyma cell of the mesophyll

1. Using the information given above, describe the **specialised features** and **role** of each of the cell types (b)-(h) below:

   (a) **Guard cell**: Features: _Curved, sausage shaped cell, unevenly thickened._

   Role in plant: _Turgor changes alter the cell shape to open or close the stoma._

   (b) **Pollen grain**: Features: _____

   Role in plant: _____

   (c) **Palisade parenchyma cell**: Features: _____

   Role in plant: _____

   (d) **Epidermal cell**: Features: _____

   Role in plant: _____

   (e) **Vessel element**: Features: _____

   Role in plant: _____

   (f) **Stone cell**: Features: _____

   Role in plant: _____

   (g) **Sieve tube member** (of phloem): Features: _____

   Role in plant: _____

   (h) **Root hair cell**: Features: _____

   Role in plant: _____

© 2015 **BIOZONE** International
ISBN: 978-1-927309-25-4
Photocopying Prohibited

LINK 88   WEB 86   **KNOW**

87 Animal Tissues

Key Idea: A tissue is a collection of related cell types that work together to carry out a specific function. Four main tissue types make up the animal body.

Tissues are formed from related cell types that carry out a specific function. They improve functional efficiency because tasks can be shared amongst specialised cells. Animal tissues fall into four broad groups: epithelial, connective, muscle, and nervous tissues. Different tissues come together to form organs. For example, the heart consists of cardiac muscle tissue, but also has epithelial tissue, which lines the heart chambers, connective tissue for strength and elasticity, and nervous tissue, which directs muscle contraction.

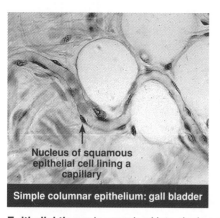
Blood

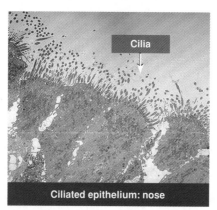
Cartilage tissue

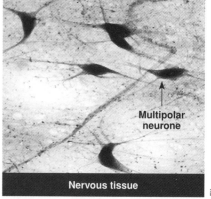
Nervous tissue

Connective tissues form the major supporting tissue of the body made up of cells within a semi-fluid matrix. Connective tissues bind structures together and provide support and protection. They include dentine (teeth), adipose (fat) tissue, bone, and cartilage (above centre), and the tissues around the organs and blood vessels. Blood is a specialised liquid tissue, made up of cells floating in a liquid matrix.

Nervous tissue contains densely packed nerve cells (neurones) which transmit information in the form of nerve impulses. There may also be supporting connective tissue and blood vessels.

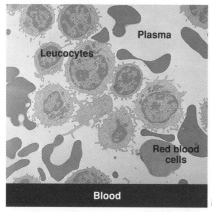
Simple columnar epithelium: gall bladder

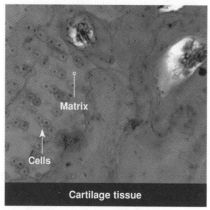
Ciliated epithelium: nose

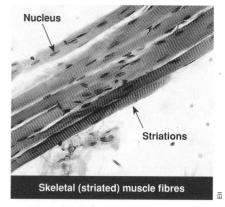
Skeletal (striated) muscle fibres

Epithelial tissue is organised into single or layered sheets. It lines internal and external surfaces (e.g. blood vessels, ducts, gut lining) and protects the structures underneath from wear, infection, or pressure. The cells may be specialised for absorption, secretion, or excretion. Examples: stratified epithelium of vagina, ciliated epithelium of respiratory tract, cuboidal epithelium of kidney ducts, columnar epithelium of the intestine, and the squamous epithelium found in capillaries, alveoli, and the glomeruli of the kidney.

Muscle tissue consists of specialised cells called fibres, held together by connective tissue. The three muscle types are cardiac, skeletal, and smooth muscle. Muscles bring about movement of body parts by contracting.

1. Explain how the development of tissues improves functional efficiency: _____

_____

_____

2. Describe the general function of each of the following broad tissue types:

   (a) Epithelial tissue: _____ (c) Muscle tissue: _____

   (b) Nervous tissue: _____ (d) Connective tissue: _____

3. Identify the particular features that contribute to the particular functional role of each of the following tissue types:

   (a) Muscle tissue: _____

   _____

   (b) Nervous tissue: _____

   _____

© 2015 **BIOZONE** International
ISBN:978-1-927309-25-4
Photocopying Prohibited

88 Plant Tissues

Key Idea: Plant tissues are either simple or complex tissues. Plant tissues are divided into simple and complex tissues. **Simple tissues** contain only one cell type and form packing and support tissues. **Complex tissues** contain more than one cell type and form the conducting and support tissues of plants. Tissues are grouped into tissue systems which make up the plant body. Vascular plants have dermal, vascular, and ground tissue systems. The **dermal system** covers the plant, providing protection and reducing water loss. The **vascular system** comprises the plant's water and nutrient transport tissues. The **ground tissue system** performs a variety of roles, including photosynthesis, storage, and support.

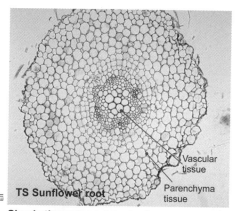

TS Sunflower root — Vascular tissue, Parenchyma tissue

Simple tissues consists of only one or two cell types. **Parenchyma tissue** is the most common and involved in storage, photosynthesis, and secretion. **Collenchyma tissue** comprises thick-walled collenchyma cells alternating with layers of intracellular substances to provide flexible support. The fibres and sclereids of **sclerenchyma** tissue have rigid cell walls which provide support.

Simple tissue	Cell type(s)	Role within the plant
Parenchyma	Parenchyma cells	Photosynthesis, storage and secretion.
Collenchyma		
Sclerenchyma		
Root endodermis	Endodermal cells	
Pericycle		

Xylem — Phloem

Complex tissues comprise more than two cell types. **Xylem** and **phloem**, which make up the plant **vascular tissue** system, are complex tissues. Each is made up of several cell types: tracheids, vessels, parenchyma, and fibres in xylem, and sieve tube members, companion cells, parenchyma and sclerenchyma in phloem.

Complex tissue	Cell type(s)	Role within the plant
Leaf mesophyll	Spongy mesophyll cells, palisade mesophyll cells	
Xylem		
Phloem		
Epidermis		

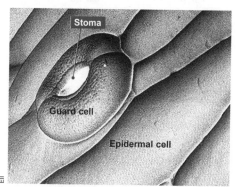

Stoma — Guard cell — Epidermal cell

Dermal tissue covers the outside of the plant. Its composition varies depending on its location. The leaf epidermis has a waxy cuticle to reduce water loss and guard cells to regulate water loss and gas exchange via pores in the leaf (stomata).

1. Identify the three tissue systems of plants:_____

_____

2. The tables above list the major types of simple and complex plant tissues. Complete the tables by filling in the cell types that make up the tissue and the role that each tissue has within the plant. The first example has been completed for you. Use the weblinks sites to help you.

89 Optical Microscopes

Key Idea: Optical microscopes use light focussed through a series of lenses to magnify objects up to several 100 times. The light (or optical) microscope is an important tool in biology and using it correctly is an essential skill. High power compound light microscopes use visible light and a combination of lenses to magnify objects up to several 100 times. The resolution of light microscopes is limited by the wavelength of light. Electron microscopes use a beam of electrons, instead of light, to produce an image. Their higher resolution is due to the shorter wavelengths of electrons.

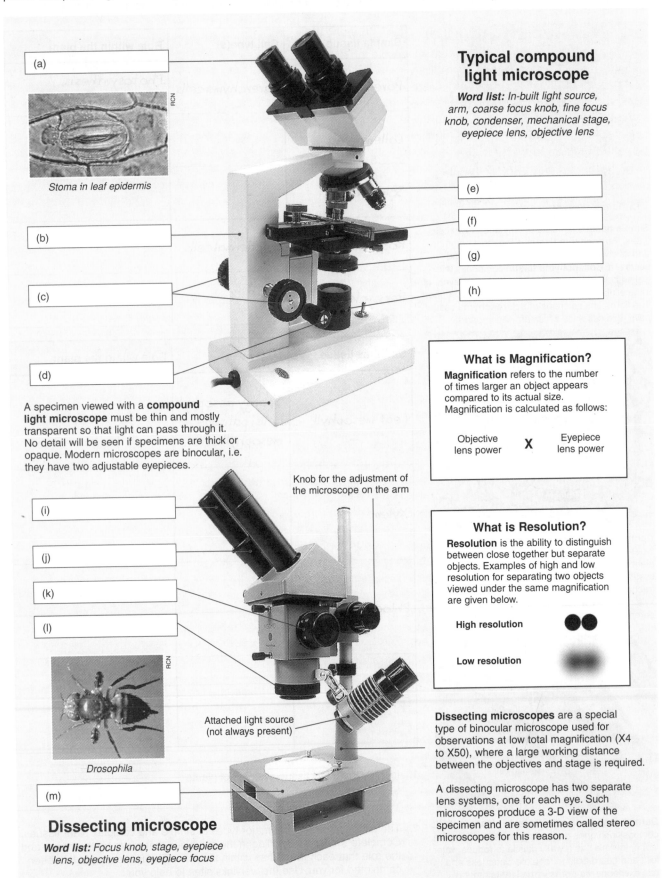

Stoma in leaf epidermis

Typical compound light microscope

Word list: *In-built light source, arm, coarse focus knob, fine focus knob, condenser, mechanical stage, eyepiece lens, objective lens*

(a)
(b)
(c)
(d)
(e)
(f)
(g)
(h)

A specimen viewed with a **compound light microscope** must be thin and mostly transparent so that light can pass through it. No detail will be seen if specimens are thick or opaque. Modern microscopes are binocular, i.e. they have two adjustable eyepieces.

What is Magnification?

Magnification refers to the number of times larger an object appears compared to its actual size. Magnification is calculated as follows:

Objective lens power **X** Eyepiece lens power

What is Resolution?

Resolution is the ability to distinguish between close together but separate objects. Examples of high and low resolution for separating two objects viewed under the same magnification are given below.

High resolution

Low resolution

Knob for the adjustment of the microscope on the arm

(i)
(j)
(k)
(l)

Drosophila

Attached light source (not always present)

Dissecting microscopes are a special type of binocular microscope used for observations at low total magnification (X4 to X50), where a large working distance between the objectives and stage is required.

A dissecting microscope has two separate lens systems, one for each eye. Such microscopes produce a 3-D view of the specimen and are sometimes called stereo microscopes for this reason.

(m)

Dissecting microscope

Word list: *Focus knob, stage, eyepiece lens, objective lens, eyepiece focus*

© 2015 **BIOZONE** International
ISBN:978-1-927309-25-4
Photocopying Prohibited

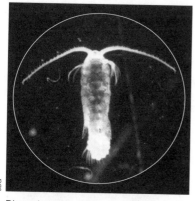

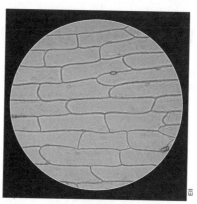

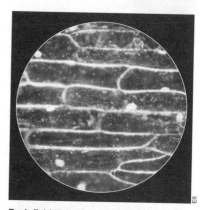

Dissecting microscopes are used for identifying and sorting organisms, observing microbial cultures, and dissections.

These onion epidermal cells are viewed with standard **bright field** lighting. Very little detail can be seen (only cell walls) and the cell nuclei are barely visible.

Dark field illumination is excellent for viewing specimens that are almost transparent. The nuclei of these onion epidermal cells are clearly visible.

1. Label the two photographs on the previous page, the compound light microscope (a) to (h) and the dissecting microscope (i) to (m). Use words from the lists supplied for each image.

2. Determine the magnification of a microscope using:

   (a) 15 X eyepiece and 40 X objective lens: _____   (b) 10 X eyepiece and 60 X objective lens: _____

3. Describe the main difference between a compound light microscope and a dissecting microscope: _____

   _____

   _____

4. What type of microscope would you use to:

   (a) Count stream invertebrates in a sample: _____   (b) Observe cells in mitosis: _____

5. (a) Distinguish between **magnification** and **resolution**: _____

   _____

   (b) Explain the benefits of a higher resolution: _____

   _____

   _____

6. Below is a list of ten key steps taken to set up a microscope and optimally view a sample. The steps have been mixed up. Put them in their **correct order** by numbering each step:

   ☐ Focus and centre the specimen using the high objective lens. Adjust focus using the fine focus knob only.

   ☐ Adjust the illumination to an appropriate level by adjusting the iris diaphragm and the condenser. The light should appear on the slide directly below the objective lens, and give an even amount of illumination.

   ☐ Rotate the objective lenses until the shortest lens is in place (pointing down towards the stage).
   This is the lowest / highest power objective lens (delete one).

   ☐ Place the slide on the microscope stage. Secure with the sample clips.

   ☐ Fine tune the illumination so you can view maximum detail on your sample.

   ☐ Focus and centre the specimen using the medium objective lens. Focus firstly with the coarse focus knob, then with the fine focus knob (if needed).

   ☐ Turn on the light source.

   ☐ Focus and centre the specimen using the low objective lens. Focus firstly with the coarse focus knob, then with the fine focus knob.

   ☐ Focus the eyepieces to adjust your view.

   ☐ Adjust the distance between the eyepieces so that they are comfortable for your eyes.

Key Idea: Graticules make it possible to measure cell size. Haemocytometers are used to count the number of cells. Measuring and counting objects to be viewed under a microscope requires precisely marked measuring equipment.

Two common pieces of equipment are the graticule and the haemocytometer. A graticule can be used to measure the size of an object whereas a haemocytometer is used to count the number of cells in a set area or volume.

Measuring cell size

A graticule is a scale placed in the eyepiece of a microscope. It is usually about 1 mm long and divided into 100 equal units. A graticule is used in combination with a stage micrometer to work out the size of an object being viewed. The stage micrometer is a slide with a scale that is exactly 1 mm long and also divided into 100 divisions (so that each division is 0.01 mm) and is placed on the microscope stage. The stage micrometer allows the graticule to be calibrated so that a precise scale can be calculated at each magnification.

The scale on the graticule is lined up with the stage micrometer. The number of graticule divisions between the divisions of the stage micrometer can then be read off. In the example right, each division of the stage micrometer is equal to four large divisions of the graticule. Each large division of the graticule is therefore 2.5×10^{-3} mm at 400x magnification.

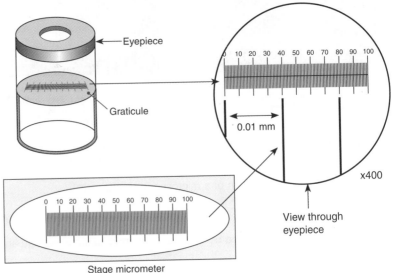

Counting cells

Microscopes can be used as a tool to count cells or other small objects (e.g pollen grains). By counting the number of cells in a known area, the total number of cells in a larger area can be calculated. A haemocytometer is commonly used to count cells viewed with a light microscope. It is a simple slide with precisely etched lines forming a grid and was developed for counting blood cells. There are a number of types of haemocytometer, including the Improved Neubauer, shown below. The slide holds a coverslip 0.1 mm above the surface of the grid, allowing volume to be calculated. The central counting grid is divided into 25 large squares, each of which is further divided into 16 squares.

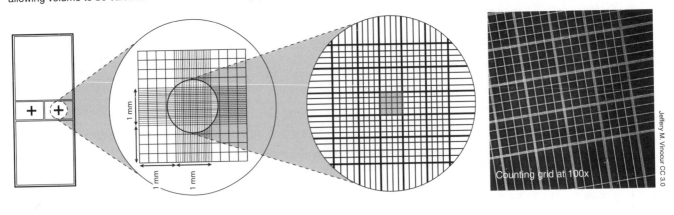

Jeffery M. Vinocur CC 3.0

Counting grid at 100x

1. A student using the graticule scale shown at the top of this page found a cell (at the same magnification) to be 56 divisions wide. Calculate the width of the cell in mm and in µm:

_____

2. A second student grew yeast cells in 5 cm³ of nutrient solution. The student used the haemocytometer shown above to count the number of yeast cells each day for 3 days.

   (a) Calculate the area and volume of the grid shown in blue: Area: _____ Volume: _____

   (b) The student counted yeast cells in the central blue grid. Complete the table below based on the counts obtained:

	Day 1	Day 2	Day 3
Number of cells counted	4	9	17
Cells in 5 cm³			

3. A botanist wished to know the number of pollen grains produced per anther by a flower with eight anthers. She cut the anthers and placed them in 3 cm³ of distilled water, shaking the mix vigorously. Using a haemocytometer she counted 6 grains in the large central counting grid (1 x 1 mm). Calculate the total number of pollen grains produced **per anther**:

_____

_____

© 2015 **BIOZONE** International
ISBN: 978-1-927309-25-4
Photocopying Prohibited

91 Calculating Linear Magnification

Key Idea: Magnification is how much larger an object appears compared to its actual size. Magnification can be calculated from the ratio of image size to object size.

Microscopes produce an enlarged (magnified) image of an object allowing it to be observed in greater detail than is possible with the naked eye. **Magnification** refers to the number of times larger an object appears compared to its actual size. Linear magnification is calculated by taking a ratio of the image height to the object's actual height. If this ratio is greater than one, the image is enlarged. If it is less than one, it is reduced. To calculate magnification, all measurements are converted to the same units. Often, you will be asked to calculate an object's actual size, in which case you will be told the size of the object and the magnification.

Calculating linear magnification: a worked example

1 Measure the body length of the bed bug image (right). Your measurement should be 40 mm (***not*** including the body hairs and antennae).

2 Measure the length of the scale line marked 1.0 mm. You will find it is 10 mm long. The magnification of the scale line can be calculated using equation 1 (below right).

The magnification of the scale line is **10** (10 mm / 1 mm)

NB: The magnification of the bed bug image will also be 10x because the scale line and image are magnified to the same degree.

3 Calculate the actual (real) size of the bed bug using equation 2 (right):

The actual size of the bed bug is **4 mm** (40 mm / 10 x magnification)

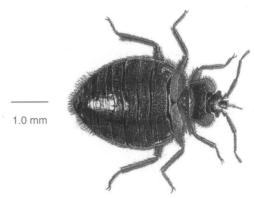

1.0 mm

Microscopy equations

1. $$\text{Magnification} = \frac{\text{measured size of the object}}{\text{actual size of the object}}$$

2. $$\text{Actual object size} = \frac{\text{size of the image}}{\text{magnification}}$$

1. The bright field microscopy image on the left is of onion epidermal cells. The measured length of the onion cell in the centre of the photograph is 52 000 µm (52 mm). The image has been magnified 140 x. Calculate the actual size of the cell:

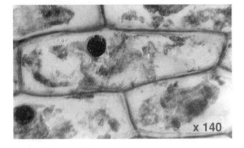

x 140

_____

_____

_____

2. The image of the flea (left) has been captured using light microscopy.

   (a) Calculate the magnification using the scale line on the image:

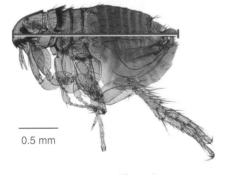

0.5 mm

   _____

   _____

   _____

   (b) The body length of the flea is indicated by a line. Measure along the line and calculate the actual length of the flea:

   _____

   _____

   _____

3. The image size of the *E.coli* cell (left) is 43 mm, and its actual size is 2 µm. Using this information, calculate the magnification of the image:

   _____

   _____

   _____

LINK
75

DATA

92 Preparing a Slide

Key Idea: Correctly preparing and mounting a specimen on a slide is important if structures are to be seen clearly under a microscope. A wet mount is suitable for most slides.

Specimens are often prepared in some way before viewing in order to highlight features and reveal details. A wet mount is a temporary preparation in which a specimen and a drop of fluid are trapped under a thin coverslip. Wet mounts are used to view thin tissue sections, live microscopic organisms, and suspensions such as blood. A wet mount improves a sample's appearance and enhances visible detail. Sections must be made very thin for two main reasons. A thick section stops light shining through making it appear dark when viewed. It also ends up with too many layers of cells, making it difficult to make out detail.

Preparing a specimen

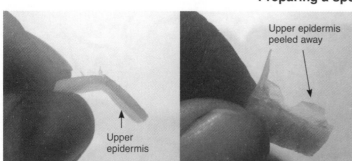

Onions make good subjects for preparing a simple wet mount. A square segment is cut from a thick leaf from the bulb. The segment is then bent towards the upper epidermis and snapped so that just the epidermis is left attached. The epidermis can then be peeled off to provide a thin layer of cells for viewing.

Sections through stems or other soft objects need to be made with a razor blade or scalpel, and must be very thin. Cutting at a slight angle to produce a wedge shape creates a thin edge. Ideally specimens should be set in wax first, to prevent crushing and make it easier to cut the specimen accurately.

Mounting a specimen

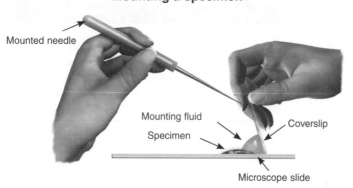

Mounting: The thin layer is placed in the centre of a clean glass microscope slide and covered with a drop of mounting liquid (e.g. water, glycerol, or stain). A coverslip is placed on top using a mounted needle to support and lower it gently over the specimen. This avoids including air in the mount.

Viewing

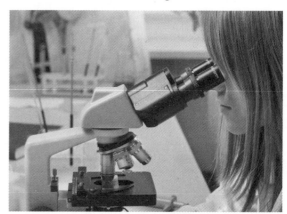

Locate the specimen or region of interest at the lowest magnification. Focus using the lowest magnification first, before switching to the higher magnifications.

1. Why must sections viewed under a microscope be very thin? _____

_____

2. What is the purpose of the coverslip? _____

_____

_____

3. Why would no chloroplasts be visible in an onion epidermis cell slide? _____

_____

4. Why is it necessary to focus on the lowest magnification first, before switching to higher magnifications? _____

_____

_____

© 2015 **BIOZONE** International
ISBN:978-1-927309-25-4
Photocopying Prohibited

93 Staining a Slide

Key Idea: Staining material to be viewed under a microscope can make it easier to distinguish particular cell structures. **Stains** and dyes can be used to highlight specific components or structures. Most stains are **non-viable**, and are used on dead specimens, but harmless viable stains can be applied to living material. Stains contain chemicals that interact with molecules in the cell. Some stains bind to a particular molecule making it easier to see where those molecules are. Others cause a change in a target molecule, which changes their colour, making them more visible.

Some commonly used stains		
Stain	Final colour	Used for
Iodine solution	blue-black	Starch
Crystal violet	purple	Gram staining
Aniline sulfate	yellow	lignin
Methylene blue	blue	Nuclei
Hematoxylin and eosin (H&E)	H=dark blue/violet E=red/pink	H=Nuclei E=Proteins

Iodine stain

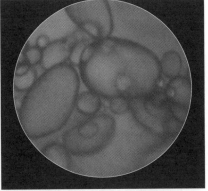

Iodine stains starch-containing organelles, such as **potato amyloplasts**, blue-black.

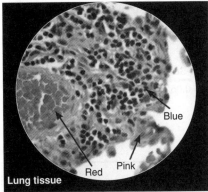

Blue

Red   Pink

Lung tissue

H&E stain is one of the most common histological stains. Nuclei stain dark blue, whereas proteins, extracellular material, and red blood cells stain pink or red.

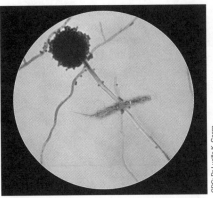

CDC: Dr Lucille K. Georg

Viable (or vital) **stains** do not immediately harm living cells. **Trypan blue** is a vital stain that stains dead cells blue but is excluded by live cells. It is also used to study fungal hyphae.

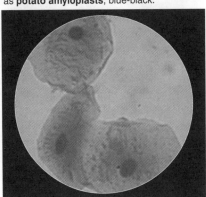

Methylene blue is a common temporary stain for animal cells, such as these **cheek cells**. It stains DNA and so makes the **nuclei** more visible. It is distinct from methyl blue, a histological stain.

How to apply a simple stain

If a specimen is already mounted, a drop of stain can be placed at one end of the coverslip and drawn through using filter paper (below). Water can be drawn through in the same way to remove excess stain.

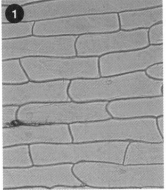

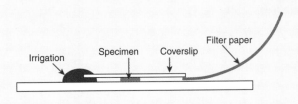

Irrigation   Specimen   Coverslip   Filter paper

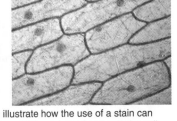

The light micrographs 1 and 2 (above) illustrate how the use of a stain can enhance certain structures. The left image (1) is unstained and only the cell wall is easily visible. Adding iodine (2) makes the cell wall and nuclei stand out.

1. What is the main purpose of using a stain? _____

_____

2. What is the difference between a viable and non-viable stain? _____

_____

3. Identify a stain that would be appropriate for distinguishing each of the following:

   (a) Live vs dead cells: _____   (c) Lignin in a plant root section: _____

   (b) Red blood cells in a tissue preparation: _____   (d) Nuclei in cheek cells: _____

LINK   WEB
77 **93**   **KNOW**

94 Practising Biological Drawings

Key Idea: Attention to detail is vital when making accurate and useful biological drawings.

In this activity, you will practise the skills required to translate what is viewed into a good biological drawing.

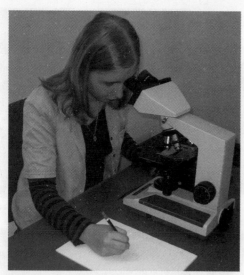

Above: Use relaxed viewing when drawing at the microscope. Use one eye (the left for right handers) to view and the right eye to look at your drawing.

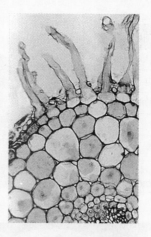

Above: Light micrograph Transverse section (TS) through a *Ranunculus* root.

Right: A biological drawing of the same section.

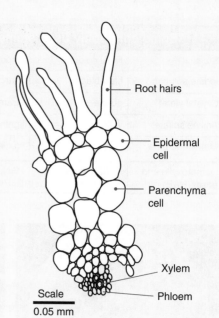

Root hairs

Epidermal cell

Parenchyma cell

Xylem

Phloem

Scale
0.05 mm

1. During your course of study, you will investigate cells and mass transport systems, and you may be required to identify and draw cells in a prepared blood smear viewed with a light microscope. It can be difficult to identify cell types in prepared smears under the magnification commonly used in school microscopes (X400). An example of what you might see is shown below.

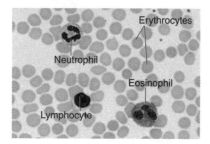

Looking at your slide, draw what you can see and try to identify as many cell types as you can. Use the picture (below, right) to help you. The drawn cells are organised from left to right in order of most common to least common. White blood cells are framed by the rectangle. Platelets are cell fragments and may not be visible. White blood cells are distinguished by the presence and staining of granules in the cytoplasm and the shape of the nucleus. Lymphocytes and monocytes do not have a granular cytoplasm.

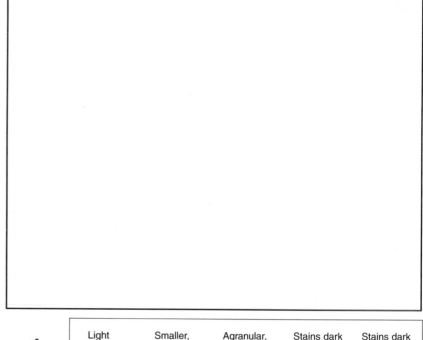

		Light staining granules	Smaller, rounder, agranular	Agranular, lobed nucleus	Stains dark pink	Stains dark purple
Platelets	Erythrocyte	Neutrophil	Lymphocyte	Monocyte	Eosinophil	Basophil

Most common

Least common

© 2015 **BIOZONE** International
ISBN: 978-1-927309-25-4
Photocopying Prohibited

95 Electron Microscopes

Key Idea: Electron microscopes use the short wavelengths of electrons to produce high resolution images of extremely small objects.

Electron microscopes (EMs) use a beam of electrons, instead of light, to produce an image. The higher resolution of EMs is due to the shorter wavelengths of electrons. There are two basic types of electron microscope: **scanning electron microscopes** (SEM) and **transmission electron microscopes** (TEM). In SEMs, the electrons are bounced off the surface of an object to produce detailed images of the external appearance. TEMs produce very clear images of specially prepared thin sections.

Transmission electron microscope (TEM)

The transmission electron microscope is used to view extremely thin sections of material. Electrons pass through the specimen and are scattered. Magnetic lenses focus the image onto a fluorescent screen or photographic plate. The sections are so thin that they have to be prepared with a special machine, called an ultramicrotome, which can cut wafers to just 30 thousandths of a millimetre thick. It can magnify several hundred thousand times.

TEM diagram labels:
- Electron gun
- Electron beam
- Electromagnetic condenser lens
- Specimen
- Electromagnetic objective lens
- Vacuum pump
- Electromagnetic projector lens
- Eyepiece
- Fluorescent screen or photographic plate

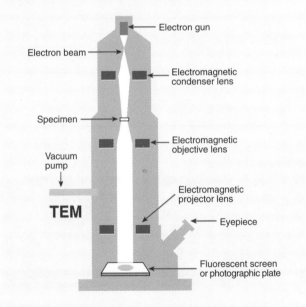

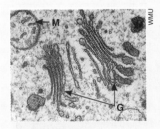

TEM photo showing the Golgi (**G**) and a mitochondrion (**M**).

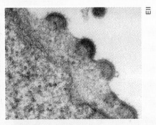

Three HIV viruses budding out of a human lymphocyte (TEM).

Scanning electron microscope (SEM)

The scanning electron microscope scans a sample with a beam of primary electrons, which knocks electrons from the sample's surface. These secondary electrons are picked up by a collector, amplified, and transmitted onto a viewing screen or photographic plate, producing a 3-D image. A microscope of this power easily obtains clear images of very small organisms such as bacteria, and small particles such as viruses. The image produced is of the outside surface only.

SEM diagram labels:
- Electron gun
- Primary electron beam
- Electromagnetic lenses
- Vacuum pump
- SEM
- Electron collector
- Amplifier
- Viewing screen
- Specimen
- Secondary electrons

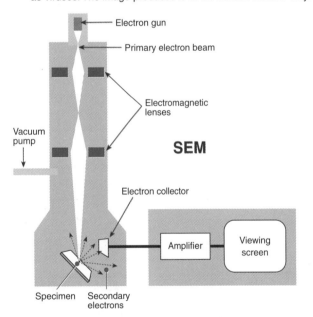

SEM photo of stoma and epidermal cells on the upper surface of a leaf.

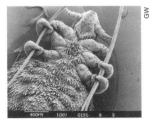

Image of hair louse clinging to two hairs on a Hooker's sealion (SEM).

	Light microscope	Transmission electron microscope (TEM)	Scanning electron microscope (SEM)
Radiation source:	light	electrons	electrons
Wavelength:	400-700 nm	0.005 nm	0.005 nm
Lenses:	glass	electromagnetic	electromagnetic
Specimen:	living or non-living supported on glass slide	non-living supported on a small copper grid in a vacuum	non-living supported on a metal disc in a vacuum
Maximum resolution:	200 nm	1 nm	10 nm
Maximum magnification:	1500 x	250 000 x	100 000 x
Stains:	coloured dyes	impregnated with heavy metals	coated with carbon or gold
Type of image:	coloured, surface or section	monochrome, section	monochrome, surface only

1. Explain why electron microscopes are able to resolve much greater detail than a light microscope:

_____

_____

_____

2. Which type of microscope [TEM, SEM, compound light microscope, or dissecting microscope] would you use for each of the following scenarios. Explain your choice in each case:

(a) Distinguishing extinct plant species on the basis of pollen surface features: _____

_____

(b) Resolving the ultrastructure of a chloroplast: _____

_____

(c) Performing a count of white blood cells from the blood of a person with an infection: _____

_____

(d) Counting the heart rate and rate of limb beating in a water flea (*Daphnia*): _____

_____

3. Identify which type of electron microscope (SEM or TEM) or optical microscope (compound light microscope or dissecting) was used to produce each of the images in the photos below (A-H):

Cardiac muscle

Plant vascular tissue

Mitochondrion

Plant epidermal cells

A _____ B _____ C _____ D _____

Head louse

Kidney cells

Alderfly larva

Tongue papilla

E _____ F _____ G _____ H _____

96 Viruses

Key Idea: A virus is an infectious, highly specialised intracellular parasite. They are acellular and non-living.
Viruses are disease-causing agents (**pathogens**), which replicate (reproduce themselves) only inside the living cells of other organisms. Viruses are acellular, meaning they are not made up of cells, so they do not conform to the existing criteria upon which a five or six kingdom classification system is based. A typical virus contains genetic material (DNA or RNA) encased in a protein coat (capsid). Some viruses have an additional membrane, called an envelope, surrounding the capsid. Many viruses have glycoprotein receptor spikes on their envelopes that help them to attach to surface of the host cell they are infecting. Viruses vary greatly in their appearance and the type of host they infect (below).

> **Viruses are not organisms!** Viruses are metabolically inert until they are inside the host cell and hijacking its metabolic machinery to make new viral particles. However, they are often called microorganisms.

Glycoprotein spikes mediate attachment to the host cells' receptors.

Two copies of single stranded RNA

Viral envelope (lipoprotein)

Reverse transcriptase forms viral DNA from viral RNA

Capsid

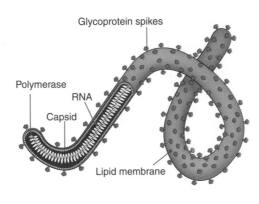

Structure of HIV, an enveloped retrovirus.

Glycoprotein spikes

Polymerase

RNA

Capsid

Lipid membrane

Structure of Ebola virus, an RNA filovirus that causes Ebola haemorrhagic fever.

Double stranded linear DNA

Capsid

Sheath

Long tail fibres help the phage attach to host cell

Base plate

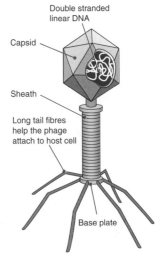

Structure of Lambda phage, a bacteriophage that infects E.coli.

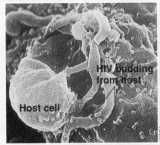

Host cell

HIV budding from host

CDC

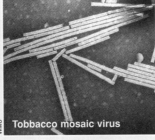

Tobbacco mosaic virus

WMU

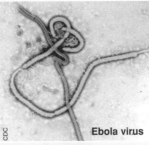

CDC

Ebola virus

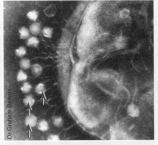

Dr Graham Beards

When viral replication is complete, new viral particles (**virons**) leave the host cell to infect more cells. In animals, enveloped viruses bud from the host cell, e.g. HIV (left). Plant viruses cannot bud from the host cell due to the rigid cell wall. Instead, plant viruses, e.g. tobacco mosaic virus (right), move through the plasmodesmata that connect neighbouring plant cells.

Viruses cause a wide variety of common human diseases, e.g. colds, influenza, and life-threatening diseases such as AIDS and Ebola (above).

Bacteriophages (arrowed) infect bacterial cells. They use tail fibres to attach to the host and a contractile region below the capsid to inject their DNA into the cell.

1. What is the significance of viruses being non-living? _____

_____

_____

2. Describe the basic structure of a generalised virus, identifying the features they all have in common: _____

_____

_____

3. Describe the purpose of the following:

(a) Glycoprotein spikes: _____

(b) A bacteriophage's tail fibres: _____

(c) Protein capsid: _____

97 Life Cycle of a Bacteriophage

Key Idea: Bacteriophages infect bacteria and have two life cycle stages: an infectious stage and a dormant stage.

A **bacteriophage** is a virus that infects a bacterial cell. Sometimes bacteriophage replication does not immediately follow infection. Instead, the virus may enter a **lysogenic cycle**, in which its genetic material is inserted into the host's DNA to form a **prophage**. The viral infection is said to be latent in this phase because the viral genes, although present, do not disrupt the bacterial cell. Eventually, a trigger causes the prophage to become active and the **lytic cycle** begins. During the lytic cycle, the host's cellular machinery is used to produce new virions. The lytic cycle results in death of the host cell through lysis (breaking) of the cell. Lysis allows the new phage to escape and infect other bacterial cells.

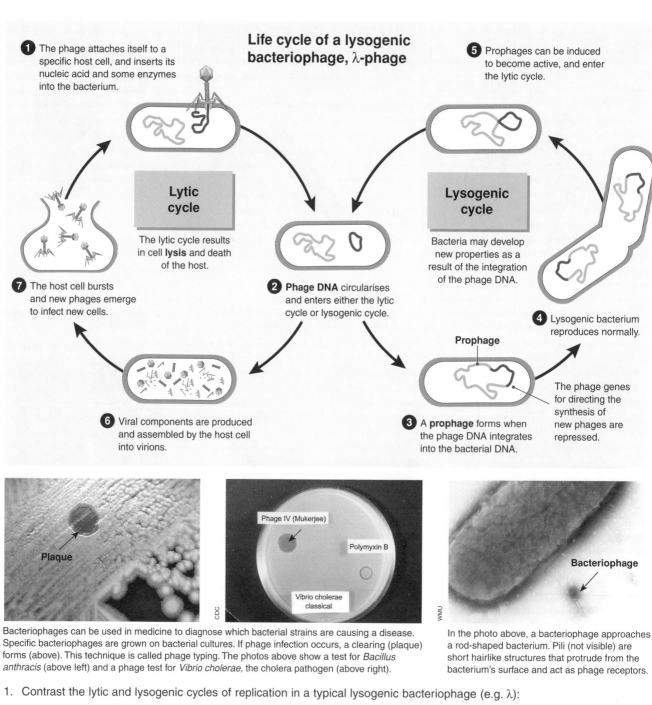

Life cycle of a lysogenic bacteriophage, λ-phage

1. The phage attaches itself to a specific host cell, and inserts its nucleic acid and some enzymes into the bacterium.

5. Prophages can be induced to become active, and enter the lytic cycle.

Lytic cycle

The lytic cycle results in cell **lysis** and death of the host.

Lysogenic cycle

Bacteria may develop new properties as a result of the integration of the phage DNA.

7. The host cell bursts and new phages emerge to infect new cells.

2. **Phage DNA** circularises and enters either the lytic cycle or lysogenic cycle.

4. Lysogenic bacterium reproduces normally.

Prophage

The phage genes for directing the synthesis of new phages are repressed.

6. Viral components are produced and assembled by the host cell into virions.

3. A **prophage** forms when the phage DNA integrates into the bacterial DNA.

Plaque

Phage IV (Mukerjee)

Polymyxin B

Vibrio cholerae classical

Bacteriophage

Bacteriophages can be used in medicine to diagnose which bacterial strains are causing a disease. Specific bacteriophages are grown on bacterial cultures. If phage infection occurs, a clearing (plaque) forms (above). This technique is called phage typing. The photos above show a test for *Bacillus anthracis* (above left) and a phage test for *Vibrio cholerae*, the cholera pathogen (above right).

In the photo above, a bacteriophage approaches a rod-shaped bacterium. Pili (not visible) are short hairlike structures that protrude from the bacterium's surface and act as phage receptors.

1. Contrast the lytic and lysogenic cycles of replication in a typical lysogenic bacteriophage (e.g. λ):

_____

_____

_____

2. Identify one possible consequence to a bacterial cell of infection with a lysogenic phage: _____

_____

_____

98 Life Cycle of a Retrovirus

Key Idea: A retrovirus can integrate into the host's genome by generating DNA from its own RNA using reverse transcription. Animal viruses exhibit a number of different mechanisms for **replicating**, i.e. entering a host cell and producing and releasing new virions. Enveloped viruses bud out from the host cell, whereas those without an envelope are released by rupture of the cell membrane. Three processes (attachment, penetration, and uncoating) are shared by both DNA- and RNA containing animal viruses. The example below describes replication in the retrovirus HIV, where the virus uses its own reverse transcriptase to synthesise viral DNA and produce **latent proviruses** or active, mature retroviruses.

How HIV infects a helper T cell

HIV, the infectious agent that causes AIDS, is a retrovirus (RNA not DNA). It is able to splice its genes into the host cell's chromosome.

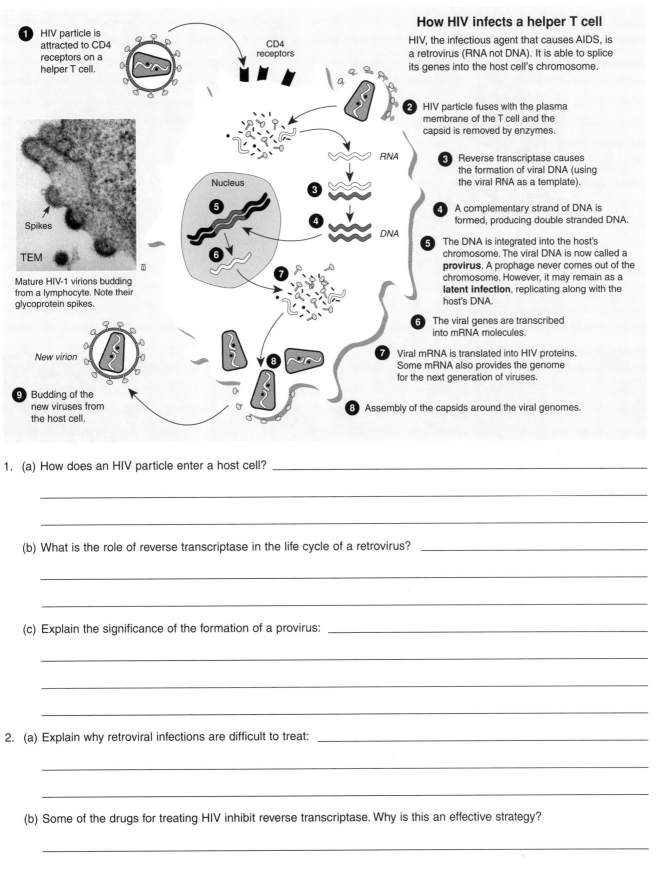

1. HIV particle is attracted to CD4 receptors on a helper T cell.

Spikes

TEM

Mature HIV-1 virions budding from a lymphocyte. Note their glycoprotein spikes.

New virion

9. Budding of the new viruses from the host cell.

CD4 receptors

Nucleus

RNA

DNA

2. HIV particle fuses with the plasma membrane of the T cell and the capsid is removed by enzymes.

3. Reverse transcriptase causes the formation of viral DNA (using the viral RNA as a template).

4. A complementary strand of DNA is formed, producing double stranded DNA.

5. The DNA is integrated into the host's chromosome. The viral DNA is now called a **provirus**. A prophage never comes out of the chromosome. However, it may remain as a **latent infection**, replicating along with the host's DNA.

6. The viral genes are transcribed into mRNA molecules.

7. Viral mRNA is translated into HIV proteins. Some mRNA also provides the genome for the next generation of viruses.

8. Assembly of the capsids around the viral genomes.

1. (a) How does an HIV particle enter a host cell? _____

_____

_____

(b) What is the role of reverse transcriptase in the life cycle of a retrovirus? _____

_____

_____

(c) Explain the significance of the formation of a provirus: _____

_____

_____

_____

2. (a) Explain why retroviral infections are difficult to treat: _____

_____

_____

(b) Some of the drugs for treating HIV inhibit reverse transcriptase. Why is this an effective strategy?

_____

_____

99 Antiviral Drugs

Key Idea: Antiviral drugs target key points in a viral life cycle. Because viruses do not display the characteristics of living things, antiviral drugs do not focus on destroying the virus itself, but on preventing completion of the viral life cycle. This is done by blocking the entry of the virus into cells or by inhibiting key steps in viral replication (below).

Actions of antiviral drugs

Currently, antiviral drugs are available for use against HIV, hepatitis, influenza, and the herpes virus. Most antiviral drugs work by inhibiting replication of the virus. The drug stops the virus replicating giving the immune system time to destroy the virus. Antiviral drugs work on several parts of virus's life cycle (right).

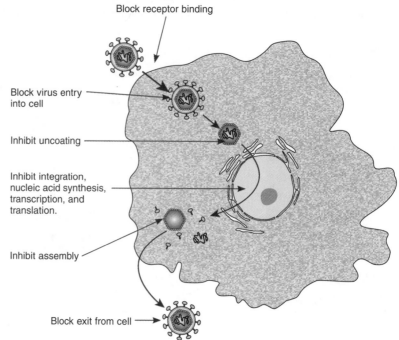

Block receptor binding

Block virus entry into cell

Inhibit uncoating

Inhibit integration, nucleic acid synthesis, transcription, and translation.

Inhibit assembly

Block exit from cell

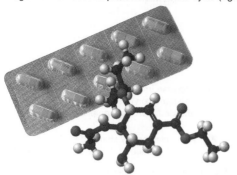

Oseltamivir (marketed as Tamiflu, above) slows the spread of influenza A and B viruses in the body by preventing a newly formed virus particle from budding from an infected cell. However, various trials have shed doubt of whether the drug produces any real benefit to flu sufferers.

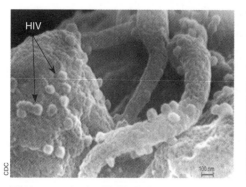

HIV is treated using Highly Active Antiretroviral Therapy (HAART). HAART usually consists of two different nucleoside analogue reverse transcriptase inhibitors (NARTIs) and a protease inhibitor. NARTIs block the reverse transcriptase enzyme used to generate DNA from viral RNA, thereby blocking the integration of viral genes into the T cell genome. Protease inhibitors block the HIV protease enzyme, which is essential to forming infectious virions.

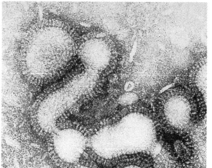

Influenza is caused by either the influenza A or influenza B virus. Influenza A is treated using the drugs amantadine and rimantadine which block the uncoating of the virus inside the host cell. Influenza B is treated using the drugs zanamivir and oseltamivir (which are also active against influenza A). These two drugs inhibit the actions of neuraminidase, a glycoprotein on the viral surface, and stops the virus from exiting the cell.

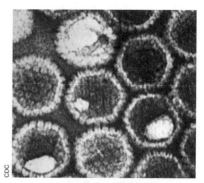

Herpesvirus (a group of viruses that includes the viruses that cause cold sores and chickenpox) is treated with drugs that interfere with DNA replication by blocking the viral polymerase enzyme. Some drugs are activated by viral enzymes and therefore are only active in infected cells, providing a targeted treatment. Others are active in all cells and are less specific.

1. For each of the following mechanisms used by antiviral drugs explain how it prevents the virus's spread:

   (a) Blocking receptor binding: _____

   _____

   (b) Inhibiting assembly: _____

   _____

2. Why is using a combination of antiviral drugs with different actions more effective that using a single drug?

   _____

   _____

© 2015 **BIOZONE** International
ISBN:978-1-927309-25-4
Photocopying Prohibited

100 Controlling Viral Disease

Key Idea: Preventing the spread of viruses in a population is important in reducing the incidence of viral disease.

Many factors can influence the spread of a viral disease, including the social climate, diet, general health, and access to medical care. Human intervention, including vaccination, and modification of behaviour (e.g. hygiene practices), can reduce the transmission rate of some diseases and inhibit their spread. Global air travel and international trade in commodities has increased the risk that diseases of humans, livestock, and crops will be spread between countries. Precautions such as quarantine, which isolates exposed individuals that may be infected, and isolation, which isolates already infected people, can help to limit the initial spread of a viral disease.

Ebola and the chain of infection

Ebola is a haemorrhagic disease caused by *Ebolavirus*. Ebola is rare but becoming less so as more people encroach on areas of rainforest in central Africa. The disease has a high mortality, killing between 50-90% of those infected. The incubation period is anywhere from 2 to 20 days. The largest outbreak, reaching epidemic scale, occurred in West Africa, beginning in early 2014 and continuing through until 2015. More than ten thousand people died in numerous countries including a number outside Africa.

Disease (viral or otherwise) follows a particular chain of infection. Controlling disease of any kind can be achieved by breaking any of the links in the chain. Some of these links are easier to break than others. Ebola exemplifies the need for measures in preventing viral spread, especially as vaccines and drug therapies are limited and still experimental.

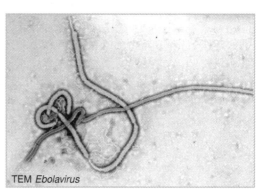

TEM *Ebolavirus*

Host susceptibility is an important link in the chain. Ebola spreads quickly in areas where people live close together and where sanitation is poor. Cultural differences between patients and medical workers and mistrust of the authorities increase the risk of spread because people fear coming into treatment clinics.

Susceptible host

Causative agent

The causative agent is the pathogen responsible for the infection, e.g. the *Ebolavirus*. Eliminating this part of the chain from the environment is often the most difficult.

A reservoir describes where the organism is normally found. The reservoir for Ebola is thought to be fruit bats, although this has yet to be confirmed.

Reservoir

Portal of entry

Chain of infection

How the is disease transmitted between people. Targeting this step is one of the most effective ways of preventing disease transmission. Prevention of infection by Ebola is based on safe hygiene practices, which includes washing hands, avoiding contact with blood or other bodily fluids, safe burial practices, and avoiding contact with contaminated items.

Portal of exit

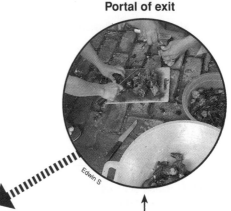

The portal of entry describes how the organism enters a host, e.g through mucous membranes or open wounds. Cleaning wounds and washing hands before eating are ways to break this link.

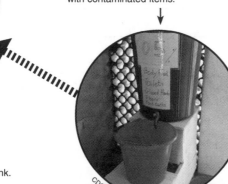

Mode of transmission

The portal of exit describes how the organism leaves the reservoir or host. Ebola leaves the host through bodily fluids including blood, urine, and faeces. Uncooked bush meat may be one portal (e.g. fruit bat meat, above).

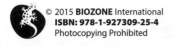

LINK 148 LINK 147 KNOW

The ethics of untested drugs

At the start of the 2014 Ebola outbreak, there was very little in the way of drug therapy that could be used to treat the disease. Vaccines are rare and mostly experimental, and antiviral drugs are even more so. The 2014 outbreak was so widespread and rapid that traditional methods of isolating infected people and tracking down all contacts were not effective. The infection of medical workers prompted the need for drugs to treat patients. However, few were available and none had been tested on humans. Questions were raised: was it ethical to give infected patients drugs that had not been through rigorous testing and had not been tested on humans?

Trials of untested drugs for the Ebola epidemic were approved by WHO on August 11 2014. There were may qualifiers added to the approval, including freedom of choice for those treated and that information gained must be freely shared. Human trials of a livestock-based vaccine began in Liberia and Guinea early in 2015 but, because the number of Ebola cases is declining, it will be difficult to determine if the vaccine is effective.

Treatment centre in Guinea

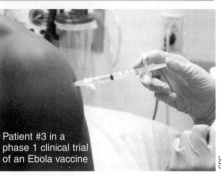
Patient #3 in a phase 1 clinical trial of an Ebola vaccine

Points on ethics:

▶ There is limited drug supply – who should be treated first? This includes questions around should it be the youngest, the sickest, or the most likely to benefit?

▶ Who should pay for the production of the drug? The countries involved in the outbreak are some of the poorest in Africa.

▶ New drugs would be used primarily in Africa, but are made outside Africa by non-African companies. Is it acceptable to treat Ebola victims in Africa as test subjects?

1. Identify two factors that increase the risk of a disease spreading between countries: _____

_____

2. Explain how Ebola spreads between people: _____

_____

3. Why are Ebola outbreaks becoming more common? _____

_____

_____

4. Give a general description for each of the following in the chain of infection and give an example for *Ebolavirus*:

(a) The causative agent: _____

_____

(b) The reservoir: _____

_____

(c) The portal of exit: _____

_____

(d) Mode of transmission: _____

_____

(e) The portal of entry: _____

_____

(f) Susceptible host: _____

_____

5. Hold a class discussion on the ethics of using untested drugs during a epidemic. Write a brief summary of the points raised here and include your own opinion on the matter:

_____

_____

_____

_____

© 2015 **BIOZONE** International
ISBN: 978-1-927309-25-4
Photocopying Prohibited

101 Cell Division

Key Idea: New cells arise from the division of existing cells. There are two types of cell division, mitosis and meiosis.

New cells are formed when existing cells divide. In eukaryotes, cell division begins with the replication of a cell's DNA followed by division of the nucleus. There are two forms of cell division. **Mitosis** produces two identical daughter cells from each parent cell. Mitosis is responsible for growth and repair processes in multicellular organisms, and asexual reproduction in some eukaryotes, e.g. yeasts. **Meiosis** is a special type of cell division concerned with producing sex cells (gametes or haploid spores) for sexual reproduction. It occurs in the sex organs of plants and animals.

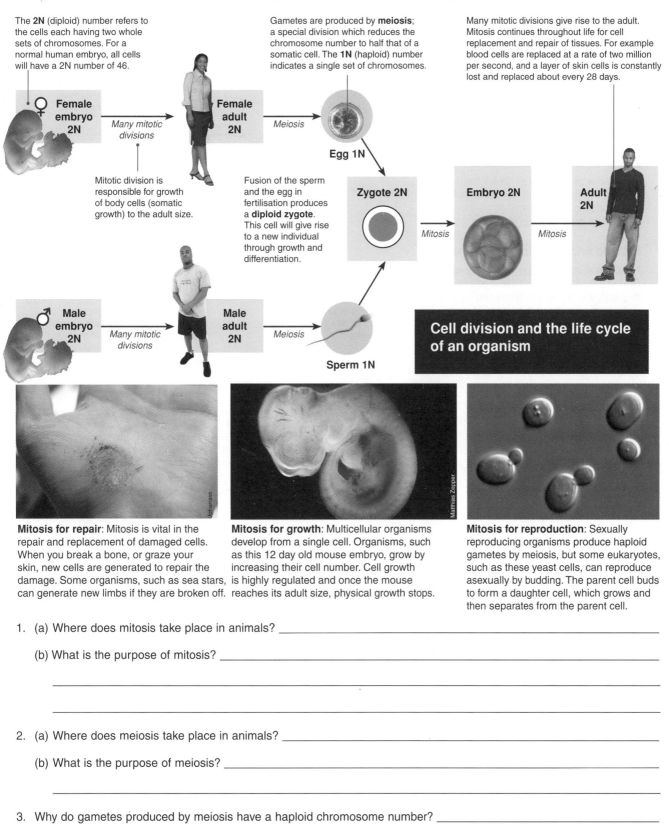

The **2N** (diploid) number refers to the cells each having two whole sets of chromosomes. For a normal human embryo, all cells will have a 2N number of 46.

Mitotic division is responsible for growth of body cells (somatic growth) to the adult size.

Gametes are produced by **meiosis**; a special division which reduces the chromosome number to half that of a somatic cell. The **1N** (haploid) number indicates a single set of chromosomes.

Fusion of the sperm and the egg in fertilisation produces a **diploid zygote**. This cell will give rise to a new individual through growth and differentiation.

Many mitotic divisions give rise to the adult. Mitosis continues throughout life for cell replacement and repair of tissues. For example blood cells are replaced at a rate of two million per second, and a layer of skin cells is constantly lost and replaced about every 28 days.

Female embryo 2N → *Many mitotic divisions* → Female adult 2N → *Meiosis* → Egg 1N

Male embryo 2N → *Many mitotic divisions* → Male adult 2N → *Meiosis* → Sperm 1N

Zygote 2N → *Mitosis* → Embryo 2N → *Mitosis* → Adult 2N

Cell division and the life cycle of an organism

Mitosis for repair: Mitosis is vital in the repair and replacement of damaged cells. When you break a bone, or graze your skin, new cells are generated to repair the damage. Some organisms, such as sea stars, can generate new limbs if they are broken off.

Mitosis for growth: Multicellular organisms develop from a single cell. Organisms, such as this 12 day old mouse embryo, grow by increasing their cell number. Cell growth is highly regulated and once the mouse reaches its adult size, physical growth stops.

Mitosis for reproduction: Sexually reproducing organisms produce haploid gametes by meiosis, but some eukaryotes, such as these yeast cells, can reproduce asexually by budding. The parent cell buds to form a daughter cell, which grows and then separates from the parent cell.

1. (a) Where does mitosis take place in animals? _____

   (b) What is the purpose of mitosis? _____

   _____

   _____

2. (a) Where does meiosis take place in animals? _____

   (b) What is the purpose of meiosis? _____

   _____

3. Why do gametes produced by meiosis have a haploid chromosome number? _____

   _____

   _____

LINK 105 LINK 102 KNOW

102 Mitosis and the Cell Cycle

Key Idea: Mitosis is an important part of the cell cycle in which the replicated chromosomes are separated and the cell divides, producing two new identical cells.

Mitosis (or M-phase) is part of the **cell cycle** in which an existing cell (the parent cell) divides into two daughter cells. Unlike meiosis, mitosis does not result in a change of chromosome numbers and the daughter cells are identical to

the parent cell. Although mitosis is part of a continuous cell cycle, it is often divided into stages to help differentiate the processes occurring. Mitosis is one of the shortest stages of the cell cycle. When a cell is not undergoing mitosis, it is said to be in interphase. Interphase accounts for 90% of the cell cycle. Cytokinesis (the division of the newly formed cells) is distinct from nuclear division.

The cell cycle

Interphase

Cells spend most of their time in interphase. Interphase is divided into three stages (right):

▶ The first gap phase (G1).
▶ The S-phase.
▶ The second gap phase (G2).

During interphase the cell grows, carries out its normal activities, and replicates its DNA in preparation for cell division.
Interphase is not a stage in mitosis.

Mitosis and cytokinesis (M-phase)

Mitosis and cytokinesis occur during M-phase. During mitosis, the cell nucleus (containing the replicated DNA) divides in two equal parts. Cytokinesis occurs at the end of M-phase. During cytokinesis the cell cytoplasm divides, and two new daughter cells are produced.

S phase: Chromosome replication (DNA synthesis).

Second gap phase: The chromosomes begin condensing.

Mitosis: Nuclear division

Cytokinesis: The cytoplasm divides and the two cells separate. Cytokinesis is part of M phase but distinct from nuclear division.

First gap phase: Cell growth and development.

The cell cycle: S, G2, M, G1

An overview of mitosis

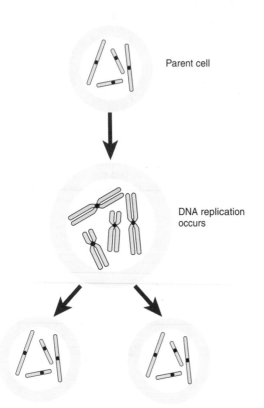

Parent cell

DNA replication occurs

The cell divides forming two identical daughter cells. The chromosome number remains the same as the parent cell.

Cytokinesis

In plant cells (below top), cytokinesis (division of the cytoplasm) involves construction of a cell plate (a precursor the new cell wall) in the middle of the cell. The cell wall materials are delivered by vesicles derived from the Golgi. The vesicles coalesce to become the plasma membranes of the new cell surfaces.

Animal cell cytokinesis (below bottom) begins shortly after the sister chromatids have separated in anaphase of mitosis. A contractile ring of microtubular elements assembles in the middle of the cell, next to the plasma membrane, constricting it to form a cleavage furrow. In an energy-using process, the cleavage furrow moves inwards, forming a region of abscission (separation) where the two cells will separate.

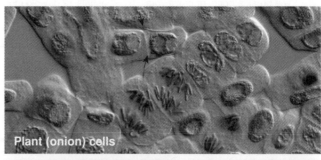

Plant (onion) cells

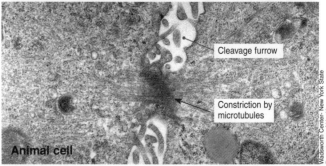

Cleavage furrow

Constriction by microtubules

Animal cell

© 2015 **BIOZONE** International
ISBN:978-1-927309-25-4
Photocopying Prohibited

The cell cycle and stages of mitosis in a plant cell

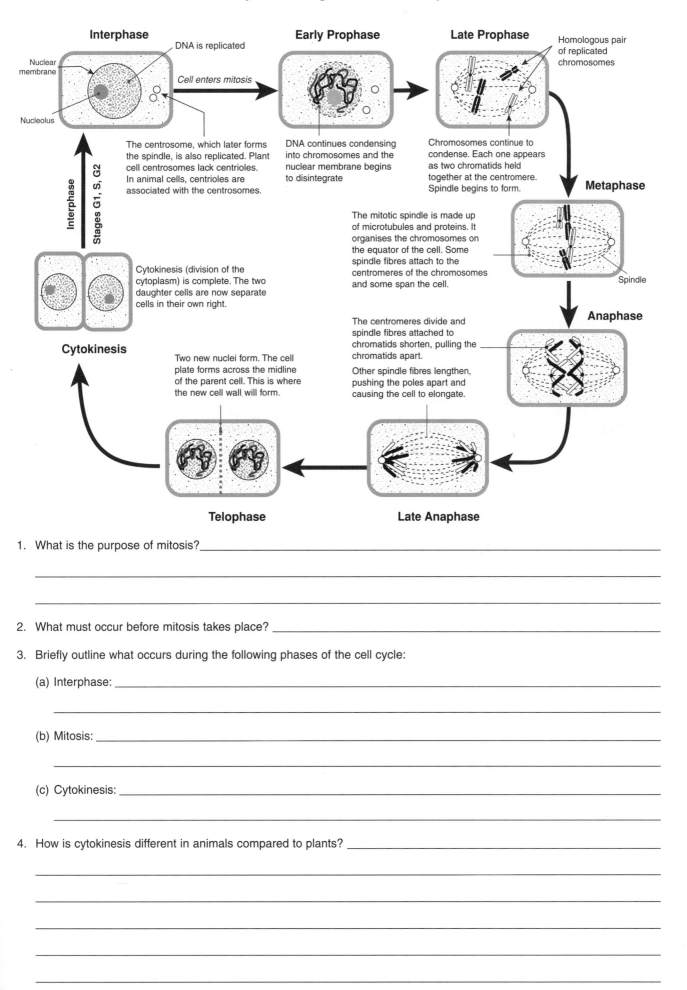

1. What is the purpose of mitosis?_____

_____

_____

2. What must occur before mitosis takes place? _____

3. Briefly outline what occurs during the following phases of the cell cycle:

   (a) Interphase: _____

   _____

   (b) Mitosis: _____

   _____

   (c) Cytokinesis: _____

   _____

4. How is cytokinesis different in animals compared to plants? _____

_____

_____

_____

_____

_____

103 Recognising Stages in Mitosis

Key Idea: The stages of mitosis can be recognised by the organisation of the cell and chromosomes.

Although mitosis is a continuous process, it is divided into four stages (prophase, metaphase, anaphase, and telophase) to more easily describe the processes occurring during its progression.

The mitotic index

The mitotic index measures the ratio of cells in mitosis to the number of cells counted. It is a measure of cell proliferation and can be used to diagnose cancer. In areas of high cell growth the mitotic index is high such as in plant apical meristems or the growing tips of plant roots. The mitotic index can be calculated using the formula:

$$\text{Mitotic index} = \frac{\text{Number of cells in mitosis}}{\text{Total number of cells}}$$

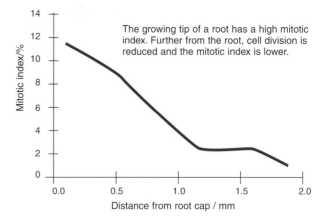

The growing tip of a root has a high mitotic index. Further from the root, cell division is reduced and the mitotic index is lower.

1. Use the information on the previous page to identify which stage of mitosis is shown in each of the photographs below:

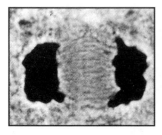 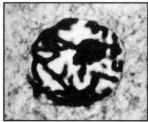  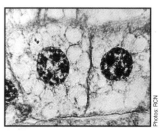

(a) _____

(b) _____

(c) _____

(d) _____

2. (a) The light micrograph (right) shows a section of cells in an onion root tip. These cells have a cell cycle of approximately 24 hours. The cells can be seen to be in various stages of the cell cycle. By counting the number of cells in the various stages it is possible to calculate how long the cell spends in each stage of the cycle. Count and record the number of cells in the image that are in mitosis and those that are in interphase. Cells in cytokinesis can be recorded as in interphase. Estimate the amount of time a cell spends in each phase.

Onion root tip cells

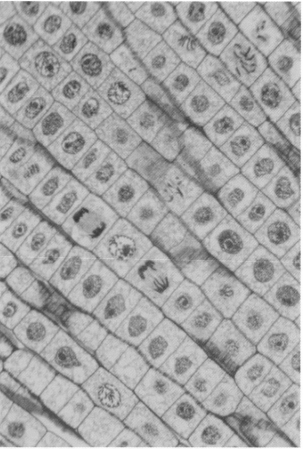

Stage	No. of cells	% of total cells	Estimated time in stage
Interphase			
Mitosis			
Total		100	

(b) Use your counts from 2(a) to calculate the mitotic index for this section of cells.

_____

_____

3. What would you expect to happen to the mitotic index of a population of cells that loses the ability to divide as they mature?

_____

_____

LINK
DATA 102

© 2015 **BIOZONE** International
ISBN: 978-1-927309-25-4
Photocopying Prohibited

104 Regulation of the Cell Cycle

Key Idea: The cell cycle is regulated by checkpoints, which ensure the cell has met certain conditions before it continues to the next phase of the cell cycle.

The cell cycle is an orderly sequence of events, but its duration varies enormously between cells of different species and between cell types in one organism. For example, human intestinal cells normally divide around twice a day, whereas cells in the liver typically divide once a year. However, if these tissues are damaged, cell division increases rapidly to repair the damage. Progression through the cell cycle is controlled by regulatory checkpoints, which ensure the cell has met the conditions required to successfully complete the next phase.

Checkpoints during the cell cycle

There are three **checkpoints** during the cell cycle. A checkpoint is a critical regulatory point in the cell cycle. At each checkpoint, a set of conditions determines whether or not the cell will continue into the next phase. For example, cell size is important in regulating whether or not the cell can pass through the G_1 checkpoint.

G_1 checkpoint
Pass this checkpoint if:
► Cell size is large enough.
► Sufficient nutrients are available.
► Signals from other cells have been received.

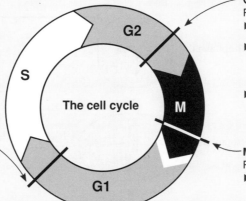

The cell cycle — S, G2, M, G1

G_2 checkpoint:
Pass this checkpoint if:
► Cell size is large enough.
► Replication of chromosomes has been successfully completed.
► Proteins required for mitosis have been synthesised.

Metaphase checkpoint
Pass this checkpoint if:
► All chromosomes are attached to the mitotic spindle.

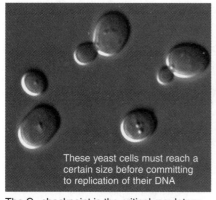

These yeast cells must reach a certain size before committing to replication of their DNA

The G_1 checkpoint is the critical regulatory point in cells. At this checkpoint, the cell decides whether to commit to the cell cycle or to enter an arrested phase called G_0. Once sufficient nutrients or cell size is reached and the checkpoint is passed the cell is committed to replication of the nuclear material. Most cells that pass G_1 complete the cell cycle.

Chromosome actively transcribing genes to make proteins

The G_2 checkpoint determines if synthesis was completed correctly, that the necessary proteins for mitosis have been synthesised, and that the cell has reached a size suitable for cell division. Damage to the DNA prevents entry to M phase. The entry into M phase is controlled by a protein called cyclin B, which reaches a concentration peak at the G_2-M phase boundary.

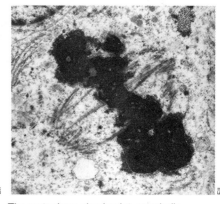

The metaphase checkpoint, or spindle checkpoint, checks that all the chromatids are attached to the spindle fibres and under the correct tension. At this point, cyclin B is degraded, ultimately resulting in the sister chromatids separating and the cell entering anaphase, pulling the chromatids apart. The cell then begins cytokinesis and produces two new daughter cells.

1. What is the general purpose of cell cycle checkpoints? _____

_____

_____

2. (a) What is the purpose of the metaphase checkpoint? _____

_____

(b) Why is this checkpoint important? _____

_____

3. What would happen if the cell cycle was not regulated? _____

_____

105 Meiosis

Key Idea: Meiosis is a special type of cell division. It produces sex cells (gametes) for the purpose of sexual reproduction. Meiosis involves a single chromosomal duplication followed by two successive nuclear divisions, and results in a halving of the diploid chromosome number. Meiosis occurs in the sex organs of plants and animals. If genetic mistakes (**gene and chromosome mutations**) occur here, they will be passed on to the offspring (they will be inherited).

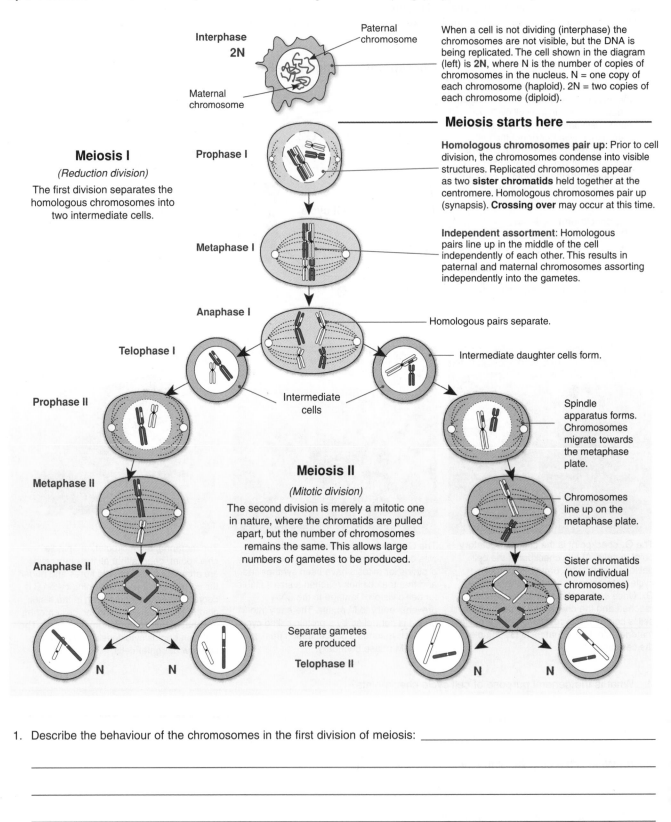

Interphase 2N

Paternal chromosome

Maternal chromosome

When a cell is not dividing (interphase) the chromosomes are not visible, but the DNA is being replicated. The cell shown in the diagram (left) is **2N**, where N is the number of copies of chromosomes in the nucleus. N = one copy of each chromosome (haploid). 2N = two copies of each chromosome (diploid).

—————————— **Meiosis starts here** ——————————

Meiosis I

(Reduction division)

The first division separates the homologous chromosomes into two intermediate cells.

Prophase I

Homologous chromosomes pair up: Prior to cell division, the chromosomes condense into visible structures. Replicated chromosomes appear as two **sister chromatids** held together at the centromere. Homologous chromosomes pair up (synapsis). **Crossing over** may occur at this time.

Metaphase I

Independent assortment: Homologous pairs line up in the middle of the cell independently of each other. This results in paternal and maternal chromosomes assorting independently into the gametes.

Anaphase I

Homologous pairs separate.

Telophase I

Intermediate daughter cells form.

Intermediate cells

Prophase II

Spindle apparatus forms. Chromosomes migrate towards the metaphase plate.

Meiosis II

(Mitotic division)

The second division is merely a mitotic one in nature, where the chromatids are pulled apart, but the number of chromosomes remains the same. This allows large numbers of gametes to be produced.

Metaphase II

Chromosomes line up on the metaphase plate.

Anaphase II

Sister chromatids (now individual chromosomes) separate.

Separate gametes are produced

Telophase II

N   **N**

N   **N**

1. Describe the behaviour of the chromosomes in the first division of meiosis: _____

_____

_____

_____

2. Describe the behaviour of the chromosomes in the second division of meiosis: _____

_____

_____

© 2015 **BIOZONE** International
ISBN:978-1-927309-25-4
Photocopying Prohibited

Crossing over and recombination

Prophase I of meiosis

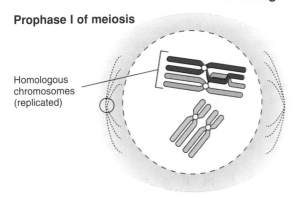

Homologous chromosomes (replicated)

Crossing over refers to the mutual exchange of pieces of chromosome (and their genes) **between the homologous chromosomes**. It can occur only during prophase in the first division of meiosis. **Recombination** as a result of crossing over is an important mechanism to increase genetic variability in the offspring and has the general effect of allowing genes to move independently of each other through the generations in a way that allows concentration of beneficial alleles.

In prophase I homologous chromosomes pair up to form **bivalents**. This process is called **synapsis**. While they are paired, the non-sister chromatids of homologous pairs may become tangled and segments may be exchanged in a process called **crossing over**. The crossing over occurs at points called chiasmata.

Crossing over results in the **recombination** of alleles, producing greater variation in the offspring than would otherwise occur.

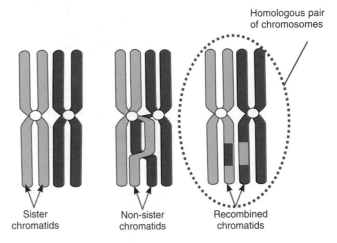

Homologous pair of chromosomes

Sister chromatids

Non-sister chromatids

Recombined chromatids

Gamete formation

Blue = paternal chromosome
Grey = maternal chromosome

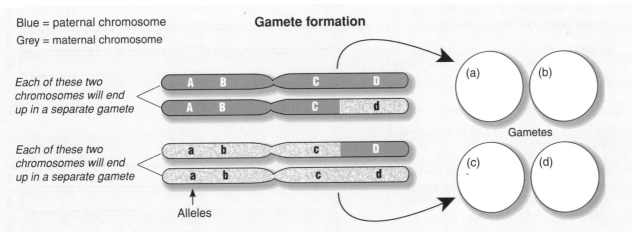

Each of these two chromosomes will end up in a separate gamete

Each of these two chromosomes will end up in a separate gamete

Alleles

Gametes

(a) (b) (c) (d)

The homologous chromosomes above have completed a crossing over event. Recombination have resulted in four different allele combinations instead the two that would appear if there was no crossing over.

3. (a) When does DNA replication occur? _____

    (b) What is the difference between a chromosome and a chromatid: _____

    _____

4. (a) Distinguish between a haploid and a diploid cell: _____

    _____

    _____

    (b) Circle the **haploid** cells in the diagram on the previous page

5. Complete the diagram above (a) - (d) by drawing the gametes formed:

6. (a) How does crossing over alter the genotype of the gametes produced by meiosis? _____

    _____

    (b) What is the consequence of this? _____

    _____

106 Crossing Over Problems

Key Idea: Crossing over can occur in multiple places in chromosomes, producing a huge amount of genetic variation. The diagram below shows a pair of homologous chromosomes about to undergo chiasma formation during the first cell division in the process of meiosis. There are known crossover points along the length of the chromatids (same on all four chromatids shown in the diagram). In the prepared spaces below, draw the gene sequences after crossing over has occurred on three unrelated and separate occasions (it would be useful to use different coloured pens to represent the genes from the two different chromosomes). See the diagrams on the previous page as a guide.

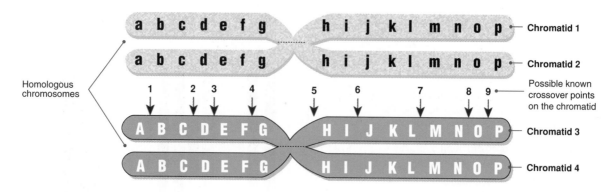

1. Crossing over occurs at a **single** point between the chromosomes above.

    (a) Draw the gene sequences for the four chromatids (on the right), after crossing over has occurred at crossover point: **2**

    (b) Which genes have been exchanged with those on its homologue (neighbour chromosome)?

    _____

2. Crossing over occurs at **two** points between the chromosomes above.

    (a) Draw the gene sequences for the four chromatids (on the right), after crossing over has occurred between crossover points: **6** and **7**.

    (b) Which genes have been exchanged with those on its homologue (neighbour chromosome)?

    _____

3. Crossing over occurs at **four** points between the chromosomes above.

    (a) Draw the gene sequences for the four chromatids (on the right), after crossing over has occurred between crossover points: **1** and **3**, and **5** and **7**.

    (b) Which genes have been exchanged with those on its homologue (neighbour chromosome)?

    _____

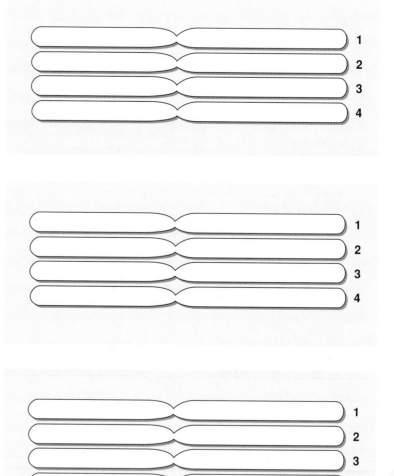

4. What would be the genetic consequences if there was no crossing over between chromatids during meiosis?

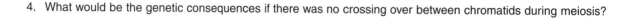

_____

_____

_____

© 2015 **BIOZONE** International
ISBN:978-1-927309-25-4
Photocopying Prohibited

KNOW

107 Modelling Meiosis

Key Idea: We can simulate crossing over, gamete production, and the inheritance of alleles during meiosis using ice-block sticks to represent chromosomes.

This practical activity simulates the production of gametes (sperm and eggs) by meiosis and shows you how crossing over increases genetic variability. This is demonstrated by studying how two of your own alleles are inherited by the child produced at the completion of the activity. Completing this activity will help you to visualise and understand meiosis. It will take 25-45 minutes.

Background

Each of your somatic cells contain 46 chromosomes. You received 23 chromosomes from your mother (**maternal chromosomes**), and 23 chromosomes from your father (**paternal chromosomes**). Therefore, you have 23 homologous (same) pairs. For simplicity, the number of chromosomes studied in this exercise has been reduced to four (two homologous pairs). To study the effect of crossing over on genetic variability, you will look at the inheritance of two of your own traits: the ability to **tongue roll** and **handedness**.

Chromosome #	Phenotype	Genotype
10	Tongue roller	TT, Tt
10	Non-tongue roller	tt
2	Right handed	RR, Rr
2	Left handed	rr

Record your phenotype and genotype for each trait in the table (right).
NOTE: If you have a dominant trait, you will not know if you are heterozygous or homozygous for that trait, so you can choose either genotype for this activity.

BEFORE YOU START THE SIMULATION: Partner up with a classmate. Your gametes will combine with theirs (fertilisation) at the end of the activity to produce a child. Decide who will be the female, and who will be the male. You will need to work with this person again at step 6.

1. Collect four ice-blocks sticks. These represent four chromosomes. Colour two sticks blue or mark them with a P. These are the paternal chromosomes. The plain sticks are the maternal chromosomes. Write your initial on each of the four sticks. Label each chromosome with their chromosome number (right).

    Label four sticky dots with the alleles for each of your phenotypic traits, and stick it onto the appropriate chromosome. For example, if you are heterozygous for tongue rolling, the sticky dots with have the alleles **T** and **t**, and they will be placed on chromosome 10. If you are left handed, the alleles will be **r** and **r** and be placed on chromosome 2 (right).

2. Randomly drop the chromosomes onto a table. This represents a cell in either the testes or ovaries. **Duplicate** your chromosomes (to simulate DNA replication) by adding four more identical ice-block sticks to the table (below). This represents **interphase**.

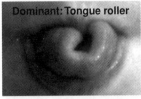

Dominant: Tongue roller

Dominant: Right hand

Recessive: Non-roller

Recessive: Left hand

Trait	Phenotype	Genotype
Handedness		
Tongue rolling		

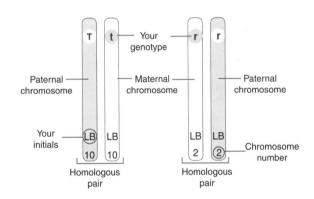

3. Simulate **prophase I** by lining the duplicated chromosome pair with their homologous pair (below). For each chromosome number, you will have four sticks touching side-by-side (A). At this stage **crossing over** occurs. Simulate this by swapping sticky dots from adjoining homologs (B).

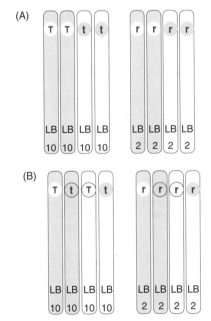

4. Randomly align the homologous chromosome pairs to simulate alignment on the metaphase plate (as occurs in **metaphase I**). Simulate **anaphase I** by separating chromosome pairs. For each group of four sticks, two are pulled to each pole.

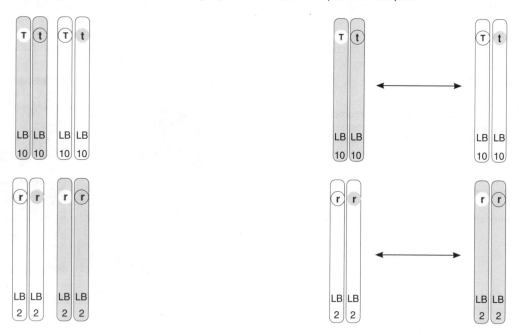

5. **Telophase I:** Two intermediate cells are formed. If you have been random in the previous step, each intermediate cell will contain a mixture of maternal and paternal chromosomes. This is the end of **meiosis 1**.

    Now that meiosis 1 is completed, your cells need to undergo **meiosis 2.** Carry out prophase II, metaphase II, anaphase II, and telophase II. Remember, there is no crossing over in meiosis II. At the end of the process each intermediate cell will have produced two haploid gametes (below).

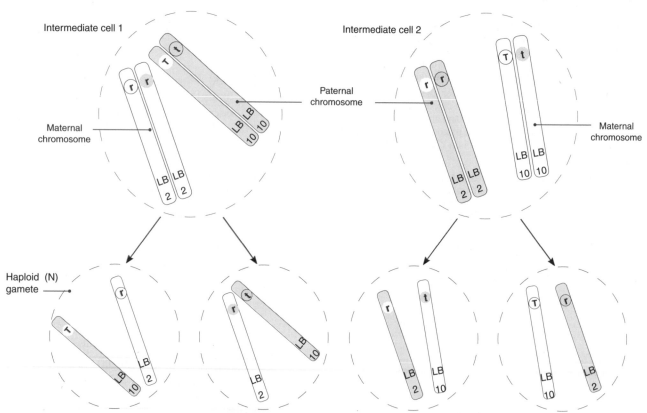

6. Pair up with the partner you chose at the beginning of the exercise to carry out **fertilisation**. Randomly select one sperm and one egg cell. The unsuccessful gametes can be removed from the table. Combine the chromosomes of the successful gametes. You have created a child! Fill in the following chart to describe your child's genotype and phenotype for tongue rolling and handedness.

Trait	Phenotype	Genotype
Handedness		
Tongue rolling		

© 2015 **BIOZONE** International
ISBN: 978-1-927309-25-4
Photocopying Prohibited

108 Mitosis vs Meiosis

Key Idea: Mitosis produces two daughter cells genetically identical to the parent cell. Meiosis produces four daughter cells that contain half the genetic information of the parent cell. Cell division is fundamental to all life, as cells arise only by the division of existing cells. All types of cell division begin with replication of the cell's DNA. In eukaryotes, this is followed by division of the nucleus. There are two forms of nuclear division: **mitosis** and **meiosis**, and they have quite different

purposes and outcomes. Mitosis is the simpler of the two and produces two identical daughter cells from each parent cell. Mitosis is responsible for growth and repair processes in multicellular organisms and reproduction in single-celled and asexual eukaryotes. Meiosis involves a **reduction division** in which haploid gametes are produced for the purposes of sexual reproduction. Fusion of haploid gametes in fertilisation restores the diploid cell number in the **zygote**.

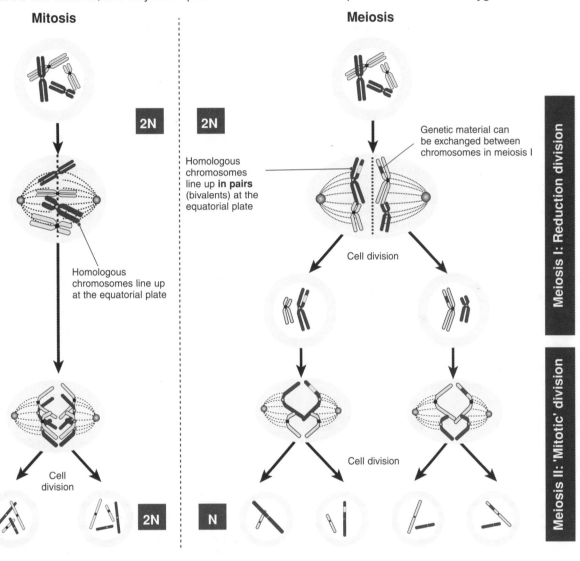

1. Explain how mitosis conserves chromosome number while meiosis reduces the number from diploid to haploid:

_____

_____

_____

2. Describe a fundamental difference between the first and second divisions of meiosis: _____

_____

_____

3. How does meiosis introduce genetic variability into gametes and offspring (following gamete fusion in fertilisation)?

_____

_____

_____

109 Chromosome Mutations

Key Idea: Large scale mutations occurring during meiosis can fundamentally change chromosome structure.

Chromosome mutations (also called block mutations) involve the rearrangement of whole blocks of genes, rather than individual bases within a gene. They commonly occur during meiosis and they alter the number or sequence of whole sets of genes on the chromosome (represented by letters below). Translocations may sometimes involve the fusion of whole chromosomes, thereby reducing the chromosome number of an organism. This is thought to be an important evolutionary mechanism by which instant speciation can occur.

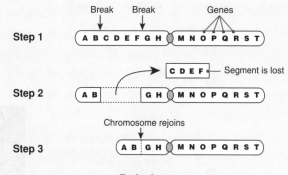

Deletion

A break may occur at two points on the chromosome and the middle piece of the chromosome falls out. The two ends then rejoin to form a chromosome deficient in some genes. Alternatively, the end of a chromosome may break off and is lost.

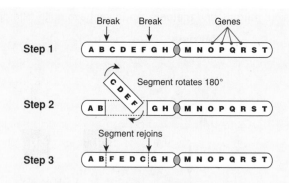

Inversion

The middle piece of the chromosome falls out and rotates through 180° and then rejoins. There is no loss of genetic material. The genes will be in a reverse order for this segment of the chromosome.

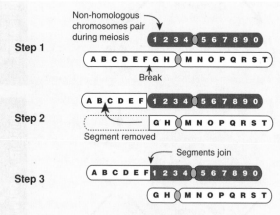

Translocation

Translocation involves the movement of a group of genes between different chromosomes. The large chromosome (white) and the small chromosome (blue) are not homologous. A piece of one chromosome breaks off and joins onto another chromosome. When the chromosomes are passed to gametes some will receive extra genes, while some will be deficient.

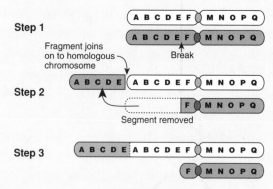

Duplication

A segment is lost from one chromosome and is added to its homologue. In this diagram, the darker chromosome on the bottom is the 'donor' of the duplicated piece of chromosome. The chromosome with the segment removed is deficient in genes. Some gametes will receive double the genes while others will have no genes for the affected segment.

1. For each of the chromosome (block) mutations illustrated above, write the original gene sequence and the new gene sequence after the mutation has occurred (the first one has been done for you):

	Original sequence(s)	Mutated sequence(s)
(a) Deletion:	A B C D E F G H M N O P Q R S T	A B G H M N O P Q R S T
(b) Inversion:		
(c) Translocation:		
(d) Duplication:		

2. Which type of block mutation is likely to be the least damaging to the organism? Explain your answer:

_____

© 2015 **BIOZONE** International
ISBN:978-1-927309-25-4
Photocopying Prohibited

110 Non-Disjunction in Meiosis

Key Idea: Non-disjunction during meiosis results in incorrect apportioning of chromosomes to the gametes.

In meiosis, chromosomes are usually distributed to daughter cells without error. Occasionally, homologous chromosomes fail to separate properly in meiosis I, or sister chromatids fail to separate in meiosis II. In these cases, one gamete receives two of the same type of chromosome and the other gamete receives no copy. This error is known as **non-disjunction** and it results in abnormal numbers of chromosomes in the gametes. The union of an aberrant and a normal gamete at fertilisation produces offspring with an abnormal chromosome number. This condition is known as **aneuploidy**.

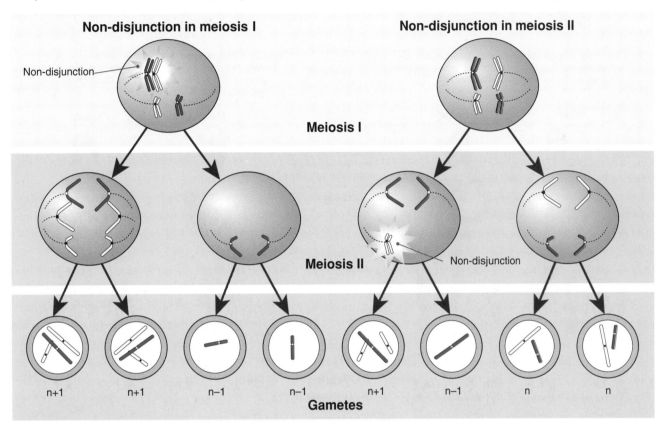

Down syndrome (trisomy 21)

Down syndrome is the most common of the human aneuploidies. The incidence rate in humans is about 1 in 800 births for women aged 30 to 31 years, with a **maternal age effect** (the rate increases rapidly with maternal age).

Nearly all cases (approximately 95%) result from **non-disjunction** of chromosome 21 during **meiosis**. When this happens, a gamete (most commonly the oocyte) ends up with 24 rather than 23 chromosomes, and fertilisation produces a trisomic offspring.

Left: Down syndrome phenotype.

Right: A karyogram for an individual with trisomy 21. The chromosomes are circled.

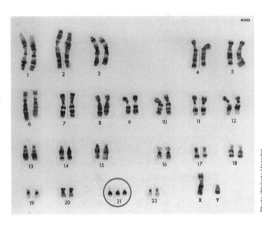

1. Describe the consequences of non-disjunction during meiosis: _____

_____

_____

2. Explain why non-disjunction in meiosis I results in a higher proportion of faulty gametes than non-disjunction in meiosis II:

_____

_____

3. What is the maternal age effect and what are its consequences? _____

_____

LINK 111 LINK 105 **KNOW**

111 Aneuploidy in Humans

Key Idea: Nondisjunction during meiosis can result in more or less than the normal number of chromosomes.

Euploidy is the condition of having an exact multiple of the haploid number of chromosomes. Normal euploid humans have 46 chromosomes (2N). **Aneuploidy** is the condition where the chromosome number is not an exact multiple of the normal haploid set for the species (e.g. 2N+2, 2N–1). **Polysomy** is aneuploidy involving reduplication of some of the chromosomes beyond the normal diploid number (e.g. 2N+1). Aneuploidy usually results from non-disjunction. The two most common forms are monosomy (e.g. Turner syndrome) and trisomy (e.g. Down and Klinefelter syndrome).

Faulty egg production	Faulty sperm production
The male has produced normal gametes, but the female has not. The two X-sex chromosomes failed to separate during the first division of meiosis.	The female has produced normal gametes, while the male has had an error during the first division of meiosis. The two sex chromosomes (**X** and **Y**) failed to separate during the first division.

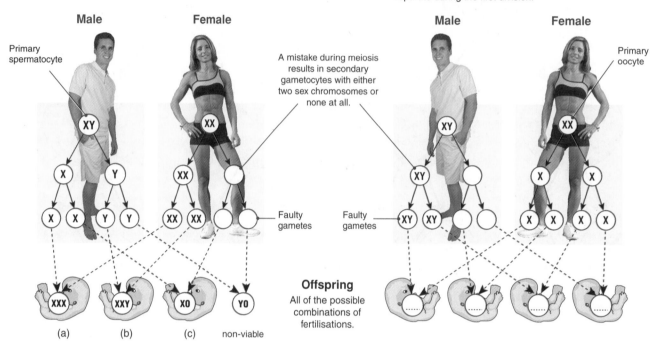

A mistake during meiosis results in secondary gametocytes with either two sex chromosomes or none at all.

Offspring
All of the possible combinations of fertilisations.

1. Identify the sex chromosomes in each of the unlabelled embryos (above, right):

2. Using the table on the next page, identify the syndrome for each of the offspring labelled (a) to (c) above:

   (a) _____ (b) _____ (c) _____

3. Why is the YO configuration (above) non-viable (i.e. there is no embryonic development)? _____

   _____

4. (a) For karyotype **A**, below, circle the sex chromosomes and state:

   Chromosome configuration: _____ Sex of individual (M/F): ___ Syndrome: _____

   (b) For karyotype **B**, below, circle the sex chromosomes and state:

   Chromosome configuration: _____ Sex of individual (M/F): ___ Syndrome: _____

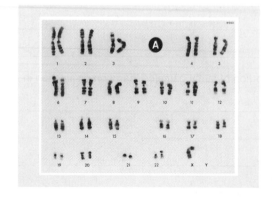

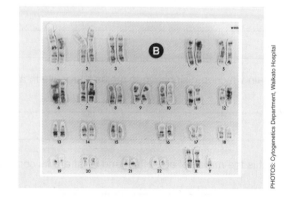

PHOTOS: Cytogenetics Department, Waikato Hospital

© 2015 **BIOZONE** International
ISBN:978-1-927309-25-4
Photocopying Prohibited

Examples of aneuploidy in human sex chromosomes

Sex chromosomes and chromosome condition	Apparent sex	Phenotype
XO, monosomic	Female	Turner syndrome
XX, disomic	Female	**Normal female**
XXX, trisomic	Female	Metafemale. Most appear normal; they have a greater tendency to criminality
XXXX, tetrasomic	Female	Rather like Down syndrome, low fertility and intelligence
XY, disomic	Male	**Normal male**
XYY, trisomic	Male	Jacob syndrome, apparently normal male, tall, aggressive
XXY, trisomic	Male	Klinefelter syndrome (infertile). Incidence rate 1 in 1000 live male births, with a maternal age effect.
XXXY, tetrasomic	Male	Extreme Klinefelter, mentally retarded

ABOVE: Features of selected aneuploidies in humans. Note that this list represents only a small sample of the possible sex chromosome aneuploidies in humans.

RIGHT: Symbolic representation of Barr body occurrence in various human karyotypes. The chromosome number is given first, and the inactive X chromosomes (Xi) are framed by a black box. Note that in aneuploid syndromes, such as those described here, all but one of the X chromosomes are inactivated, regardless of the number present.

If extra copies of X are inactivated, why do extra copies still produce the aneuploidy syndromes? This is because some of the genes on the Xi escape inactivation so the dosage of these non-silenced genes will differ as they escape inactivation.

Barr bodies

In the nucleus of any non-dividing somatic cell, one of the X chromosomes condenses to form a visible piece of chromatin, called a **Barr body**. This chromosome is inactivated (Xi), so that only one X chromosome in a cell ever has its genes expressed. The inactivation is random, so Xi may be either the maternal homologue (from the mother) or the paternal homologue (from the father).

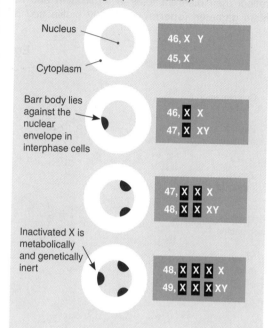

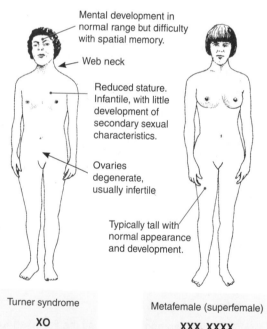

Jacob syndrome	Klinefelter syndrome	Turner syndrome	Metafemale (superfemale)
XYY	**XXY, XXXY**	**XO**	**XXX, XXXX**

5. State how many Barr bodies are present in each somatic cell for each of the following syndromes:

   (a) Jacob syndrome: _____ (b) Klinefelter syndrome: _____ (c) Turner syndrome: _____

6. Explain the consequence of X-chromosome inactivation in terms of the proteins encoded by the X chromosome genes:

   _____

   _____

7. State how many chromosomes for each set of homologues are present for the following forms of aneuploidy:

   (a) Nullisomy: _____ (c) Trisomy: _____

   (b) Monosomy: _____ (d) Polysomy: _____

112 Gametes

Key Idea: Gametes are the sex cells of organisms. Male and female gametes differ in their size, shape, and number.

Gametes (sex cells) are produced for the purposes of sexual reproduction. The gametes of male and female mammals differ greatly in size, shape, and number. These differences reflect their different roles in fertilisation and reproduction. Male gametes (**sperm**) are highly motile and produced in large numbers. Female gametes (**eggs** or **ova**) are large, few in number, and immobile. They move as a result of the wave-like motion produced by the ciliated cells lining the Fallopian tube. Egg cells contain some food sources to nourish the developing embryo. In mammals, this food source is small because, once implanted into the uterine lining, the embryo derives its nutrients from the mother's blood supply.

Egg structure and function

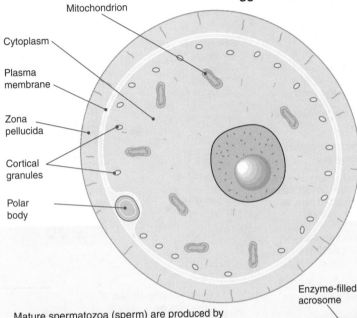

Mitochondrion
Cytoplasm
Plasma membrane
Zona pellucida
Cortical granules
Polar body

The ovum has no propulsion mechanism and is a simpler structure than the sperm cell. It is required to survive for a much longer time than a sperm, so it contains many more nutrients and metabolites and, as a result, it is much larger than a sperm cell (up to 100 μm).

The contents of the ovum are similar to that of a typical mammalian cell, although it is externally surrounded by a jelly-like glycoprotein called the zona pellucida. A small polar body (the remnants of a sister cell) lies between the plasma membrane and zona pellucida. Cortical granules around the inner edge of the plasma membrane contain enzymes that are released once a sperm has penetrated the egg, forming a block to prevent further sperm entry (the cortical reaction).

Sperm structure and function

Mature spermatozoa (sperm) are produced by **spermatogenesis** in the testes. Meiotic division of spermatocytes produces spermatids, which then differentiate into mature sperm.

The sperm's structure reflects its purpose, which is to swim along the fluid environment of the female reproductive tract to the ovum, penetrate the ovum's protective barrier, and donate its genetic material. A sperm cell comprises three regions: a headpiece, containing the nucleus and penetrative enzymes, an energy-producing mid-piece, and a tail for propulsion.

Human sperm live only about 48 hours, but they swim quickly and there are so many of them (millions per ejaculation) that usually some are able to reach the egg to fertilise it.

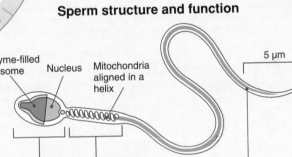

Enzyme-filled acrosome   Nucleus   Mitochondria aligned in a helix

5 μm

The **mid-piece** has many mitochondria to generate the energy for swimming.

The **headpiece** contains the nucleus and the acrosome, which contains the enzymes that help penetrate the egg.

The **tail** is a long flagellum that propels the sperm in its swim to the egg.

1. Why do sperm need to be motile? _____

_____

_____

2. (a) How does an egg move along the Fallopian tube? _____

_____

_____

   (b) Why does a mature egg need to be so many times larger than a sperm? _____

_____

_____

3. Why does a sperm cell have a large number of mitochondria? _____

_____

_____

© 2015 **BIOZONE** International
ISBN:978-1-927309-25-4
Photocopying Prohibited

113 Spermatogenesis

Key Idea: Sperm are the male gametes. They are produced by spermatogenesis in the testes.

Sperm are produced by a process called **spermatogenesis** in the testis. Mammalian sperm are highly motile and produced in large numbers. In human males, sperm production begins at puberty and continues throughout life, but does decline with age. Thousands of sperm are produced every second, and take approximately two months to fully mature.

Spermatogenesis

Spermatogenesis is the process by which mature spermatozoa (sperm) are produced in the testis. In humans, they are produced at the rate of about 120 million per day. Spermatogenesis is regulated by the hormones **follicle stimulating hormone** (FSH) (from the anterior pituitary) and testosterone (secreted from the testes in response to **luteinising hormone** (LH) (from the anterior pituitary). Spermatogonia, in the outer layer of the seminiferous tubules, multiply throughout reproductive life. Some of them divide by meiosis into spermatocytes, which produce spermatids. These are transformed into mature sperm by the process of spermiogenesis in the seminiferous tubules of the testis. Full sperm motility is achieved in the epididymis.

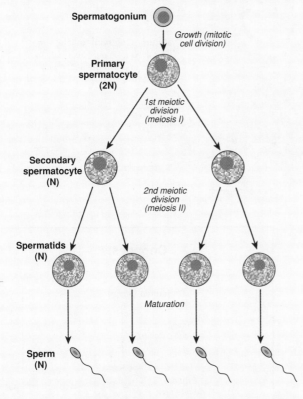

Cross section through seminiferous tubule

The photograph below shows maturing sperm (arrowed) with tails projecting into the lumen of the seminiferous tubule. Their heads are embedded in the Sertoli cells in the tubule wall and they are ready to break free and move to the epididymis where they complete their maturation. The same cross-section is illustrated diagrammatically (bottom).

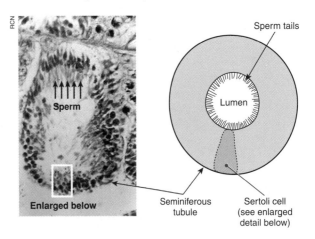

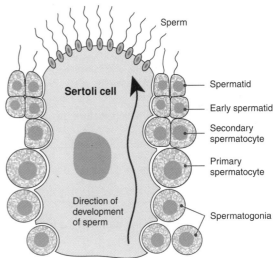

1. (a) Name the process by which mature sperm are formed: _____

   (b) Identify where this process takes place: _____

   (c) State how many mature sperm form from one primary spermatocyte: _____

   (d) State the type of cell division which produces mature sperm cells: _____

2. Describe the role of FSH and LH in sperm cell production: _____

   _____

   _____

3. Each ejaculation of a healthy, fertile male contains 100-400 million sperm. Suggest why so many sperm are needed:

   _____

   _____

114 Oogenesis

Key Idea: Eggs are the female gametes. They are produced by oogenesis, which takes place in the ovaries.

Egg cell (ovum, plural ova) production in females occurs by **oogenesis**. Unlike spermatogenesis, no new eggs are produced after birth. Instead, a human female is born with her entire complement of immature eggs. These remain in prophase of meiosis I throughout childhood. After puberty, most commonly a single egg cell is released from the ovaries at regular monthly intervals as part of the menstrual cycle. These egg cells are arrested in metaphase of meiosis II. This second meiotic division is only completed upon fertilisation. The release of egg cells from the ovaries takes place from the onset of puberty until menopause, when menstruation ceases and the woman is no longer fertile.

Development of the ovarian follicle and egg cell within the ovary

Primordial follicle: A follicle is an aggregation of cells containing a single immature egg. Follicles are periodically initiated to grow and develop. This process culminates in ovulation of (usually) a single competent oocyte.

Primary follicle: supports the **primary oocyte**. This is arrested before birth prior to the first meiotic division.

Secondary follicle

Secondary oocyte: derived from the primary oocyte shortly before ovulation. It is arrested at metaphase of meiosis II and will only complete meiosis II if fertilised.

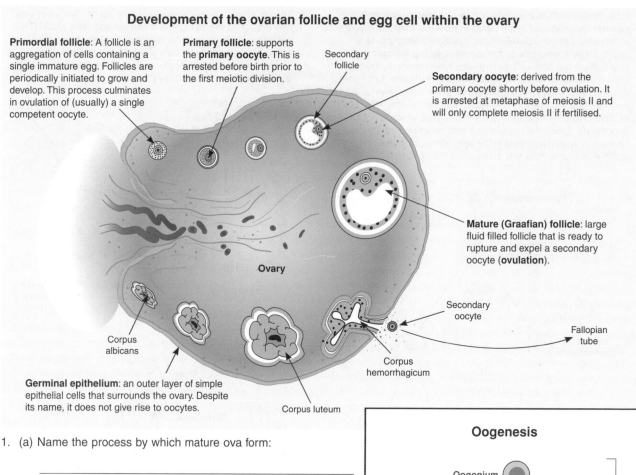

Ovary

Mature (Graafian) follicle: large fluid filled follicle that is ready to rupture and expel a secondary oocyte (**ovulation**).

Secondary oocyte

Fallopian tube

Corpus albicans

Corpus hemorrhagicum

Corpus luteum

Germinal epithelium: an outer layer of simple epithelial cells that surrounds the ovary. Despite its name, it does not give rise to oocytes.

1. (a) Name the process by which mature ova form:

   _____

   (b) Name the place(s) where this takes place:

   _____

2. Discuss the main differences between the production of male gametes and female gametes:

   _____

   _____

   _____

   _____

3. Explain why males can be potentially fertile all their life, while female fertility decreases and eventually ceases with age:

   _____

   _____

   _____

   _____

   _____

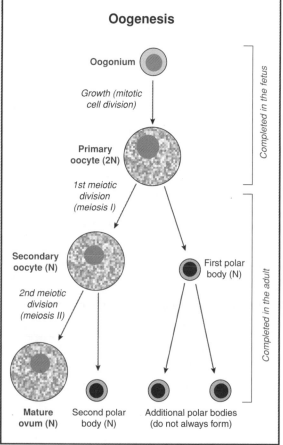

Oogenesis

Oogonium

Growth (mitotic cell division)

Primary oocyte (2N)

1st meiotic division (meiosis I)

Secondary oocyte (N)

First polar body (N)

2nd meiotic division (meiosis II)

Mature ovum (N)

Second polar body (N)

Additional polar bodies (do not always form)

Completed in the fetus

Completed in the adult

© 2015 **BIOZONE** International
ISBN:978-1-927309-25-4
Photocopying Prohibited

115 Fertilisation and Early Growth

Key Idea: Fertilisation occurs when a male and female gamete fuse to form a zygote.

Fertilisation occurs when a sperm penetrates an egg cell at the secondary oocyte stage and the sperm and egg nuclei unite to form the zygote. In mammals, the entry of a sperm into the egg triggers specific mechanisms to prevent polyspermy (fertilisation of the egg by more than one sperm). These include a change in membrane potential, and the cortical reaction (see below). A zygote resulting from polyspermy contains too many chromosomes, and is not viable (does not develop). Fertilisation is seen as time 0 in a period of gestation (pregnancy) and has five stages (below). After fertilisation, the zygote begins its development, i.e. its growth and differentiation into a multicellular organism.

Fertilisation (time 0)

The stages in fertilisation are represented below in a numbered sequence (1-5)

1. Capacitation
The surface of the sperm cell undergoes changes that are essential to enabling the acrosome reaction and sperm entry.

2. The acrosome reaction
Enzymes from the acrosome (an enzyme-filled bag at the tip of the sperm) are released and digest a pathway through the follicle cells (not shown) and the jelly-like zona pellucida surrounding the egg cell (secondary oocyte).

3. Fusion of sperm head
The plasma membranes of the sperm and egg fuse, and the nucleus of the sperm enters the egg cytoplasm. Fusion causes a sudden membrane depolarisation that acts as a "fast block" to further sperm entry. The fusion of the two plasma membranes also triggers the completion of meiosis II in the egg cell and induces the cortical reaction (below).

4. The cortical reaction
The fusion of the two plasma membranes induces a permanent change in the egg surface that prevents further sperm entry. Cortical granules in the egg cytoplasm release their contents into the space between the plasma membrane and the vitelline layer. Substances released from the granules raise and harden the vitelline layer to form a slow (permanent) block to further sperm entry.

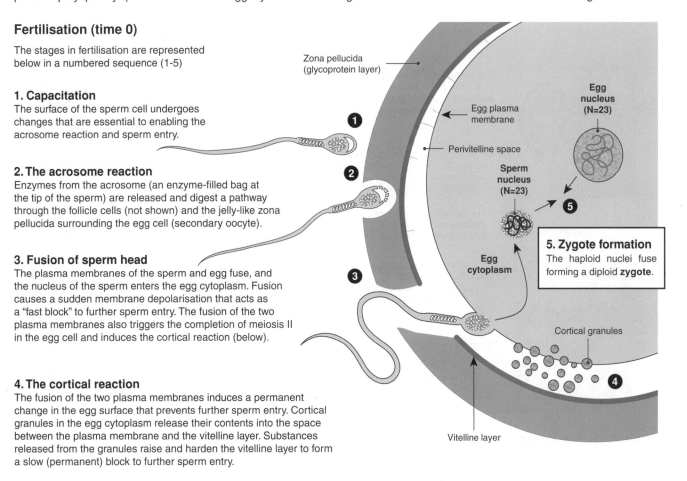

Zona pellucida (glycoprotein layer)

Egg plasma membrane

Perivitelline space

Egg nucleus (N=23)

Sperm nucleus (N=23)

Egg cytoplasm

5. Zygote formation
The haploid nuclei fuse forming a diploid **zygote**.

Cortical granules

Vitelline layer

---

1. Briefly describe the significant events (and their importance) occurring at each of the following stages of fertilisation:

(a) Capacitation: _____

_____

(b) The acrosome reaction: _____

_____

(c) Fusion of egg and sperm plasma membranes: _____

_____

(d) The cortical reaction: _____

_____

(e) Fusion of egg and sperm nuclei: _____

_____

2. Why is it important that fertilisation of the egg by more than one sperm (polyspermy) does not occur? _____

_____

_____

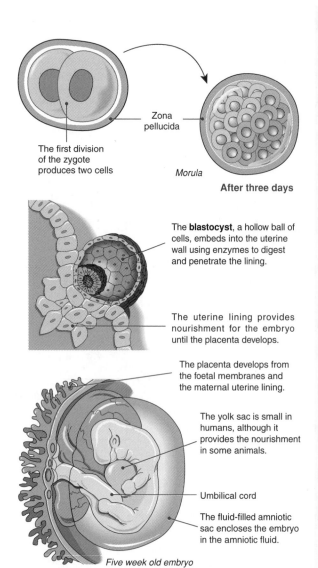

The first division of the zygote produces two cells

Zona pellucida

Morula

After three days

The **blastocyst**, a hollow ball of cells, embeds into the uterine wall using enzymes to digest and penetrate the lining.

The uterine lining provides nourishment for the embryo until the placenta develops.

The placenta develops from the foetal membranes and the maternal uterine lining.

The yolk sac is small in humans, although it provides the nourishment in some animals.

Umbilical cord

The fluid-filled amniotic sac encloses the embryo in the amniotic fluid.

Five week old embryo

Early growth and development

Cleavage and the development of the morula

Immediately after fertilisation, rapid cell division takes place. These early cell divisions are called **cleavage** and they increase the number of cells, but not the size of the zygote. The first cleavage is completed after 36 hours, and each succeeding division takes less time. After 3 days, successive cleavages have produced a solid mass of cells called the **morula**, (left) which is still about the same size as the original zygote.

Implantation of the blastocyst (after 6-8 days)

After several days in the uterus, the morula develops into the blastocyst. It makes contact with the uterine lining and pushes deeply into it, ensuring a close maternal-fetal contact. Blood vessels provide early nourishment as they are opened up by enzymes secreted by the blastocyst. The embryo produces **HCG** (human chorionic gonadotropin), which prevents degeneration of the corpus luteum and signals that the woman is pregnant.

The embryo at 5-8 weeks

Five weeks after fertilisation, the embryo is only 4-5 mm long, but already the central nervous system has developed and the heart is beating. The embryonic membranes have formed; the amnion encloses the embryo in a fluid-filled space, and the allanto-chorion forms the fetal portion of the placenta. From two months the embryo is called a fetus. It is still small (30-40 mm long), but the limbs are well formed and the bones are beginning to harden. The face has a flat, rather featureless appearance with the eyes far apart. Fetal movements have begun and brain development proceeds rapidly. The placenta is well developed, although not fully functional until 12 weeks. The umbilical cord, containing the fetal umbilical arteries and vein, connects fetus and mother.

3. (a) Explain why the egg cell, when released from the ovary, is termed a secondary oocyte: _____

_____

   (b) At which stage is its meiotic division completed? _____

4. What contribution do the sperm and egg cell make to each of the following:

   (a) The nucleus of the zygote?   Sperm contribution: _____   Egg contribution: _____

   (b) The cytoplasm of the zygote?   Sperm contribution: _____   Egg contribution: _____

5. What is meant by cleavage? Explain its significance to the early development of the embryo:_____

_____

_____

6. (a) What is the importance of implantation to the early nourishment of the embryo?_____

_____

   (b) What is the purpose of HCG production by the embryo? _____

_____

_____

7. Why is the fetus particularly prone to damage from drugs towards the end of the first trimester (2-3 months):

_____

© 2015 **BIOZONE** International
ISBN: 978-1-927309-25-4
Photocopying Prohibited

116 Reproduction in Plants

Key Idea: The life cycle of plants includes alternation between a haploid (N) gametophyte generation and a diploid (2N) sporophyte generation.

The life cycles of all plants are characterised by **alternation of** **generations**, in which a haploid (N) gametophyte generation alternates with a diploid (2N) sporophyte generation, each giving rise to the other. In vascular plants, the sporophyte generation is dominant.

▶ The sporophyte and gametophyte generations are named for the type of reproductive cells they produce. Haploid gametophytes (N) produce gametes by mitosis, whereas diploid sporophytes (2N) produce spores by meiosis.

▶ Spores develop directly into organisms. Gametes (egg and sperm) unite during fertilisation to form a zygote which gives rise to an organism.

▶ Pollen carries the gametes from the male reproductive structures to the female reproductive structures.

In seed plants, the pollen is the gametophyte...

... and the sporophyte is the plant that we are familiar with.

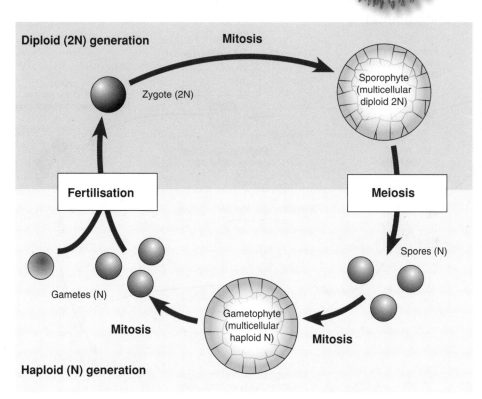

Diploid (2N) generation

Mitosis

Zygote (2N)

Sporophyte (multicellular diploid 2N)

Fertilisation

Meiosis

Spores (N)

Gametes (N)

Gametophyte (multicellular haploid N)

Mitosis

Mitosis

Haploid (N) generation

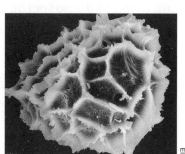
Dandelion pollen

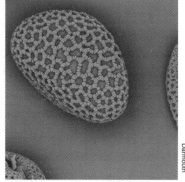
Lily pollen

1. Describe the alternation of generations in plants: _____

_____

_____

2. (a) Give an example of a sporophyte: _____

(b) Give an example of a gametophyte: _____

3. Complete the table below to show what produces each structure:

Structure	Spores	Gametes	Zygote
Produced by			
Process			

LINK 118 LINK 117 KNOW

117 Reproduction in Angiosperms

Key Idea: Angiosperms are flowering plants. The sporophyte produces flowers, which house the tiny gametophytes. Fertilisation of the gametes gives rise to the seed. Angiosperms are flowering seed plants. In seed plants, pollen is the vehicle that carries the male gametes to the female gametes. The leafy plant that bears the flowers represents the sporophyte generation of the life cycle. The flowers contain specialised male and female structures (anthers and ovules), in which the haploid male and female gametophytes are formed by meiosis.

▶ The pollen grain is the male gametophyte and the embryo sac is the female gametophyte. Each mature pollen grain contains two sperm nuclei and each mature embryo sac contains the egg and two polar nuclei.

▶ The typical life cycle of angiosperms (below) involves the formation of gametes (egg and sperm) from the haploid gametophytes, the fertilisation of the egg by a sperm cell to form the zygote, the production of fruit around the seed, and the germination of the seed and its growth by mitosis.

▶ Fertilisation in angiosperms is characterised by the double fertilisation event which produces a 2N zygote and 3N endosperm.

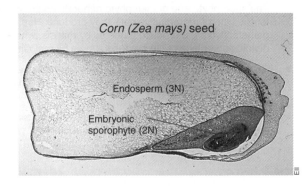

Corn (Zea mays) seed

Endosperm (3N)

Embryonic sporophyte (2N)

Life cycle of angiosperms (flowering plants)

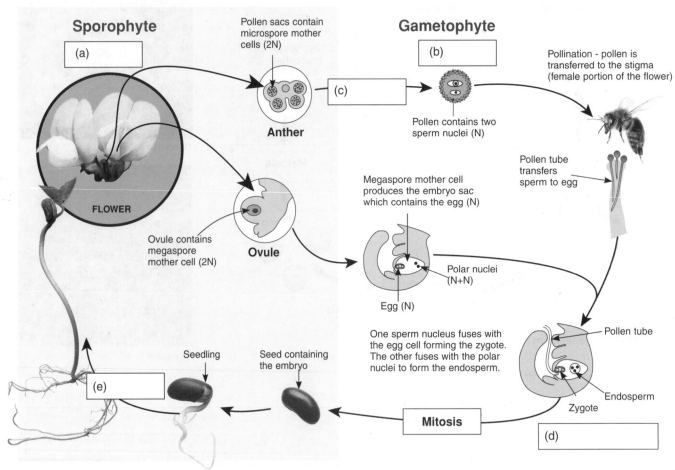

Sporophyte

(a)

FLOWER

Pollen sacs contain microspore mother cells (2N)

Anther

(c)

Ovule contains megaspore mother cell (2N)

Ovule

Gametophyte

(b)

Pollen contains two sperm nuclei (N)

Pollination - pollen is transferred to the stigma (female portion of the flower)

Pollen tube transfers sperm to egg

Megaspore mother cell produces the embryo sac which contains the egg (N)

Polar nuclei (N+N)

Egg (N)

One sperm nucleus fuses with the egg cell forming the zygote. The other fuses with the polar nuclei to form the endosperm.

Pollen tube

Endosperm

Zygote

(d)

Seedling

Seed containing the embryo

(e)

Mitosis

1. (a) - (e) Complete the diagram above using the labels *N, 2N, fertilisation, meiosis, mitosis*:

2. (a) In which part of a flowering plant do the male gametophytes develop? _____

   (b) In which part of a flowering plant do the female gametophytes develop? _____

3. Identify one way in which pollen is transferred to the stigma: _____

4. What cells contribute to the endosperm? _____

5. The endosperm is: haploid / diploid / triploid (circle the correct answer)

6. How do the sperm nuclei reach the egg cell? _____

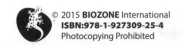
© 2015 **BIOZONE** International
ISBN:978-1-927309-25-4
Photocopying Prohibited

118 Pollination and Fertilisation

Key Idea: In plants, pollination is essential to ensure fertilisation and production of seeds.

Before fertilisation, the pollen (which contains the male gametes) must be transferred from the male anthers to the female stigma in pollination. Plants rarely self-pollinate. Most often the stigma of one plant receives pollen from other plants in cross pollination (pollination between different plants). Cross pollination is beneficial because it maximises variation in the offspring (reduces inbreeding). Adaptations to ensure cross-pollination include structural and physiological mechanisms associated with the flowers themselves, and reliance on wind and animal pollinators. After pollination, the sperm nuclei can enter the ovule and fertilise the egg. In angiosperms, there is a double fertilisation: one to produce the embryo and the other to produce the endosperm (the food store for the embryonic plant).

Pollen formation

Pollen forms in pollen sacs found within the anther. Each pollen sac contains cells called **microspore mother cells**. These cell undergo meiosis and produce four haploid **microspores**. Mitosis of these microspores forms the pollen grain (the male gametophyte). Each pollen grain contains a **generative cell**. After pollination, this cell will divide to produce two sperm cells.

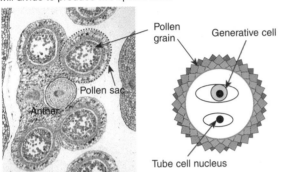

Pollen grain · Generative cell · Pollen sac · Anther · Tube cell nucleus

Embryo sac formation

Egg cells develop in the ovule. Each ovule contains a **megaspore mother cell**. Meiosis of the megaspore mother cell produces four haploid **megaspores**. One of these survives and undergoes mitosis, producing eight nuclei enclosed within an embryo sac. One nucleus located near the opening of the embryo sac forms the **egg cell**. Two other nuclei near the middle of the sac form the **polar nuclei**.

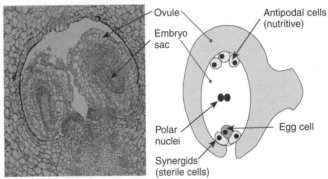

Ovule · Embryo sac · Antipodal cells (nutritive) · Polar nuclei · Egg cell · Synergids (sterile cells)

Mechanisms to ensure cross-pollination

Male willow catkin

An effective way of ensuring cross pollination is to have separate male and female plants. This occurs in about 6% of angiosperms including willows and holly.

Male flowers · Female flowers

Male and female flower on sweet gum

Other plants produce separate male and female flowers or cones on the same plant. They may develop at different times so pollen does not fertilise the same plant.

Tulip anthers and stigma

Some angiosperms have flowers that house both male and female structures. They can ensure cross pollination if the anthers and stigma mature at different times or are structurally isolated.

Germinating pollen grains

In many plants, pollen that lands on the stigma of the same plant will not germinate. This ensures that the egg cells are not fertilised by sperm from the same plant.

1. (a) What is the purpose of the microspore mother cell? _____

_____

(b) How many pollen grains arise from a microspore mother cell: _____

2. (a) What is the purpose of the megaspore mother cell? _____

_____

(b) How many egg cells arise from the megaspore mother cell? _____

3. What is the purpose of the generative cell: _____

4. Where does the pollen tube enter the ovule? _____

5. Explain why plants, in general, have evolved to limit self pollination (maximise cross pollination): _____

_____

_____

LINK 118 LINK 117 WEB 118 KNOW

Growth of the pollen tube and double fertilisation

Pollen grains are immature male gametophytes, formed by mitosis of haploid microspores within the pollen sac. Pollination is the actual transfer of the pollen from the anthers to the stigma. Pollen grains cannot move independently. They are usually carried by wind (**anemophily**) or animals (**entomophily**). After landing on the sticky stigma, the pollen grain is able to complete development, germinating and growing a pollen tube that extends down to the ovary. Directed by chemicals (usually calcium), the pollen tube enters the ovule through the micropyle, a small gap in the ovule. A **double fertilisation** takes place. One sperm nucleus fuses with the egg to form the zygote. A second sperm nucleus fuses with the two polar nuclei within the embryo sac to produce the endosperm tissue (3N). There are usually many ovules in an ovary, therefore many pollen grains (and fertilisations) are needed before the entire ovary can develop.

Different pollens are variable in shape and pattern, and genera can be easily distinguished on the basis of their distinctive pollen. This feature is exploited in the relatively new field of forensic botany; the tracing of a crime through botanical evidence. The species specific nature of pollen ensures that only genetically compatible plants will be fertilised. Some species, such as *Primula*, produce two pollen types, and this assists in cross pollination between different flower types.

SEM: *Primula* (primrose) pollen

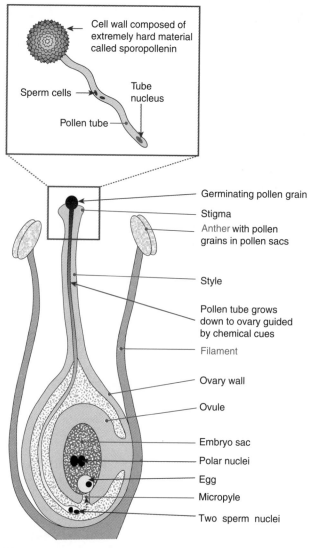

Cell wall composed of extremely hard material called sporopollenin

Sperm cells

Tube nucleus

Pollen tube

Germinating pollen grain

Stigma

Anther with pollen grains in pollen sacs

Style

Pollen tube grows down to ovary guided by chemical cues

Filament

Ovary wall

Ovule

Embryo sac

Polar nuclei

Egg

Micropyle

Two sperm nuclei

Stigma, style, ovary and ovule = pistil (female)
Filament and anther = stamen (male)

6. Name the main chemical responsible for pollen tube growth: _____

7. Identify three ways in which plants avoid self pollination:

   (a) _____

   (b) _____

   (c) _____

8. Distinguish clearly between **pollination** and **fertilisation**: _____

   _____

   _____

   _____

   _____

9. Describe the role of the double fertilisation in angiosperms: _____

   _____

   _____

10. In what way is the ovary shown in the diagram above not typical of most ovaries: _____

   _____

© 2015 **BIOZONE** International
ISBN: 978-1-927309-25-4
Photocopying Prohibited

119 Sucrose Concentration and Pollen Tube Growth

Key Idea: Once the pollen had reached the stigma it develops a tube through which the sperm cells will pass to the ovule. A concentration gradient guides the tube to its destination. The sugars produced by flowers act as a natural germinating compound for pollen tubes. Once the pollen reaches the pistil, the sugars present there stimulate the germination of the pollen tube. The sugar concentrations affect the germination rate and speed of pollen tube growth.

Aim:

To observe the effect of sucrose concentration on pollen tube germination and growth.

Method:

Five solutions were made containing 100 ppm borate (borate was added to prevent pollen grains bursting and to help initiate pollen germination) and 5% to 25% sucrose. Pollen samples from *Lawsonia inermis* (the henna tree) were sown on haemocytometer slides and irrigated with one of the sucrose solutions. Pollen grains were examined under a microscope and the percentage of grains germinated calculated after 1, 2, and 3 hours. The length of the pollen tubes was also measured.

Results:

Percentage germination and mean pollen tube length

Sucrose concentration	% pollen grains germinated	Mean pollen tube length / μm
0%	0	0
5%	36	512
10%	58	884
15%	92	1144
20%	86	1084
25%	58	762

S. Mondal and R. Ghanta Advances in Bioresearch 3:3 2012

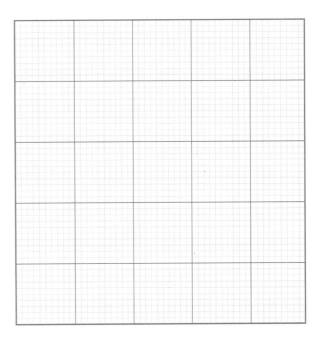

As well as measuring pollen tube length and the number and percentage of pollen grains germinating, the rate of growth of the pollen tubes was measured over three hours. The results are below:

Rate of pollen tube growth

Sucrose concentration	1 hour / μm	2 hours / μm	3 hours / μm
0%	0	0	0
5%	308	416	512
10%	414	688	884
15%	544	890	1144
20%	480	800	1084
25%	410	611	762

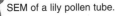

SEM of a lily pollen tube.

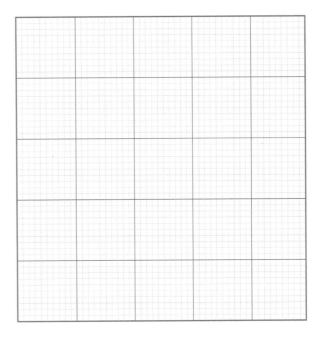

1. On the grid at the top of the page, draw a line graph of the results of the experiment (use a dual axis):

2. On the next grid, draw a line graph with a key to show pollen tube growth at 1, 2, and 3 hours in different sucrose solutions:

3. State the concentration at which:

   (a) The most pollen tubes germinated: _____

   (b) The longest pollen tube was produced: _____

4. What is the purpose of the borate in the sucrose solution? _____

120 Chapter Review

Summarise what you know about this topic under the headings provided. You can draw diagrams or mind maps, or write short notes. Use the images and hints to help you and refer back to the introduction to check the points covered:

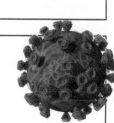

Eukaryotic and prokaryotic cells
HINT: Describe differences between prokaryotic and eukaryotic cells. Describe use of microscopy, including staining, to study cells.

Viruses:
HINT: Describe replication in bacteriophages and retroviruses

Eukaryotic cell cycle and division
HINT: Describe mitosis and meiosis

Sexual reproduction in mammals
HINT: Describe spermatogenesis and oogenesis. Describe the events in fertilisation.

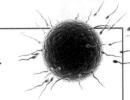

Sexual reproduction in plants
HINT: Describe the alternation of generations in plants and pollination and fertilisation in angiosperms.

121 KEY TERMS: Did You Get It?

1. (a) Label the cell cycle right with the following: G_1, G_2, M, S, cytokinesis, G_1 checkpoint, G_2 checkpoint, metaphase checkpoint.

   (b) Briefly describe what happens in each of the following phases:

   G_1: _____

   _____

   _____

   G_2: _____

   _____

   _____

   M
   phase: _____

   _____

   S phase: _____

   _____

2. (a) Identify the process occurring in the circled chromosomes right: _____

   (b) Does this occur during mitosis or meiosis? _____

   (c) At what stage of your answer in (b) does this occur? _____

3. Matching each term below to its definition, as identified by its preceding letter code:

cell cycle	A	The stage in the cell cycle between divisions.
cell wall	B	The phase of a cell cycle involving nuclear division in which the replicated chromosomes in a cell nucleus are separated into two identical sets.
cell division	C	Process by which a parent cell divides into two or more cells.
endosperm	D	A structural and functional part of the cell usually bound within its own membrane. Examples include the mitochondria and chloroplasts.
fertilisation	E	The changes that take place in a cell in the period between its formation as a product of cell division and its own subsequent division.
interphase	F	A non-cellular obligate intracellular parasite, requiring a living host to reproduce.
latency	G	A structure, present in plants and bacteria, which is found outside the plasma membrane and gives rigidity to the cell.
meiosis	H	The transfer of the male gametophyte from the anther to the stigma.
mitosis	I	Triploid nutritive tissue found in the seed of flowering plants.
organelle	J	The process of double nuclear division (reduction division) to produce four nuclei, each containing half the original number of chromosomes (haploid).
pollination	K	The union of two haploid gametes to form a diploid zygote.
virus	L	A feature of viral life cycles in which viral DNA is integrated into the host's genome and replicated along with it.

4. (a) Identify organelle 1: _____

   (b) The organelle in (a) is found in a plant cell / animal cell / both plant and animal cells (circle the correct answer).

   (c) Identify organelle 2: _____

   (d) The organelle in (c) is found in a plant / animal cell / plant and animal cell (circle the correct answer).

© 2015 **BIOZONE** International
ISBN: 978-1-927309-25-4
Photocopying Prohibited

Topic 3

Classification and Biodiversity

Key terms

adaptation

allopatric speciation

antimicrobial drug

binomial nomenclature

biodiversity

bioinformatics

biological species

class

conservation

diversity indices

DNA sequencing

domain

ecological niche

ecosystem services

ex-situ conservation

family

fitness

gel electrophoresis

genetic diversity

genotype

genus

in-situ conservation

kingdom

natural selection

order

peer review

phenotype

phylogenetic species

phylogeny

reproductive isolation

species

species diversity

species evenness

species richness

sympatric speciation

variation

3.1 Classification

Learning outcomes

☐ i Describe the biological classification of species with reference to the taxonomic hierarchy of domain, kingdom, phylum, class, order, family, genus, and species. — 122

☐ ii Give a definition of a biological species. Understand the limitations of this definition, e.g. for asexual or extinct organisms, and for species that interbreed to produce fertile hybrids. How else could we define species? — 124 125

☐ iii Understand and explain why it is often difficult to assign organisms to any one species, or to identify new species, e.g. in the case of cryptic species. — 123

☐ iv Understand and explain how gel electrophoresis can be used to distinguish between species and to determine evolutionary relationships (phylogenies). — 126 127

☐ v Understand the basis of DNA sequencing and bioinformatics and explain how they can be used to distinguish between species and to determine phylogenies. — 128-131

☐ vi Understand the role of scientific literature, peer review, and scientific conferences in validating new evidence supporting the accepted scientific theory of evolution. — 132

☐ vii Outline the evidence for a three domain classification system as an alternative to the five kingdom classification. Explain the role of the scientific community in validating this evidence. — 133-134

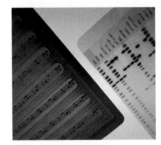
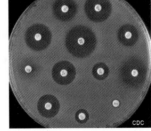

3.2 Natural selection

Learning outcomes

☐ i Describe how evolution can come about through natural selection acting on the natural variation in populations. Include reference to the sources of variation, the heritability of variation, and differential survival of the best adapted phenotypes. Know that adaptations are the result of natural selection and contribute to fitness. — 135 138 139

☐ ii Explain how organisms occupy niches according to their anatomical (structural), physiological, and behavioural adaptations of organisms to their environment. — 136 137

☐ iii Describe how species become reproductively isolated. Explain how reproductive isolation can lead to speciation in allopatric or sympatric populations. — 140-144

☐ iv Using examples, e.g. in bacteria and viruses, describe and explain the link between pathogen evolution and the development of antimicrobial drugs. — 145-1489

3.3 Biodiversity

Learning outcomes

☐ i Describe how biodiversity can be assessed at different scales, e.g. within a habitat at the species level using a diversity index, or within a species at the genetic level by quantifying the diversity of alleles in a population's gene pool. — 149-154

☐ ii Understand the reasons for loss of biodiversity and the role of human activity in this. Describe the ethical and economic reasons for maintaining biodiversity. — 155 156

☐ iii Explain the principles of *ex-situ* and *in-situ* conservation and the advantages and disadvantages associated with each method. — 157-159

122 Classification Systems

Key Idea: Organisms are named and assigned to taxa based on their shared characteristics and evolutionary relationships. Organisms are categorised into a hierarchical system of taxonomic groups (taxa) based on features they share that distinguish them from other taxa. The fundamental unit of classification is the **species**, and each member of a species is assigned a unique two part (binomial) name that identifies it. Classification systems are nested, so that with increasing taxonomic rank, related taxa at one hierarchical level are combined into more inclusive taxa at the next higher level.

Naming an organism: genus and species

Most organisms have a common name as well a scientific name. Common names may change from place to place as people from different areas name organisms differently based on both language and custom. Scientifically, every organism is given a classification that reflects its known lineage (i.e. its evolutionary history). The last two (and most specific) parts of that lineage are the **genus** and **species** names. Together these are called the scientific name and every species has its own. This two-part naming system is called **binomial nomenclature**. When typed the name is always *italicised*. If handwritten, it should be <u>underlined</u>.

What are subspecies?

A monotypic species has no distinct populations but, for some species, scientists recognise morphologically and genetically distinct subspecies (in animals) or varieties (in plants, algae, and fungi). Subspecies could interbreed but do not generally do so because they are isolated by geography or habitat (e.g. subspecies of tiger). Subspecies are identified by a third name after the species name (but never with the subspecies name alone). The type specimen carries the same specific and subspecific name. Species with defined subspecies are called polytypic species.

The animal *Rangifer tarandus* is known as caribou in North America, but as reindeer in Europe. The scientific name is unambiguous.

The Bengal tiger *Panthera tigris tigris* (India)   The Siberian tiger *Panthera tigris altaica* (Russia)

1. Complete the classification for humans (*Homo sapiens*) in the table below using the **principal taxa** of classification. Note that the taxonomic rank of Domain is not generally included within a five kingdom system, so it has been provided for you. Use the classification of the European hedgehog (opposite) and activity 133 to help you.

Taxonomic rank	Human classification
1. Domain	Eukarya
2. _____	_____
3. _____	_____
4. _____	_____
5. _____	_____
6. _____	_____
7. _____	_____
8. _____	_____

2. Construct an acronym or mnemonic to help you remember the principal taxonomic groupings (KPCOFGS):

_____

_____

3. Which is the type specimen in the tiger examples above?_____

4. (a) What is the two part naming system for classifying organisms called?_____

   (b) What are the two parts of the name? _____

5. What are the advantages of a scientific name (as opposed to a common name)? _____

_____

_____

© 2015 **BIOZONE** International
ISBN:978-1-927309-25-4
Photocopying Prohibited

Classification of the European hedgehog

The classification for the **European hedgehog** is described below to show the levels that can be used in classifying an organism. Not all possible subdivisions have been shown here (taxa such as **sub-family** often appear). The only natural category is the **species**, which may be separated into **sub-species**, based on molecular and morphological data.

Kingdom: **Animalia**
Animals; one of five kingdoms

Phylum: **Chordata**
Animals with a notochord (supporting rod of cells along the upper surface)
tunicates, salps, lancelets, and vertebrates

23 other phyla

Sub-phylum: **Vertebrata**
Animals with backbones
fish, amphibians, reptiles, birds, mammals

Class: **Mammalia**
Animals that suckle their young on milk from mammary glands
placentals, marsupials, monotremes

Infra-class: **Eutheria or Placentals**
Mammals whose young develop for some time in the female's reproductive tract gaining nourishment from a placenta
placental mammals

Order: **Eulipotyphla**
The insectivore-type mammals. Once part of the now abandoned order Insectivora, the order also includes shrews, moles, desmans, and solenodons.

20 other orders

Family: **Erinaceidae**
Comprises two subfamilies: the true or spiny hedgehogs and the moonrats (gymnures). Representatives in the family include the Ethiopian hedgehog, desert hedgehog, and the moonrats. The molecular evidence supports the Eulipotyphla being a monophyletic group (a common ancestor and all its descendants) but other classifications are common, e.g. sometimes the order is given as Erinaceomorpha with Erinaceidae as its only family.

4 other families

Genus: *Erinaceus*
One of twelve genera in this family. The genus *Erinaceus* includes four species.

11 other genera

Species: *europaeus*
The European hedgehog. Among the largest of the spiny hedgehogs. Characterised by a dense covering of spines on the back, the presence of a big toe (hallus) and 36 teeth.

3 other species

The advent of DNA sequencing and other molecular techniques for classification has resulted in the reclassification of many species. There is now considerable debate over the classification of species at almost all levels of classification. The now-defunct order, Insectivora, is one example. This order included a range of mammals with unspecialised features. The order was abandoned in 1956 but persisted (and still persists) in many textbooks. Over the years, families were moved out, merged, split apart again and reformed in other ways based on new evidence or interpretations. Do not be surprised if you see more than one classification for hedgehogs (or any other organism for that matter).

European hedgehog
Erinaceus europaeus

123 How Do We Assign Species?

Key Idea: Assigning species on the basis of appearance alone can be inaccurate. Molecular analysis allows distinct species with a similar appearance to be distinguished.

Humans have always tried to identify and classify organisms. Traditional classifications were based simply on similarities in morphology, (appearance) but modern taxonomy relies heavily on biochemical data as well in an attempt to classify species on the basis of their evolutionary relationships. Assigning an organism to a particular species is not a trivial matter. Organisms within a single species may have very different appearances and, conversely, different species may be morphologically indistinguishable. How we identify and define species has ecological and economic implications because we cannot conserve what we cannot recognise.

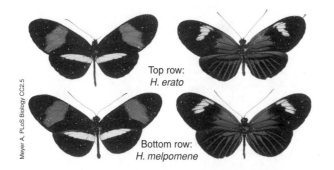

Top row:
H. erato

Bottom row:
H. melpomene

Meyer A, PLoS Biology CC2.5

Different species may look the same

Assigning species based on morphology alone can lead to mis-classification. Some organisms may be morphologically indistinguishable but DNA analysis or a close examination of their biology may prove them to be different species. DNA analysis is becoming increasingly important in distinguishing species.

Example: The butterfly genus *Heliconius* comprises 39 species, many of which mimic each others' patterns and colours. *Heliconius* is a **species complex**, a group of closely related or sibling species with similar appearances and unclear boundaries between them. Their appearance varies with geographical location, but different species often adopt a similar pattern in the same location (left) making species determination based on appearance alone extremely difficult.

African bush elephant
Loxodonta africana
Yathin S Krishnappa CC3.0

African forest elephant
Loxodonta cyclotis
Thomas Breuer cc2.5

Molecular analysis can distinguish cryptic species

DNA variation occurs within species as well as between species, so scientists must determine what level of variation is acceptable within a species before a new species classification is made. If such boundaries were not set, every molecular variation observed would result in the classification of a new species.

Example: Molecular studies have been important in identifying **cryptic species**, i.e. two or more distinct species disguised under one species name. The African bush elephant and the African forest elephant were once considered subspecies, but recent genetic analysis has confirmed they are separate species, which diverged from each other 2-7 million years ago. Analysis of morphological differences, including skull anatomy, supports this.

Conservation and species assignment

The recognition of species complexes and cryptic species has important implications to our estimates of biodiversity, and affects decisions made in species conservation and in the management of economically important species (including pests and medically important organisms). DNA analyses indicate that cryptic species are far more common than previously thought, providing a strong argument for whole ecosystem (*in-situ*) management of biodiversity.

Example: The fly agaric mushroom (*Amanita muscaria*, left) comprises several cryptic species. Genetic analyses in 2006 and 2008 showed at least four groups or clades that are genetically distinct enough to be considered separate species. The varieties identified left include the type specimen (far left) and two of the subspecies now considered to be separate species.

Tony Willis CC3.0   Ron Pastorino CC3.0   The High Fin Sperm Whale CC3.0

A. muscaria muscaria   *Amanita m. var. formosa*   *Amanita m. var. guessowii*

1. In what way have traditional methods of classification based on morphology been inadequate? _____

_____

_____

_____

2. What are the implications of species complexes and cryptic species in conservation? _____

_____

_____

124 The Biological Species Concept

Key Idea: A biological species is defined by the ability of its members to interbreed and produce fertile offspring.

One of the best recognised definitions of a biological species is as "*a group of actually or potentially interbreeding natural populations that is reproductively isolated from other such groups*" (Ernst Mayr). However, the concept of a biological species is not always simple to apply. The concept is difficult to apply to fossil species and to organisms that reproduce asexually. The occurrence of cryptic species and closely related species that interbreed to produce fertile hybrids (e.g. species of *Canis*), indicate that the boundaries of a species **gene pool** (i.e. all the genes in a population) can be unclear.

Geographical distribution of selected *Canis species*

The global distribution of most of the species of *Canis* (dogs and wolves) is shown on the map, right. The grey wolf inhabits the forests of North America, northern Europe, and Siberia. The red wolf and Mexican wolf (original distributions shown) were once distributed more widely, but are now extinct in the wild except for reintroduction efforts. In contrast, the coyote has expanded its original range and is now found throughout North and Central America. The range of the three jackal species overlap in the open savannah of Eastern Africa. The dingo is distributed throughout the Australian continent. Distribution of the domesticated dog is global as a result of the spread of human culture. The dog has been able to interbreed with all other members of the genus listed here to form fertile hybrids.

Interbreeding between *Canis* species

The *Canis* species illustrate problems with the traditional species concept. The domesticated dog is able to breed with other members of the same genus to produce fertile hybrids. Red wolves, grey wolves, Mexican wolves, and coyotes are all capable of interbreeding to produce fertile hybrids. Red wolves are very rare, and it is possible that hybridisation with coyotes has been a factor in their decline. By contrast, the ranges of the three distinct species of jackal overlap in the Serengeti of Eastern Africa. These animals are highly territorial, but simply ignore members of the other jackal species and no interbreeding takes place.

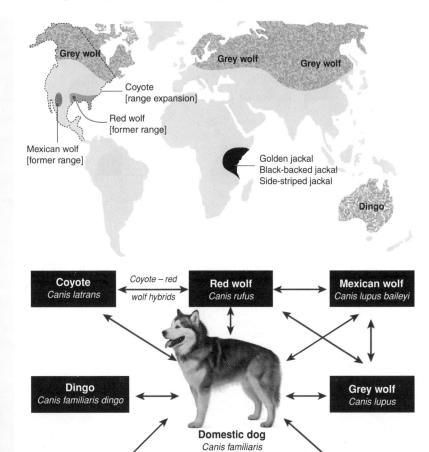

1. What type of barrier prevents interbreeding between the three jackal species? _____

2. Describe the barrier preventing interbreeding between the dingo and other *Canis* species (apart from the dog):

   _____

3. Describe a possible contributing factor to the occurrence of interbreeding between the coyote and red wolf:

   _____

4. The grey wolf is a widely distributed species. Explain why the North American and the northern European and Siberian populations are considered to be the same species:

   _____

   _____

5. Explain what you understand by the term species, identifying examples where the definition is problematic:

   _____

   _____

   _____

LINK 125   LINK 122   WEB 124   KNOW

125 The Phylogenetic Species Concept

Key Idea: Phylogenetic species are determined on the basis of shared derived characters.

For situations in which the biological species concept is difficult to apply, the **phylogenetic species concept** (PSC) can be useful. It does not rely on the criterion of successful interbreeding and can be applied to organisms that reproduce asexually and to extinct organisms. Phylogenetic species are defined by their shared evolutionary history (phylogeny), which is determined on the basis of **shared derived characters**. These are characters that evolved in the ancestor of a group

and are present in all of its descendents (the group, or clade, is therefore monophyletic, meaning of one phylogeny). They may be morphological, especially for higher taxonomic ranks, or biochemical (e.g. DNA differences). The PSC defines a species as the smallest group that all share a derived character state. It is less restrictive than the biological species concept (BSC) because reproductive isolation is not a criterion for assigning species. However, it can result in species being divided into smaller and smaller groups simply because differences between them can be detected.

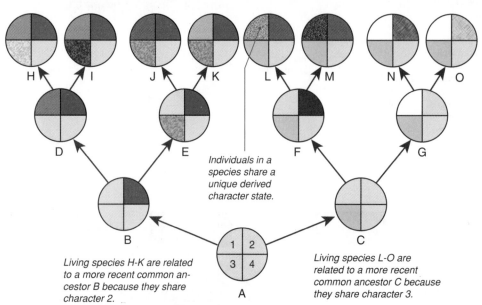

Individuals in a species share a unique derived character state.

Living species H-K are related to a more recent common ancestor B because they share character 2.

Living species L-O are related to a more recent common ancestor C because they share character 3.

This simplified phylogenetic tree (left) traces four characters among 15 species (8 present and 7 ancestral). The 8 modern species (species H-O) share a character (4) derived from a distant common ancestor (A). Although the primitive character unites all 8 species, the branching of the tree is based on characters derived from the ancestral ones. Classification on the basis of shared derived characters defines the species as the smallest group diagnosable by a unique combination of characters. If large numbers of characters are included in the analysis, it is easy to see how this method results in a proliferation of species that may or may not be meaningful. Under the PSC model, there are no subspecies; either a population is a phylogenetic species or it is not taxonomically distinguishable.

Tree sparrows (*P. montanus*) are ~10% smaller than the similar house sparrow but the two species hybridise freely.

House sparrows (*P. domesticus*) are widespread with many intermediate "subspecies" of unknown status.

Mallards are infamous for their ability to hybridise freely with a large number of other duck "species".

True sparrows all belong to the genus *Passer*. There are a large number of species distinguished on the basis of song, plumage, and size. A vestigial dorsal outer primary feather and an extra bone in the tongue are ancestral characters. Many populations are not good biological species in that they hybridise freely to produce fertile offspring. A similar situation exists within the genus *Anas* of dabbling ducks (which includes the mallards). Many birds are best described using the PSC rather than the BSC.

1. (a) Explain the basis by which species are assigned under the PSC: _____

_____

_____

(b) Describe one problem with the use of the PSC: _____

_____

(c) Describe situations where the use of the PSC might be more appropriate than the BSC: _____

_____

_____

2. Suggest how genetic techniques could be used to clarify the phylogeny of a cluster of related phylogenetic species:

_____

_____

126 Gel Electrophoresis

Key Idea: Gel electrophoresis is used to separate DNA fragments on the basis of size.

DNA can be loaded onto an electrophoresis gel and separated by size. DNA has an overall negative charge, so when an electrical current is run through a gel, the DNA moves towards the positive electrode. The rate at which the DNA molecules move through the gel depends primarily on their size and the strength of the electric field. The gel they move through is full of pores (holes). Smaller DNA molecules move through the pores more quickly than larger ones. At the end of the process, the DNA molecules can be stained and visualised as a series of bands. Each band contains DNA molecules of a particular size. The bands furthest from the start of the gel contain the smallest DNA fragments.

Analysing DNA using gel electrophoresis

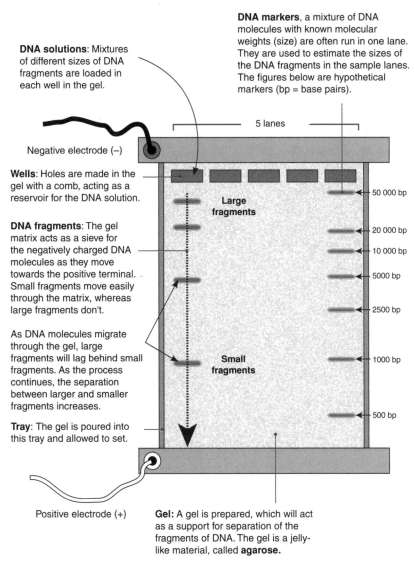

DNA solutions: Mixtures of different sizes of DNA fragments are loaded in each well in the gel.

DNA markers, a mixture of DNA molecules with known molecular weights (size) are often run in one lane. They are used to estimate the sizes of the DNA fragments in the sample lanes. The figures below are hypothetical markers (bp = base pairs).

5 lanes

Negative electrode (−)

Wells: Holes are made in the gel with a comb, acting as a reservoir for the DNA solution.

Large fragments

DNA fragments: The gel matrix acts as a sieve for the negatively charged DNA molecules as they move towards the positive terminal. Small fragments move easily through the matrix, whereas large fragments don't.

As DNA molecules migrate through the gel, large fragments will lag behind small fragments. As the process continues, the separation between larger and smaller fragments increases.

Small fragments

Tray: The gel is poured into this tray and allowed to set.

50 000 bp
20 000 bp
10 000 bp
5000 bp
2500 bp
1000 bp
500 bp

Positive electrode (+)

Gel: A gel is prepared, which will act as a support for separation of the fragments of DNA. The gel is a jelly-like material, called **agarose.**

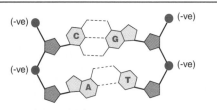

DNA is **negatively charged** because the phosphates (blue) that form part of the backbone of a DNA molecule have a negative charge.

Steps in the process of gel electrophoresis of DNA

1. A tray is prepared to hold the gel matrix.

2. A gel comb is used to create holes in the gel. The gel comb is placed in the tray.

3. Agarose gel powder is mixed with a buffer solution (this stabilises the DNA). The solution is heated until dissolved and poured into the tray and allowed to cool.

4. The gel tray is placed in an electrophoresis chamber and the chamber is filled with buffer, covering the gel. This allows the electric current from electrodes at either end of the gel to flow through the gel.

5. DNA samples are mixed with a "loading dye" to make the DNA sample visible. The dye also contains glycerol or sucrose to make the DNA sample heavy so that it will sink to the bottom of the well.

6. The gel is covered, electrodes are attached to a power supply and turned on.

7. When the dye marker has moved through the gel, the current is turned off and the gel is removed from the tray.

8. DNA molecules are made visible by staining the gel with **methylene blue** or ethidium bromide which binds to DNA and will fluoresce in UV light.

1. What is the purpose of gel electrophoresis? _____

_____

_____

2. Describe the two forces that control the speed at which fragments pass through the gel:

(a) _____

(b) _____

3. Why do the smallest fragments travel through the gel the fastest? _____

_____

_____

© 2015 **BIOZONE** International
ISBN: 978-1-927309-25-4
Photocopying Prohibited

LINK
130
LINK
128
WEB
126
KNOW

127 The Principles of DNA Sequencing

Key Idea: DNA sequencing techniques are used to determine the nucleotide (base) sequence of DNA.

The Sanger method (below) is a manual method for determining a DNA sequence. It uses modified nucleotides, which prematurely stop DNA replication when they are incorporated into the nucleotide sequence. Different lengths of DNA are produced and these can be put in order to reveal the original sequence. Four separate reactions are run, each containing a modified nucleotide mixed with

its normal counterpart, as well as the three other normal nucleotides. When a modified nucleotide is added to the growing complementary DNA, synthesis stops. The fragments of DNA produced from the four reactions are separated by electrophoresis and analysed by autoradiography to determine the DNA sequence. For large scale genome analyses, Sanger sequencing has largely been replaced by automated (so-called Next-Gen) sequencing methods, but it is still widely used for small scale projects.

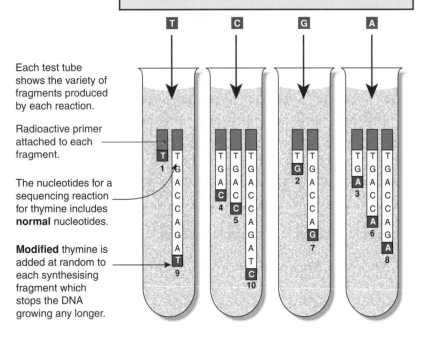

1% modified T, C, G, or A nucleotides (dideoxyribonucleic acids) are added to each reaction vessel. Only one kind of modified nucleotide is added per reaction vessel to cause termination of replication at random T, C, G, or A sites.

Each test tube shows the variety of fragments produced by each reaction.

Radioactive primer attached to each fragment.

The nucleotides for a sequencing reaction for thymine includes **normal** nucleotides.

Modified thymine is added at random to each synthesising fragment which stops the DNA growing any longer.

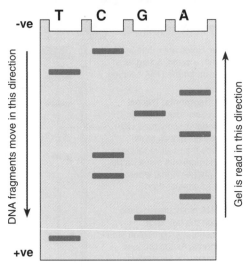

The fragments are placed on an electrophoresis gel to separate them so they can be read.

DNA fragments move in this direction

Gel is read in this direction

1. (a) In the Sanger method, what type of molecule is added to stop replication? _____

   (b) Analyse the gel diagram, above right, and write the sequence of the bands as they would appear in the DNA:

   _____

   (c) On the diagram circle the shortest fragment:

   (d) Write the sequence of the copied DNA: _____

   (e) Write the sequence of the original DNA: _____

2. Why must this method of DNA sequencing use four separate reaction vessels? _____

   _____

   _____

   _____

3. Why is only 1% of the reaction mix modified DNA? _____

   _____

   _____

   _____

   _____

© 2015 **BIOZONE** International
ISBN:978-1-927309-25-4
Photocopying Prohibited

128 Distinguishing Species by Gel Electrophoresis

Key Idea: The banding pattern on an electrophoresis gel can give information about genetic variation and relationships.

Once made, an electrophoresis gel must be interpreted. If a specific DNA base sequence was being investigated, then the band pattern can be used to determine the DNA sequence and the protein that it encoded. Alternatively, depending on how the original DNA was treated, the banding pattern may be used as a profile for a species or individual. Commonly, the gene for cytochrome oxidase I (COXI), a mitochondrial protein, is used to distinguish animal species. The genetic information from this gene is both large enough to measure differences between species and small enough to have the differences make sense (i.e. the differences occur in small regions and aren't hugely varied).

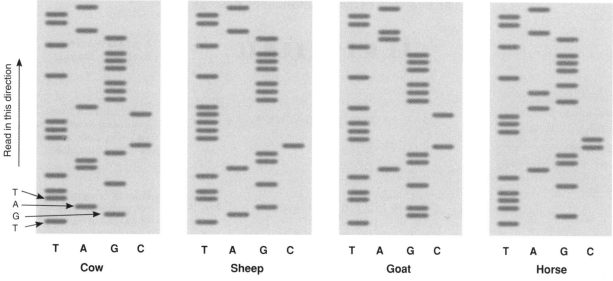

Read in this direction

T
A
G
T

| T A G C | T A G C | T A G C | T A G C |
| Cow | Sheep | Goat | Horse |

1. For each of the species above:

   (a) Determine the sequence of **synthesised DNA** in the gel in the photographs above. The synthesised DNA is what is visible on the gel. It is complementary to the sample DNA.
   (b) Convert it to the complementary sequence of the sample DNA. This is the DNA that is being investigated.

   Cow: **synthesised DNA**: _____

   sample DNA: _____

   Sheep: **synthesised DNA**: _____

   sample DNA: _____

   Goat: **synthesised DNA**: _____

   sample DNA: _____

   Horse: **synthesised DNA**: _____

   sample DNA: _____

   Based on the number of differences in the DNA sequences:

   (c) Identify the two species that are most closely related: _____

   (d) Identify the two species that are the least closely related: _____

   Calibration A   B   C   D   E

2. Determine the relatedness of each individual (A-E) using each banding pattern on the set of DNA profiles (left). When you have done this, complete the phylogenetic tree by adding the letter of each individual.

LINK
127

KNOW

129 Bioinformatics

Key Idea: Bioinformatics is the science of collecting, storing and analysing biological data using computer science.

Bioinformatics involves the collection, analysis, and storage of biochemical information (e.g. DNA sequences) using computer science and mathematics. The advancement of techniques in molecular biology is providing increasingly large amounts of information about the genetic makeup of organisms. Bioinformatics allows this information to be stored in databases where it can be easily retrieved, analysed, and compared. Comparison of DNA or protein sequences between species enables researchers to investigate and better understand their evolutionary relationships.

An overview of the bioinformatics process

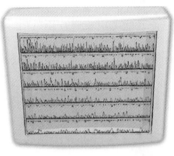

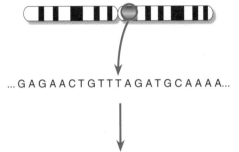

A gene of interested is selected for analysis.

...G A G A A C T G T T T A G A T G C A A A A...

High throughput 'Next-Gen' sequencing technologies allow the DNA sequence of the gene to be quickly determined.

Organism 1 ...G A G A A C T G T T T A G A T G C A A A A..

Organism 2 ...G A G A T C T G T G T A G A T G C A G A A..

Organism 3 ...G A G T T C T G T G T C G A T G C A G A A..

Organism 4 ...G A G T T C T G T T T C G A T G C A G A G..

Powerful computer software can quickly compare the DNA sequences of many organisms. Commonalities and differences in the DNA sequence can help to determine the evolutionary relationships of organisms. The blue boxes indicate differences in the DNA sequences.

Once sequence comparisons have been made, the evolutionary relationships can be displayed as a phylogenetic tree. The example (right) shows the evolutionary relationships of the whales to some other land mammals.

Bioinformatics has played an important role in determining the origin of whales and their transition from a terrestrial (land) form to a fully aquatic form. This phylogenetic tree was determined by comparing retropositional events in whales and some of their closest relatives. Retroposons are repetitive DNA fragments that are inserted into chromosomes after they have been reverse transcribed from a mRNA molecule. Retroposons and their locations are predictable and stable, so they make reliable markers for determining species relationships. If two species have the same retroposons in the same location, they probably share a common ancestor.

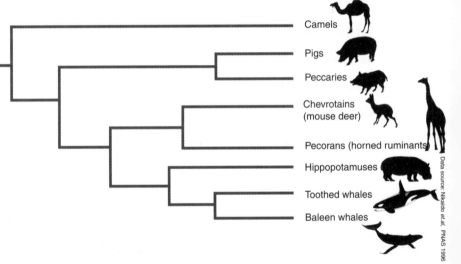

Camels
Pigs
Peccaries
Chevrotains (mouse deer)
Pecorans (horned ruminants)
Hippopotamuses
Toothed whales
Baleen whales

Data source: Nikaido et al. PNAS 1996

1. How has bioinformatics helped scientists determine the evolutionary relationship of organisms? _____

_____

_____

2. The diagram above shows the relatedness of several mammals as determined by DNA sequencing of 10 genes:

(a) Which land mammal are whales most related to? _____

(b) Mark with an arrow on the diagram above where whales and the organism in (a) last shared a common ancestor.

(c) Pigs were once considered to the most closely related land ancestor to the whales. Use the phylogenetic tree above to describe the currently accepted relationship.

_____

_____

© 2015 **BIOZONE** International
ISBN:978-1-927309-25-4
Photocopying Prohibited

130 Using DNA Probes

Key Idea: DNA probes use attached markers (tags) to identify the presence and location of individual genes.

A DNA probe is a single stranded DNA sequence, with a base sequence that is complementary to a gene of interest. DNA probes target specific DNA sequences so they can be used to determine whether a person has a gene for a specific genetic disease, or to construct a gene map of a chromosome. DNA probes have either a radioactive label (e.g. ^{32}P) or a fluorescent dye so that they can be visualised on an electrophoresis gel or X-ray film.

Making and using a DNA probe

1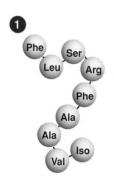

The protein product of a gene is isolated and its amino acid sequence is determined.

2 A tag is added. This can be one of two types:
Fluorescent dye: Shows up as a fluorescent band when exposed to ultraviolet light.

Radioactive tag: Shows up as a dark band when exposed to X-ray film.

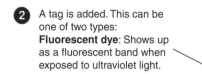

ATTTTT

The DNA sequence for the protein product is identified from the amino acid sequence. The DNA sequence is artificially manufactured.

3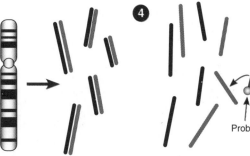

The DNA sequence being probed is cut into fragments using restriction enzymes.

4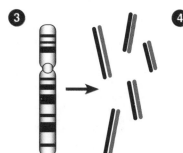

Probe

The DNA fragments are denatured, forming single stranded DNA. The probe is added to the DNA fragments.

5 If a complementary sequence is present, the probe will bind to it by base pairing.

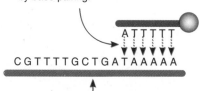

ATTTTT
CGTTTTGCTGATAAAAA

Target DNA strand (contains the complementary sequence to that of the probe).

6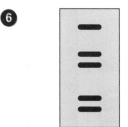

The DNA fragments are run on an electrophoresis gel. The fragments are separated by size.

7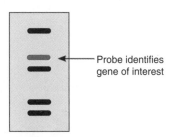

Probe identifies gene of interest

The gel is viewed by fluorescent light or on X-ray film (depending on the type of probe used). If the probe has bound to a gene, the tag makes it visible.

1. What is the purpose of a DNA probe? _____

2. Explain why a DNA probe can be used to identify a gene or DNA sequence: _____

3. Why does the DNA have to be denatured before adding the probe? _____

4. How is the presence of a specific DNA sequence or gene visualised? _____

131 Investigating Genetic Diversity

Key Idea: Genetic analysis of springtails in Taylor Valley has been able to separate morphologically cryptic species.

Genetic analysis is now widely used to investigate dispersal and divergence in all kinds of species. **Springtails** are tiny arthropods and have a limited capacity to move between locations. For this reason, they are good candidates for studying evolutionary phenomena. Researchers wanted to investigate the genetic relatedness of springtails in a Dry Valley in Antarctica. Results of a mtDNA study show two distinct genetic 'types' of springtail in Taylor Valley (see map, blue and white squares below). The two types have different DNA bases at a number of positions in a mitochondrial gene.

They also coexist in an area of **sympatry** in the middle of Taylor Valley. The results of the research are summarised on the following page. It shows an order of separation based on the genetic differences between the two types (TV1-14) compared with other populations of the same species (from Cape Evans, Cape Royds, and Beaufort Is). One other Antarctic species of springtail (*Biscoia sudpolaris)* is included on the diagram as an 'outgroup' (reference point). The genetic difference between populations is indicated by the distance to the 'branching point'. Groups that branch apart early in the tree are more different genetically than groups that branch later.

The springtail *Gomphiocephalus hodgsoni* (above) is a small arthropod, just over 1 mm long. It occupies the Dry Valleys region of Antarctica, particularly in Taylor Valley (below).

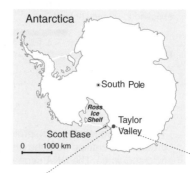

Sampling sites (below):
A total of 14 sampling sites was used to build up a picture of the genetic diversity of springtails in an area of Taylor Valley. They were named TV1 through TV14 (TV = Taylor Valley). Bluesquares represent one genetic 'type' of springtail, while white squares represent another.

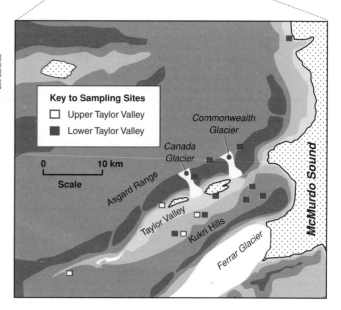

Taylor Valley (above) is one of the Dry Valleys in Antarctica, and is clear of snow virtually the whole year round. Any snow that falls in it soon melts as the dark rock surface heats up in the sun.

The process of DNA analysis of springtails:

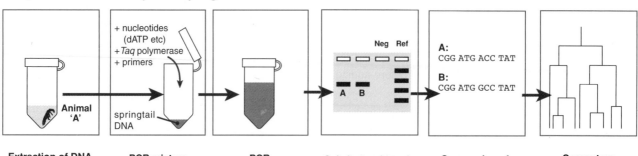

Extraction of DNA	**PCR mixture**	**PCR**	**Gel electrophoresis**	**Sequencing of**	**Computers**
Proteinase enzyme dissolves the tissues of the springtail to release DNA	Primers anneal to the start and end of the gene in the mitochondrial DNA	DNA amplification 92°C, 45°C, 72°C 45 cycles	of PCR product	PCR products	**calculate** relationships between springtail DNA

Source: Many thanks to **Liam Nolan**, teacher at Tauranga Girls' College, for supplying the information for these pages. Liam studied with the Centre for Biodiversity and Ecology Research (University of Waikato, Hamilton, New Zealand), whilst the recipient of a study award from the NZ Ministry of Education.

KNOW

Genetic relationship between samples of springtail *Gomphiocephalus hodgsoni* in Taylor Valley, Antarctica

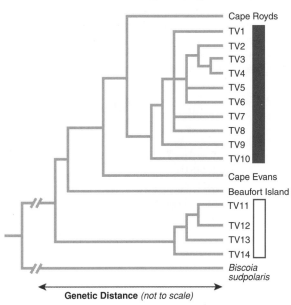

Cape Royds
TV1
TV2
TV3
TV4
TV5
TV6
TV7
TV8
TV9
TV10
Cape Evans
Beaufort Island
TV11
TV12
TV13
TV14
Biscoia sudpolaris

← **Genetic Distance** *(not to scale)* →

Mosses (right) are the tallest plants in Antarctica. They provide ideal habitats for springtails. Although springtails have antifreeze (glycerol) in their blood, they are still vulnerable to freezing. Antarctic springtails do not possess the proteins that some Antarctic fish have to help them avoid freezing.

Burkhard Budel

This photo taken in **Taylor Valley** (left) shows an ephemeral stream (it dries up at certain times of the year) emerging from one of the many "hanging glaciers" that line the margins of the valley. Such streams provide the moisture essential for springtails to survive amongst rocks, moss, lichen, and algae.

Leo Sanchez

1. Study the diagram of genetic relationships between samples of springtails (above). Describe what you notice about the branching point of the populations from the upper (TV11-14) and lower (TV1-10) Taylor Valley:

_____

_____

2. Studies of the enzymes from the two 'types' of springtails indicate that the springtails do not interbreed. Explain why this is significant:

_____

_____

_____

3. Springtails cannot fly and in Antarctica quickly dry out and die if they are blown by the wind. Discuss the significance of these two features for gene flow between populations:

_____

_____

_____

_____

4. Taylor Valley was once (thousands of years ago) covered in ice, with the only habitats available for springtails being the mountain tops lining both sides of the valley. Explain how this, together with low dispersal rates and small population size, could result in the formation of two species from one original species of springtail:

_____

_____

_____

_____

_____

_____

_____

_____

132 Validating New Evidence

Key Idea: Peer review of scientific data is used to verify the accuracy and validity of new scientific evidence.

Scientists present their research during conferences and in scientific journals. This enables information to be shared with others and provides an opportunity for the scientific community to review and validate new research. Before a scientific article can be accepted for publication in a peer reviewed journal, it is reviewed by experts in the field of study.

The process ensures that only research of a high quality is published and aims to prevent the publishing of substandard or falsified research. A double blind review of the research, in which the author and reviewer are anonymous, prevents an opportunity for the process to be manipulated or influenced by either, and ensures the paper is reviewed on its content only. Such reviews have been important in assessing and validating new data to support Darwin's theory of evolution.

The review process

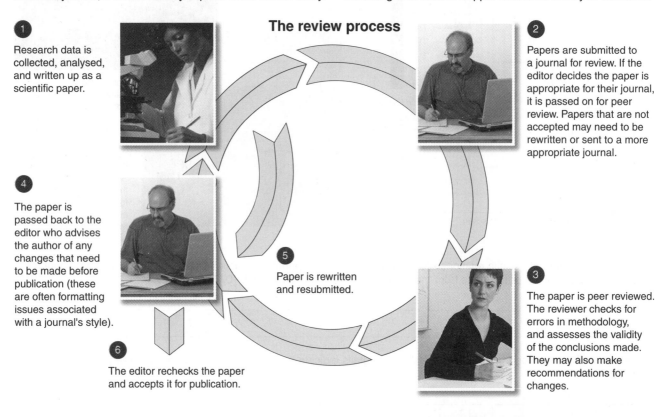

1. Research data is collected, analysed, and written up as a scientific paper.

2. Papers are submitted to a journal for review. If the editor decides the paper is appropriate for their journal, it is passed on for peer review. Papers that are not accepted may need to be rewritten or sent to a more appropriate journal.

3. The paper is peer reviewed. The reviewer checks for errors in methodology, and assesses the validity of the conclusions made. They may also make recommendations for changes.

4. The paper is passed back to the editor who advises the author of any changes that need to be made before publication (these are often formatting issues associated with a journal's style).

5. Paper is rewritten and resubmitted.

6. The editor rechecks the paper and accepts it for publication.

Peter and Rosemary Grant, both Professors Emeritus at Princeton University, have spent more than four decades researching and documenting evolutionary change in the finches of the Galápagos. Their many peer reviewed publications, which include a recent book, contribute to the body of data validating the fundamental principles of Darwin's theory of evolution by natural selection.

There is no doubt about the fact of evolution, because genetic change in populations is well documented, but the work of scientists in many different scientific disciplines continues to develop our understanding of the mechanisms by which evolutionary change occurs.

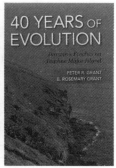

Princeton University, Office of Communications, Denise Applewhite (2005)

1. Why is the peer review process so important when publishing scientific research? _____

_____

_____

2. Information presented to the public (e.g. in the media or the internet) is not always peer reviewed. What problems could be associated with disseminating information that has not been through the peer review process?

_____

_____

3. How has the peer review process been important in validating Darwin's theory of evolution by natural selection? _____

_____

_____

© 2015 **BIOZONE** International
ISBN:978-1-927309-25-4
Photocopying Prohibited

133 Classification Systems: The Old and The New

Key Idea: The classification of life into specific groups, or taxa, is constantly being updated in light of new information. Taxonomy is the science of classification and, like all science, is constantly changing as new information is discovered. With the advent of DNA sequencing technology, scientists began to analyse the genomes of many bacteria. In 1996, the results of a scientific collaboration examining DNA evidence confirmed that life comprises three major evolutionary lineages (domains) and not two as was the convention. The recognised lineages are the Bacteria, the Eukarya, and the Archaea. The new classification better reflects the evolutionary history of life on Earth. Molecular evidence has since led to the reclassification of many other taxa, including birds, reptiles, many plants, and primates.

A changing view of classification

Before DNA sequencing, taxonomists divided life into five kingdoms based mainly on visible characteristics. The five kingdom system places all prokaryotes in one kingdom, with protoctists, fungi, plants, and animals being the other four. This system is dated and seriously at odds with molecular evidence. In particular, it does not fairly represent the diversity or evolutionary history of the prokaryotic organisms or unicellular eukaryotes.

A new view of the world

In 1996, scientists deciphered the full DNA sequence of the thermophilic bacterium *Methanococcus jannaschii*. The data supported the hypothesis of three major evolutionary lineages and gave rise to a modified six kingdom classification. This was further revised to the current three domain system (below), which more properly represents the phylogeny of life on Earth.

Whittaker 1969 **Five kingdoms**	Woese *et al.* 1977 **Six kingdoms**	Woese *et al.* 1990 **Three domains**
Monera	Eubacteria	Bacteria
	Archaebacteria	Archaea
Protoctista	Protoctista	Eukarya
Fungi	Fungi	
Plantae	Plantae	
Animalia	Animalia	

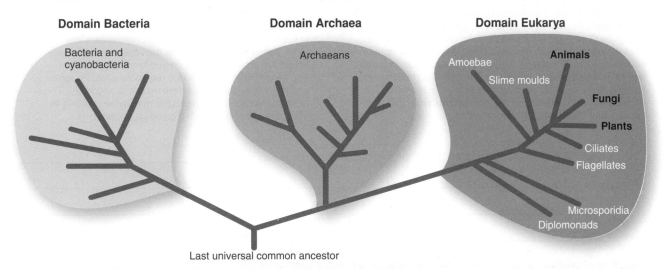

Domain Bacteria

Bacteria and cyanobacteria

Domain Archaea

Archaeans

Domain Eukarya

Amoebae
Slime moulds
Animals
Fungi
Plants
Ciliates
Flagellates
Microsporidia
Diplomonads

Last universal common ancestor

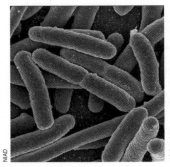

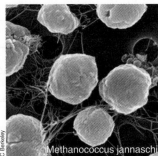

Methanococcus jannaschii

M. jannaschii was isolated from a deep sea hydrothermal vent.

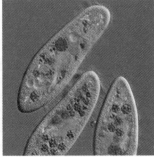

Domain Bacteria

Lack a distinct nucleus and cell organelles. Present in most of Earth's habitats and vital to its ecology. Includes well-known pathogens, many harmless and beneficial species, and the cyanobacteria (photosynthetic bacteria containing the pigments chlorophyll a and phycocyanin).

Domain Archaea

Methanococcus jannaschii was the first archaean genome to be sequenced. The sequencing identified many genes unique to Archaea and provided strong evidence for three evolutionary lineages. Although archaeans may resemble bacteria, they posses several metabolic pathways that are more similar to eukaryotes. Other aspects of their structure and metabolism, such their membrane lipids and respiratory pathways, are unique. Although once regarded as organisms of extreme environments, such as volcanic springs, archaeans are now known to be widespread, including in the ocean and soil.

Domain Eukarya

Complex cell structure with organelles and nucleus. The three domain classification recognises the diversity and different evolutionary paths of the unicellular eukaryotes (formerly Protoctista), which have little in common with each other. The fungi, animals, and plants form the remaining lineages.

LINK 134 | WEB 133 | **KNOW**

Scientists can use the tools at their disposal, including anatomical and molecular evidence, to construct a branching diagram to illustrate how the species in a taxonomic group are related. These '**phylogenetic trees**' represent a hypothesis for the evolutionary history of the taxon and will be supported to greater or lesser extents by the evidence. Increasingly, DNA and protein analyses are indicating that many traditional phylogenies do not accurately portray evolutionary relationships. This is true at all levels of classification including class (e.g. reptiles and birds) and order e.g. primates. To illustrate this, the traditional classification of primates is compared with the revised classification based on cladistic analysis (a newer method of determining evolutionary relationships based on molecular evidence).

A classical taxonomic view

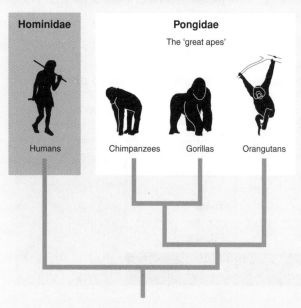

On the basis of overall anatomical similarity (e.g. bones and limb length, teeth, musculature), apes were grouped into a family (Pongidae) that is separate from humans and their immediate ancestors (Hominidae). The family Pongidae (the great apes) is not monophyletic (of one phylogeny with one common ancestor and all its descendents), because it stems from an ancestor that also gave rise to a species in another family (i.e. humans). This traditional classification scheme is now at odds with schemes derived after considering genetic evidence.

A view based on molecular evidence

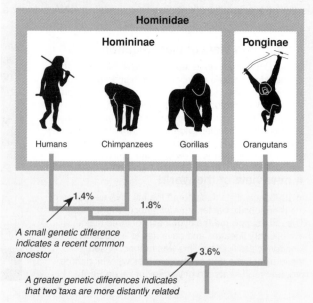

Based on the evidence of genetic differences (% values above), chimpanzees and gorillas are more closely related to humans than to orangutans, and chimpanzees are more closely related to humans than they are to gorillas. Under this scheme there is no true family of great apes. The family Hominidae includes two subfamilies: Ponginae and Homininae (humans, chimpanzees, and gorillas). This classification is monophyletic: the Hominidae includes all the species that arise from a common ancestor.

1. (a) Outline the evidence supporting a three domain classification system: _____

    _____

    _____

    _____

    (b) In what respects is the five kingdom classification system inadequate? _____

    _____

    _____

    (c) How has molecular evidence contributed to the taxonomic revisions described in this activity: _____

    _____

    _____

2. Suggest why classifications based on molecular evidence might provide a more likely phylogeny than one based on appearance alone:

    _____

    _____

    _____

3. What evidence has led to the reclassification of the primates? _____

    _____

134 Constructing Cladograms

Key Idea: Cladograms are phylogenetic trees constructed on the basis of shared derived characteristics.

A **cladogram** is a phylogenetic tree constructed using a taxonomic tool called cladistics. Cladistics groups organisms on the basis of their shared derived characters (features arising in an ancestor and shared by all its descendents) and ignores features that are not the result of shared ancestry. A clade, or branch on the tree, includes a common ancestor and all its descendents (i.e. it is monophyletic). Increasingly, cladistic methods rely on molecular data (e.g. DNA sequences) to determine the evolutionary history of a taxon. Highly conserved DNA sequences (those that change very little over time) are used because changes are likely to signal a significant evolutionary divergence.

Derived vs ancestral characters

When constructing cladograms, shared derived characters are used to separate the clades (branches on the tree). Using ancestral characters (those that arise in a species that is ancestral to more than one group) would result in distantly related organisms being grouped together and would not help to determine the evolutionary relationships within a clade. Whether or not a character is derived depends on the taxonomic level being considered. For example, a backbone is an ancestral character for mammals, but a derived character for vertebrates. Production of milk is a derived character shared by all mammals but no other taxa.

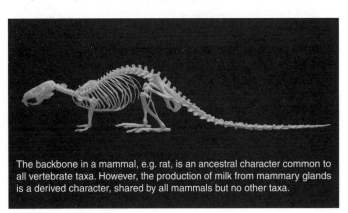

The backbone in a mammal, e.g. rat, is an ancestral character common to all vertebrate taxa. However, the production of milk from mammary glands is a derived character, shared by all mammals but no other taxa.

Constructing a simple cladogram

A table listing the features for comparison allows us to identify where we should make branches in the **cladogram**. An outgroup (one which is known to have no or little relationship to the other organisms) is used as a basis for comparison.

Taxa

Comparative features	Jawless fish (outgroup)	Bony fish	Amphibians	Lizards	Birds	Mammals
Vertebral column	✔	✔	✔	✔	✔	✔
Jaws	✘	✔	✔	✔	✔	✔
Four supporting limbs	✘	✘	✔	✔	✔	✔
Amniotic egg	✘	✘	✘	✔	✔	✔
Diapsid skull	✘	✘	✘	✔	✔	✘
Feathers	✘	✘	✘	✘	✔	✘
Hair	✘	✘	✘	✘	✘	✔

The table above lists features shared by selected taxa. The outgroup (jawless fish) shares just one feature (vertebral column), so it gives a reference for comparison and the first branch of the cladogram (phylogenetic tree). As the number of taxa in the table increases, the number of possible trees that could be drawn increases exponentially. To determine the most likely relationships, the rule of **parsimony** is used. This assumes that the tree with the least number of evolutionary events is most likely to show the correct evolutionary relationship.

Three possible cladograms are shown on the right. The top cladogram requires six events while the other two require seven events. Applying the rule of parsimony, the top cladogram must be taken as correct.

Parsimony can lead to some confusion. Some evolutionary events have occurred multiple times. An example is the evolution of the four chambered heart, which occurred separately in both birds and mammals. The use of fossil evidence and DNA analysis can help to solve problems like this.

Possible cladograms

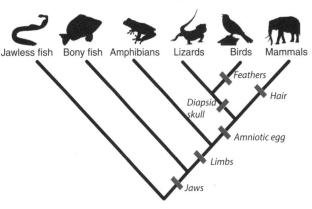

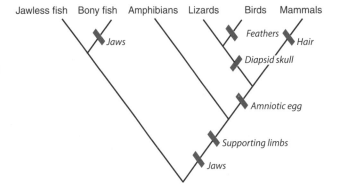

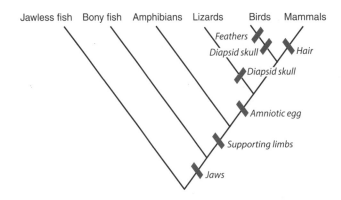

© 2015 **BIOZONE** International
ISBN: 978-1-927309-25-4
Photocopying Prohibited

LINK 130 LINK 125 WEB 134 **KNOW**

Using DNA data to construct cladograms

DNA analysis has allowed scientists to confirm many phylogenies and refute or redraw others. DNA sequences can be tabulated and analysed in a similar way to morphological differences. The ancestry of whales has been in debate since Darwin. The radically different morphologies of whales and other mammals makes it difficult to work out the correct phylogenetic tree. However, recently discovered fossil ankle bones, as well as DNA studies, show whales are more closely related to hippopotami than to any other mammal. When coupled with molecular clocks, DNA data can also give the time between each split in the lineage.

The DNA sequences on the right show part of a the nucleotide subset 141-200 and some of the matching nucleotides used to draw the cladogram. Although whales were once thought to be most closely related to pigs, based on the DNA analysis, the most parsimonious tree disputes this. Note how this phylogenetic tree agrees with that constructed using data from retropositional events as described in the activity 'Bioinformatics'.

← Difference in DNA

AGTCC... CTATGGTTCCTAAGCACA...TTCCC

AGTCC... CTATCCTTCCTAAGCATA... TTCCC

AGTCC... CTATCCTTCCTAAGCATA... TTCTC

AGATT... CCATTGTTCCCAAGCGTA...TTCCC

TGTCC... CCATCATTCCTAAGCGCA...TTCCT

1   2   3   4   5
DNA matches

1. (a) Distinguish between a shared derived characteristic and a shared ancestral characteristic: _____

_____

_____

   (b) Why are ancestral characteristics not useful in constructing evolutionary histories? _____

_____

_____

2. What assumption is made when applying the rule of parsimony in constructing a cladogram? _____

_____

_____

3. (a) What is the advantage of using DNA analysis to construct a cladogram over morphological comparisons? _____

_____

_____

   (b) Why do you think highly conserved DNA sequences are used to construct cladograms? _____

_____

_____

4. (a) In the DNA data for the whale cladogram (above) identify the DNA match that shows a mutation event must have happened twice in evolutionary history.

_____

   (b) Explain your reasoning for your choice in (a): _____

_____

_____

5. A phylogenetic tree is a hypothesis for an evolutionary history. How could you test it? _____

_____

_____

© 2015 **BIOZONE** International
ISBN: 978-1-927309-25-4
Photocopying Prohibited

135 Mechanism of Natural Selection

Key Idea: Natural selection is the mechanism by which organisms that are better adapted to their environment survive to produce a greater number of offspring.
Evolution is the change in inherited characteristics in a population over generations. Evolution is the consequence of interaction between four factors: (1) The potential for populations to increase in numbers, (2) Genetic variation as a result of mutation and sexual reproduction, (3) competition for resources, and (4) proliferation of individuals with better survival and reproduction.

Natural selection is the term for the mechanism by which better adapted organisms survive to produce a greater number of viable offspring. This has the effect of increasing their proportion in the population so that they become more common. This is the basis of Darwin's theory of evolution by natural selection.

We can demonstrate the basic principles of evolution using the analogy of a 'population' of M&M's candy.

#1

In a bag of M&M's, there are many colours, which represents the variation in a population. As you and a friend eat through the bag of candy, you both leave the blue ones, which you both dislike, and return them to bag.

#2

The blue candy becomes more common...

#3

Eventually, you are left with a bag of blue M&M's. Your selective preference for the other colours changed the make-up of the M&M's population. This is the basic principle of selection that drives evolution in natural populations.

Darwin's theory of evolution by natural selection

Darwin's theory of evolution by natural selection is outlined below. It is widely accepted by the scientific community today and is one of founding principles of modern science.

Overproduction
Populations produce too many young: many must die

Populations generally produce more offspring than are needed to replace the parents. Natural populations normally maintain constant numbers. A certain number will die without reproducing.

Variation
Individuals show variation: some variations more favourable than others

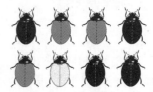

Individuals have different **phenotypes** (appearances) and therefore **genotypes** (genetic makeup). Some phenotypes have better survival and reproductive success in the environment.

Natural selection
Natural selection favours the individuals best suited to the prevailing environment (the environment at the time)

Individuals in the population compete for limited resources. Those with favourable variations will be more likely to survive. Relatively more of those without favourable variations will die.

Inherited
Variations are inherited: the best suited variants leave more offspring

The variations (both favourable and unfavourable) are passed on to offspring. Each generation will contain proportionally more descendants of individuals with favourable characters.

1. Identify the four factors that interact to bring about evolution in populations: _____

_____

_____

_____

LINK 139 LINK 138 LINK 136 WEB 135 KNOW

Variation, selection, and population change

Natural populations, like the ladybug population above, show genetic variation. This is a result of **mutation** (which creates new alleles) and sexual reproduction (which produces new combinations of alleles). Some variants are more suited to the environment of the time than others. These variants will leave more offspring, as described for the hypothetical population (right).

1. Variation through mutation and sexual reproduction:
In a population of brown beetles, mutations independently produce red colouration and 2 spot marking on the wings. The individuals in the population compete for limited resources.

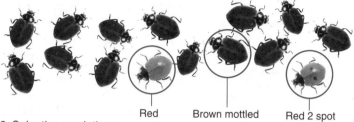

Red   Brown mottled   Red 2 spot

2. Selective predation:
Brown mottled beetles are eaten by birds but red ones are avoided. Any factor that affects reproductive success like this is called a **selection pressure**.

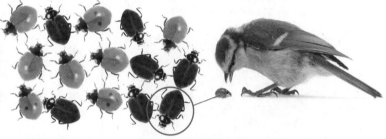

3. Change in the genetics of the population:
Red beetles have better survival and fitness and become more numerous with each generation. Brown beetles have poor fitness and become rare.

2. What produces the genetic variation in populations? _____

3. Define evolution: _____

_____

4. Explain how the genetic make-up of a population can change over time: _____

_____

_____

_____

_____

_____

_____

_____

5. Complete the table below by calculating the percentage of beetles in the example above right.

Beetle population	% Brown beetles	% Red beetles	% Red beetles with spots
1			
2			
3			

136 What is Adaptation?

Key Idea: Adaptations are inherited traits that have evolved and are maintained by natural selection. They have a functional role in an organism's life and enhance an individual's fitness. An **adaptation** (or adaptive feature) is any heritable trait that equips an organism to its functional position in the environment (its niche). These traits may be structural, physiological, or behavioural and reflect ancestry as well as adaptation.

Adaptation is important in an evolutionary sense because adaptive features promote fitness. **Fitness** is a measure of an organism's ability to maximise the numbers of offspring surviving to reproductive age. Genetic adaptation must not be confused with physiological adjustment (acclimatisation), which refers to an organism's ability to adjust during its lifetime to changing environmental conditions.

Ear length in rabbits and hares

The external ears of many mammals are used as important organs to assist in thermoregulation (controlling loss and gain of body heat). The ears of rabbits and hares native to hot, dry climates, such as the jack rabbit of south-western USA and northern Mexico, are relatively very large. The Arctic hare lives in the tundra zone of Alaska, northern Canada and Greenland, and has ears that are relatively short. This reduction in the size of the extremities (ears, limbs, and noses) is typical of cold adapted species.

Arctic hare: *Lepus arcticus*

Black-tail jackrabbit: *Lepus californicus*

Body size in relation to climate

Regulation of body temperature requires a large amount of energy and mammals exhibit a variety of structural and physiological adaptations to increase the effectiveness of this process. Heat production in any endotherm depends on body volume (heat generating metabolism), whereas the rate of heat loss depends on surface area. Increasing body size minimises heat loss to the environment by reducing the surface area to volume ratio. Animals in colder regions therefore tend to be larger overall than those living in hot climates. This relationship is well documented in many mammalian species. Cold adapted species also tend to have more compact bodies and shorter extremities than related species in warmer climates.

The **fennec fox** of the Sahara illustrates the adaptations typical of mammals living in hot climates: a small body size and lightweight fur, and long ears, legs, and nose. These features facilitate heat dissipation and reduce heat gain.

The Arctic fox shows the physical characteristics typical of cold adapted mammals: a stocky, compact body shape with small ears, short legs and nose, and dense fur. These features reduce heat loss to the environment.

Number of horns in rhinoceroses

Not all differences between species can be convincingly interpreted as adaptations to particular environments. Rhinoceroses charge rival males and predators, and the horn(s), when combined with the head-down posture, add effectiveness to this behaviour. Horns are obviously adaptive, but it is not clear if having one (Indian rhino) or two (black rhino) horns is related to the functionality in the environment or a reflection of evolution from a small hornless ancestor.

Great Indian rhino

African black rhino

1. Distinguish between adaptation and acclimatisation: _____

_____

_____

2. Explain the nature of the relationship between the length of extremities (such as limbs and ears) and climate: ___

_____

_____

3. Explain the adaptive value of a compact body with a relatively small surface area in a colder climate: _____

_____

_____

© 2015 **BIOZONE** International
ISBN: 978-1-927309-25-4
Photocopying Prohibited

137 Adaptation and Niche

Key Idea: Adaptations allow an organism to function effectively in its niche, increasing survival and fitness. The morphological, physiological, and behavioural adaptations of species are the result of selection pressures acting on them over the course of their evolution. They enable effective exploitation of the species' ecological niche.

Moles are solitary and territorial except during the breeding season.

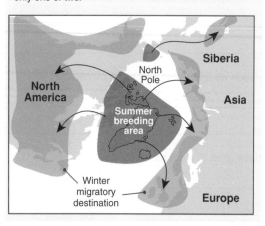

Mole hill

Nest lined with dry grass

Pups

Moles (above) spend most of the time underground and are rarely seen at the surface. Mole hills are piles of soil excavated from the tunnels and pushed to the surface. Surface tunnels occur where the prey is concentrated at the surface. Deeper, permanent tunnels form a complex network used for feeding and nesting, sometimes for several generations.

Northern or common mole *(Talpa europaea)*

The northern (common) mole is a small insectivore (70-130 g) found throughout most of Britain and Europe, apart from Ireland, The are found in most habitats but are less common in coniferous forest, moorland, and sand dunes, where their prey (earthworms and insect larvae) are rare. They are well adapted to life underground and burrow extensively, using enlarged, spade-like feet for digging. Their small size, tubular body shape, and heavily buttressed head and neck are typical of burrowing species.

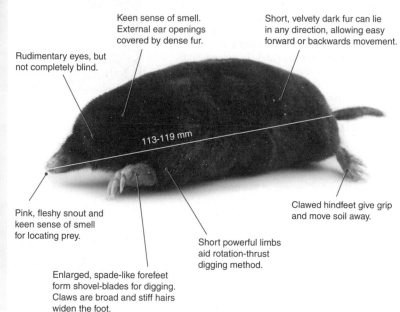

Keen sense of smell. External ear openings covered by dense fur.

Short, velvety dark fur can lie in any direction, allowing easy forward or backwards movement.

Rudimentary eyes, but not completely blind.

113-119 mm

Clawed hindfeet give grip and move soil away.

Pink, fleshy snout and keen sense of smell for locating prey.

Short powerful limbs aid rotation-thrust digging method.

Enlarged, spade-like forefeet form shovel-blades for digging. Claws are broad and stiff hairs widen the foot.

Snow bunting *(Plectrophenax nivalis)*

The snow bunting is a small ground feeding bird that lives and breeds in the Arctic and sub-Arctic islands. Although migratory, snow buntings do not move to traditional winter homes but prefer winter habitats that resemble their Arctic breeding grounds, such as bleak shores or open fields of northern Britain and the eastern United States (below).

Snow buntings have the unique ability to moult very rapidly after breeding. During the warmer months, they are a brown colour, changing to white in winter. They must complete this colour change quickly, so that they have a new set of feathers before the onset of winter and before migration. To achieve this, snow buntings lose as many as four or five of their main flight wing feathers at once, as opposed to most birds, which lose only one or two.

Very few small birds breed in the Arctic, because most small birds lose more heat than larger ones. In addition, birds that breed in the Arctic summer must migrate before the onset of winter, often travelling over large expanses of water. Large, long winged birds are better able to do this. However, the snow bunting is superbly adapted to survive in the extreme cold of the Arctic region.

Less heat is lost from the white plumage compared to dark plumage.

White feathers are hollow and filled with air, which acts as an insulator. In the dark-coloured feathers, the internal spaces are filled with pigmented cells.

During snow storms or periods of high wind, snow buntings will burrow into snowdrifts for shelter.

The male bird feeds his mate during the incubation period and helps to feed the young.

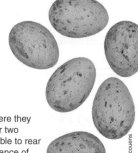

Siberia

North Pole

North America

Asia

Summer breeding area

Winter migratory destination

Europe

The snow bunting's eggs (right) are laid amongst stones where they are well camouflaged. Snow buntings lay, on average, one or two more eggs than equivalent species further south. They are able to rear more young because the continuous daylight and the abundance of insects at high latitudes enables them to feed their chicks around the clock, resting for only 2-3 hours in any 24 hour period.

Didier Descouens

© 2015 **BIOZONE** International
ISBN:978-1-927309-25-4
Photocopying Prohibited

1. Describe a structural, physiological, and behavioural adaptation of the **common mole**, explaining how each adaptation assists survival:

   (a) Structural adaptation: _____

   _____

   (b) Physiological adaptation: _____

   _____

   (c) Behavioural adaptation: _____

   _____

2. Describe a structural, physiological, and behavioural adaptation of the **snow bunting**, explaining how each adaptation assists survival:

   (a) Structural adaptation: _____

   _____

   (b) Physiological adaptation: _____

   _____

   (c) Behavioural adaptation: _____

   _____

3. The rabbit is a colonial mammal, which lives underground in warrens (burrow systems) and feeds on grasses, cereal crops, roots, and young trees. Rabbits are a hugely successful species worldwide and often reach plague proportions. Through discussion, or your own knowledge and research, describe **six adaptations** of rabbits, identifying them as structural (S), physiological (P), or behavioural (B). The examples below are typical:

   Structural: Widely spaced eyes gives wide field of vision for surveillance and detection of danger.

   Physiological: High reproductive rate; short gestation and high fertility aids rapid population increases when food is available.

   Behavioural: Freeze behaviour when startled reduces the chance of detection by wandering predators.

   (a) _____

   (b) _____

   (c) _____

   (d) _____

   (e) _____

   (f) _____

4. Examples of adaptations are listed below. Identify them as predominantly structural, physiological, and/or behavioural:

   (a) Relationship of body size and shape to latitude (tropical or Arctic): _____

   (b) The production of concentrated urine in desert dwelling mammals: _____

   (c) The summer and winter migratory patterns in birds and mammals: _____

   (d) The C4 photosynthetic pathway and CAM metabolism of plants: _____

   (e) The thick leaves and sunken stomata of desert plants: _____

   (f) Hibernation or torpor in small mammals over winter: _____

   (g) Basking in lizards and snakes: _____

138 Natural Selection in Pocket Mice

Key Idea: The need to blend into their surroundings to avoid predation is an important selection pressure acting on the coat colour of rock pocket mice.

Rock pocket mice are found in the deserts of southwestern United States and northern Mexico. They are nocturnal, foraging at night for seeds, while avoiding owls (their main predator). During the day they shelter from the desert heat in their burrows. The coat colour of the mice varies from light brown to very dark brown. Throughout the desert environment in which the mice live there are outcrops of dark volcanic rock. The presence of these outcrops and the mice that live on them present an excellent study in natural selection.

▶ The coat colour of the Arizona rock pocket mice is controlled by the Mc1r gene (a gene that in mammals is commonly associated with the production of the pigment melanin).

There are variations for the gene that controls coat colour. These variations are called alleles. Homozygous dominant (DD)and heterozygous mice (Dd) have dark coats, while homozygous recessive mice (dd) have light coats. Coat colour of mice in New Mexico is not related to the Mc1r gene.

▶ 107 rock pocket mice from 14 sites were collected and their coat colour and the rock colour they were found on were recorded by measuring the percentage of light reflected from their coat (low percentage reflectance equals a dark coat). The data is presented right:

Site	Rock type (V volcanic)	Percent reflectance / %	
		Mice coat	Rock
KNZ	V	4	10.5
ARM	V	4	9
CAR	V	4	10
MEX	V	5	10.5
TUM	V	5	27
PIN	V	5.5	11
AFT		6	30
AVR		6.5	26
WHT		8	42
BLK	V	8.5	15
FRA		9	39
TIN		9	39
TUL		9.5	25
POR		12	34.5

1. (a) What are the genotypes of the dark coloured mice? _____

   (b) What is the genotype of the light coloured mice? _____

2. Using the data in the table above and the grids below and on the facing page, draw column graphs of the percent reflectance of the mice coats and the rocks at each of the 14 collection sites.

© 2015 **BIOZONE** International
ISBN: 978-1-927309-25-4
Photocopying Prohibited

3. (a) What do you notice about the reflectance of the rock pocket mice coat colour and the reflectance of the rocks they were found on?

_____

_____

_____

(b) Suggest a cause for the pattern in 3(a). How do the phenotypes of the mice affect where the mice live?

_____

_____

_____

(c) What are two exceptions to the pattern you have noticed in 3(a)? _____

_____

_____

_____

(d) How might these exceptions have occurred? _____

_____

_____

4. The rock pocket mice populations in Arizona use a different genetic mechanism to control coat colour than the New Mexico populations. What does this tell you about the evolution of the genetic mechanism for coat colour?

_____

_____

_____

_____

139 Selection for Skin Colour in Humans

Key Idea: Skin colour is an evolutionary response to the need to synthesise vitamin D which requires sunlight, and to conserve folate which breaks down in sunlight.

Pigmented skin of varying tones is a feature of humans that evolved after early humans lost the majority of their body hair. However, the distribution of skin colour globally is not random; people native to equatorial regions have darker skin tones than people from higher latitudes. For many years, biologists postulated that this was because darker skins had evolved to protect against skin cancer. The problem with this explanation was that skin cancer is not tied to evolutionary fitness because it affects post-reproductive individuals and cannot therefore provide a mechanism for selection. More complex analyses of the physiological and epidemiological evidence has shown a more complex picture in which selection pressures on skin colour are finely balanced to produce a skin tone that regulates the effects of the sun's ultraviolet radiation on the nutrients vitamin D and folate, both of which are crucial to successful human reproduction, and therefore evolutionary fitness. The selection is stabilising within each latitudinal region.

Skin colour in humans: A product of natural selection

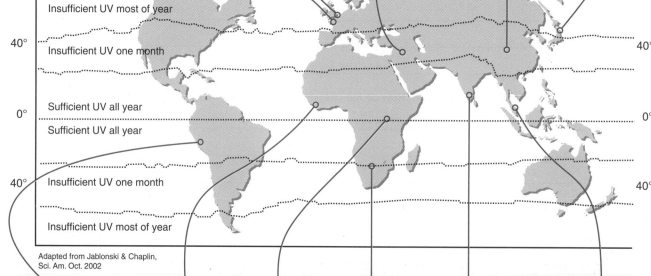

Alaska · France · The Netherlands · Iraq · China · Japan

80° No data

Insufficient UV most of year

40° Insufficient UV one month

0° Sufficient UV all year

Sufficient UV all year

40° Insufficient UV one month

Insufficient UV most of year

Adapted from Jablonski & Chaplin, Sci. Am. Oct. 2002

Peru

Liberia

Burundi

Botswana

Southern India

Malaysia

Human skin colour is the result of two opposing selection pressures. Skin pigmentation has evolved to protect against destruction of folate from ultraviolet light, but the skin must also be light enough to receive the light required to synthesise vitamin D. Vitamin D synthesis is a process that begins in the skin and is inhibited by dark pigment. Folate is needed for healthy neural development in humans and a deficiency is associated with fatal neural tube defects. Vitamin D is required for the absorption of calcium from the diet and therefore normal skeletal development.

Women also have a high requirement for calcium during pregnancy and lactation. Populations that live in the tropics receive enough ultraviolet (UV) radiation to synthesise vitamin D all year long. Those that live in northern or southern latitudes do not. In temperate zones, people lack sufficient UV light to make vitamin D for one month of the year. Those nearer the poles lack enough UV light for vitamin D synthesis most of the year (above). Their lighter skins reflect their need to maximise UV absorption (the photos show skin colour in people from different latitudes).

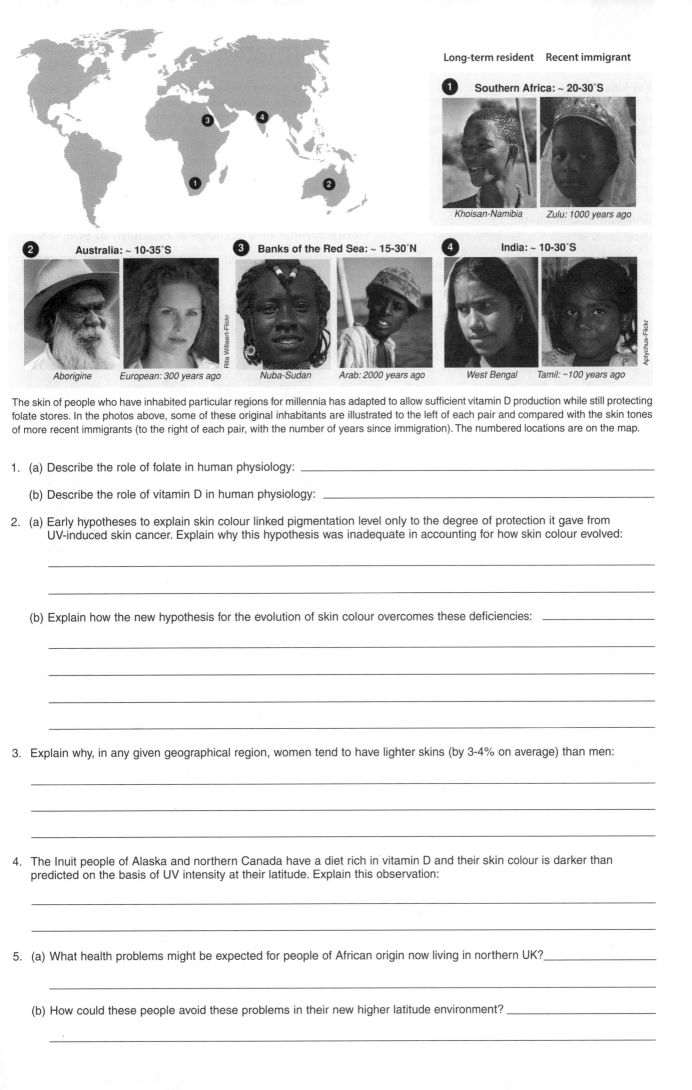

Long-term resident   Recent immigrant

1 **Southern Africa: ~ 20-30˚S**

Khoisan-Namibia   Zulu: 1000 years ago

2 **Australia: ~ 10-35˚S**

Aborigine   European: 300 years ago

3 **Banks of the Red Sea: ~ 15-30˚N**

Nuba-Sudan   Arab: 2000 years ago

4 **India: ~ 10-30˚S**

West Bengal   Tamil: ~100 years ago

The skin of people who have inhabited particular regions for millennia has adapted to allow sufficient vitamin D production while still protecting folate stores. In the photos above, some of these original inhabitants are illustrated to the left of each pair and compared with the skin tones of more recent immigrants (to the right of each pair, with the number of years since immigration). The numbered locations are on the map.

1. (a) Describe the role of folate in human physiology: _____

   (b) Describe the role of vitamin D in human physiology: _____

2. (a) Early hypotheses to explain skin colour linked pigmentation level only to the degree of protection it gave from UV-induced skin cancer. Explain why this hypothesis was inadequate in accounting for how skin colour evolved:

   _____

   _____

   (b) Explain how the new hypothesis for the evolution of skin colour overcomes these deficiencies: _____

   _____

   _____

   _____

   _____

3. Explain why, in any given geographical region, women tend to have lighter skins (by 3-4% on average) than men:

   _____

   _____

   _____

4. The Inuit people of Alaska and northern Canada have a diet rich in vitamin D and their skin colour is darker than predicted on the basis of UV intensity at their latitude. Explain this observation:

   _____

   _____

5. (a) What health problems might be expected for people of African origin now living in northern UK?_____

   _____

   (b) How could these people avoid these problems in their new higher latitude environment? _____

   _____

140 Isolation and Species Formation

Key Idea: Ecological and geographical isolation are important in separating populations prior to reproductive isolation.
Isolating mechanisms are barriers to successful interbreeding between species. **Reproductive isolation** is fundamental to the biological species concept, which defines a species by its inability to breed with other species to produce fertile offspring. **Geographical barriers** are not regarded as reproductive isolating mechanisms because they are not part of the species' biology, although they are often a necessary precursor to reproductive isolation in sexually reproducing populations. Ecological isolating mechanisms are those that isolate gene pools on the basis of ecological preferences, e.g. habitat selection. Although ecological and geographical isolation are sometimes confused, they are quite distinct, as ecological isolation involves a component of the species biology.

Geographical isolation

Geographical isolation describes the isolation of a species population (gene pool) by some kind of physical barrier, for example, mountain range, water body, isthmus, desert, or ice sheet. Geographical isolation is a frequent first step in the subsequent reproductive isolation of a species. For example, geological changes to the lake basins has been instrumental in the subsequent proliferation of cichlid fish species in the rift lakes of East Africa (right). Similarly, many Galapagos Island species (e.g. iguanas, finches) are now quite distinct from the Central and South American species from which they arose after isolation from the mainland.

Geographical and ecological isolation of species

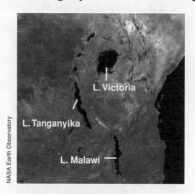
L. Victoria
L. Tanganyika
L. Malawi

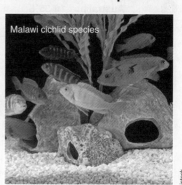
Malawi cichlid species

Red-browed treecreeper

Brown treecreeper

Ecological (habitat) isolation

Ecological isolation describes the existence of a **prezygotic reproductive barrier** between two species (or sub-species) as a result of them occupying or breeding in different habitats within the same general geographical area. Ecological isolation includes small scale differences (e.g. ground or tree dwelling) and broad differences (e.g. desert vs grasslands). The red-browed and brown **treecreepers** (*Climacteris* spp.) are sympatric in south-eastern Australia and both species feed largely on ants. However the brown spends most of its time foraging on the ground or on fallen logs while the red-browed forages almost entirely in the trees. Ecological isolation often follows geographical isolation, but in many cases the geographical barriers may remain in part. For example, five species of **antelope squirrels** occupy different habitat ranges throughout the southwestern United States and northern Mexico, a region divided in part by the Grand Canyon. The white tailed antelope squirrel is widely distributed in desert areas to the north and south of the canyon, while the smaller, more specialised Harris' antelope squirrel has a much more limited range only to the south in southern Arizona. The Grand Canyon still functions as a barrier to dispersal but the species are now ecologically isolated as well.

White-tailed antelope squirrel

The Grand Canyon - a massive rift in the Colourado Plateau

Harris' antelope squirrel

1. Describe the role of isolating mechanisms in maintaining the integrity of a species: _____

2. (a) Why is geographical isolation not regarded as a reproductive isolating mechanism? _____

   (b) Explain why, despite this, it often precedes reproductive isolation: _____

3. Distinguish between geographical and ecological isolation: _____

141 Reproductive Isolation

Key Idea: Reproductive isolating mechanisms acting before and after fertilisation, prevent interbreeding between species. Reproductive isolation is a defining feature of biological species. Any mechanism that prevents two species from producing viable, fertile hybrids contributes to reproductive isolation. Single barriers to gene flow (such as geographical barriers) are usually insufficient to isolate a gene pool, so most species commonly have more than one type of barrier. Most reproductive isolating mechanisms (RIMs) are prezygotic and operate before fertilisation. Postzyotic RIMs, which act after fertilisation, are important in maintaining the integrity of closely related species.

Prezygotic isolating mechanisms

Temporal Isolation

Individuals from different species do not mate because they are active during different times of the day or in different seasons. Plants flower at different times of the year or at different times of the day to avoid hybridisation (e.g. species of the orchid genus *Dendrobium* occupy the same location but flower on different days). Closely related animal species may have different breeding seasons or periods of emergence. Species of **periodical cicadas** (*Magicicada*) in a particular region are developmentally synchronised, despite very long life cycles. Once their underground period of development (13 or 17 years depending on the species) is over, the entire population emerges at much the same time to breed.

Gamete Isolation

The gametes from different species are often incompatible, so even if they meet they do not survive. Where fertilisation is internal, the sperm may not survive in the reproductive tract of another species. If the sperm does survive and reach the ovum, chemical differences in the gametes prevent fertilisation. Gamete isolation is particularly important in aquatic environments where the gametes are released into the water and fertilised externally, such as in reproduction in frogs. Chemical recognition is also used by flowering plants to recognise pollen from the same species.

Behavioural isolation

Behavioural isolation operates through differences in species courtship behaviours. Courtship is a necessary prelude to mating in many species and courtship behaviours are species specific. Mates of the same species are attracted with distinctive dances, vocalisations, and body language. Courtship behaviours are not easily misinterpreted and will be unrecognised and ignored by individuals of another species. Birds exhibit a remarkable range of courtship displays. The use of song is widespread but ritualised movements, including nest building, are also common. For example, the elaborate courtship bowers of bowerbirds are well known, and Galápagos frigatebirds have an elaborate display in which they inflate a bright red gular pouch (right). Amongst insects, empid flies have some of the most elaborate of courtship displays. They are aggressive hunters so ritualised behaviour involving presentation of a prey item facilitates mating. The sexual organs of the flies are also like a lock-and-key, providing mechanical reproductive isolation as well (see below).

Mechanical (morphological) isolation

Structural differences (incompatibility) in the anatomy of reproductive organs prevents sperm transfer between individuals of different species. This is an important isolating mechanism preventing breeding between closely related species of arthropods. Many flowering plants have coevolved with their animal pollinators and have flowers structures to allow only that insect access. Structural differences in the flowers and pollen of different plant species prevents cross breeding because pollen transfer is restricted to specific pollinators and the pollen itself must be species compatible.

Temporal isolation: periodical cicadas

Cicada emergence

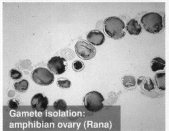
Gamete isolation: amphibian ovary (Rana)

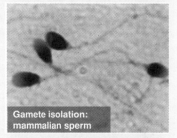
Gamete isolation: mammalian sperm

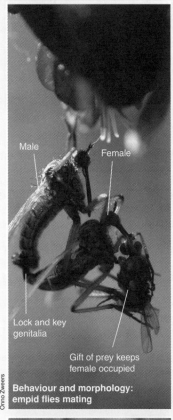
Male
Female
Lock and key genitalia
Gift of prey keeps female occupied
Behaviour and morphology: empid flies mating

Behaviour: male frigatebird display

Behaviour: male tree frog calling

Behaviour: wing beating in male sage grouse

Mechanical: Damselflies mating

Mechanical: flower shape in orchids

Postzygotic isolating mechanisms

Hybrid sterility

Even if two species mate and produce hybrid offspring that are vigorous, the species are still reproductively isolated if the hybrids are sterile (genes cannot flow from one species' gene pool to the other). Such cases are common among the horse family (such as the zebra and donkey shown on the right). One cause of this sterility is the failure of meiosis to produce normal gametes in the hybrid. This can occur if the chromosomes of the two parents are different in number or structure (see the "**zebronkey**" karyotype on the right). The **mule**, a cross between a donkey stallion and a horse mare, is also an example of **hybrid vigour** (they are robust) as well as **hybrid sterility**. Female mules sometimes produce viable eggs but males are infertile.

Hybrid inviability

Mating between individuals of two species may produce a zygote, but genetic incompatibility may stop development of the zygote. Fertilised eggs often fail to divide because of mis-matched chromosome numbers from each gamete. Very occasionally, the hybrid zygote will complete embryonic development but will not survive for long. For example, although sheep and goats seem similar and can be mated together, they belong to different genera. Any offspring of a sheep-goat pairing is generally stillborn.

Hybrid breakdown

Hybrid breakdown is common feature of some plant hybrids. The first generation (F₁) may be fertile, but the second generation (F₂) are infertile or inviable. Examples include hybrids between cotton species (near right), species within the genus *Populus*, and strains of the cultivated rice *Oryza* (far right)

Zebra stallion (2N = 44) **X** Donkey jenny (2N = 62)

Karyotype of '**Zebronkey**' offspring (2N = 53)

Chromosomes contributed by zebra stallion

Chromosomes contributed by donkey jenny

Sheep (*Ovis*) 54 chromosomes

Goat (*Capra*) 60 chromosomes

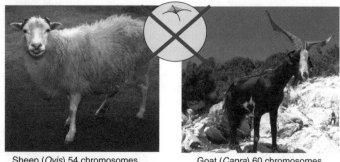

1. In the following examples, classify the reproductive isolating mechanism as either **prezygotic** or **postzygotic** and describe the mechanisms by which the isolation is achieved (e.g. structrual isolation, hybrid sterility etc.):

   (a) Some different cotton species can produce fertile hybrids, but breakdown of the hybrid occurs in the next generation when the offspring of the hybrid die in their seeds or grow into defective plants:

   Prezygotic / postzygotic (delete one)   Mechanism of isolation: _____

   (b) Many plants have unique arrangements of their floral parts that stops transfer of pollen between plants:

   Prezygotic / postzygotic (delete one)   Mechanism of isolation: _____

   (c) Two skunk species do not mate despite having habitats that overlap because they mate at different times of the year:

   Prezygotic / postzygotic (delete one)   Mechanism of isolation: _____

   (d) Several species of the frog genus *Rana*, live in the same regions and habitats, where they may occasionally hybridise. The hybrids generally do not complete development, and those that do are weak and do not survive long:

   Prezygotic / postzygotic (delete one)   Mechanism of isolation: _____

2. Postzygotic isolating mechanisms are said to reinforce prezygotic ones. Explain why this is the case:

   _____

   _____

   _____

   _____

142 Allopatric Speciation

Key Idea: Allopatric speciation is the genetic divergence of a population after it becomes subdivided and isolated.

Allopatric speciation refers to the genetic divergence of a species after a population becomes split and then isolated geographically. It is probably the most common mechanism by which new species arise and has certainly been important in regions where there have been cycles of geographical fragmentation, e.g. as a result of ice expansion and retreat (and accompanying sea level changes) during glacial and interglacial periods.

Stage 1: Moving into new environments

There are times when the range of a species expands for a variety of different reasons. A single population in a relatively homogeneous environment will move into new regions of their environment when they are subjected to intense competition (whether it is interspecific or intraspecific). The most severe form of competition is between members of the same species since they are competing for identical resources in the habitat. In the diagram on the right there is a 'parent population' of a single species with a common gene pool with regular 'gene flow' (theoretically any individual has access to all members of the opposite sex for mating purposes).

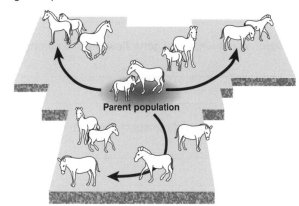

Parent population

Stage 2: Geographical isolation

Isolation of parts of the population may occur due to the formation of **physical barriers**, such as mountains, deserts, or stretches of water. These barriers may cut off those parts of the population that are at the extremes of the range and gene flow is prevented or rare. The rise and fall of the sea level has been particularly important in functioning as an isolating mechanism. Climatic change can leave 'islands' of habitat separated by large inhospitable zones that the species cannot traverse.

Example: In mountainous regions, alpine species can populate extensive areas of habitat during cool climatic periods. During warmer periods, they may become isolated because their habitat is reduced to 'islands' of high ground surrounded by inhospitable lowland habitat.

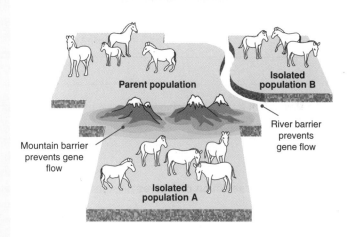

Parent population

Isolated population B

River barrier prevents gene flow

Mountain barrier prevents gene flow

Isolated population A

Stage 3: Different selection pressures

The isolated populations (A and B) may be subjected to quite different selection pressures. These will favour individuals with traits that suit each particular environment. For example, population A will be subjected to selection pressures that relate to drier conditions. This will favour those individuals with phenotypes (and therefore genotypes) that are better suited to dry conditions. They may for instance have a better ability to conserve water. This would result in improved health, allowing better disease resistance and greater reproductive performance (i.e. more of their offspring survive). Finally, as allele frequencies for certain genes change, the population takes on the status of a subspecies. Reproductive isolation is not yet established but the **subspecies** are significantly different genetically from other related populations.

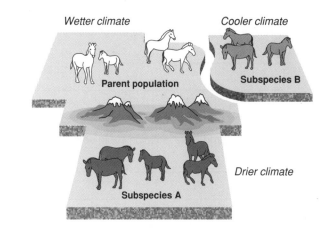

Wetter climate

Cooler climate

Parent population

Subspecies B

Subspecies A

Drier climate

Stage 4: Reproductive isolation

The separated populations (isolated subspecies) undergo genetic and behavioural changes. These ensure that the gene pool of each population remains isolated and 'undiluted' by genes from other populations, even if the two populations should be able to remix (due to the removal of the geographical barrier). Gene flow does not occur. The arrows (diagram, right) indicate the zone of overlap between two species after Species B has moved back into the range inhabited by the parent population. Closely-related species whose distribution overlaps are said to be **sympatric species**. Those that remain geographically isolated are called **allopatric species**.

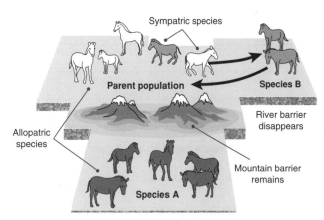

Sympatric species

Parent population

Species B

River barrier disappears

Allopatric species

Mountain barrier remains

Species A

LINK 144   LINK 140   WEB 142 KNOW

1. Why do some animals, given the opportunity, move into new environments? _____

_____

_____

2. Plants are unable to move. How might plants disperse to new environments? _____

_____

3. Describe the amount of **gene flow** within a parent population prior to and during the expansion of a species' range:

_____

_____

4. Explain how cycles of climate change can cause large changes in **sea level** (up to 200 m):

_____

_____

5. (a) What kinds of **physical barriers** could isolate different parts of the same population? _____

_____

_____

_____

(b) How might emigration achieve the same effect as geographical isolation? _____

_____

_____

6. (a) How might **selection pressures** differ for a population that becomes isolated from the parent population?

_____

_____

(b) Describe the general effect of the change in selection pressures on the **allele frequencies** of the isolated gene pool:

_____

_____

_____

7. Explain how reproductive isolation could develop in geographically separated populations (see previous pages):

_____

_____

_____

_____

_____

_____

_____

_____

8. What is the difference between an allopatric and sympatric species? _____

_____

_____

© 2015 **BIOZONE** International
ISBN: 978-1-927309-25-4
Photocopying Prohibited

143 Sympatric Speciation

Key Idea: Sympatric speciation is speciation occurring in the absence of physical barriers between gene pools.
Sympatric speciation is rarer than allopatric speciation, although it is not uncommon in plants, which can form polyploids. There are two situations in which sympatric speciation is thought to commonly occur (described below).

Speciation through niche differentiation

Niche isolation

In a heterogeneous environment (one that is not the same everywhere), a population exists within a diverse collection of **microhabitats**. Some organisms prefer to occupy one particular type of 'microhabitat' most of the time, only rarely coming in contact with fellow organisms that prefer other microhabitats. Some organisms become so dependent on the resources offered by their particular microhabitat that they never meet up with their counterparts in different microhabitats.

Reproductive isolation

Finally, the individual groups have remained genetically isolated for so long because of their microhabitat preferences, that they have become reproductively isolated. They have become new species that have developed subtle differences in behaviour, structure, and physiology. Gene flow (via sexual reproduction) is limited to organisms that share a similar microhabitat preference (as shown in the diagram on the right).

Example: Some beetles prefer to find plants identical to the species they grew up on, when it is time for them to lay eggs. Individual beetles of the same species have different preferences.

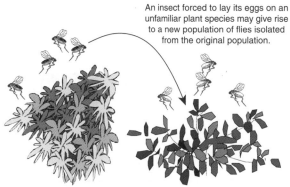

An insect forced to lay its eggs on an unfamiliar plant species may give rise to a new population of flies isolated from the original population.

Original host plant species   **New host plant species**

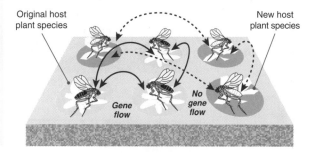

Original host plant species   New host plant species

Gene flow   *No gene flow*

Instant speciation by polyploidy

Polyploidy may result in the formation of a new species without isolation from the parent species. This event, occurring during meiosis, produces sudden reproductive isolation for the new group. Because the sex-determining mechanism is disturbed, animals are rarely able to achieve new species status this way (they are effectively sterile, e.g. tetraploid XXXX). Many plants, on the other hand, are able to reproduce vegetatively, or carry out self pollination. This ability to reproduce on their own enables such polyploid plants to produce a breeding population.

Speciation by allopolyploidy

This type of polyploidy usually arises from the doubling of chromosomes in a hybrid between two different species. The doubling often makes the hybrid fertile.

Examples: Modern wheat. Swedes are polyploid species formed from a hybrid between a type of cabbage and a type of turnip.

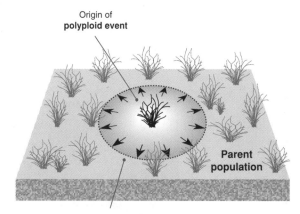

Origin of **polyploid event**

Parent population

New polyploid plant species spreads outwards through the existing parent population

---

1. Explain what is meant by **sympatric speciation** (do not confuse this with sympatric species):

   _____

   _____

2. Explain how **polyploidy** can result in the formation of a new species: _____

   _____

   _____

3. Identify an example of a species that has been formed by polyploidy: _____

4. Explain how **niche differentiation** can result in the formation of a new species: _____

   _____

   _____

144 Stages in Species Development

Key Idea: Species may develop in stages marked by increasing isolation of diverging gene pools. Physical separation is followed by increasing reproductive isolation.

The diagram below shows a possible sequence of events in the origin of two new species from an ancestral population. Over time, the genetic differences between two populations increase and the populations become increasingly isolated from each other. The isolation of the two gene pools may begin with a geographical barrier. This may be followed by progressively greater reduction in gene flow between the populations until the two gene pools are isolated and they each attain species status.

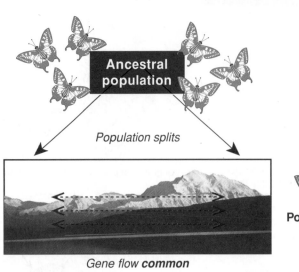

Ancestral population

Population splits

Evolutionary development or time

A species of butterfly lives on a plateau. The plateau is covered with grassland strewn with boulders. During colder weather, some butterflies sit on the sun-heated boulders to absorb the heat, while others retreat to the lower altitude grassland to avoid the cold.

Population A   **Population B**

*Gene flow **common***

Continued mountain building raises the altitude of the plateau, separating two populations of butterflies, one in the highlands the other in the lowlands.

Race A   **Race B**

*Gene flow **uncommon***

In the highlands, boulder-sitting butterflies (BSBs) do better than grass-sitting butterflies (GSBs). In the lowlands, the opposite is true. BSBs only mate on boulders with other BSBs. Darker BSBs have greater fitness than light BSBs. (they can absorb more heat from the boulders). In the lowlands, light GSBs blend in with the grass and survive better than darker butterflies.

Subspecies A   **Subspecies B**

*Gene flow **very rare***

Over time, only boulder-sitting butterflies are found in the highlands and grass-sitting butterflies in the lowlands. Occasionally wind brings members of the two groups together, but if they mate, the offspring are usually not viable or have a much lowered fitness.

Species A   **Species B**

Separate species

Eventually gene flow between separated populations ceases as variation between the populations increases. They fail to recognise each other as members of the same species.

1. Identify the variation in behaviour in the original butterfly population: _____

_____

2. What were the selection pressures acting on BSBs in the highlands and GSBs in the lowlands respectively?

_____

_____

_____

LINK
142

145 The Evolution of Antibiotic Resistance

Key Idea: Current widespread use of antibiotics has created a selective environment for the proliferation of antibiotic resistance in bacterial populations.

Antibiotic resistance arises when a genetic change allows bacteria to tolerate levels of antibiotic that would normally inhibit growth. This resistance may arise spontaneously, through mutation or copying error, or by transfer of genetic material between microbes. Genomic analyses from 30 000 year old permafrost sediments show that the genes for antibiotic resistance are not new. They have long been present in the bacterial genome, predating the modern selective pressure of antibiotic use. In the current selective environment, these genes have proliferated and antibiotic resistance has spread. For example, methicillin resistant strains of *Staphylococcus aureus* (MRSA) have acquired genes for resistance to all penicillins. Such strains are called superbugs.

The evolution of drug resistance in bacteria

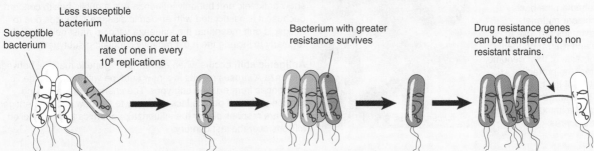

Susceptible bacterium

Less susceptible bacterium

Mutations occur at a rate of one in every 10^8 replications

Bacterium with greater resistance survives

Drug resistance genes can be transferred to non resistant strains.

Any population, including bacterial populations, includes variants with unusual traits, in this case reduced sensitivity to an antibiotic. These variants arise as a result of mutations in the bacterial chromosome.

When a person takes an antibiotic, only the most susceptible bacteria will die. The more resistant cells remain alive and continue dividing. Note that the antibiotic does not create the resistance; it provides the environment in which selection for resistance can take place.

If the amount of antibiotic delivered is too low, or the course of antibiotics is not completed, a population of resistant bacteria develops. Within this population too, there will be variation in susceptibility. Some will survive higher antibiotic levels than others.

A highly resistant population has evolved. The resistant cells can exchange genetic material with other bacteria (via horizontal gene transmission), passing on the genes for resistance. The antibiotic initially used against this bacterial strain will now be ineffective.

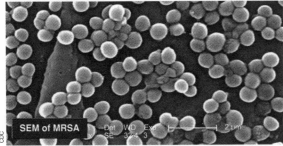

SEM of MRSA   Det WD Exp   2 µm
SE 32.1 3

Staphylococcus aureus is a common bacterium responsible for skin infections in humans. MRSA is a strain that has evolved resistance to penicillin and related antibiotics. MRSA is troublesome in hospital-associated infections because patients with open wounds, invasive devices (e.g. catheters), or poor immunity are at greater risk for infection than the general public.

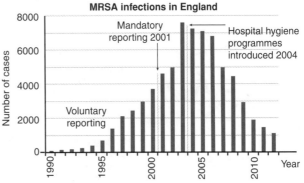

MRSA infections in England

Mandatory reporting 2001

Hospital hygiene programmes introduced 2004

Voluntary reporting

In the UK, MRSA cases rose sharply during the early-mid 1990s, but are now declining as a result of mandatory reporting and the implementation of stringent hospital hygiene programmes.

1. What does **antibiotic resistance** mean? _____

_____

2. (a) How does antibiotic resistance arise in a bacterial population? _____

_____

(b) Describe two ways in which antibiotic resistance can become widespread: _____

_____

_____

_____

3. With reference to MRSA, describe the implications to humans of widespread antibiotic resistance: _____

_____

_____

146 Antigenic Variability in Influenzavirus

Key Idea: The rapid mutation rate of *Influenzavirus* causes its surface proteins to continually change from year to year. **Influenza** (flu) is a disease of the upper respiratory tract caused by *Influenzavirus*. Globally, flu kills up to half a million people every year and it is estimated that up to 20% of Britons are affected annually. High mutation rates in influenzaviruses result in small sequential changes in the viral envelope over time. This phenomenon is called **antigenic drift**. The most virulent strain, *Influenzavirus* A, periodically also undergoes **antigenic shifts** as a result of two or more different viral strains combining to form a new subtype. These new subtypes are associated with increased virulence.

Influenzavirus

Three strains of *Influenzavirus*. (A, B, and C) affect humans, distinguished on the basis of their nuclear material. Influenzaviruses are able to combine and rearrange the 8 RNA segments of their genome, which alters the protein composition of their glycoprotein spikes. The changes make it difficult for the immune system to detect the virus.

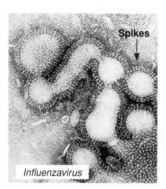

Spikes

Influenzavirus

Structure of *Influenzavirus*

Viral strains are identified by the variation in their H and N surface **antigens**. Antigens are foreign proteins that alert the immune system to the presence of a pathogen. Viruses are able to combine and rearrange their RNA segments, producing new variants of their H and N glycoprotein spikes (designated by numbers. e.g. H1N2).

The influenzavirus is surrounded by an **envelope** containing protein and lipids.

The genetic material is actually closely surrounded by protein capsomeres (these have been omitted here in order to illustrate the changes in the RNA more clearly).

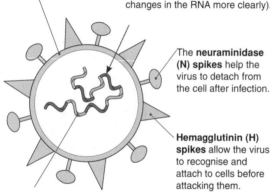

The **neuraminidase (N) spikes** help the virus to detach from the cell after infection.

Hemagglutinin (H) spikes allow the virus to recognise and attach to cells before attacking them.

The viral genome is contained on **eight RNA segments**, which enables the exchange of genes between different viral strains.

How does the *Influenzavirus* change?

Antigenic drifts are small, sequential changes within a virus subtype caused by point mutations in a gene. All strains of *Influenzavirus* show antigenic drift but only influenza A is a public health concern because it is associated with epidemic disease. Changes due to antigenic drift mean that the influenza vaccine must be adjusted regularly to include the most recently circulating subtypes.

Antigenic shift occurs when exchange of genetic material between influenza A viruses results in a new subtype with major antigenic differences from existing subtypes. The changes are large and sudden and most people lack immunity to the new subtype. Antigenic shifts are responsible for the influenza pandemics that have killed millions over the last century.

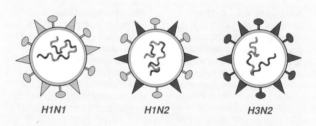

H1N1   H1N2   H3N2

Influenza A virus subtypes currently circulating among humans

Type A influenza has a number of subtypes that are determined (and named) by the surface antigens hemagglutinin (H) and neuraminidase (N). Type A is harboured in wild fowl populations and periodically (every 10-40 years) undergoes an antigenic shift to produce a novel subtype.

The 2009 "swine flu" epidemic

In 2009, a new strain of the H1N1 influenza subtype was identified. It appeared to be the result of a reassortment of the genes originally found in human and swine flu. The H protein on the surface was one that until 2009 had been seen only in pigs. This meant it was far more likely to avoid the human immune response, including people vaccinated against regular flu. The strain was first identified in North America but quickly spread to the rest of the world and was declared a pandemic in April 2009. Partly due to health measures taken world wide, the pandemic was declared over in August 2010.

1. The *Influenzavirus* is able to mutate readily and alter the composition of H and N spikes on its surface.

   (a) Why can the virus mutate so readily? _____

   _____

   _____

   (b) How does this affect the ability of the immune system to recognize and respond to the virus? _____

   _____

   _____

2. Why is a virus capable of antigenic shift is more dangerous to humans than a virus undergoing antigenic drift:

   _____

   _____

147 Resistance in HIV

Key Idea: HIV mutates rapidly, making vaccine production difficult and the chances of drug resistance high.

Although many diseases are treated effectively with drugs, the emergence of drug resistant pathogens is increasingly undermining the ability to treat and control diseases such as HIV/AIDS. HIV's high mutation rate and short generation times contribute to the rapid spread of drug resistance. Rapid evolution in pathogens is exacerbated by the strong selection pressures created by the wide use and misuse of antiviral drugs, the poor quality of available drugs in some sectors of the population, and lack of education on drug use. The most successful treatment for several diseases, including HIV/AIDS, appears to be a multi-pronged attack using a cocktail of drugs to target the pathogen in several different ways.

HIV

The human immunodeficiency virus (HIV) infects the T lymphocytes of the immune system, eventually causing AIDS, a fatal disease, which acts by impairing the body's ability to fight disease.

HIV replicates quickly, producing billions of copies of itself each day, so its ability to infect new cells (and new hosts) is high. HIV shows high genetic variability and mutates frequently. It can also combine its genetic material with other HIV viruses to form new strains. These factors have important consequences for the prevention and treatment of HIV. Any vaccine would quickly become ineffective because the virus changes so rapidly and so many different strains are present. Resistance to drugs used for treatment also arises quickly because of rapid mutation rates and short generation times. Preventing new HIV infections is critical to halting the spread of the disease.

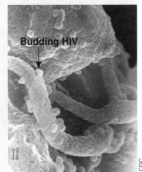
Budding HIV

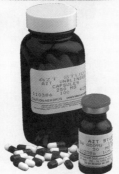

Drug resistance in HIV

Strains of drug-resistant HIV arise when the virus mutates during replication. Resistance may develop as a result of a single mutation, or through a step-wise accumulation of specific mutations. These mutations may alter drug binding capacity or increase viral fitness, or they may be naturally occurring polymorphisms (which occur in untreated patients). Drug resistance is likely to develop in patients who do not follow their treatment schedule closely, as the virus has an opportunity to adapt more readily to a "non-lethal" drug dose. The best practice for managing the HIV virus is to treat it with a cocktail of anti-retroviral drugs with different actions to minimise the number of viruses in the body. This minimises the replication rate, and also the chance of a drug resistant mutation being produced.

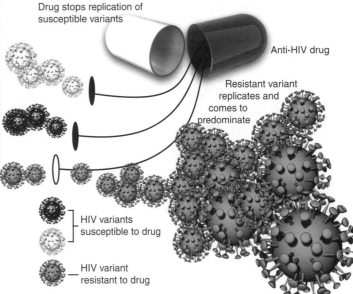

Drug stops replication of susceptible variants
Anti-HIV drug
Resistant variant replicates and comes to predominate
HIV variants susceptible to drug
HIV variant resistant to drug

Drug resistance in HIV

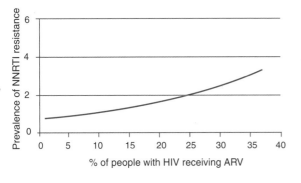

In general, resistance to drug treatment in HIV increases as the percentage of patients receiving drug therapy increases. A 2012 WHO study found that 10-17% of patients in Western nations had resistance to at least one anti-retroviral drug. In Africa this number was much lower, but increasing.

1. What is the basis of drug resistance in HIV?

2. Explain why a producing a vaccine for HIV is difficult:

3. Explain why a combination drug therapy is used to treat HIV:

LINK 98 LINK 96 WEB 147 KNOW

148 Chloroquine Resistance in Protozoa

Key Idea: Resistance to chloroquine in the protozoan that causes malaria has spread ever since chloroquine's introduction in the 1940s.

Chloroquine is an antimalarial drug, discovered in 1934, and first used clinically to prevent malaria in 1946. Chloroquine was widely used because it was cheap to produce, safe, and very effective against the malarial parasite, *Plasmodium*. Chloroquine resistance in *P. falciparum* first appeared in the late 1950s, and the subsequent spread of resistance has significantly decreased chloroquine's effectiveness. The WHO regularly update the global status on anti-malarial drug efficacy and drug resistance. Their 2010 report shows that when chloroquine is used as a monotherapy, it is still effective at preventing malaria in Central American countries (chloroquine resistance has not yet developed there). In 30 other countries, chloroquine failure rates ranged between 20-100%. In some regions, chloroquine used in combination with other anti-malarial drugs is still an effective treatment.

Global spread of chloroquine resistance

Areas of chloroquine resistance in *P. falciparum*.

Malaria in humans is caused by various species of *Plasmodium*, a protozoan parasite transmitted by *Anopheles* mosquitoes. The inexpensive antimalarial drug **chloroquine** was used successfully to treat malaria for many years, but its effectiveness has declined since resistance to the drug was first recorded in the 1950s. Chloroquine resistance has spread steadily (above) and now two of the four *Plasmodium* species, *P. falciparum* and *P. vivax* are chloroquine-resistant. *P. falciparum* alone accounts for 80% of all human malarial infections and 90% of the deaths, so this rise in resistance is of global concern. New anti-malarial drugs have been developed, but are expensive and often have undesirable side effects. Resistance to even these newer drugs is already evident, especially in *P. falciparum*, although this species is currently still susceptible to artemisinin, a derivative of the medicinal herb *Artemisia annua*.

Recent studies have demonstrated a link between mutations in the chloroquine resistance transporter (PfCRT) gene, and resistance to chloroquine in *P. falciparum*. PfCRT is a membrane protein involved in drug and metabolite transport.

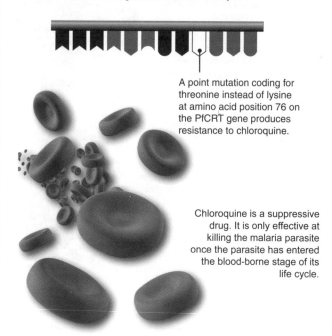

A point mutation coding for threonine instead of lysine at amino acid position 76 on the PfCRT gene produces resistance to chloroquine.

Chloroquine is a suppressive drug. It is only effective at killing the malaria parasite once the parasite has entered the blood-borne stage of its life cycle.

The use of chloroquine in many African countries was halted during the 1990s because resistance developed in *P. falciparum*. Recent studies in Malawi and Kenya have revealed a significant decrease in chloroquine resistance since the drug was withdrawn. There may be a significant fitness cost to the PfCRT mutants in the absence of anti-malaria drugs, leading to their decline in frequency once the selection pressure of the drugs is removed. This raises the possibility of re-introducing chloroquine as an anti-malarial treatment in the future.

1. Describe the benefits of using chloroquine to prevent malaria: _____

_____

_____

2. With reference to *Plasmodium falciparum*, explain how chloroquine resistance arises: _____

_____

_____

3. Describe two strategies to reduce the spread of chloroquine resistance while still treating malaria:

   (a) _____

   _____

   (b) _____

   _____

© 2015 **BIOZONE** International
ISBN:978-1-927309-25-4
Photocopying Prohibited

149 Biodiversity

Key Idea: Biodiversity is the sum of all biotic variation from the level of genes to ecosystems. All organisms within an ecosystem contribute to its functioning, but keystone species have a disproportionate effect on ecosystem functioning.

Biodiversity is defined as the sum of all biotic variation from the level of genes to ecosystems. Species diversity describes species richness (the number of species), genetic diversity is the diversity of genes within a species, and

ecosystem diversity (of which habitat diversity is a part) refers to the diversity at the ecosystem level. Total biodiversity is threatened by the loss of just one of these components. While every species plays a role in ecosystem function, **keystone species** have a disproportionate effect on ecosystem stability because of their pivotal role in some aspect of ecosystem functioning, e.g. as predators or in nutrient cycling. The loss of a keystone species can result in rapid ecosystem change.

Habitat diversity

Habitat diversity (the presence of many different types of habitat) is important for maintaining biodiversity. Specific habitats are occupied by different organisms and, in general, the greater the number of habitats, the greater the species diversity. Within habitats, microhabitats (smaller areas with specific characteristics) further increase biodiversity. For example, in a stream habitat, microhabitats exist under the rocks, in riffles, in pools, and in vegetation at the stream edges. Some common English habitats are shown (right).

Habitat protection is important to maintain species biodiversity. Habitat loss is one of the biggest threats to biodiversity and is the most common cause of extinction. Examples of habitat destruction include clear cutting forests for logging and agriculture, ploughing natural meadows to make way for agriculture, draining wetland and peatlands, and creating dams that alter river flows.

Coastal sand dunes, Wales

Stream, Peak district

Bluebell woodland

Meadow, Yorkshire

Measuring biodiversity

Biodiversity is quantified for a variety of reasons, e.g. to assess the success of conservation work or to measure the impact of human activity.

One measure of biodiversity is to simply count all the species present (the **species richness**). Species richness (S) is directly related to the number of species in a sampled area. It is a crude measure of the homogeneity of a community but it does not give any information about the relative abundance of particular species and so is relatively meaningless by itself. Thus a sample area with 500 daisies and 3 dandelions has the same species richness as a sample area with 200 daisies and 300 dandelions.

Species evenness measures the proportion of individuals of each species in an area (the relative abundance). Species evenness is highest when the proportions of all species are the same and decreases as the proportions of species become less similar.

Sample of freshwater invertebrates in a stream			
Common name	Site 1 / $n\,m^{-2}$	Site 2 / $n\,m^{-2}$	Site 3 / $n\,m^{-2}$
Freshwater shrimp	67	20	5
Freshwater mite	4	15	1
Flat mayfly	23	21	0
Bighead stonefly	12	18	2
Blackfly	78	40	100
Bloodworm	21	22	43

Data for species richness and species evenness can be obtained by sampling, e.g. using quadrats. In the example above, three sites in a stream were sampled using quadrats and the species and number of individuals per m² recorded for each site. Using Site 1 as an example, species richness is 6, since $S = n$. Measures of species evenness are an integral component of biodiversity indices, such as Simpson's Index of biodiversity, but can also be estimated from the numbers of individuals of each species. In terms of species evenness, site 2 > site 1 > site 3.

High species richness

Low species richness

Stephen Moore

1. Distinguish between species diversity and genetic diversity and explain the importance of both of these to our definition of total biological diversity:

_____

_____

_____

_____

Keystone species in Europe and the UK

Grey wolf

European beaver

Scots pine

Grey or timber wolves (*Canis lupus*) are a keystone predator and were once widespread through North America, Europe, and Eurasia. Historically they have been eliminated because of their perceived threat to humans and livestock, and now occupy only a fraction of their former range. As a top predator, the wolf is a keystone species. When they are absent, populations of their prey (e.g. red deer) increase to the point that they adversely affect other flora and fauna.

The European beaver (*Caster fiber*) was originally distributed throughout most of Europe and northern Asia but populations have been decimated as a result of hunting and habitat loss. Where they occur, beavers are critical to ecosystem function and a number of species depend partly or entirely on beaver ponds for survival. Their tree-felling activity is akin to a natural coppicing process and promotes vigorous regrowth, while historically they helped the spread of alder (a water-loving species) in Britain.

Scots pine (*Pinus sylvestris*) is the most widely distributed conifer in the world. In the Scots pine forests in Scotland, this species occupies a unique position, both because of the absence of other native conifers and because it directly or indirectly supports so many other species. Among those dependent on Scots pine for survival are blaeberries, wood ants, pine martens, and a number of bird species including the capercaillie (wood grouse) and the UK's only endemic bird, the Scottish crossbill.

2. Why is habitat diversity important to maintaining species biodiversity? _____

_____

_____

3. (a) Distinguish between the two measures of biodiversity: species richness and species evenness: _____

_____

_____

_____

(b) Why is it is important to incorporate both these measures when considering species conservation? _____

_____

_____

4. Why are keystone species are so important to ecosystem function? _____

_____

_____

_____

5. On a separate sheet of paper, discuss the biological features of the grey wolf, European beaver, and Scots pine that contribute to their position as a keystone species. Attach the sheet to this workbook.

© 2015 **BIOZONE** International
ISBN: 978-1-927309-25-4
Photocopying Prohibited

150 Sampling Populations

Key Idea: A population's characteristics may be inferred from data collected by sampling. Random sampling methods are preferred as they provide unbiased data.

In most ecological studies, it is not possible to measure or count all the members of a population. Instead, information is obtained through sampling in a manner that provides a fair (unbiased) representation of the organisms present and their distribution. This is usually achieved through **random** **sampling**, a technique in which each individual has the same probability of being selected at any stage during the sampling process. Sometimes researchers collect information by **non-random sampling**, a process that does not give all the individuals in the population an equal chance of being selected. While faster and cheaper to carry out than random sampling, non-random sampling may not give a true representation of the population.

Sampling strategies

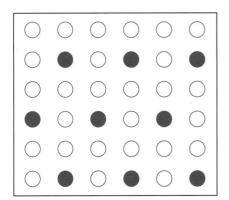

Systematic sampling

Samples from a larger population are selected according to a random starting point and a fixed, periodic sampling interval. For the example above, the sampling period is every fourth individual. Systematic sampling is a random sampling method, provided the periodic interval is determined beforehand and the starting point is random.

Example: Selecting individuals from a patient list.

Stratified sampling

Stratified sampling divides the population into subgroups before sampling. The strata should be mutually exclusive, and individuals must be assigned to only one stratum. Stratified sampling is used to highlight a specific subgroup within the population. Individuals are then randomly sampled from the strata to study.

Example: Dividing the population into males and females.

Opportunistic sampling

A non-random sampling technique in which subjects are selected because of they are easily accessible to the researcher. Opportunistic sampling excludes a large proportion of the population and is usually not representative of the population. It is sometimes used in pilot studies to gather data quickly and with little cost.

Example: Selecting 13 people at a cafe where you are having lunch.

1. Why do we sample populations? _____

_____

_____

2. Why is random sampling preferable to non-random sampling? _____

_____

3. (a) Why can stratified sampling be considered a random sampling method?_____

_____

(b) Describe a situation where its use might be appropriate? _____

_____

4. A student wants to investigate the incidence of asthma in their school. Describe how they might select samples from the school population using:

(a) Systematic sampling: _____

_____

(b) Stratified sampling: _____

_____

(c) Opportunistic sampling: _____

_____

LINK LINK WEB
153 **151** **150** KNOW

151 Interpreting Samples

Key Idea: If sample data are collected without bias and in sufficient quantity, even a simple analysis can provide useful information about the composition of a community and the possible physical factors influencing this.

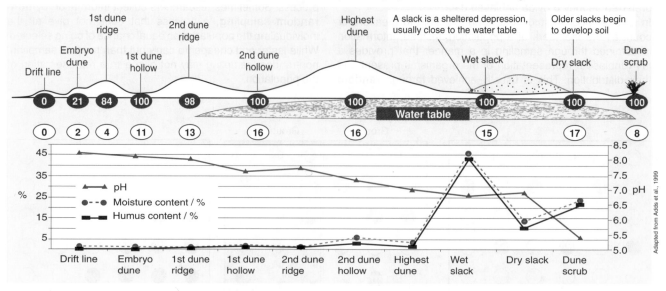

1. The beach dune profile (top) shows transect sampling points at fixed morphological features (e.g. dune ridges). The blue ovals on the dune profile represent the percentage vegetation cover at each sampling point. The white ovals record the number of plant species. Some physical data for each sampling site are presented in the graph below the profile.

   (a) What is the trend in pH from drift line to dune scrub? _____

   (b) Suggest why moisture and humus content increase along the transect? _____

   _____

   _____

   _____

2. The figure below shows changes in vegetation cover along a 2 m vertical transect up the trunk of an oak tree. Changes in the physical factors light, humidity, and temperature along the same transect were also recorded.

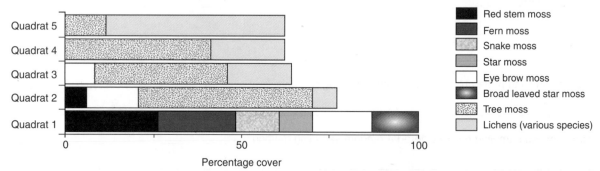

Legend	
■	Red stem moss
■	Fern moss
▨	Snake moss
▨	Star moss
□	Eye brow moss
◉	Broad leaved star moss
▨	Tree moss
▨	Lichens (various species)

Percentage cover

QUADRAT	1	2	3	4	5
Height / m	0.4	0.8	1.2	1.6	2.0
Light / arbitrary units	40	56	68	72	72
Humidity / percent	99	88	80	76	78
Temperature / °C	12.1	12.2	13	14.3	14.2

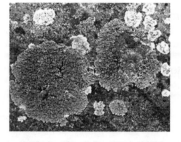 

   (a) At which height were mosses most diverse and abundant? _____

   (b) What plant type predominates at 2.0 m height? _____

   (c) What can you deduce about the habitat preferences of most mosses and lichens from this study? _____

   _____

152 Assessing Species Diversity

Key Idea: Diversity indices allow a quantitative analysis of diversity of an ecosystem and can be used as an indicator of ecosystem change (degradation or recovery).

Measures of biodiversity are commonly used as the basis for making conservation decisions, identifying environmental degradation, or monitoring ecosystem recovery. Species diversity indices may be used to quantify biodiversity and are often used in conjunction with the presence or absence of particular indicator species (species typical of certain conditions) to monitor ecosystem health.

Calculation and use of diversity indices

Diversity can be quantified using a diversity index. Diversity indices account for both species richness and species evenness and can be useful in identifying environmental degradation (or recovery). Most indices of diversity are easy to use and they are widely used in ecological work. One example, which is a derivation of the Simpson's Index, is described below. Other indices produce values ranging between 0 and almost 1. These are more easily interpreted because of the more limited range of values but no single index offers the 'best' measure of diversity. They are chosen on the basis of their suitability to different situations.

$$D = \frac{N(N-1)}{\sum n(n-1)}$$

This formula is called Simpson's index for finite populations

D = Diversity index
N = Total number of individuals (of all species) in the sample
n = Number of individuals of each species in the sample

Example of species diversity in a stream

Species	n
A (backswimmer)	12
B (stonefly larva)	7
C (silver water beetle)	2
D (caddisfly larva)	6
E (water spider)	5
F (mayfly larva)	8

$$n = 40$$

The table left records the results from a survey of stream invertebrates. It is not necessary to know the species to calculate a diversity index as long as the different species can be distinguished.

Calculation of d using the formula (left) is:

$$D = \frac{40 \times 39}{(12\times11) + (7\times6) + (2\times1) + (6\times5) + (5\times4) + (8\times7)} = \frac{1560}{282} = 5.53$$

A value of 5.53 can only really be evaluated relative to a previous state or another community. Communities with a wide range of species produce a higher score than communities dominated by larger numbers of only a few species.

Using diversity indices: the role of indicator species

To be properly interpreted, indices are usually evaluated with reference to earlier measurement or a standard ecosystem measure. The photographs left show samples from two stream communities, a high diversity community with a large number of macroinvertebrate species (top) and a low diversity community (lower photograph) with fewer species in large numbers. These photographs also show indicator species. The top image shows a stonefly (1) and an alderfly larva (2). These species (together with mayfly larvae) are typical of clean, well oxygenated water. The lower image is dominated by snails (3), which are tolerant of a wide range of conditions, included degraded environments.

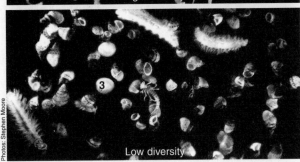
High diversity

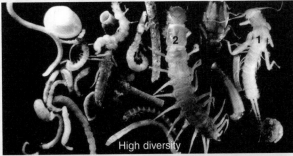
Low diversity

Photos: Stephen Moore

Photo: C Johnson-Walker, c 3.0

The aptly named rat-tail maggot is the larva of the drone fly. This species is an indicator of gross pollution. Its prominent feature is a long snorkel-like breathing siphon.

---

1. (a) An area of forest floor was sampled and six invertebrate species were recorded, with counts of 7, 10, 11, 2, 4, and 3 individuals. Using Simpson's index for finite populations, calculate *d* for this community:

    D = _____   *D* = _____

   (b) The same study also sampled near the margin of the forest and the same six invertebrates were recorded, with counts of 16, 4, 1, 3, 4, and 2 individuals. Use Simpson's index for finite populations, calculate *d* for this community:

    D = _____   *D* = _____

   (c) Comment on the diversity of these communities relative to each other: _____

   _____

   _____

153 Investigating Biodiversity

Key Idea: Sampling must be carefully planned in order to obtain meaningful results.

Careful planning is needed before sampling to ensure sound, unbiased data are obtained. If your sampling technique, assumptions, sample size, or sample unit are inadequate, your results will not provide a true representation of the community under study. The Simpson's index of diversity can be used to compare species diversity at two different sites.

Observation

Walking through a conifer plantation, a student observed that there seemed to be only a few different invertebrate species in the forest leaf litter. She wondered if more invertebrate species would be found in a nearby oak woodland.

Hypothesis

The oak woodland has a more varied leaf litter composition than the conifer plantation, so will support a wider variety of invertebrate species.

The **null hypothesis** is that there is no difference between the diversity of invertebrate species in oak woodland and coniferous plantation litter.

Oak woodland

Conifer plantation

Sampling programme

The student designed a sampling programme to test the prediction that there would be a greater diversity of invertebrates in the leaf litter of oak woodlands than in coniferous plantation.

Equipment and procedure

Sites: For each of the two forest types, an area 20 x 8 m was chosen and marked out in 2 x 2 m grids. Eight sampling sites were selected, evenly spaced along the grid as shown (right).

- The two general sampling areas for the study (oak and conifer) were **randomly selected**.
- Eight sites were chosen as the largest number feasible to collect and analyse in the time available.
- The two areas were sampled on sequential days.

Capture of invertebrates: At each site, a 0.4 x 0.4 m quadrat was placed on the forest floor and the leaf litter within the quadrat was collected. Leaf litter invertebrates were captured using a simple gauze lined funnel containing the leaf litter from within the quadrat. A lamp was positioned over each funnel for two hours and the invertebrates in the litter moved down and were trapped in the collecting jar.

- After two hours, each jar was labelled with the site number and returned to the lab for analysis.
- The litter in each funnel was bagged, labelled with the site number and returned to the lab for weighing.
- The number of each invertebrate species at each site was recorded.
- After counting and analysis of the samples, all the collected invertebrates were returned to the sites.

Assumptions

- The areas chosen in each forest were representative in terms of invertebrate abundance.
- Eight sites were sufficient to adequately sample the invertebrate populations in each forest.
- A quadrat size of 0.4 x 0.4 m contained enough leaf litter to adequately sample the invertebrates at each sample site.
- The invertebrates did not prey on each other once captured in the collecting jar.
- All the invertebrates within the quadrat were captured.
- Invertebrates moving away from the light are effectively captured by the funnel apparatus and cannot escape.
- Two hours was long enough for the invertebrates to move down through the litter and fall into the trap.

Note that these last two assumptions could be tested by examining the bagged leaf litter for invertebrates after returning to the lab.

Oak woodland or coniferous plantation

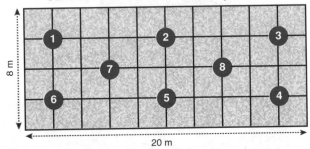

8 m

20 m

1 Sampling sites numbered 1-8 at evenly spaced intervals on a 2 x 2 m grid within an area of 20 m x 8 m.

Sampling equipment: leaf litter light trap

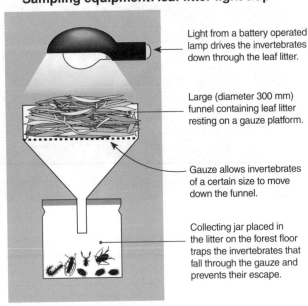

Light from a battery operated lamp drives the invertebrates down through the leaf litter.

Large (diameter 300 mm) funnel containing leaf litter resting on a gauze platform.

Gauze allows invertebrates of a certain size to move down the funnel.

Collecting jar placed in the litter on the forest floor traps the invertebrates that fall through the gauze and prevents their escape.

The importance of sample size

In any field study, two of the most important considerations are the **sample size** (the number of samples you will take) and the size of the **sampling unit** (e.g. quadrat size). An appropriate choice will enable you to collect sufficient, unbiased data to confidently test your hypothesis. The number of samples you take will be determined largely by the resources and time that you have available to collect and analyse your data (your **sampling effort**).

LINK 150   LINK 152
DATA

Results

The results from the student's study are presented in the tables and images below. The invertebrates are not drawn to scale.

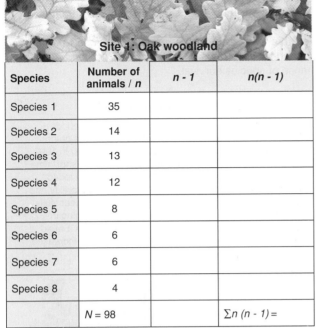

Site 1: Oak woodland

Species	Number of animals / n	n - 1	n(n - 1)
Species 1	35		
Species 2	14		
Species 3	13		
Species 4	12		
Species 5	8		
Species 6	6		
Species 7	6		
Species 8	4		
	N = 98		$\sum n(n-1) =$

Site 2: Conifer plantation

Species	Number of animals / n	n - 1	n(n - 1)
Species 1	74		
Species 2	16		
Species 3	4		
Species 4	2		
Species 5	2		
Species 6	1		
Species 7	0		
Species 8	1		
	N = 100		$\sum n(n-1) =$

Species 1	Species 2	Species 3	Species 4	Species 5	Species 6	Species 7	Species 8
Mite	Ant	Earwig	Woodlice	Centipede	Longhorn beetle	Small beetle	Pseudoscorpion

1. What type of sampling design is used in this study? _____

2. Explain the importance of each of the following in field studies:

   (a) Appropriately sized sampling unit: _____

   _____

   (b) Recognising any assumptions that you are making: _____

   _____

   (c) Appropriate consideration of the environment: _____

   _____

   (d) Return of organisms to the same place after removal: _____

   _____

   (e) Appropriate size of total sampling area within which the sites are located: _____

   _____

3. (a) Complete the two tables above to calculate the values for *n(n-1)* for the student's two sampling sites:

   (b) Calculate **D** for site 1: _____

   (c) Calculate **D** for site 2: _____

   (d) Compare the diversity of the two sites and suggest any reasons for it: _____

   _____

   _____

   _____

154 Assessing Genetic Diversity

Key Idea: Genetic diversity can be measured by calculating the allele diversity in a population. Species with low genetic diversity may be at risk of extinction.

Genetic diversity refers to the variety of alleles and genotypes present in a population. Genetic diversity is important to the survival and adaptability of a species.

Populations with low genetic diversity may not be able to respond to environmental change and are at greater risk of extinction. In contrast, species with greater genetic diversity are more likely to have the genetic resources to adapt and respond to environmental change. This increases their chance of species survival.

Measuring genetic diversity

Measuring genetic diversity can help identify at-risk populations and prioritise conservation efforts for rare breeds or animals in captive breeding programmes. Pedigree animals may be tested for genetic diversity to assist in planning breeding programmes so that loss of genetic diversity is minimised. Eukaryotic chromosomes contain many genes and, in any one population, each gene may have a number of versions called alleles. The presence of more than one allele at a specific gene location (locus) is called polymorphism. When only one allele is present the locus is said to be monomorphic. One of the simplest measures of genetic diversity involves calculating the proportions polymorphic loci across a genome or a species. The following equation can be used:

$$\text{Proportion of polymorphic gene loci} = \frac{\text{number of polymorphic gene loci}}{\text{total number of loci}}$$

Measuring genetic diversity in African lions

Allele variation at 26 enzyme loci in an African lion population was studied (below). Twenty loci showed no variation (they were monomorphic) and six loci showed variation (they were polymorphic).

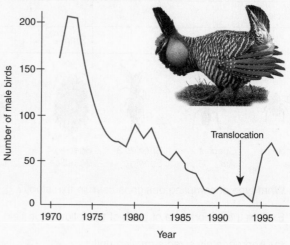

Enzyme locus	Allele		
	1	2	3
ADA	0.56	0.33	0.11
DIAB	0.61	0.39	
ESI	0.88	0.12	
GPI	0.85	0.15	
GPT	0.89	0.11	
MPI	0.92	0.08	
20 Monomorphic loci	1.00		

Data: Newman et al. 1985

The effects of low genetic diversity

Until 1992, the Illinois prairie chicken was destined for extinction. The population had fallen from millions before European arrival to 25 000 in 1933 and then to 50 in 1992. The dramatic decline in the population in such a short time resulted in a huge loss of genetic diversity, which led to inbreeding and in turn resulted in a decrease in fertility and an ever-decreasing number of eggs hatching successfully. In 1992, a translocation programme began, bringing in 271 birds from Kansas and Nebraska. There was a rapid population response, as fertility and egg viability increased. The population is now recovering.

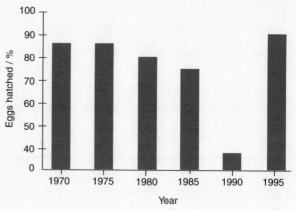

1. What is genetic diversity? _____

_____

_____

_____

_____

_____

2. (a) For the lion data, identify the enzyme locus with the highest genetic diversity: _____

(b) Calculate the genetic diversity for the 26 loci studied above: _____

3. (a) Describe the factors contributing to the loss of diversity in the Illinois prairie chicken: _____

_____

_____

(b) Why did the translocation of 271 birds from outside Illinois into the Illinois population halt the population decline?

_____

© 2015 **BIOZONE** International
ISBN:978-1-927309-25-4
Photocopying Prohibited

155 Why is Biodiversity Important?

Key Idea: Maintaining biodiversity enhances ecosystem stability and functioning and also provides economic and aesthetic benefits to humans.

Ecosystems provide both material and non-material benefits to humans. These benefits, or ecosystem services, are best provided by healthy, diverse systems. As a general rule, high diversity ecosystems are ecologically more stable (constant in character over time) and resistant to disturbance (**resilient**) than systems with low diversity. Maintaining diversity therefore has economic benefits to humans through their use of ecosystem resources and through the generation of income from tourism to ecologically significant areas. Although often discussed as individual benefits, the ecological, aesthetic, and economic reasons for maintaining biodiversity overlap.

Ecological reasons for maintaining biodiversity

Evidence from both experimental and natural systems indicates that the most diverse ecosystems are generally the most stable, most probably because the complex network of species interactions has a buffering effect against change. Maintaining biodiversity is therefore critical to maintaining key ecological functions such as nutrient cycling and water purification.

Ecosystems include many interdependent species (e.g. flowering plants and their pollinators, hosts and parasites). The loss of even one species can detrimentally alter ecosystem dynamics, especially if the species is a keystone species. For example, in the Caledonian forest in Scotland, the Scots pine is key to the survival of many of the species present there. Its loss would affect the survival of those species and compromise the stability of the ecosystem.

Genetic diversity is an important component of ecosystem stability and resilience. A loss of genetic diversity is associated with an increased risk of extinction and a greater chance that an ecosystem will become impoverished and degraded. Genetic diversity effectively represents genetic resources, i.e. those genes in living organisms that may have benefits to humans (e.g. medicinal plants). Once an organism is extinct, those genetic resources are also lost.

Rainforest

Monoculture of soy beans

Rainforests represent the highest diversity systems on Earth. Whilst they are generally resistant to disturbance (resilient), once degraded (e.g. by deforestation), they have little ability to recover. Monocultures, which provide the majority of the world's food supply, represent very low diversity systems and are particularly susceptible to diseases, pests, and disturbance.

Aesthetic reasons for maintaining biodiversity

Many people enjoy looking at, or spending time in areas of natural beauty. Viewing aesthetically pleasing landscapes provides satisfaction and enjoyment to the individual. Nature can also provide inspiration for artists, photographers, and writers, as well as economic benefits from tourism. As countries become more populated and development increases, it becomes more important to maintain and protect natural landscapes as areas of natural beauty. The UK has several programmes designed to protect habitat and landscape for a variety of reasons, including aesthetics.

The images below show two coral reefs. Reef A has high biodiversity, many different species are represented and it is full of colour and life. Reef B is an area of coral bleaching and supports far fewer species. Imagine you were a tourist paying to visit the reef. Which would you rather visit?

A

B

1. What is the most likely reason for high diversity ecosystems being more stable than ecosystems with low biodiversity?

_____

_____

_____

2. Describe two aesthetic benefits of maintaining biodiversity: _____

_____

_____

3. (a) What is a genetic resource? _____

_____

   (b) Many medicines are derived from plants. How does tropical rainforest destruction reduce genetic resources?

_____

_____

LINK WEB
156 155 KNOW

Economic reasons for maintaining biodiversity

A variety of economic benefits (goods and services) are generated by biodiversity. These benefits are commonly called **ecosystem services** and are split into four categories: provisioning, regulating, and cultural services, which directly affect people, and supporting services, which maintain the other three services. The provisioning services are sometimes referred to as goods because they can be sold and their economic value can easily be calculated as they have a monetary value. Estimating the total economic value of total ecosystem services is difficult and contentious, but some estimates place their value at £81 trillion per year.

Provisioning services

(Products obtained from ecosystems)

- Food
- Water
- Fuel wood
- Fibres
- Biochemicals
- Genetic resources

Regulating services

(Benefits obtained from the regulation of ecosystem processes)

- Climate regulation
- Disease regulation
- Water regulation
- Water purification
- Pollination

Cultural services

(Nonmaterial benefits people obtain from ecosystems)

- Spiritual and religious
- Recreation and ecotourism
- Aesthetic
- Inspirational
- Educational
- Cultural heritage

Supporting services

(Services necessary for the production of all other ecosystem services)

- Soil formation
- Nutrient cycling
- Primary production

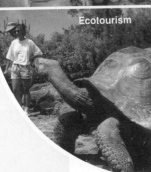

Food production

Pollination

Ecotourism

Soil formation

The economic cost of soil depletion

Soil depletion refers to the decline in soil fertility due to the removal of nutrients. Some definitions of soil depletion also include the physical loss (erosion) of soil.

The increase of continuous monoculture farming practices has contributed to a rapid loss of nutrients from the soil over the last few decades. Farmers must make an economic choice: spend money on fertilisers to add nutrients back to the soil or do nothing and suffer the economic consequences of low crop yields.

4. The 17th century Irish potato famine is an example of how low biodiversity can threaten our food supply. Farmers planted only one potato variety with limited genetic diversity. Most potato crops were destroyed by the fungal disease late blight and, exacerbated by the political environment at the time, there was widespread famine. How could have this situation have been prevented?

Blight affected potato

_____

_____

_____

5. Summarise the economic benefits of maintaining biodiversity: _____

_____

_____

_____

_____

_____

_____

156 How Humans Affect Biodiversity

Key Idea: The activities of an expanding human population are contributing to an increase in extinction rates above the natural level and a local and global reduction in biodiversity. The natural environment provides humans with the resources that sustain us, including food, water, fuel, and shelter. As the human population grows, demand on natural resources increases and land is cleared to build the houses and infrastructure associated with servicing a growing population. As a consequence of human demand, pressure on habitats and their natural populations increases and biodiversity declines. Humans rely heavily on biodiversity for survival, so a loss of biodiversity has a negative effect on us all.

The different species of Heliconius butterflies are difficult to distinguish because they mimic each other

Natural extinction rates for all organisms are estimated to be 10-100 species a year. The actual extinction rate is 100-1000 times higher, mainly due to the effects of human activity. The pool frog (above) is endangered in Britain due to habitat loss.

As the human population increases, cities expand, fragmenting or destroying the natural ecosystems surrounding them. Careful management of urban development and resource use will be needed to prevent local extinctions and loss of biodiversity.

The true loss biodiversity is unknown, partly because many species remain undiscovered or unrecognised because they cannot be distinguished from related species (above). *In-situ* conservation of ecosystems has a vital role in conserving species like these.

Most industry depends on the combustion of fossil fuels and this contributes to **global warming**, the continuing rise in the average temperature of the Earth's surface. Global warming and associated shifts in climate will affect species distributions, breeding cycles, and patterns of migration. Species unable to adapt are at risk of extinction.

Eighty percent of Earth's documented species are found in tropical rainforests. These rainforests are being destroyed rapidly as land is cleared for agriculture or cattle ranching, to supply logs, for mining, or to build dams. Deforestation places a majority of the Earth's biodiversity at risk and threatens and stability of important ecosystems.

Demand for food increases as the population grows. Modern farming techniques favour **monocultures** to maximise yield and profit. However monocultures, in which a single crop type is grown year after year, are a low diversity system and food supplies are vulnerable if the crop fails. The UN estimates that 12 plant species provide 75% of our total food supply.

1. The human population is growing at a rapid rate and as a result the demand for resources in increasing. Discuss how human activities are affecting biodiversity on Earth:

_____

_____

_____

_____

_____

_____

_____

_____

Loss of biodiversity

Insects make up 80% of all known animal species. There are an estimated 6-10 million insect species on Earth, but only 900 000 have been identified. Some 44 000 species may have become extinct over the last 600 years. The Duke of Burgundy butterfly (*Hamearis lucina*), right, is an endangered British species.

About 5% of the 8225 reptile species are at risk. These include the two tuatara species (right) from New Zealand, which are the only living members of the order Sphenodontia, and the critically endangered blue iguana. Only about 200 blue iguanas remain, all in the Grand Caymans.

	Total number of species*	Number of IUCN listed species
Plants	310 000 - 422 000	8474
Insects	6 -10 million	622
Fish	28 000	126
Amphibians	5743	1809
Reptiles	8225	423
Birds	10 000	1133
Mammals	5400	1027

* Estimated numbers

The giant panda (above), is one of many critically endangered terrestrial mammals, with fewer than 2000 surviving in the wild. Amongst the 120 species of marine mammals, approximately 25% (including the humpback whale and Hector's dolphin) are on the ICUN's red list.

Prior to the impact of human activity on the environment, one bird species became extinct every 100 years. Today, the rate is one every year, and may increase to 10 species every year by the end of the century. Some at risk birds, such as the Hawaiian crow (right), are now found only in captivity.

Current estimates suggest as many as 47% of plant species may be endangered. Some, such as the South African cycad *Encephalartos woodii* (above), is one of the rarest plants in the world. It is extinct in the wild and all remaining specimens are clones.

2. (a) Comment on the actual extinction rate compared with the estimated background extinction rate: _____

_____

_____

(b) What factor is attributed to this difference? _____

3. The International Union for Conservation (IUCN) has established a Red List Index (RLI) for four taxonomic groups: reef forming corals, amphibians, birds, and mammals. This index focusses on the genuine status of changes. An RLI of 1.0 equates to all species qualifying as Least Concern (unlikely to become extinct in the near future). An RLI of 0 means that all species have become extinct. The figure right shows the trends in risk for the four taxonomic groups currently completed.

(a) Which taxon is moving most rapidly towards extinction risk?

_____

(b) Which taxon is, on average, the most threatened?

_____

(c) Why would an index like this be useful and how could it help to highlight environmental issues of concern?

_____

_____

_____

Graph: IUCN Red List Index of species survival (y-axis, 0.70 to 1.00) vs Year (x-axis, 1980 to 2010). Lines shown for Corals, Birds, Mammals, and Amphibians. Adapted from IUCN Red List of Endangered Species: www.iucnredlist.org/

4. Of the nearly 45 000 species assessed for the IUCN's red list, nearly 17 000 are threatened with extinction (endangered, critically endangered or vulnerable). The weblinks for this activity provide links to information on four British species. Select one and, on a separate sheet of paper, describe its conservation status, the reasons for its current status, and what is being done to assist its conservation. Attach the summary to this page.

157 *In-Situ* Conservation

Key Idea: *In-situ* (on site) conservation methods manage ecosystems to protect diversity within the natural environment. A variety of strategies are used to protect at-risk species and help the recovery of those that are threatened. *In-situ* conservation means conservation on site and it focuses on ecological restoration and legislation to protect ecosystems of special value. Ecological restoration is a long term process and often involves collaboration between scientific institutions and the local communities involved. Some examples of *in-situ* conservation methods in the UK are shown below.

Conservation and action plans are in place for many UK species that are at risk of extinction or their numbers are in decline. As at 2009, 1150 species and 65 habitats were identified by the UK biodiversity action plan (BAP) as needing conservation or protective measures. The natterjack toad (above left) and the New Forest cicada (top right) are two such species.

White-backed vulture

Hazel dormouse

The British and Irish Association of Zoos and Aquariums (BIAZA) is a strong supporter of *in-situ* conservation nationally and internationally, developing, managing, and funding a diverse range of field conservation projects. BIAZA supports *in-situ* management of the white backed vulture in South Africa and locally is involved in the Hazel Dormouse Recovery Programme and Biodiversity Action Plan.

A case study in *in-situ* conservation

The East Midland Ancient Woodland Project is a government project to restore ancient woodland sites in the Northants Forest District in central England. England was once extensively wooded, but much native woodland was cleared or replanted last century, mostly with Norway spruce. The project, which was launched in 2000, aims to restore ancient woodland sites (those dating back to 1600 or before) to native woodland. The project will focus on key species.

The objectives

▸ To identify key features of ancient woodlands.
▸ To draw up design plans (with input from the public) for existing woodlands.
▸ To establish groups to monitor and review progress.
▸ To promote the value of the woodlands for recreation, ecology, and heritage.

How the project will proceed

▸ Restore plantations of ancient woodland sites to semi-natural woodland.
▸ Remove conifers and exotic broadleaf species.
▸ Expand the size and range of key species.
▸ Restore and manage the woodland to reflect its culture and history, while recognising current uses.
▸ To generate income to contribute to the costs of the long term management.

Source: UK Clearing House Mechanisms for Biodiversity

Advantages of *in-situ* conservation

- Species left in the protected area have access to their natural resources and breeding sites.
- Species will continue to develop and evolve in their natural environment thus conserving their natural behaviour.
- *In-situ* conservation is able to protect more species at once and allow them greater space than those in captivity.
- *In-situ* conservation preserves unrecognised species.
- *In-situ* conservation protects larger breeding populations.
- *In-situ* conservation is less expensive and requires fewer specialised facilities than captive breeding.

Disadvantages of *in-situ* conservation

- Controlling illegal exploitation of *in-situ* populations is difficult.
- Habitats that shelter *in-situ* populations may need extensive restoration, including pest eradication and ongoing control.
- Populations may continue to decline during restoration.

In-situ conservation requires a lot of effort initially to restore sites and eradicate pests.

Source: UK Clearing House Mechanisms for Biodiversity

Bluebell woodland in Buckinghamshire

Woodland-pond restoration (UK)

Orangutan (endangered species)

Confiscated ivory, Kenya

Habitat protection and restoration

Most countries have a system of reserve lands focused on ecosystem conservation. These areas aim to protect and restore habitats of special importance and they may be intensively managed through pest and weed control, revegetation, reintroduction of threatened species, and site specific management practices (such as coppicing).

Convention on international trade in endangered species (CITES)

CITES is an international agreement between governments which aims to ensure that trade in species of wild animals and plants does not threaten their survival. CITES comprises more than 150 member nations and includes virtually all important wildlife producing and consuming countries. Trade in over 40 000 species is controlled or prohibited depending on their level of threat. In 1989, CITES imposed a global ban on the international trade in ivory and ivory products (above) in a move that has helped enormously in reducing the slaughter of elephants.

Micheal Apel CC 3.0

Snake's head fritillaries

Simon Carey CC 2.0

Pagham Harbour

Cymothoa exigua C 3.0

Starlet sea anemone

National Nature Reserves (NNRs)

The UK has 364 National Nature Reserves (NNRs), which are areas designated as having wildlife, habitat, or natural formations needing protection. NNRs often contain rare or nationally important species of plants or animals. The North Meadow NNR in Wiltshire is home to snake's head fritillaries (*Fritillaria meleagris*) a plant that is now rarely found in the English countryside.

Marine Conservation Zones (MCZs)

The UK has several types of Marine Protected Areas, each giving different levels of protection. Recently, Marine Conservation Zone (MCZ) were added. MCZs aim to conserve the diversity of rare and threatened marine species or habitats. They protect nationally important marine wildlife, habitats, and geology while allowing some sustainable activities within their boundaries. Pagham Harbour, West Sussex was designated a MCZ to protect the seagrass beds, lagoon sand shrimp, Defolin's lagoon snail, and the starlet sea anemone found there.

1. (a) What are the advantages of *in-situ* conservation? _____

   _____

   _____

   _____

   (b) Why is *in-situ* conservation quite difficult? _____

   _____

   _____

   _____

2. Explain why *in-situ* conservation commonly involves both ecosystem restoration and legislation to protect species:

   _____

   _____

   _____

   _____

3. Choose an endangered species in your area. Research what conservation efforts are being undertaken to protect it, and determine if these efforts are effective. Write a short summary and attach it to this page.

© 2015 **BIOZONE** International
ISBN: 978-1-927309-25-4
Photocopying Prohibited

158 Hedgerows

Key Idea: Hedgerows provide food, shelter and transport corridors for many species so are important for biodiversity. Since the 1940s, many thousands of kilometres of hedgerows have been removed from the British landscape each year as traditional mixed farms have been converted to farms with larger fields. In addition, neglect and improper management have been responsible for almost half of lost hedgerows every year. Hedgerows require maintenance and management in order to remain viable, yet hedge-laying and trimming skills are rapidly becoming lost. In 1997, legislation was introduced to control the destruction of hedgerows in rural settings. In England and Wales, landowners must apply to the local authority for permission to remove a hedgerow of greater than 20 metres in length, and this can be refused if the hedge is shown to be significant in terms of its age, environmental, or historical importance.

Hedgerows are important because...

▸ Hedges may support up to 80% of England's birds, 50% of its mammals, and 30% of its butterflies.

▸ The ditches and banks associated with hedgerows provide habitat for amphibians and reptiles.

▸ Hedges provide habitat, nesting material and food for birds and mammals.

▸ Some small mammals, e.g. dormice, once used hay ricks as overwintering habitat. With the loss of hay ricks, hedgerows are virtually their only alternative.

▸ They act as corridors, along which animals (e.g. pheasants) can safely move between areas of woodland.

▸ They provide overwintering habitat for predatory insects which move into crops to control pest insects in spring.

▸ Hedges provide shelter for stock and crops and reduce wind speed, which prevents erosion.

▸ Hedges act as barriers for windborne pests.

Photo courtesy, Kimberley Mallady

Bjorn Schulz

Hazel dormouse

Hedgerows commonly comprise hawthorn, blackthorn, field maple, hazel, and bramble. A hedgerow is essentially a linear wood and many of the associated plants are woodland species. At least 30 bird species nest in hedges. Hedgerows of different heights are preferred by different bird species, so management to provide a range of hedge heights and tree densities provides the best option for increasing diversity. For example, bullfinches prefer well-treed hedgerows over 4 m tall, whereas whitethroats, linnets, and yellowhammers favour shorter hedgerows (2-3 m) with fewer trees. The hedge base is important for ground-nesting species like the grey partridge. Hedgerows are important habitat for dormice and are used as dispersal corridors linking copses that are too small to support a viable populations on their own. Crucially they also support breeding populations independent of other habitats.

1. From an environmental perspective, describe three benefits of hedgerows to biodiversity:

    (a) _____

    (b) _____

    (c) _____

2. Explain why hedgerows might be regarded as undesirable from the perspective of a modern farmer: _____

    _____

    _____

3. Outline a brief argument to convince a farmer to retain and manage hedgerows, rather than remove them:

    _____

    _____

    _____

    _____

    _____

LINK WEB
157 158 KNOW

159 *Ex-Situ* Conservation

Key Idea: *Ex-situ* conservation methods operate away from the natural environment and are useful where species are critically endangered.

Ex-situ conservation is the process of protecting an endangered species outside its natural habitat. It is used when a species has become critically low in numbers or *in-situ* methods have been, or are likely to be, unsuccessful. Zoos,

aquaria, and botanical gardens are the most conventional facilities for *ex-situ* conservation. They house and protect specimens for breeding and can reintroduce them into the wild to restore natural populations. The maintenance of seedbanks by botanic gardens and breeding registers by zoos ensures that efforts to conserve species are not impaired by problems of inbreeding.

M. Betley

Captive breeding and relocation

Individuals are captured and bred under protected conditions. If breeding programmes are successful and there is suitable habitat available, captive individuals may be relocated to the wild where they can establish natural populations. Zoos now have an active role in captive breeding. There are problems with captive breeding; individuals are inadvertently selected for fitness in a captive environment and their survival in the wild may be compromised. This is especially so for marine species. However, for some taxa, such as reptiles, birds, and small mammals, captive rearing is very successful.

Above: England is home to a rare sub-species of sand lizard (*Lacerta agilis*). It is restricted to southern heathlands and the coastal sand dunes of north west England. The UK Herpetological Conservation Trust is the lead partner in the action plan for this species and Chester Zoo hosts a captive breeding colony.

Right: A puppet 'mother' shelters a takahe chick. Takahe, a rare rail species native to New Zealand, were brought back from the brink of extinction through a successful captive breeding program.

The important role of zoos and aquaria

As well as keeping their role in captive breeding programs and as custodians of rare species, zoos have a major role in public education. They raise awareness of the threats facing species in their natural environments and engender public empathy for conservation work. Modern zoos tend to concentrate on particular species and are part of global programs that work together to help retain genetic diversity in captive bred animals.

D. Eason (DOC)

In New Zealand, introduced predatory mammals, including weasels and stoats, have decimated native bird life. Relocation of birds on to predator-free islands or into areas that have been cleared of predators has been instrumental in the recovery of some species such as the North Island kokako. Sadly, others have been lost forever.

I Flux, DOC

Above: The okapi is a species of rare forest antelope related to giraffes. Okapi are only found naturally in the Ituri Forest, in the northeastern rainforests of the Democratic Republic of Congo (DRC), Africa, an area at the front line of an ongoing civil war. A okapi calf was born to Bristol Zoo Gardens in 2009, one of only about 100 okapi in captivity.

1. Describe the key features of ex-situ conservation methods: _____

_____

_____

_____

_____

2. Explain why some animal species are more well suited to *ex-situ* conservation efforts than others: _____

_____

_____

_____

© 2015 **BIOZONE** International
ISBN:978-1-927309-25-4
Photocopying Prohibited

The role of botanic gardens

Botanic gardens have years of collective expertise and resources and play a critical role in plant conservation. They maintain seed banks, nurture rare species, maintain a living collection of plants, and help to conserve indigenous plant knowledge. They also have an important role in both research and education. The Royal Botanic Gardens at Kew (above) contain an estimated 25 000 species, 2700 of which are classified by the ICUN as rare, threatened, or endangered. Kew Gardens are involved in both national and international projects associated with the conservation of botanical diversity and are the primary advisors to CITES on threatened plant species. Kew's Millennium Seed Bank partnership is the largest ex situ plant conservation project in the world; working with a network in over 50 countries they have banked 10% of the world's wild plant species.

Seedbanks and gene banks

Seedbanks and gene banks around the world have a role in preserving the genetic diversity of species. A seedbank (above) stores seeds as a source for future planting in case seed reserves elsewhere are lost. The seeds may be from rare species whose genetic diversity is at risk, or they may be the seeds of crop plants, in some cases of ancient varieties no longer used in commercial production.

3. Describe three key roles of zoos and aquaria and explain the importance of each:

(a) _____

_____

(b) _____

_____

(c) _____

_____

4. Explain the importance of gene and seed banks, both to conservation and to agriculture: _____

_____

_____

_____

5. Compare and contrast *in-situ* and *ex-situ* methods of conservation, including reference to the advantages and disadvantages of each approach:

_____

_____

_____

_____

_____

_____

_____

_____

_____

_____

_____

160 Chapter Review

Summarise what you know about this topic under the headings provided. You can draw diagrams or mind maps, or write short notes to organise your thoughts. Use the images and hints to help you and refer back to the introduction to check the points covered:

Classification: biological classification
HINT: What are species and how do we classify them?

Classification: bioinformatics and phylogenetics
HINT: How can molecular data be used to determine evolutionary relationships?

© 2015 BIOZONE International
ISBN: 978-1-927309-25-4
Photocopying Prohibited

Natural selection

HINT: How does natural selection bring about evolutionary change? How do species form and remain distinct? How are pathogens evolving and what selection pressures are involved?

Biodiversity:

HINT: What is biodiversity? How is it measured, why is it important, and how do we conserve it?

161 KEY TERMS: Did You Get It?

1. Test your vocabulary by matching each term to its correct definition, as identified by its preceding letter code.

adaptation _____

allopatric speciation _____

biodiversity _____

bioinformatics _____

binomial nomenclature _____

conservation _____

diversity indices _____

domain _____

ex situ conservation _____

fitness _____

in-situ conservation _____

natural selection _____

phylogeny _____

reproductive isolation _____

species _____

sympatric speciation _____

A Statistics used to quantify the heterogeneity of a system. Often used in ecological studies to assess environmental health.

B A formal system of naming species of organisms by giving each a Latin name composed of two parts

C Speciation in which the populations are physically separated.

D The number or variety of species living within given ecosystem, biome, or on the entire Earth. The species richness.

E The science of collecting, storing and analysing biological data using computer science.

F A heritable characteristic of a species, which is shaped by natural selection and equips the species for its functional role in the environment.

G Conservation methods that operate away from the natural environment (e.g. zoo breeding programmes).

H The evolutionary history of a species or other taxon, hypothesised on the basis of morphological or molecular data.

I A measure of an organism's genetic contribution to the next generation.

J The act of preserving, protecting, or restoring something (e.g. an organism or habitat).

K The situation in which members of a group of organisms breed with each other but not with members of other groups.

L Speciation as a result of reproductive isolation without any physical separation of the populations, i.e. populations remain within the same range.

M Group of organisms capable of breeding together to produce viable and fertile offspring.

N The process by which heritable traits become more or less common in a population through differential survival and reproduction.

O Conservation efforts that take place on site involving whole ecosystem management.

P The highest taxonomic rank in the revised classification of life based on recognition of prokaryote diversity.

2. Describe in words the species richness and evenness of ecosystem A and B (below):

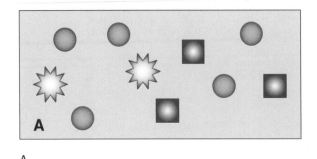

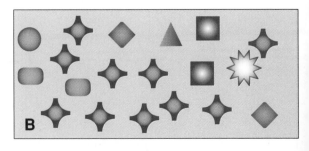

A _____

_____

B _____

_____

TEST

Exchange and Transport

Key terms

active transport
alveolus (pl. alveoli)
artery
ATP
blood
Bohr effect
capillary
capillary network
cardiac cycle
cohesion-tension hypothesis
concentration gradient
cotransport
countercurrent exchange
diffusion
endocytosis
exocytosis
facilitated diffusion
fluid mosic model
gas exchange
gills
haemoglobin
heart
ion pump
lungs
mass flow hypothesis
osmotic potential
oxyhaemoglobin dissociation curve
phloem
potometer
respiratory gas
solute
stomata
surface area: volume ratio
surfactant
tissue fluid
tracheal system
translocation
transpiration
turgor pressure
vein
ventilation (breathing)
venule
water potential
xylem

4.1 Surface area to volume ratio

Learning outcomes

		Activity number
☐	i Using model cells if you wish, explain how surface area to volume ratio affects transport of molecules in living organisms.	170
☐	ii Explain that mass transport systems and specialised gas exchange surfaces are adaptations to facilitate exchanges with the environment as organisms become larger and their surface area to volume ratio reduces.	176 185

4.2 Cell transport mechanisms

Learning outcomes

		Activity number
☐	i Describe the fluid mosaic model of membrane structure. Include reference to the significance of phospholipid orientation and the role of transmembrane proteins in the integral structure of the membrane.	162 163
☐	ii Describe the movement of molecules across membranes by diffusion, facilitated diffusion, and osmosis. Explain the movement of water across membranes by osmosis with reference to gradients in water potential. Describe factors affecting diffusion rates across membranes: membrane thickness, surface area, and concentration gradient.	165 166 167 176
☐	iii Explain how the properties of molecules, including size, solubility, and charge, affects how they are transported across membranes.	162

CP-5	Investigate factors affecting membrane permeability, e.g. the effect of temperature on beetroot membrane permeability.	164
CP-6	Determine the water potential of a plant tissue using a calibration curve for a solute and the equation: water potential = turgor pressure and osmotic (or solute) potential.	168 169

☐	iv Explain how endocytosis and exocytosis transports large molecules into and out of the cell in membrane-bound vesicles. Know that cytosis is an active process.	171 173
☐	v Using examples, explain active transport in cells, including the role of ATP, e.g in ion pumps or in establishing an ion gradient for the cotransport of molecules.	171-174
☐	vi Explain the phosphorylation of ADP to form ATP. Explain how the hydrolysis of ATP provides energy for biological processes (metabolism).	175

4.3 Gas exchange

Learning outcomes

		Activity number
☐	i Explain how insects, fish, and mammals are adapted for gas exchange (including adaptations for ventilation of the gas exchange surfaces).	176-179 181 183
☐	**CP-7** Dissect an insect to show the gas exchange system.	182
☐	ii Explain how gases are exchanged in flowering plants, including the role of stomata, gas exchange surfaces in the leaf, and lenticels.	176 184

4.4   Circulation

Learning outcomes

Activity number

☐ i Describe the structure of the mammalian heart including the heart chambers, valves, and the main blood vessels. Describe and explain differences in the structure and role of blood vessels in mammals (arteries, capillaries, and veins).

188-191
193

AT ▶ Use dissection equipment safely for the dissection of an animal organ.

194

☐ ii Compare and contrast double and single circulatory systems, including with respect to maintenance of higher blood pressure and separation of oxygenated and deoxygenated blood.

186 187

☐ iii Describe the cardiac cycle, including the pressure and volume changes and the associated valve movements.

195

☐ iv Describe the myogenic nature of the heart beat, including the roles of the sinoatrial node, atrioventricular nodes, and bundle of His.

196

☐ v Analyse and interpret data showing ECG traces and pressure (and volume) changes during the cardiac cycle.

195

AT ▶ Safely and ethically measure physiological functions.

180 197

☐ vi Describe blood as a liquid tissue, identifying its components: plasma, platelets, erythrocytes, and leucocytes (neutrophils, eosinophils, monocytes, lymphocytes).

199

☐ vii Describe the roles of blood in transport, internal defence, and in the formation of lymph and tissue fluid.

192 199

☐ viii Explain blood clotting including the roles of platelets and blood proteins in the formation of a fibrin clot.

2001

☐ ix Describe the stages leading to atherosclerosis, describe its effect on health, and outline the factors that increase the risk of its development.

201-203

4.5   Transport of gases in the blood

Learning outcomes

Activity number

☐ i Describe the structure of haemoglobin (Hb) and its role in the transport of respiratory gases. Include reference to the Bohr effect and its significance.

204 205

☐ ii Interpret the oxygen dissociation curve for haemoglobin.

205

☐ iii Compare and contrast the structure and function of haemoglobin and myoglobin.

204 205

☐ iv Compare the oxygen dissociation curves for fetal and adult haemoglobins and explain the significance of the differences.

204 205

4.6   Transfer of material between the blood and cells

Learning outcomes

Activity number

☐ i Describe the role of tissue fluid in the interchange of substances between the blood and tissues. Explain the formation and reabsorption of tissue fluid with reference to the varying influences of hydrostatic and oncotic pressures.

192

☐ ii Explain how the unabsorbed tissue fluid is returned to general circulation.

192

4.7   Transport in plants

Learning outcomes

Activity number

☐ i Describe the structure of phloem and xylem tissue in relation to their respective roles in plant transport.

206 -210

☐ ii Describe the movement of water through the plant. Include reference to the apoplastic and symplastic pathways and their relative importance.

211

☐ iii Describe the cohesion-tension model as an explanation for the movement of water in the xylem from the roots to the shoots.

212

☐ iv Describe and explain the effect of temperature, light, humidity, and air movement on transpiration rate.

213

☐ v Describe the mass-flow hypothesis for the transport of sugars in the phloem. Explain strengths and weaknesses of the hypothesis based on evidence.

214 215

☐ **CP-7** ▶ Use a potometer to investigate factors affecting water uptake by plant shoots. Interpret data from investigations of transpiration.

213

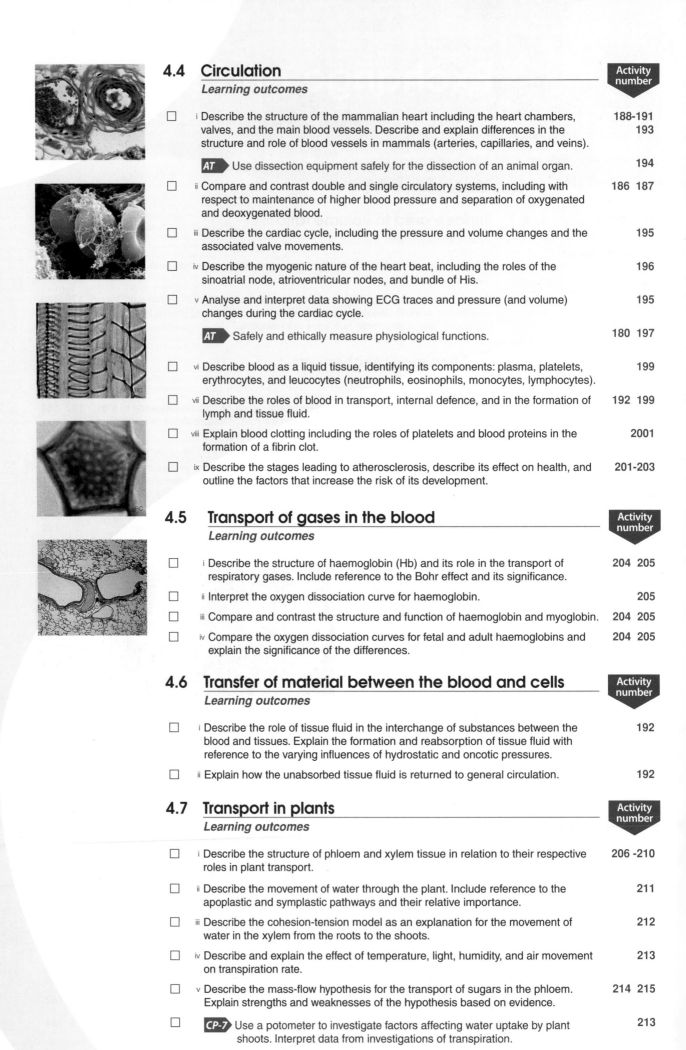

162 The Structure of Membranes

Key Idea: The plasma membrane is composed of a lipid bilayer with proteins moving freely within it.

All cells have a plasma membrane, which forms the outer limit of the cell and regulates the passage of materials into and out of the cell. A cell wall, if present, lies outside this, and it is quite distinct from it. Membranes are also found inside eukaryotic cells as part of membranous organelles. The original model of membrane structure was as a lipid bilayer coated with protein. This model was modified after the discovery that the protein molecules were embedded within the bilayer rather than coating the outside. The now-accepted **fluid-mosaic model** of membrane structure (below) satisfies the observed properties of membranes. The self-orientating properties of the phospholipids allows cellular membranes to reseal themselves when disrupted. The double layer of lipids is also quite fluid, and proteins move quite freely within it.

The fluid mosaic model of membrane structure

Glycolipids in membranes are phospholipids with attached carbohydrate. Like glycoproteins, they are involved in cell signalling and cell-cell recognition. They also help to stabilise membrane structure.

Cholesterol is a packing molecule and interacts with the phospholipids to regulate membrane consistency, keeping it firm but fluid.

Water molecules pass between the phospholipid molecules by osmosis.

Glycoproteins are proteins with attached carbohydrate. They are important in membrane stability, in cell-cell recognition, and in cell signalling, acting as receptors for hormones and neurotransmitters.

Attached carbohydrate

CO_2

Phospholipids naturally form a bilayer.

Some integral proteins do not span the lipid bilayer.

Phosphate head is hydrophilic

Fatty acid tail is hydrophobic

Carrier proteins permit the passage of specific molecules by facilitated diffusion or active transport.

α-helical transmembrane glycoprotein

Phospholipid

A molecule's solubility, size, and charge affects how it is transported across a plasma membrane. In general, the smaller the molecule and the more hydrophobic it is, the more rapidly it will diffuse. Charged molecules, such as ions, are unable to diffuse through a phospholipid bilayer regardless of size. They must cross the lipid bilayer via membrane proteins.

Channel proteins form a pore through the hydrophobic interior of the membrane to enable water soluble molecules to pass by facilitated diffusion.

Lipid soluble molecules, e.g. gases and steroids, can move through the membrane by diffusion, down their concentration gradient.

Based on a diagram in Biol. Sci. Review, Nov. 2009, pp. 20-21

Intracellular environment

1. Identify the component(s) of the plasma membrane involved in:

   (a) Facilitated diffusion: _____

   (b) Active transport: _____

   (c) Cell signalling: _____

   (d) Regulating membrane fluidity: _____

2. How do the properties of phospholipids contribute to their role in forming the structural framework of membranes?

   _____

   _____

3. (a) Describe the modern fluid mosaic model of membrane structure: _____

   _____

   _____

   _____

LINK LINK WEB
164 **163** **162** KNOW

(b) Explain how the fluid mosaic model accounts for the observed properties of cellular membranes:

_____

_____

_____

_____

_____

_____

4. Explain the importance of each of the following to cellular function:

(a) Carrier proteins in the plasma membrane: _____

_____

(b) Channel proteins in the plasma membrane: _____

_____

5. Non-polar (lipid-soluble) molecules diffuse more rapidly through membranes than polar (lipid-insoluble) molecules:

(a) Explain the reason for this: _____

_____

(b) Discuss the implications of this to the transport of substances into the cell through the plasma membrane:

_____

_____

6. Describe the purpose of cholesterol in plasma membranes: _____

_____

7. List three substances that need to be transported **into** all kinds of animal cells, in order for them to survive:

(a) _____ (b) _____ (c) _____

8. List two substances that need to be transported **out** of all kinds of animal cells, in order for them to survive:

(a) _____ (b) _____

9. Use the symbol for a phospholipid molecule (below) to draw a **simple labelled diagram** to show the structure of a plasma membrane (include features such as lipid bilayer and various kinds of proteins):

Symbol for phospholipid

163 How Do We Know? Membrane Structure

Key Idea: The freeze-fracture technique for preparing and viewing cellular membranes has provided evidence to support the fluid mosaic model of the plasma membrane.

Cellular membranes play many extremely important roles in cells and understanding their structure is central to understanding cellular function. Moreover, understanding the structure and function of membrane proteins is essential to understanding cellular transport processes, and cell recognition and signalling. Cellular membranes are far too small to be seen clearly using light microscopy, and certainly any detail is impossible to resolve. Since early last century, scientists have known that membranes were composed of a lipid bilayer with associated proteins. The original model of membrane structure, proposed by Davson and Danielli, was the unit membrane (a lipid bilayer coated with protein). This model was later modified by Singer and Nicolson after the discovery that the protein molecules were embedded *within* the bilayer rather than coating the outside. But how did they find out just how these molecules were organised?

The answers were provided with electron microscopy, and one technique in particular – **freeze fracture**. As the name implies, freeze fracture, at its very simplest level, is the freezing of a cell and then fracturing it so the inner surface of the membrane can be seen using electron microscopy. Membranes are composed of two layers of phospholipids held together by weak intermolecular bonds. These split apart during fracture.

The procedure involves several steps:

▶ Cells are immersed in chemicals that alter the strength of the internal and external regions of the plasma membrane and immobilise any mobile macromolecules.

▶ The cells are passed through a series of glycerol solutions of increasing concentration. This protects the cells from bursting when they are frozen.

▶ The cells are mounted on gold supports and frozen using liquid propane.

▶ The cells are fractured in a helium-vented vacuum at -150°C. A razor blade cooled to -170° C acts as both a cold trap for water and the fracturing instrument.

▶ The surface of the fractured cells may be evaporated a little to produce some relief on the surface (known as etching) so that a three-dimensional effect occurs.

▶ For viewing under an electron microscope (EM), a replica of the cells is made by coating them with gold or platinum to ~3 nm thick. A layer of carbon around 30 nm thick is used to provide contrast and stability for the replica.

▶ The samples are then raised to room temperature and placed into distilled water or digestive enzymes, which separates the replica from the sample. The replica is then rinsed in distilled water before it is ready for viewing.

The freeze fracture technique provided the necessary supporting evidence for the current fluid mosaic model of membrane structure. When cleaved, proteins in the membrane left impressions that showed they were embedded into the membrane and not a continuous layer on the outside as earlier models proposed.

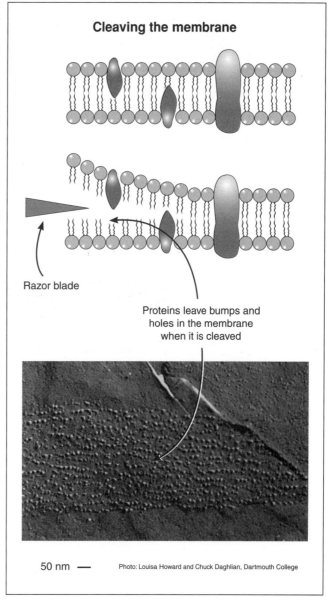

Cleaving the membrane

Razor blade

Proteins leave bumps and holes in the membrane when it is cleaved

50 nm —   Photo: Louisa Howard and Chuck Daghlian, Dartmouth College

1. Explain how freeze-fracture studies provided evidence for our current model of membrane structure:

_____

_____

_____

2. The Davson and Danielli model of membrane structure was the unit membrane; a phospholipid bilayer with a protein coat. Explain how the freeze-fracture studies showed this model to be flawed:

_____

_____

_____

164 Factors Altering Membrane Permeability

Key Idea: Temperature and solvents can disrupt the structure of cellular membranes and alter their permeability.

Membrane permeability can be disrupted if membranes are subjected to high temperatures or solvents. At temperatures above the optimum, the membrane proteins become denatured. Alcohols, e.g. ethanol, can also denature proteins. In both instances, the denatured proteins no longer function properly and the membrane loses its selective permeability and becomes leaky. In addition, the combination of alcohol and high temperature can also dissolve lipids.

Beetroot cubes

The aim and hypothesis

To investigate the effect of temperature on membrane permeability. The students hypothesised that the amount of pigment leaking from the beetroot cubes would increase with increasing temperature.

Experimental method

Raw beetroot was cut into uniform cubes using a cork borer with a 4 mm internal diameter. The cubes were trimmed to 20 mm lengths and placed in a beaker of distilled water for 30 minutes.

Five cm³ of distilled water was added to 15 clean test tubes. Three were placed into a beaker containing ice. These were the 0°C samples. Three test tubes were placed into water baths at 20, 40, 60, or 90°C and equilibrated for 30 minutes. Once the tubes were at temperature, the beetroot cubes were removed from the distilled water and blotted dry on a paper towel. One beetroot cube was added to each of the test tubes. After 30 minutes, they were removed. The colour of the solution in each test tube was observed by eye and then the absorbance of each sample was measured at 530 nm. Results are given in the table below.

Background

Plant cells often contain a large central vacuole surrounded by a membrane called a **tonoplast**. In beetroot plants, the vacuole contains a water-soluble red pigment called betacyanin, which gives beetroot its colour. If the tonoplast is damaged, the red pigment leaks out into the surrounding environment. The amount of leaked pigment relates to the amount of damage to the tonoplast.

Temperature / °C	Absorbance of beetroot samples at varying temperatures				Mean
	Observation	Sample 1	Sample 2	Sample 3	
0	No colour	0	0.007	0.004	
20	Very pale pink	0.027	0.022	0.018	
40	Very pale pink	0.096	0.114	0.114	
60	Pink	0.580	0.524	0.509	
90	Red	3	3	3	

Absorbance / 530 nm

1. Why is it important to wash the beetroot cubes in distilled water prior to carrying out the experiment? _____

_____

2. (a) Complete the table above by calculating the mean absorbance for each temperature:

(b) Based on the results in the table above, describe the effect of temperature on membrane permeability: _____

_____

_____

_____

(c) Explain how temperature affects the permeability of the tonoplast: _____

_____

_____

_____

DATA

Method for determining effect of ethanol concentration on membrane permeability

Beetroot cubes were prepared the same way as described on the previous page. The following ethanol concentrations were prepared using serial dilution: 0, 6.25, 12.5, 25, 50, and 100%. Eighteen clean test tubes were divided into six groups of three and labelled with one of the six ethanol concentrations. Three cm^3 of the appropriate ethanol solution was placed into each test tube. A dried beetroot cube was added to each test tube. The test tubes were covered with parafilm (plastic paraffin film with a paper backing) and left at room temperature. After one hour the beetroot cubes were removed and the absorbance measured at 477 nm.
Results are given in the table, right.

Ethanol concentration / %	Absorbance / 477 nm			Mean
	Sample 1	Sample 2	Sample 3	
0	0.014	0.038	0.038	
6.25	0.009	0.015	0.023	
12.5	0.010	0.041	0.018	
25	0.067	0.064	0.116	
50	0.945	1.100	0.731	
100	1.269	1.376	0.907	

Absorbance of beetroot samples at varying ethanol concentrations

3. What was the purpose of the 0% ethanol solution in the experiment described above?

_____

_____

_____

4. (a) Why do you think the tubes were covered in parafilm?

_____

_____

_____

_____

(b) How could the results have been affected if the test tubes were not covered with parafilm?

_____

_____

_____

_____

5. (a) Complete the table above by calculating the mean absorbance for each ethanol concentration:

(b) Plot a line graph of ethanol concentration against mean absorbance on the grid (above):

(c) Describe the effect of ethanol concentration on the membrane permeability of beetroot: _____

_____

_____

_____

_____

6. How does ethanol affect membrane permeability? _____

_____

165 Diffusion

Key Idea: Diffusion is the movement of molecules from higher concentration to a lower concentration (i.e. down a concentration gradient).

The molecules that make up substances are constantly moving about in a random way. This random motion causes molecules to disperse from areas of high to low concentration. This dispersal is called **diffusion** and it requires no energy. Each type of molecule moves down its own concentration gradient. Diffusion is important in allowing exchanges with the environment and in the regulation of cell water content.

What is diffusion?

Diffusion is the movement of particles from regions of high concentration to regions of low concentration (down a concentration gradient). Diffusion is a **passive process**, meaning it needs no input of energy to occur. During diffusion, molecules move randomly about, becoming evenly dispersed.

Factors affecting the rate of diffusion

Concentration gradient	The rate of diffusion is higher when there is a greater difference between the concentrations of two regions.
The distance moved	Diffusion over shorter distance occurs at a greater rate than over a larger distance.
The surface area involved	The larger the area across which diffusion occurs, the greater the rate of diffusion.
Barriers to diffusion	Thick barriers have a slower rate of diffusion than thin barriers.
Temperature	Particles at a high temperature diffuse at a greater rate than at a low temperature.

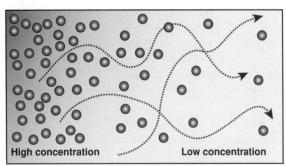

High concentration   **Low concentration**

Concentration gradient

If molecules can move freely, they move from high to low concentration (down a concentration gradient) until evenly dispersed.

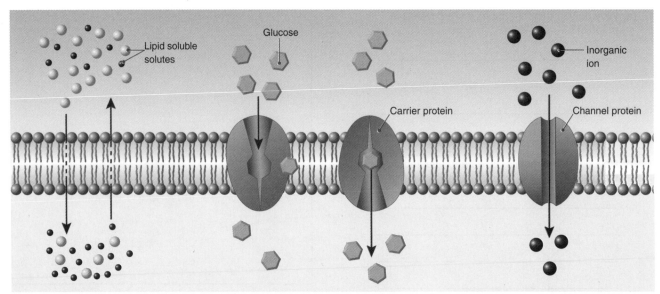

Lipid soluble solutes

Glucose

Inorganic ion

Carrier protein

Channel protein

Simple diffusion
Molecules move directly through the membrane without assistance.
<u>Example</u>: O_2 diffuses into the blood and CO_2 diffuses out.

Carrier-mediated facilitated diffusion
Carrier proteins allow large lipid-insoluble molecules that cannot cross the membrane by simple diffusion to be transported into the cell.
<u>Example</u>: the transport of glucose into red blood cells.

Channel-mediated facilitated diffusion
Channels (hydrophilic pores) in the membrane allow inorganic ions to pass through the membrane.
<u>Example</u>: K^+ ions exiting nerve cells to restore resting potential.

1. What is diffusion? _____

_____

2. What do the three types of diffusion described above all have in common? _____

_____

3. How does facilitated diffusion differ from simple diffusion? _____

_____

© 2015 **BIOZONE** International
ISBN:978-1-927309-25-4
Photocopying Prohibited

166 Osmosis

Key Idea: Osmosis is the term describing the diffusion of water molecules down their concentration gradient across a partially permeable membrane.

The diffusion of water down its concentration gradient across a partially permeable membrane is called **osmosis** and it is the principal mechanism by which water moves in and out of living cells. A partially permeable membrane, such as the plasma membrane, allows some molecules, but not others, to pass through. Water molecules can diffuse directly through the lipid bilayer, but movement is aided by specific protein channels called aquaporins. There is a net movement of water molecules until an equilibrium is reached and net movement is then zero. Osmosis is a passive process and does not require any energy input.

Demonstrating osmosis

Osmosis can be demonstrated using dialysis tubing in a simple experiment (described below). Dialysis tubing, like all cellular membranes, is a partially permeable membrane.

A sucrose solution (high solute concentration) is placed into dialysis tubing, and the tubing is placed into a beaker of water (low solute concentration). The difference in concentration of sucrose (solute) between the two solutions creates an osmotic gradient. Water moves by osmosis into the sucrose solution and the volume of the sucrose solution inside the dialysis tubing increases.

The dialysis tubing acts as a partially permeable membrane, allowing water to pass freely, while keeping the sucrose inside the dialysis tubing.

Glass capillary tube

Dialysis tubing containing sucrose solution

Dialysis tubing (partially permeable membrane)

Sucrose molecule

Water molecule

Water

Net water movement

Osmotic potential

Osmotic potential is a term often used when studying animal cells. The presence of solutes (dissolved substances) in a solution increases the tendency of water to move into that solution. This tendency is called the osmotic potential or osmotic pressure. The greater a solution's concentration (i.e. the more total dissolved solutes it contains) the greater the osmotic potential.

Describing solutions

Water movements in cells, particularly plant cells, are often explained in terms of water potential (see next activity). But you will often see other terms used to compare solutions of different solute concentration, especially in animal biology:

Isotonic solution: Having the same solute concentration relative to another solution (e.g. the cell's contents).

Hypotonic solution: Having a lower solute concentration relative to another solution.

Hypertonic solution: Having a higher solute concentration relative to another solution.

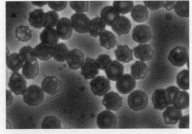

The red blood cells above were placed into a hypertonic solution. As a result, the cells have lost water and have begun to shrink, losing their usual discoid shape.

1. What is osmosis? _____

_____

_____

2. (a) In the blue box on the diagram above, draw an arrow to show the direction of net water movement.

(b) Why did water move in this direction? _____

_____

_____

3. What would happen to the height of the water in the capillary tube if the sucrose concentration was increased?

_____

© 2015 **BIOZONE** International
ISBN: 978-1-927309-25-4
Photocopying Prohibited

LINK 167 WEB 166 KNOW

167 Water Movement in Plant Cells

Key Idea: Water potential explains the tendency of water to move from one region to another by osmosis. Water molecules moves to regions of lower water potential.

The water potential of a solution (denoted by ψ) is the term given to the tendency for water molecules to enter or leave a solution by osmosis. The tendency for water to move in any particular direction can be calculated on the basis of the water potential of the cell sap relative to its surrounding environment. The use of water potential to express the water relations of plant cells is used in preference to osmotic potential and osmotic pressure although these terms are still frequently used in areas of animal physiology and medicine.

Water potential and water movement

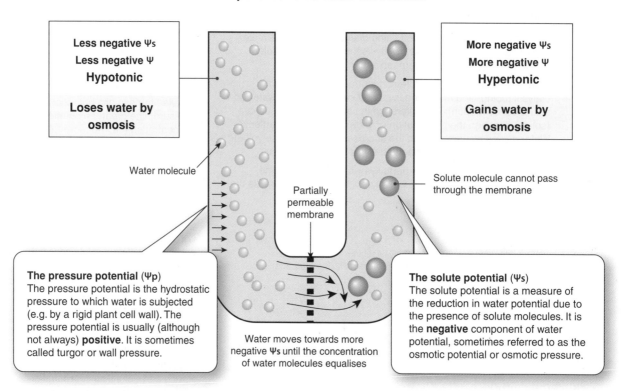

Less negative ψs
Less negative ψ
Hypotonic

Loses water by osmosis

More negative ψs
More negative ψ
Hypertonic

Gains water by osmosis

Water molecule

Solute molecule cannot pass through the membrane

Partially permeable membrane

The pressure potential (ψp)
The pressure potential is the hydrostatic pressure to which water is subjected (e.g. by a rigid plant cell wall). The pressure potential is usually (although not always) **positive**. It is sometimes called turgor or wall pressure.

Water moves towards more negative ψs until the concentration of water molecules equalises

The solute potential (ψs)
The solute potential is a measure of the reduction in water potential due to the presence of solute molecules. It is the **negative** component of water potential, sometimes referred to as the osmotic potential or osmotic pressure.

As water molecules move around some collide with the plasma membrane and create pressure on the membrane called **water potential (ψ)**. The greater the movement of water molecules, the higher their water potential. The presence of solutes (e.g. sucrose) lowers water potential because the solutes restrict the movement of water molecules. Pure water has the highest water potential (zero). Dissolving any solute in water lowers the water potential (makes it more negative).

Water always diffuses from regions of less negative to more negative water potential. Water potential is determined by two components: the **solute potential**, ψs (of the cell sap) and the **pressure potential**, ψp, expressed by:

$$\psi\text{cell} = \psi\text{s} + \psi\text{p}$$

The closer a value is to zero, the higher its water potential.

1. What is the water potential of pure water? _____

2. The diagrams below show three hypothetical situations where adjacent cells have different water potentials. Draw arrows on each pair of cells (a)-(c) to indicate the net direction of water movement and calculate ψ for each side:

(a)

A	B
ψs = −400 kPa	ψs = −500 kPa
ψp = 300 kPa	ψp = 300 kPa

(b)

A	B
ψs = −500 kPa	ψs = −600 kPa
ψp = 100 kPa	ψp = 100 kPa

(c)

A	B
ψs = −600 kPa	ψs = −500 kPa
ψp = 200 kPa	ψp = 300 kPa

ψ for side A: _____ _____ _____

ψ for side B: _____ _____ _____

When the contents of a plant cell push against the cell wall they create **turgor** (tightness) which provides support for the plant body. When cells lose water, there is a loss of turgor and the plant wilts. Complete loss of turgor from a cell is called plasmolysis and is irreversible. The diagram below shows two situations: when the external water potential is less negative than the cell and when it is more negative than the cell. When the external water potential is the same as that of the cell, there is no net movement of water.

Plasmolysis in a plant cell

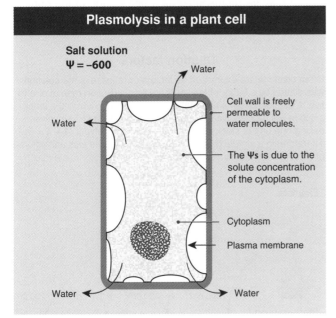

Salt solution
$\Psi = -600$

Water

Water

Cell wall is freely permeable to water molecules.

The Ψs is due to the solute concentration of the cytoplasm.

Cytoplasm

Plasma membrane

Water

Water

Turgor in a plant cell

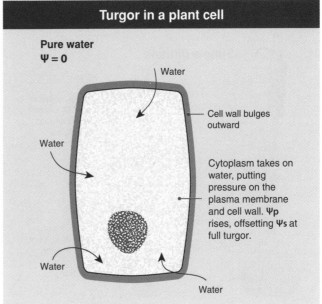

Pure water
$\Psi = 0$

Water

Water

Cell wall bulges outward

Cytoplasm takes on water, putting pressure on the plasma membrane and cell wall. Ψp rises, offsetting Ψs at full turgor.

Water

Water

When external water potential is more negative than the water potential of the cell (Ψcell = Ψs + Ψp), water leaves the cell and, because the cell wall is rigid, the plasma membrane shrinks away from the cell wall. This process is termed **plasmolysis** and the cell becomes flaccid (Ψp = 0). Full plasmolysis is irreversible; the cell cannot recover by taking up water.

When the external water potential is less negative than the Ψcell, water enters the cell. A pressure potential is generated when sufficient water has been taken up to cause the cell contents to press against the cell wall. Ψp rises progressively until it offsets Ψs. Water uptake stops when the Ψcell = 0. The rigid cell wall prevents cell rupture. Cells in this state are **turgid**.

3. What is the effect of dissolved solutes on water potential? _____

_____

_____

4. Why don't plant cells burst when water enters them? _____

_____

_____

5. (a) Distinguish between plasmolysis and turgor: _____

_____

_____

(b) Describe the state of the plant in the photo on the right and explain your reasoning:

_____

_____

6. (a) Explain the role of pressure potential in generating cell turgor in plants: _____

_____

_____

(b) Explain the purpose of cell turgor to plants: _____

_____

_____

© 2015 **BIOZONE** International
ISBN: 978-1-927309-25-4
Photocopying Prohibited

168 Making Dilutions

Key Idea: Dilution reduces the concentration of a stock solution by a known factor.

A dilution reduces the concentration of a solution by a known value. **Simple dilutions** are based on ratios, and involve taking a volume of stock solution and adding it to an appropriate volume of solvent to achieve the desired dilution. Simple dilutions are often used to produce calibration curves from which to determine the concentration of unknowns. The dilution may be represented as a percentage of the original solution, a dilution factor, or a ratio.

Simple dilution

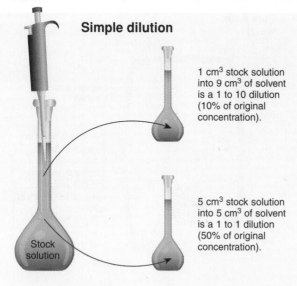

1 cm³ stock solution into 9 cm³ of solvent is a 1 to 10 dilution (10% of original concentration).

5 cm³ stock solution into 5 cm³ of solvent is a 1 to 1 dilution (50% of original concentration).

The following equation is used to calculate the volume needed to make a simple dilution:

$$C1 \times V1 = C2 \times V2$$

C1 = initial concentration of stock solution

V1 = initial volume of stock solution

C2 = final concentration required

V2 = final volume required

You will always know three of the values, so by rearranging the equation you can determine what volume of stock solution is needed to achieve the desired final concentration.

$$V1 = (C2 \times V2) / C1$$

Dilution factors

Often dilutions are expressed as factors or ratios, e.g. the solution was diluted by a factor of five, or there was a dilution ratio of one to five. A dilution factor is the total number of units in which the stock solution will be dissolved, e.g. a one to five dilution (1:5) involves mixing one unit of stock solution with 4 units of solvent (1 + 4 = 5). Therefore: in a simple dilution, add the stock to *one less* unit volume of solvent than the dilution factor required.

Example

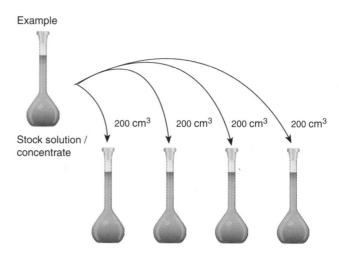

Stock solution / concentrate

200 cm³   200 cm³   200 cm³   200 cm³

A technician has 1 dm³ of stock solution. This provides enough concentrate for him to produce five solutions of equal concentration to be used by groups in his lab. The stock solution represents one solution and he needs four others, into which 200 cm³ of stock solution will be added. The five solutions are then topped up with water to reach the final (diluted) concentration in all five solutions.

1. A student had a 1.00 mol dm⁻³ stock solution of sucrose. Calculate the dilutions required to produce 5 cm³ of sucrose solution at the following concentrations:

   (a) 0.75 mol dm⁻³: _____

   (b) 0.50 mol dm⁻³: _____

   (c) 0.25 mol dm⁻³: _____

2. (a) Use the equation below to calculate the solute potential (ψ_s) of the solutions in (1) and also of the 1.00 mol dm⁻³ solution (the solutions were at 22°C):

   0.75 mol dm⁻³: _____   0.50 mol dm⁻³: _____

   0.25 mol dm⁻³: _____   1.00 mol dm⁻³: _____

   $$\psi_s = -iCRT$$

   i = ionisation constant (for sucrose, this is 1)
   C = molar concentration
   R = pressure constant = 8.31 dm³ kPa K⁻¹mol⁻¹
   T = temperature (°K) = 273 + °C of solution.

   (b) Plot sucrose concentration vs solute potential on the grid.

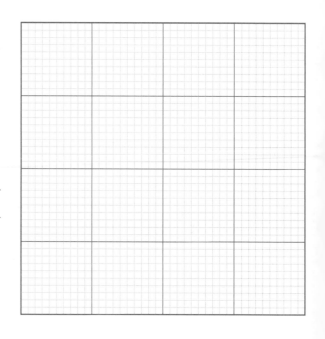

LINK

DATA 8

© 2015 **BIOZONE** International
ISBN: 978-1-927309-25-4
Photocopying Prohibited

169 Estimating Osmolarity

Key Idea: A cell placed in a hypotonic solution will gain water while a cell placed in a hypertonic solution will lose water. The osmolarity (which is directly proportional to the solute potential) of a cell or tissue can be estimated by placing the tissue into a series of solutions of known concentration and observing if the tissue loses (hypertonic solution) or gains (hypotonic solution) water. The solution in which the tissue remains unchanged indicates the osmolarity of the tissue.

Potato cubes

The aim
To determine the solute potential of potatoes by placing potato cubes in varying solutions of sucrose, $C_{12}H_{22}O_{11}$ (table sugar).

The method
Fifteen identical 1.5 cm^3 cubes of potato where cut and weighed in grams to two decimal places. Five solutions of sucrose were prepared in the following range (in mol dm^{-3}): 0.00, 0.25, 0.50, 0.75, 1.00. Three potato cubes were placed in each solution, at 22°C, for two hours, stirring every 15 minutes. The cubes were then retrieved, patted dry on blotting paper and weighed again.

1. Complete the table (right) by calculating the total mass of the potato cubes, the total change in mass, and the total % change in mass for all the sucrose concentrations:

2. Use the grid below to draw a line graph of the sucrose concentration vs total percentage change in mass:

The results

	Potato sample	Initial mass (I) / g	Final mass (F) / g
[Sucrose] 0.00 mol dm^{-3}	1	5.11	6.00
	2	5.15	6.07
	3	5.20	5.15
Total			
Change (C) (F-I) / g			
% Change (C/I x 100)			
[Sucrose] 0.25 mol dm^{-3}	1	6.01	4.98
	2	6.07	5.95
	3	7.10	7.00
Total			
Change (C) (F-I) / g			
% Change (C/I x 100)			
[Sucrose] 0.50 mol dm^{-3}	1	6.12	5.10
	2	7.03	6.01
	3	5.11	5.03
Total			
Change (C) (F-I) / g			
% Change (C/I x 100)			
[Sucrose] 0.75 mol dm^{-3}	1	5.03	3.96
	2	7.10	4.90
	3	7.03	5.13
Total			
Change (C) (F-I) / g			
% Change (C/I x 100)			
[Sucrose] 1.00 mol dm^{-3}	1	5.00	4.03
	2	5.04	3.95
	3	6.10	5.02
Total			
Change (C) (F-I) / g			
% Change (C/I x 100)			

3. (a) Use this graph to estimate the osmolarity of the potato (the point where there is no change in mass):

_____

(b) Use the calibration curve (opposite) to determine the solute potential (ψs) of your potato (in kPa):

_____

(c) What is the pressure potential (ψp) of the potato cells at equilibrium?

_____

(d) Use the equation $\psi = \psi$s $+ \psi$p to determine the water potential of the potato cells at equilibrium:

_____

LINK
168 DATA

170 Diffusion and Cell Size

Key Idea: Diffusion is less efficient in cells with a small surface area relative to their volume than in cells with a large surface area relative to their volume.

When an object (e.g. a cell) is small it has a large surface area in comparison to its volume. Diffusion is an effective way to transport materials (e.g. gases) into the cell. As an object becomes larger, its surface area compared to its volume is smaller. Diffusion is no longer an effective way to transport materials to the inside. This places a physical limit on the size a cell can grow, with the effectiveness of diffusion being the controlling factor. Larger organisms overcome this constraint by becoming multicellular.

Single-celled organisms

Single-celled organisms (e.g. *Amoeba*), are small and have a large surface area relative to the cell's volume. The cell's requirements can be met by the diffusion or active transport of materials into and out of the cell (below).

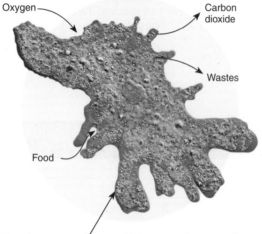

Oxygen

Carbon dioxide

Wastes

Food

The **plasma membrane**, which surrounds every cell, regulates movements of substances into and out of the cell. For each square micrometre of membrane, only so much of a particular substance can cross per second.

Multicellular organisms

Multicellular organisms (e.g. plants and animals) are often quite large and large organisms have a small surface area compared to their volume. They require specialised systems to transport the materials they need to and from the cells and tissues in their body.

In a multicellular organism, such as an elephant, the body's need for respiratory gases cannot be met by diffusion through the skin.

A specialised gas exchange surface (lungs) and circulatory (blood) system are required to transport substances to the body's cells.

The diagram below shows four hypothetical cells of different sizes. They range from a small 2 cm cube to a 5 cm cube. This exercise investigates the effect of cell size on the efficiency of diffusion.

2 cm cube   3 cm cube   4 cm cube   5 cm cube

1. Calculate the volume, surface area and the ratio of surface area to volume for each of the four cubes above (the first has been done for you). When completing the table below, show your calculations.

Cube size	Surface area	Volume	Surface area to volume ratio
2 cm cube	$2 \times 2 \times 6 = 24 \ cm^2$ (2 cm x 2 cm x 6 sides)	$2 \times 2 \times 2 = 8 \ cm^3$ (height x width x depth)	24 to 8 = 3:1
3 cm cube			
4 cm cube			
5 cm cube			

LINK
DATA 10

© 2015 **BIOZONE** International
ISBN: 978-1-927309-25-4
Photocopying Prohibited

2. Create a graph, plotting the surface area against the volume of each cube, on the grid on the right. Draw a line connecting the points and label axes and units.

3. Which increases the fastest with increasing size: the **volume** or the **surface area**?

   _____

4. Explain what happens to the ratio of surface area to volume with increasing size.

   _____

   _____

   _____

   _____

   _____

5. The diffusion of molecules into a cell can be modelled by using agar cubes infused with phenolphthalein indicator and soaked in sodium hydroxide (NaOH). Phenolphthalein turns a pink colour when in the presence of a base. As the NaOH diffuses into the agar, the phenolphthalein changes to pink and thus indicates how far the NaOH has diffused into the agar. By cutting an agar block into cubes of various sizes, it is possible to show the effect of cell size on diffusion.

   (a) Use the information below to fill in the table on the right:

   NaOH solution

   Agar cubes infused with phenolphthalein

   Cube 1

   2 cm

   Cube 2

   1 cm

   4 cm

   Cube 3

   Region of no colour change

   Region of colour change

   Cubes shown to same scale

Cube	1	2	3
1. Total volume / cm³			
2. Volume not pink / cm³			
3. Diffused volume / cm³ (subtract value 2 from value 1)			
4. Percentage diffusion			

   (b) Diffusion of substances into and out of a cell occurs across the plasma membrane. For a cuboid cell, explain how increasing cell size affects the effective ability of diffusion to provide the materials required by the cell:

   _____

   _____

   _____

   _____

6. Explain why a single large cell of 2 cm x 2 cm x 2 cm is less efficient in terms of passively acquiring nutrients than eight cells of 1 cm x 1 cm x 1 cm:

   _____

   _____

   _____

   _____

© 2015 **BIOZONE** International
ISBN: 978-1-927309-25-4
Photocopying Prohibited

171 Active Transport

Key Idea: Active transport uses energy to transport molecules against their concentration gradient across a partially permeable membrane.

Active transport is the movement of molecules (or ions) from regions of low concentration to regions of high concentration across a cellular membrane by a transport protein. Active transport needs energy to proceed because molecules are being moved against their concentration gradient.

▶ The energy for active transport comes from **ATP** (adenosine triphosphate). Energy is released when ATP is hydrolysed (water is added) forming ADP (adenosine diphosphate) and inorganic phosphate (Pi).

▶ Transport (carrier) proteins in the membrane are used to actively transport molecules from one side of the membrane to the other (below).

▶ Active transport can be used to move molecules into and out of a cell.

▶ Active transport can be either primary or secondary. Primary active transport directly uses ATP for the energy to transport molecules. In secondary active transport, energy is stored in a concentration gradient. The transport of one molecule is coupled to the movement of another down its concentration gradient, ATP is not directly involved in the transport process.

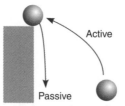

A ball falling is a passive process (it requires no energy input). Replacing the ball requires active energy input.

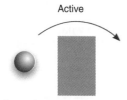

It requires energy to actively move an object across a physical barrier.

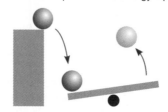

Sometimes the energy of a passively moving object can be used to actively move another. For example, a falling ball can be used to catapult another (left).

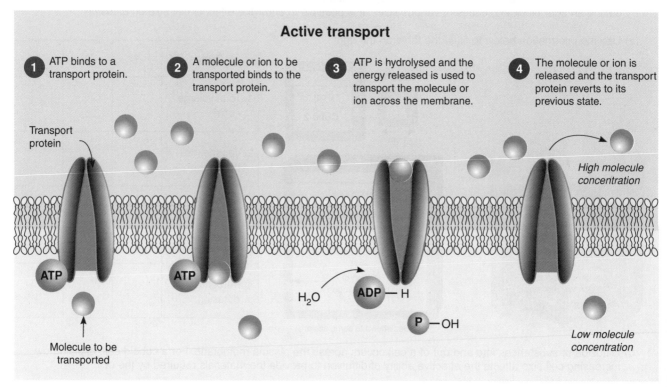

Active transport

1 ATP binds to a transport protein.

2 A molecule or ion to be transported binds to the transport protein.

3 ATP is hydrolysed and the energy released is used to transport the molecule or ion across the membrane.

4 The molecule or ion is released and the transport protein reverts to its previous state.

Transport protein

High molecule concentration

ATP

ATP

H_2O

ADP — H

P — OH

Molecule to be transported

Low molecule concentration

1. What is **active transport**? _____

_____

_____

_____

2. Where does the energy for active transport come from? _____

3. What is the difference between primary active transport and secondary active transport? _____

_____

_____

_____

© 2015 **BIOZONE** International
ISBN:978-1-927309-25-4
Photocopying Prohibited

172 Ion Pumps

Key Idea: Ion pumps are transmembrane proteins that use energy to move ions and molecules across a membrane against their concentration gradient.

Sometimes molecules or ions are needed in concentrations that diffusion alone cannot supply to the cell, or they cannot diffuse through the plasma membrane. In this case ion pumps move ions (and some molecules) across the plasma membrane. The sodium-potassium pump (below) is found in almost all animal cells and is common in plant cells also. The concentration gradient created by ion pumps is often coupled to the transport of other molecules such as glucose across the membrane.

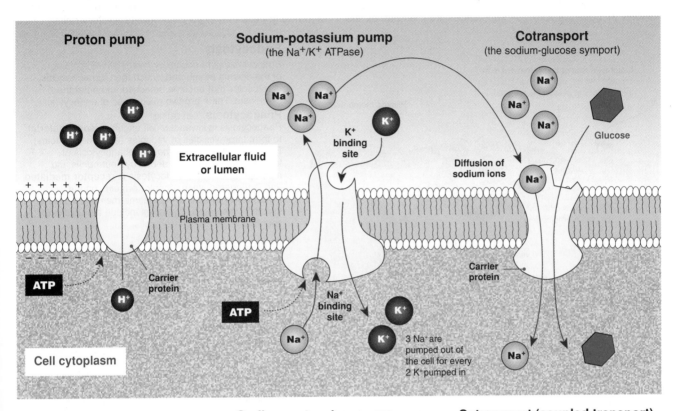

Proton pumps

ATP driven proton pumps use energy to remove hydrogen ions (H+) from inside the cell to the outside. This creates a large difference in the proton concentration either side of the membrane, with the inside of the plasma membrane being negatively charged. This potential difference can be coupled to the transport of other molecules.

Sodium-potassium pump

The sodium-potassium pump is a specific protein in the membrane that uses energy in the form of ATP to exchange sodium ions (Na+) for potassium ions (K+) across the membrane. The unequal balance of Na+ and K+ across the membrane creates large concentration gradients that can be used to drive transport of other substances (e.g. cotransport of glucose).

Cotransport (coupled transport)

A gradient in sodium ions drives the active transport of **glucose** in intestinal epithelial cells. The specific transport protein couples the return of Na+ down its concentration gradient to the transport of glucose into the intestinal epithelial cell. A low intracellular concentration of Na+ (and therefore concentration gradient) is maintained by a sodium-potassium pump.

1. Why is ATP required for membrane pump systems to operate? _____

_____

2. (a) Explain what is meant by cotransport: _____

_____

   (b) How is cotransport used to move glucose into the intestinal epithelial cells? _____

_____

_____

   (c) What happens to the glucose that is transported into the intestinal epithelial cells? _____

_____

3. Describe two consequences of the extracellular accumulation of sodium ions: _____

_____

_____

© 2015 **BIOZONE** International
ISBN: 978-1-927309-25-4
Photocopying Prohibited

LINK 214   LINK 175   WEB 172   KNOW

173 Exocytosis and Endocytosis

Key Idea: Endocytosis and exocytosis are active transport processes. Endocytosis involves the cell engulfing material. Exocytosis involves the cell expelling material.

Most cells carry out **cytosis**, a type of active transport in which the plasma membrane folds around a substance to transport it across the plasma membrane. The ability of cells to do this is a function of the flexibility of the plasma membrane. Cytosis results in bulk transport of substances into or out of the cell and is achieved through the energy-requiring localised activity of the cell's cytoskeleton. **Endocytosis** involves material being engulfed and taken into the cell. It typically occurs in protozoans and the phagocytic white blood cells of the mammalian defence system. **Exocytosis** is the reverse of endocytosis and involves expelling material from the cell in vesicles that fuse with the plasma membrane. Exocytosis is common in cells that export material (secretory cells).

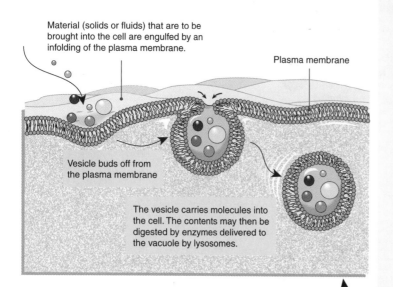

Material (solids or fluids) that are to be brought into the cell are engulfed by an infolding of the plasma membrane.

Plasma membrane

Vesicle buds off from the plasma membrane

The vesicle carries molecules into the cell. The contents may then be digested by enzymes delivered to the vacuole by lysosomes.

Both endocytosis and exocytosis require energy in the form of ATP.

Endocytosis

Endocytosis (left) occurs by invagination (infolding) of the plasma membrane, which then forms vesicles or vacuoles that become detached and enter the cytoplasm. There are two main types of endocytosis:

Phagocytosis: 'cell-eating'
Phagocytosis involves the cell engulfing **solid material** to form large vesicles or vacuoles (e.g. food vacuoles). **Examples:** Feeding in *Amoeba*, phagocytosis of foreign material and cell debris by neutrophils and macrophages. Some endocytosis is **receptor mediated** and is triggered when receptor proteins on the extracellular surface of the plasma membrane bind to specific substances. <u>Examples</u> include the uptake of lipoproteins by mammalian cells.

Pinocytosis: 'cell-drinking'
Pinocytosis involves the non-specific uptake of **liquids** or fine suspensions into the cell to form small pinocytic vesicles. Pinocytosis is used primarily for absorbing extracellular fluid. <u>Examples</u>: Uptake in many protozoa, some cells of the liver, and some plant cells.

Areas of enlargement

The contents of the vesicle are expelled into the intercellular space.

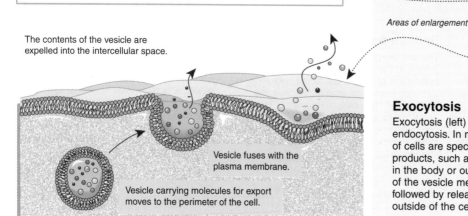

Vesicle fuses with the plasma membrane.

Vesicle carrying molecules for export moves to the perimeter of the cell.

Exocytosis

Exocytosis (left) is the reverse process to endocytosis. In multicellular organisms, various types of cells are specialised to manufacture and export products, such as proteins, from the cell to elsewhere in the body or outside it. Exocytosis occurs by fusion of the vesicle membrane and the plasma membrane, followed by release of the vesicle contents to the outside of the cell.

1. Distinguish between **phagocytosis** and **pinocytosis**: _____

_____

_____

2. Describe an example of phagocytosis and identify the cell type involved: _____

_____

3. Describe an example of exocytosis and identify the cell type involved: _____

_____

4. How does each of the following substances enter a living macrophage:

(a) Oxygen: _____ (c) Water: _____

(b) Cellular debris: _____ (d) Glucose: _____

© 2015 **BIOZONE** International
ISBN:978-1-927309-25-4
Photocopying Prohibited

174 Active and Passive Transport Summary

Key Idea: Cells move materials into and out of the cell by either passive transport, which does not require energy, or by active transport which requires energy, often as ATP.

Cells need to move materials into and out of the cell. Molecules needed for metabolism must be accumulated from outside the cell, where they may be in low concentration. Waste products and molecules for use in other parts of the

organism must be 'exported' out of the cell. Some materials (e.g. gases and water) move into and out of the cell by passive transport processes, without energy expenditure. Other molecules (e.g. sucrose) are moved into and out of the cell using active transport. Active transport processes involve the expenditure of energy in the form of ATP, and therefore use oxygen.

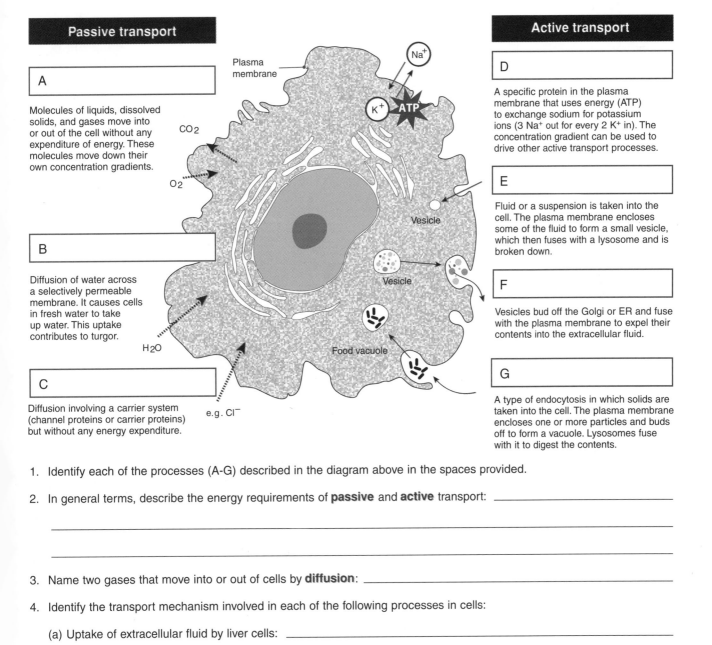

Passive transport

A

Molecules of liquids, dissolved solids, and gases move into or out of the cell without any expenditure of energy. These molecules move down their own concentration gradients.

B

Diffusion of water across a selectively permeable membrane. It causes cells in fresh water to take up water. This uptake contributes to turgor.

C

Diffusion involving a carrier system (channel proteins or carrier proteins) but without any energy expenditure.

Active transport

D

A specific protein in the plasma membrane that uses energy (ATP) to exchange sodium for potassium ions (3 Na$^+$ out for every 2 K$^+$ in). The concentration gradient can be used to drive other active transport processes.

E

Fluid or a suspension is taken into the cell. The plasma membrane encloses some of the fluid to form a small vesicle, which then fuses with a lysosome and is broken down.

F

Vesicles bud off the Golgi or ER and fuse with the plasma membrane to expel their contents into the extracellular fluid.

G

A type of endocytosis in which solids are taken into the cell. The plasma membrane encloses one or more particles and buds off to form a vacuole. Lysosomes fuse with it to digest the contents.

Diagram labels: Plasma membrane, Na$^+$, K$^+$, ATP, CO$_2$, O$_2$, Vesicle, Vesicle, Food vacuole, H$_2$O, e.g. Cl$^-$

1. Identify each of the processes (A-G) described in the diagram above in the spaces provided.

2. In general terms, describe the energy requirements of **passive** and **active** transport: _____

_____

_____

3. Name two gases that move into or out of cells by **diffusion**: _____

4. Identify the transport mechanism involved in each of the following processes in cells:

   (a) Uptake of extracellular fluid by liver cells: _____

   (b) Capture and destruction of a bacterial cell by a white blood cell: _____

   (c) Movement of water into the cell: _____

   (d) Secretion of digestive enzymes from cells of the pancreas: _____

   (e) Uptake of lipoproteins in the blood by mammalian cells: _____

   (f) Ingestion of a food particle by a protozoan: _____

   (g) Transport of chloride ions into a cell: _____

   (h) Uptake of glucose into red blood cells: _____

   (i) Establishment of a potential difference across the membrane of a nerve cell: _____

TEST

175 ATP Supplies Energy for Work

Key Idea: ATP transports chemical energy within the cell for use in metabolic processes.

ATP is one of a group of phosphorylated nucleosides that generally provide energy and a phosphate group for phosphorylations. ATP is the universal energy carrier in cells, transferring chemical energy within the cell for use in metabolic processes such as biosynthesis, cell division, cell signalling, cell mobility, and active transport of substances across membranes. ATP is produced during cellular respiration from the coupling of an inorganic phosphate to an ADP.

The structure of ATP

The ATP molecule is a nucleotide derivative. It consists of three components; a purine base (adenine) and a pentose sugar (ribose), which form the nucleoside component, and three phosphate groups, which attach to the 5' carbon of the pentose sugar. The structure of ATP is shown as a schematic (right) and as a three dimensional space filling molecule (far right).

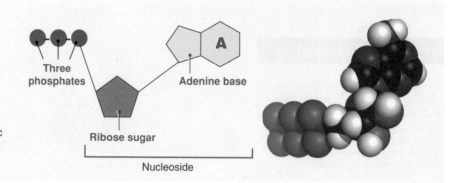

Three phosphates

A

Adenine base

Ribose sugar

Nucleoside

How does ATP provide energy?

ATP releases its energy during hydrolysis. Water is split and added to the terminal phosphate group resulting in ADP and Pi. For every mole of ATP hydrolysed **30.7 kJ** of energy is released. Note that energy is released during the formation of chemical bonds not from the breaking of chemical bonds.

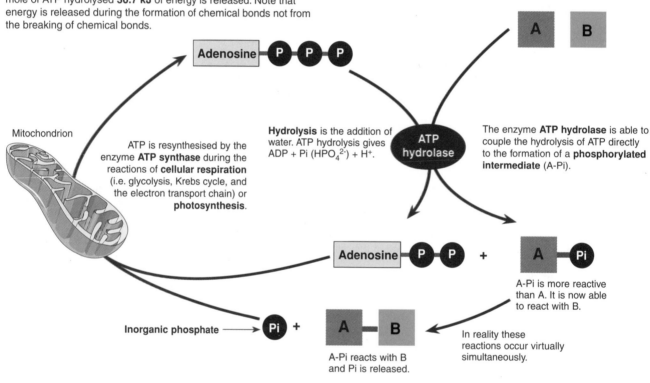

The reaction of A + B is endergonic. It requires energy to proceed and will not occur spontaneously.

A   **B**

Adenosine P P P

Mitochondrion

ATP is resynthesised by the enzyme **ATP synthase** during the reactions of **cellular respiration** (i.e. glycolysis, Krebs cycle, and the electron transport chain) or **photosynthesis**.

Hydrolysis is the addition of water. ATP hydrolysis gives $ADP + Pi (HPO_4^{2-}) + H^+$.

ATP hydrolase

The enzyme **ATP hydrolase** is able to couple the hydrolysis of ATP directly to the formation of a **phosphorylated intermediate** (A-Pi).

Adenosine P P + A Pi

A-Pi is more reactive than A. It is now able to react with B.

Inorganic phosphate ⟶ Pi + A B

In reality these reactions occur virtually simultaneously.

A-Pi reacts with B and Pi is released.

---

1. In which organelle is ATP produced in the cell? _____

2. Which enzyme catalyses the hydrolysis of ATP? _____

3. Which enzyme catalyses the synthesis of ATP? _____

4. On the space filling model of ATP at the top right of the page:

   (a) Label the three components of an ATP molecule:

   (b) Show which phosphate bond is hydrolysed to provide the energy for cellular work:

5. In what way is the ADP/ATP system like a rechargeable battery? _____

   _____

   _____

LINK 171   LINK 172   LINK 214

KNOW

© 2015 **BIOZONE** International
ISBN:978-1-927309-25-4
Photocopying Prohibited

176 Introduction to Gas Exchange

Key Idea: Gas exchange is the process by which respiratory gases are exchanged between the cells of an organism and the environment. Large, complex organisms require special adaptations to ensure adequate gas exchange.

Energy is released in cells by the breakdown of sugars and other substances in cellular respiration. As a consequence of this process, respiratory gases (carbon dioxide and oxygen) need to be exchanged by diffusion. Gas are exchanged in opposite directions across a gas exchange surface between the lungs (or gills) and the external environment. Diffusion gradients are maintained by transport of gases away from the gas exchange surface. Gas exchange surfaces must be in close proximity to the blood for this to occur effectively.

The need for gas exchange

Gas exchange is the process by which respiratory gases (oxygen and carbon dioxide) enter and leave the body by diffusion across **gas exchange surfaces**. To achieve effective gas exchange rates, gas exchange surfaces must be thin, they must have a high surface area, and there must be a concentration gradient for diffusion. The concentration gradients for diffusion are maintained by transport of gases away from the gas exchange surface. Because gases must be in solution to cross the membrane, gas exchange surfaces are also moist.

Gas exchange surfaces provide a means for gases to enter and leave the body. Some organisms use the body surface as the sole gas exchange surface, but many have specialised gas exchange structures (e.g. lungs, gills, or stomata). Amphibians use the body surface and simple lungs to provide for their gas exchange requirements.

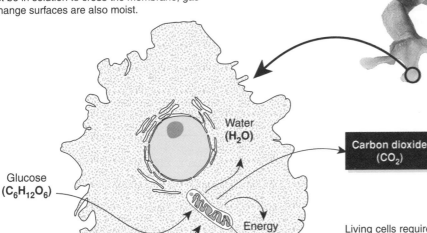

Carbon dioxide gas

Oxygen gas

Cellular respiration takes place in every cell of an organism's body. Cellular respiration creates a constant demand for oxygen (O_2) and a need to eliminate carbon dioxide gas (CO_2).

Water (H_2O)

Carbon dioxide (CO_2)

Glucose ($C_6H_{12}O_6$)

Energy

Oxygen (O_2)

Living cells require energy for the activities of life. **Mitochondria** are the main sites where glucose is broken down to release energy. In the process, oxygen is used to make water, and carbon dioxide is released as a waste product.

Features of gas exchange surfaces

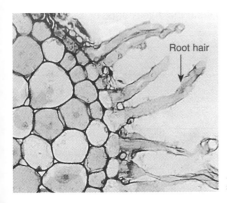

Root hair

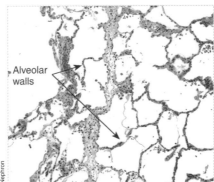

Alveolar walls

Blood cells within a capillary. The blood cells carry O_2 and CO_2

Root hair cells are thin-walled extensions of the root epidermis that greatly increase the surface area over which the plant can absorb minerals and dissolved gases. A study of the roots of a four-month old rye plant (*Secale cereale*) found the root system covered 639 m² (of which the root hair cells made up 401 m²), 130 times the area of the shoot system. It was estimated there were 14 billion root hair cells. The volume of space occupied by the root system was just 6 dm³.

In mammalian lungs, the surface area for gas exchange is greatly increased by alveoli, the microscopic air sacs at the terminal ends of the airways. The walls of the alveoli are only one cell thick and are enveloped by capillaries. Oxygen diffuses across the alveolar walls into the blood in the capillaries and is transported away to the body's cells. Carbon dioxide is brought from the body's cells to the alveoli, where it diffuses into the alveolar space and is breathed out.

Effective gas exchange relies on maintaining a concentration gradient for the diffusion of gases. Oxygen is transported from the alveoli or gills by the blood, reducing its concentration relative to the environmental side of the gas exchange surface (respiratory membrane). Carbon dioxide is transported to the alveoli or gills, increasing its concentration relative to the environmental side of the membrane. It then diffuses out of the blood, across the membrane, and into the external environment.

LINK 184   LINK 177   LINK 165   WEB 176   **KNOW**

Gas exchange in unicellular and multicellular organisms

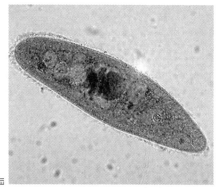

Gills

Spiracle

Single celled organisms are small enough that gases can diffuse into their interior without the need for gas exchange or transport systems. Oxygen and carbon dioxide diffuse into and out of the cell over the cell's entire surface.

Larger animals require specialised systems to obtain and transport oxygen to the cells of the body and remove carbon dioxide. Aquatic animals have gills, thin feathery structures, which remain moist and functional in water.

Terrestrial animals protect their respiratory membranes internally. Insects exchange gases by way of tubes called tracheae, which open to the outside through spiracles. Terrestrial vertebrates have lungs, which are ventilated to maintain gas exchange rates.

Fick's law of diffusion expresses the rate of diffusion of a given molecule across a membrane at a given temperature. At a given temperature the rate is affected by three main factors:

▶ **Concentration gradient**: The greater the concentration gradient, the greater the diffusion rate.

▶ **Surface area**: The larger the area across which diffusion occurs, the greater the rate of diffusion.

▶ **Barriers to diffusion**: Thicker barriers slow diffusion rate. Pores in a barrier enhance diffusion.

Fick's law

The diffusion rate across gas exchange surfaces is described by Fick's law:

$$\frac{\text{Surface area of membrane} \quad X \quad \text{Difference in concentration across the membrane}}{\text{Thickness of the membrane}}$$

---

1. Distinguish between cellular respiration and gas exchange: _____

_____

_____

2. (a) What gases are involved in cellular respiration? _____

(b) How do these gases move across the gas exchange surface? _____

3. What is the main function of a gas exchange surface? _____

_____

4. Describe the three properties that all gas exchange surfaces have in common and state the significance of each:

(a) _____

(b) _____

(c) _____

5. Explain the function of root hairs: _____

_____

6. State the effect on diffusion rate in the following situations:

(a) The surface area for diffusion is increased: _____

(b) The thickness of the membrane is decreased: _____

(c) The difference in concentration on either side of the membrane is decreased: _____

7. Explain how mammals maintain a gradient for oxygen uptake across the gas exchange surface: _____

_____

_____

177 Gas Exchange in Animals

Key Idea: Animal gas exchange systems are suited to the animal's environment, body form, and metabolic needs.

The way an animal exchanges gases with its environment is influenced by the animal's body form and by the environment in which the animal lives. Small or flat organisms in moist or aquatic environments, such as sponges and flatworms, require no specialised structures for gas exchange. Larger or more complex animals have specialised systems to supply the oxygen to support their metabolic activities. The type and complexity of the exchange system reflects the demands of metabolism for gas exchange (oxygen delivery and carbon dioxide removal) and the environment (aquatic or terrestrial).

1. Describe two reasons for the development of gas exchange structures and systems in animals:

   (a) _____

   _____

   (b) _____

   _____

2. Describe two ways in which air breathers manage to keep their gas exchange surfaces moist:

   (a) _____

   _____

   (b) _____

   _____

3. Explain why gills would not work in a terrestrial environment:

   _____

   _____

   _____

   _____

   _____

   _____

   _____

4. Explain why mammals must ventilate their lungs (breathe in and out):

   _____

   _____

   _____

   _____

   _____

   _____

Representative gas exchange systems

Simple organisms

The high surface area to volume ratio of very flat or very small organisms, such as this nematode, enables them to use the body surface as the gas exchange surface.

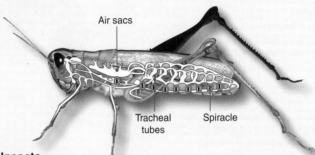

Insects

Insects transport gases via a system of branching tubes called **tracheae** (or tracheal tubes). The tracheae deliver oxygen directly to the tissues. Larger insects can increase the air moving in and out of these tubes by contracting and expanding the abdomen.

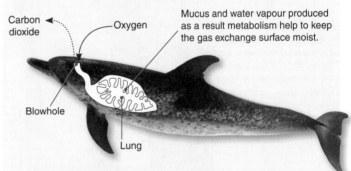

Mucus and water vapour produced as a result metabolism help to keep the gas exchange surface moist.

Air breathing vertebrates

The gas exchange surface in mammals and other air breathing vertebrates is located in internal **lungs**. Their internal location within the body keeps the exchange surfaces moist and prevents them from drying out. The many alveoli of the lungs provide a large surface area for maximising gas exchange. For example, human lungs have 600 million alveoli with a total surface area of 100 m^2.

Gills under gill cover (operculum).

Bony fish, sharks, and rays

Fish extract oxygen dissolved in water using **gills**. Gills achieve high extraction rates of oxygen from the water which is important because there is less oxygen in water than air. Bony fish ventilate the gill surfaces by movements of the gill cover. The water supports the gills, and the gill lamellae (the gas exchange surface) can be exposed directly to the environment without drying out.

© 2015 **BIOZONE** International
ISBN: 978-1-927309-25-4
Photocopying Prohibited

LINK 183   LINK 181   LINK 178   WEB 177

KNOW

178 The Human Gas Exchange System

Key Idea: Lungs are internal sac-like organs connected to the outside by a system of airways. The smallest airways end in thin-walled alveoli, where gas exchange occurs.

The gas exchange (or respiratory system) includes all the structures associated with exchanging respiratory gases with the environment. In humans, this system consists of paired lungs connected to the outside air by way of a system of tubular passageways: the trachea, bronchi, and bronchioles. The details of exchanges across the gas exchange membrane are described on the next page.

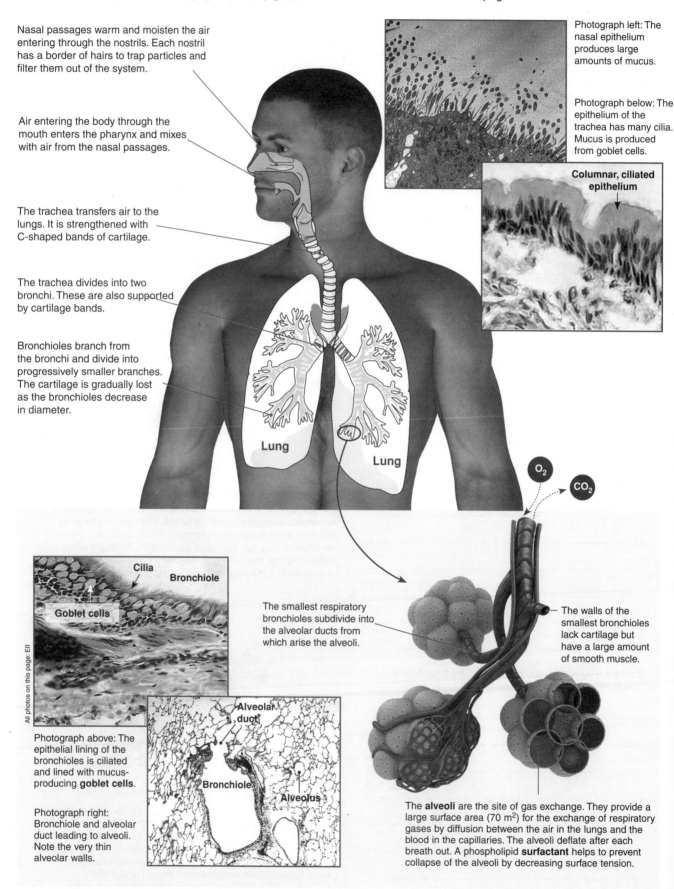

Nasal passages warm and moisten the air entering through the nostrils. Each nostril has a border of hairs to trap particles and filter them out of the system.

Air entering the body through the mouth enters the pharynx and mixes with air from the nasal passages.

The trachea transfers air to the lungs. It is strengthened with C-shaped bands of cartilage.

The trachea divides into two bronchi. These are also supported by cartilage bands.

Bronchioles branch from the bronchi and divide into progressively smaller branches. The cartilage is gradually lost as the bronchioles decrease in diameter.

Photograph left: The nasal epithelium produces large amounts of mucus.

Photograph below: The epithelium of the trachea has many cilia. Mucus is produced from goblet cells.

Columnar, ciliated epithelium

Lung

Lung

O_2

CO_2

The walls of the smallest bronchioles lack cartilage but have a large amount of smooth muscle.

The smallest respiratory bronchioles subdivide into the alveolar ducts from which arise the alveoli.

Cilia

Bronchiole

Goblet cells

All photos on this page: EII

Photograph above: The epithelial lining of the bronchioles is ciliated and lined with mucus-producing **goblet cells**.

Photograph right: Bronchiole and alveolar duct leading to alveoli. Note the very thin alveolar walls.

Alveolar duct

Bronchiole

Alveolus

The **alveoli** are the site of gas exchange. They provide a large surface area (70 m^2) for the exchange of respiratory gases by diffusion between the air in the lungs and the blood in the capillaries. The alveoli deflate after each breath out. A phospholipid **surfactant** helps to prevent collapse of the alveoli by decreasing surface tension.

© 2015 **BIOZONE** International
ISBN:978-1-927309-25-4
Photocopying Prohibited

Cross section through an alveolus

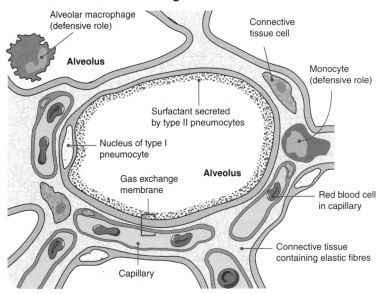

Alveolar macrophage (defensive role)

Connective tissue cell

Alveolus

Monocyte (defensive role)

Surfactant secreted by type II pneumocytes

Nucleus of type I pneumocyte

Gas exchange membrane

Alveolus

Red blood cell in capillary

Connective tissue containing elastic fibres

Capillary

The gas exchange membrane

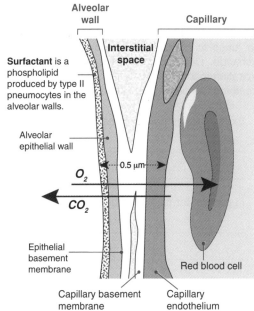

Alveolar wall

Capillary

Interstitial space

Surfactant is a phospholipid produced by type II pneumocytes in the alveolar walls.

Alveolar epithelial wall

0.5 μm

O_2

CO_2

Epithelial basement membrane

Red blood cell

Capillary basement membrane

Capillary endothelium

The alveoli are very close to the blood-filled capillaries. The alveolus is lined with alveolar epithelial cells or **pneumocytes**. Type I pneumocytes (90-95% of aveolar cells) contribute to the gas exchange membrane (right). Type II pneumocytes secrete a **surfactant**, which decreases surface tension within the alveoli and prevents them from collapsing and sticking to each other. Macrophages and monocytes defend the lung tissue against pathogens. Elastic connective tissue gives the alveoli their ability to expand and recoil.

The **gas exchange membrane** is the term for the layered junction between the alveolar epithelial cells (pneumocytes), the endothelial cells of the capillary, and their associated basement membranes (thin, collagenous layers that underlie the epithelial tissues). Gases move freely across this membrane.

1. (a) Explain how the basic structure of the human gas exchange system provides such a large area for gas exchange:

    _____

    _____

    (b) Identify the general region of the lung where exchange of gases takes place: _____

2. Describe the structure and purpose of the alveolar-capillary membrane: _____

    _____

    _____

3. Describe the role of the surfactant in the alveoli: _____

    _____

4. Using the information above and opposite, complete the table below summarising the **histology of the gas exchange pathway**. Name each numbered region and use a tick or cross to indicate the presence or absence of particular tissues.

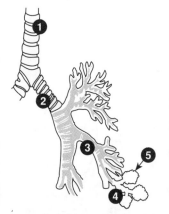

	Region	Cartilage	Ciliated epithelium	Goblet cells (mucus)	Smooth muscle	Connective tissue
1						✓
2						
3		gradually lost				
4	Alveolar duct		✗	✗		
5					very little	

5. Babies born prematurely are often deficient in surfactant. This causes respiratory distress syndrome; a condition where breathing is very difficult. From what you know about the role of surfactant, explain the symptoms of this syndrome:

    _____

    _____

179 Breathing in Humans

Key Idea: Breathing provides a continual supply of air to the lungs to maintain the concentration gradients for gas exchange. Different muscles are used in inspiration and expiration to force air in and out of the lungs.

Breathing (ventilation) provides a continual supply of oxygen-rich air to the lungs and expels air high in carbon dioxide. Together with the cardiovascular system, which transports respiratory gases between the alveolar and the cells of the body, breathing maintains concentration gradients for gas exchange. Breathing is achieved by the action of muscles.

1. Explain the purpose of breathing: _____

   _____

   _____

2. In general terms, how is breathing achieved?

   _____

   _____

   _____

   _____

3. (a) Describe the sequence of events involved in quiet breathing:

   _____

   _____

   _____

   _____

   _____

   (b) What is the essential difference between this and the situation during forced breathing:

   _____

   _____

   _____

4. During inspiration, which muscles are:

   (a) Contracting: _____

   _____

   (b) Relaxed: _____

   _____

5. During forced expiration, which muscles are:

   (a) Contracting: _____

   _____

   (b) Relaxed: _____

   _____

6. Explain the role of antagonistic muscles in breathing:

   _____

   _____

   _____

Breathing and muscle action

Muscles can only do work by contracting, so they can only perform movement in one direction. To achieve motion in two directions, muscles work as antagonistic pairs. Antagonistic pairs of muscles have opposing actions and create movement when one contracts and the other relaxes. Breathing in humans involves two sets of antagonistic muscles. The external and internal intercostal muscles of the ribcage, and the diaphragm and abdominal muscles.

Inspiration (inhalation or breathing in)

During quiet breathing, inspiration is achieved by increasing the thoracic volume (therefore decreasing the pressure inside the lungs). Air then flows into the lungs in response to the decreased pressure inside the lung. Inspiration is always an active process involving muscle contraction.

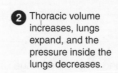

1 External intercostal muscles contract causing the ribcage to expand and move up. Diaphragm contracts and moves down.

2 Thoracic volume increases, lungs expand, and the pressure inside the lungs decreases.

3 Air flows into the lungs in response to the pressure gradient.

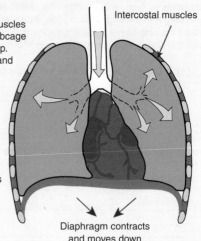

Intercostal muscles

Diaphragm contracts and moves down

Expiration (exhalation or breathing out)

In quiet breathing, expiration is a passive process, achieved when the external intercostals and diaphragm relax and thoracic volume decreases. Air flows passively out of the lungs to equalise with the air pressure. In active breathing, muscle contraction is involved in bringing about both inspiration and expiration.

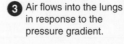

1 In **quiet breathing**, external intercostals and diaphragm relax. The elasticity of the lung tissue causes recoil.

In **forced breathing**, the internal intercostals and abdominal muscles contract to compress the thoracic cavity and increase the force of the expiration.

2 Thoracic volume decreases and the pressure inside the lungs increases.

3 Air flows passively out of the lungs in response to the pressure gradient.

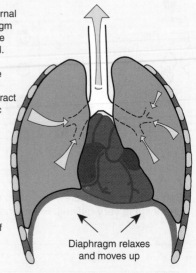

Diaphragm relaxes and moves up

© 2015 **BIOZONE** International
ISBN:978-1-927309-25-4
Photocopying Prohibited

180 Investigating Ventilation in Humans

Key Idea: Vital capacity can be affected by several factors including age, gender, height, ethnicity, and physical condition. Vital capacity is the greatest volume of air that can be expelled from the lungs after taking the deepest possible breath. It is easily measured using a spirometer or a bell jar system (as described below). In healthy adults, vital capacity ranges between 4-6 dm^3, but is influenced by factors such as gender, age, height, ethnicity, and physical condition.

Measuring vital capacity

Vital capacity can be measured using a 6 dm^3 calibrated glass bell jar, supported in a sink of water (right). The jar is calibrated by inverting it, pouring in known volumes of water, and marking the level on the bell jar with a marker pen.

To measure vital capacity, a person breathes in as far as possible (maximal inhalation), and then exhales as far as possible (maximal exhalation) into a mouth piece connected to tubing. The drop in volume within the bell jar is measured (this is the vital capacity in dm^3).

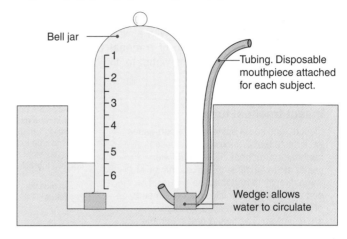

Bell jar

Tubing. Disposable mouthpiece attached for each subject.

Wedge: allows water to circulate

Investigating vital capacity

A class of high school biology students investigated the vital capacity of the whole class using the bell jar method described above.

The students recorded their heights as well as their vital capacity. The results are presented on the table (right).

1. Calculate the mean vital capacity for:

   (a) Females: _____

   (b) Males: _____

   (c) Explain if these results are what you would expect?

   _____

   _____

   _____

   _____

Females		Males	
Height / cm	Vital capacity / dm^3	Height / cm	Vital capacity / dm^3
156	2.75	181	4.00
145	2.50	163	2.50
155	3.25	167	4.00
170	4.00	174	4.00
162	2.75	177	4.00
164	2.75	177	3.75
163	3.40	176	3.75
158	2.75	177	3.25
167	4.00	178	4.00
165	3.00	178	3.75

2. (a) Plot height versus vital capacity as a scatter graph on the grid provided (right). Use different symbols or colours for each set of data (female and male).

   (b) Draw a line of best fit through each set of points. For a line of best fit, the points should fall equally either side of the line.

   (c) Describe the relationship between height and vital capacity:

   _____

   _____

   _____

   _____

   _____

   _____

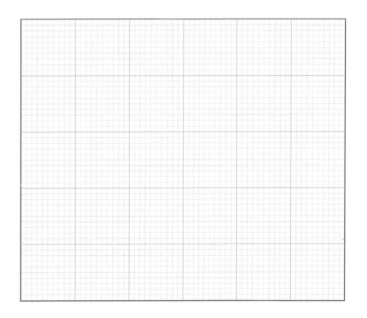

LINK 179   LINK 19

DATA

181 Gas Exchange in Insects

Key Idea: Insects transport air throughout their bodies via a system of tracheal tubes. Spiracles allow air to enter and leave the body.

Terrestrial air breathers lose water from their gas exchange surfaces to the environment. Most terrestrial insects have a large surface area to volume ratio and so are at risk of drying out. They minimise water losses with a waxy outer layer to their exoskeleton and a system of **tracheal tubes** for gas exchange that loses very little water to the environment.

Tracheal systems, which open to the air via paired openings (**spiracles**) in the body wall, are the most common gas exchange organs of insects. Filtering devices stop the system clogging and valves control the degree to which the spiracles are open. In small insects, diffusion is the only mechanism needed to exchange gases, because it occurs so rapidly through the air-filled tubules. Larger, active insects, such as locusts, have air sacs, which can be compressed and expanded to assist in moving air through the tubules.

Insect tracheal tubes

Insects, and some spiders, transport gases via a system of branching tubes called tracheae or tracheal tubes. Respiratory gases move by diffusion across the moist lining directly to and from the tissues. The end of each tube contains a small amount of fluid in which the respiratory gases are dissolved. The fluid is drawn into the muscle tissues during their contraction, and is released back into the tracheole when the muscle rests. Insects ventilate their tracheal system by making rhythmic body movements to help move the air in and out of the tracheae.

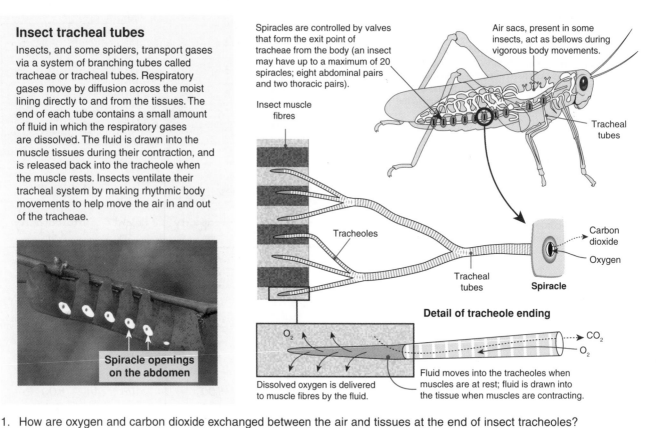

Spiracles are controlled by valves that form the exit point of tracheae from the body (an insect may have up to a maximum of 20 spiracles; eight abdominal pairs and two thoracic pairs).

Insect muscle fibres

Air sacs, present in some insects, act as bellows during vigorous body movements.

Tracheal tubes

Tracheoles

Carbon dioxide

Oxygen

Tracheal tubes

Spiracle

Detail of tracheole ending

O_2

CO_2

O_2

Dissolved oxygen is delivered to muscle fibres by the fluid.

Fluid moves into the tracheoles when muscles are at rest; fluid is drawn into the tissue when muscles are contracting.

Spiracle openings on the abdomen

1. How are oxygen and carbon dioxide exchanged between the air and tissues at the end of insect tracheoles?

_____

_____

_____

_____

2. Valves in the spiracles can regulate the amount of air entering the tracheal system. Suggest a reason for this adaptation:

_____

_____

3. How is ventilation achieved in a terrestrial insect? _____

_____

_____

4. Even though most insects are small, they have evolved an efficient and highly developed gas exchange system that is independent of diffusion across the body surface. Why do you think this is the case?

_____

_____

_____

© 2015 **BIOZONE** International
ISBN:978-1-927309-25-4
Photocopying Prohibited

182 Dissection of an Insect

Key Idea: The insect tracheal system can be readily exposed during a dissection of a generalised insect.

The tracheal system of insects comprises extensively branching tubes that allow the transport of oxygen and carbon dioxide to and from all parts of the insect's body. A dissection of an insect with a generalised body plan, such as a cockroach, provides an appreciation of how extensively these tubes ramify throughout the body.

The insect is first euthanased using chloroform. The cockroach being used here is *Drymaplaneta semivitta*, a wingless species. If the insect you are dissecting has wings, these will need to be removed.

Place the insect on its side to observe the spiracles. This can be made easier by removing the legs. The spiracles can be seen as small dark areas where the dorsal and ventral surfaces of the abdomen join.

After removing the legs, carefully cut the insect along both sides of the exoskeleton with sharp scissors. Try to cut with the points of the scissors facing up to limit damage. Pin the insect on a wax dish on its ventral surface. Do not pin through the dorsal surface.

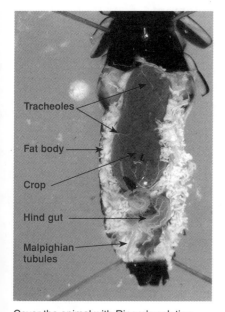

Cover the animal with Ringer's solution (an isotonic solution) and then carefully remove the dorsal exoskeleton with forceps. Observe the fat body, crop, and hind gut. Note the excretory (Malpighian) tubules branching from the hind-gut.

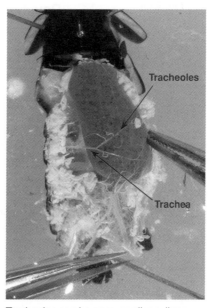

Tracheoles can be seen as silvery lines crossing the dorsal surface of the crop. Carefully pull the crop to the side to reveal the larger tracheal tubes where they join the spiracles.

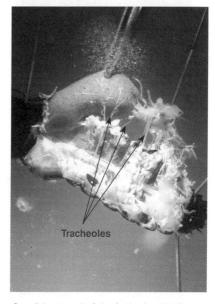

Careful removal of the fat body will allow better viewing of the tracheal system. Even under a low power dissecting microscope, the rings around the tracheal tubes can be seen. Use the microscope to trace the system to the finest tubes.

1. What is the function of the spiracles? _____

_____

2. (a) Where do the tracheoles end? _____

   (b) What does this mean about the direction of air flow? _____

_____

LINK
181

PRAC

183 Gas Exchange in Fish

Key Idea: The gills of fish exchange gases between the blood and the environment. Gills are thin filamentous, vascular structures located just behind the head.

Fish obtain the oxygen they need from the water using gills, which are membranous structures supported by cartilaginous or bony struts. Gill surfaces are very large and as water flows over the gill surface, respiratory gases are exchanged between the blood and the water. The percentage of dissolved oxygen in a volume of water is much less than in the same volume of air. Air is 21% oxygen, whereas in water, dissolved oxygen is about 1% by volume. Active organisms with gills must therefore be able to extract oxygen efficiently from the water. In fish, high oxygen extraction rates are achieved using countercurrent mechanisms and by pumping water across the gill surface (bony fish) or swimming continuously with the mouth open (sharks and rays).

Fish gills

The gills of fish have a great many folds, which are supported and kept apart from each other by the water. This gives them a high surface area for gas exchange. The outer surface of the gill is in contact with the water, and blood flows in vessels inside the gill. Gas exchange occurs by diffusion between the water and blood across the gill membrane and capillaries. The operculum (gill cover) permits exit of water and acts as a pump, drawing water past the gill filaments. The gills of fish are very efficient and achieve an 80% extraction rate of oxygen from water; over three times the rate of human lungs from air.

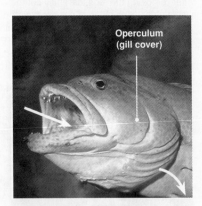

Operculum (gill cover)

Ventilation of the gills

Bony fish ventilate the gills by opening and closing the mouth in concert with opening and closing the operculum. The mouth opens, increasing the volume of the buccal (mouth) cavity and causing water to enter. The operculum bulges slightly, moving water into the opercular cavity. The mouth closes and the operculum opens and water flows out over the gills. These continual pumping movements keep oxygenated water flowing over the gills, maintaining the concentration gradient for diffusion.

Breathing in bony fish

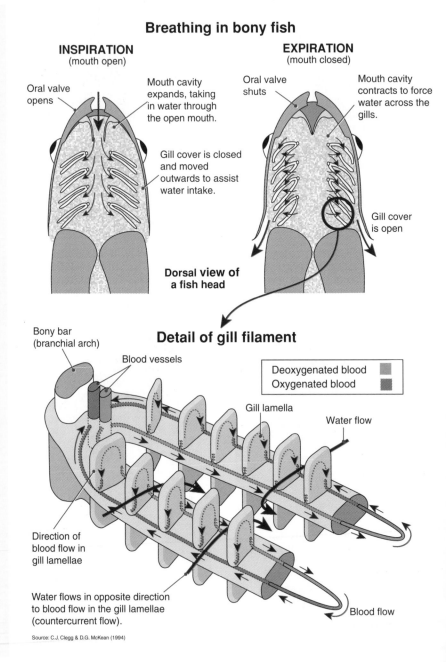

INSPIRATION (mouth open)

Oral valve opens

Mouth cavity expands, taking in water through the open mouth.

Gill cover is closed and moved outwards to assist water intake.

EXPIRATION (mouth closed)

Oral valve shuts

Mouth cavity contracts to force water across the gills.

Gill cover is open

Dorsal view of a fish head

Detail of gill filament

Bony bar (branchial arch)

Blood vessels

| Deoxygenated blood | |
| Oxygenated blood | |

Gill lamella

Water flow

Direction of blood flow in gill lamellae

Water flows in opposite direction to blood flow in the gill lamellae (countercurrent flow).

Blood flow

Source: C.J. Clegg & D.G. McKean (1994)

1. Describe three features of a fish gas exchange system (gills and related structures) that facilitate gas exchange:

(a) _____

(b) _____

(c) _____

2. Why do fish need to ventilate their gills? _____

_____

_____

© 2015 **BIOZONE** International
ISBN:978-1-927309-25-4
Photocopying Prohibited

Countercurrent flow

▶ The structure of fish gills and their physical arrangement in relation to the blood flow maximises gas exchange rates. A constant stream of oxygen-rich water flows over the gill filaments in the opposite direction to the blood flowing through the gill filaments.

▶ This is called countercurrent flow (below left) and it is an adaptation for maximising the amount of O_2 removed from the water. Blood flowing through the gill capillaries encounters water of increasing oxygen content.

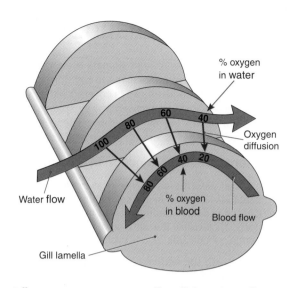

The concentration gradient (for oxygen uptake) across the gill is maintained across the entire distance of the gill lamella and oxygen continues to diffuse into the blood (CO_2 diffuses out at the same time).

A parallel current flow would not achieve the same oxygen extraction rates because the concentrations across the gill would quickly equalise (far right).

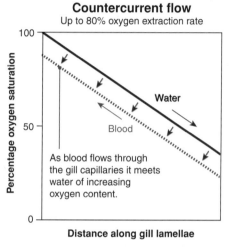

Countercurrent flow
Up to 80% oxygen extraction rate

As blood flows through the gill capillaries it meets water of increasing oxygen content.

Parallel current flow
Up to 50% oxygen extraction rate

At this point, blood and water have the same O_2 concentration and no more O_2 exchange takes place.

3. Describe how bony fish achieve adequate ventilation of the gills through:

(a) Pumping (mouth and operculum): _____

(b) Continuous swimming (mouth open): _____

4. Describe countercurrent flow: _____

5. (a) How does the countercurrent system in a fish gill increase the efficiency of oxygen extraction from the water?

(b) Explain why parallel flow would not achieve the same rates of oxygen extraction: _____

6. In terms of the amount of oxygen available in the water, explain why fish are very sensitive to increases in water temperature or suspended organic material in the water:

184 Gas Exchange in Plants

Key Idea: Gas exchange through stomata is associated with water losses. Plants have adaptations to limit this loss.

The leaf epidermis of angiosperms is covered with tiny pores, called **stomata**. Angiosperms have many air spaces between the cells of the stems, leaves, and roots. These air spaces are continuous and gases are able to move freely through them and into the plant's cells via the stomata. Each stoma is bounded by two **guard cells**, which together regulate the entry and exit of gases and water vapour. Although stomata permit gas exchange between the air and the photosynthetic cells inside the leaf, they are also the major routes for water loss through transpiration.

Gas exchanges and the function of stomata

Gases enter and leave the leaf by way of stomata. Inside the leaf (as illustrated by a dicot, right), the large air spaces and loose arrangement of the spongy mesophyll facilitate the diffusion of gases and provide a large surface area for gas exchanges.

Respiring plant cells use oxygen (O_2) and produce carbon dioxide (CO_2). These gases move in and out of the plant and through the air spaces by diffusion.

When the plant is photosynthesising, the situation is more complex. Overall there is a net consumption of CO_2 and a net production of oxygen. The fixation of CO_2 maintains a gradient in CO_2 concentration between the inside of the leaf and the atmosphere. Oxygen is produced in excess of respiratory needs and diffuses out of the leaf. These **net** exchanges are indicated by the arrows on the diagram.

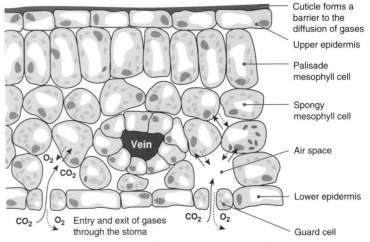

Cuticle forms a barrier to the diffusion of gases

Upper epidermis

Palisade mesophyll cell

Spongy mesophyll cell

Air space

Lower epidermis

Guard cell

CO_2 O_2 Entry and exit of gases through the stoma

Net gas exchanges in a photosynthesising dicot leaf

Wood prevents gas exchange. A lenticel is a small area in the bark where the loosely arranged cells allow the entry and exit of gases into the stem tissue underneath.

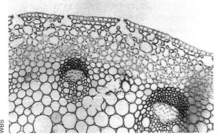

The stems of some plants (e.g. the buttercup above) are photosynthetic. Gas exchange between the stem tissues and the environment occurs through stomata in the outer epidermis.

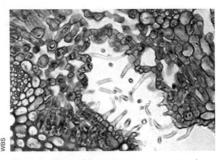

Oleander (above) has many water conserving features. The stomata are in pits on the leaf underside. The pits restrict water loss to a greater extent than they reduce CO_2 uptake.

The cycle of opening and closing of stomata

The opening and closing of stomata shows a daily cycle that is largely determined by the hours of light and dark.

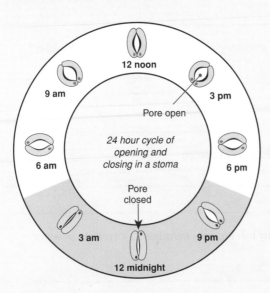

24 hour cycle of opening and closing in a stoma

Pore open

Pore closed

12 noon
9 am
3 pm
6 am
6 pm
3 am
9 pm
12 midnight

The image left shows a scanning electron micrograph (SEM) of a single stoma from the leaf epidermis of a dicot. Note the guard cells (G), which are swollen tight and open the pore (S) to allow gas exchange between the leaf tissue and the environment.

Factors influencing stomatal opening

Stomata	Guard cells	Daylight	CO_2	Soil water
Open	Turgid	Light	Low	High
Closed	Flaccid	Dark	High	Low

The opening and closing of stomata depends on environmental factors, the most important being light, CO_2 concentration in the leaf tissue, and water supply. Stomata tend to open during daylight in response to light, and close at night (left and above). Low CO_2 levels also promote stomatal opening. Conditions that induce water stress cause the stomata to close, regardless of light or CO_2 level.

© 2015 **BIOZONE** International
ISBN:978-1-927309-25-4
Photocopying Prohibited

The guard cells on each side of a stoma control the diameter of the pore by changing shape. When the guard cells take up water by osmosis they swell and become turgid, making the pore wider. When the guard cells lose water, they become flaccid, and the pore closes up. By this mechanism a plant can control the amount of gas entering, or water leaving, the plant. The changes in turgor pressure that open and close the pore result mainly from the reversible uptake and loss of potassium ions (and thus water) by the guard cells.

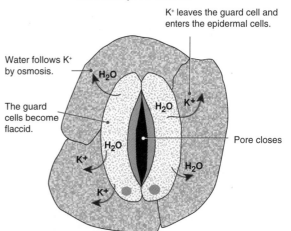

Stomatal pore open

K^+ enters the guard cells from the epidermal cells (active transport coupled to a proton pump).

Water follows K^+ by osmosis.

Thickened ventral wall

Guard cell swells and becomes turgid.

Pore opens

Nucleus of guard cell

Stomatal pore closed

K^+ leaves the guard cell and enters the epidermal cells.

Water follows K^+ by osmosis.

The guard cells become flaccid.

Pore closes

Ψguard cell < Ψepidermal cell: water enters the guard cells
Stomata open when the guard cells actively take up K^+ from the neighboring epidermal cells. The ion uptake causes the water potential (Ψ) to become more negative in the guard cells. As a consequence, water is taken up by the cells and they swell and become turgid. The walls of the guard cells are thickened more on the inside surface (the ventral wall) than the outside wall, so that when the cells swell they buckle outward, opening the pore.

ψepidermal cell < ψguard cell: water leaves the guard cells
Stomata close when K^+ leaves the guard cells. The loss causes the water potential (Ψ) to become less negative in the guard cells, and more negative in the epidermal cells. As a consequence, water is lost by osmosis and the cells sag together and close the pore. The K^+ movements in and out of the guard cells are thought to be triggered by blue-light receptors in the plasma membrane, which activate the active transport mechanisms involved.

1. Describe two adaptive features of leaves:

    (a) _____

    (b) _____

2. With respect to a mesophytic, terrestrial flowering plant:

    (a) Describe the **net** gas exchanges between the air and the cells of the mesophyll in the dark (no photosynthesis):

    _____

    (b) Explain how this situation changes when a plant is photosynthesising: _____

    _____

    _____

3. Describe two ways in which the continuous air spaces through the plant facilitate gas exchange:

    (a) _____

    (b) _____

4. Outline the role of stomata in gas exchange in an angiosperm: _____

    _____

5. Summarise the mechanism by which the guard cells bring about:

    (a) Stomatal opening: _____

    _____

    _____

    (b) Stomatal closure: _____

    _____

    _____

© 2015 **BIOZONE** International
ISBN: 978-1-927309-25-4
Photocopying Prohibited

185 Transport in Multicelluar Organisms

Key Idea: Internal transport systems in animals move materials between exchange surfaces by mass transport.

Living cells require a constant supply of nutrients and oxygen, and continuous removal of wastes. Simple, small organisms achieve this through diffusion. Larger, more complex organisms require specialised systems to facilitate

exchanges as their surface area to volume ratio decreases. **Mass transport** (also known as mass flow or bulk flow) describes the movement of materials at equal rates or as a single mass. Mass transport accounts for the long distance transport of fluids in living organisms. It includes the movement of blood in the circulatory systems of animals.

Exchanges across a body surface

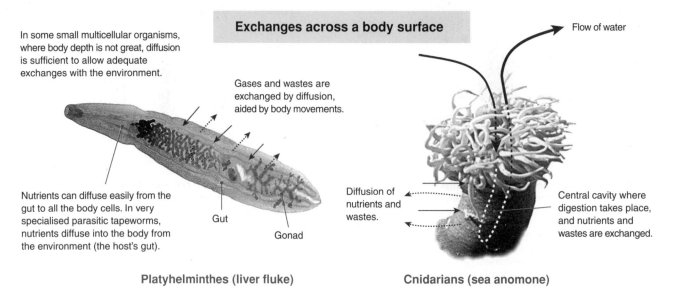

In some small multicellular organisms, where body depth is not great, diffusion is sufficient to allow adequate exchanges with the environment.

Gases and wastes are exchanged by diffusion, aided by body movements.

Nutrients can diffuse easily from the gut to all the body cells. In very specialised parasitic tapeworms, nutrients diffuse into the body from the environment (the host's gut).

Gut

Gonad

Flow of water

Diffusion of nutrients and wastes.

Central cavity where digestion takes place, and nutrients and wastes are exchanged.

Platyhelminthes (liver fluke)

Cnidarians (sea anomone)

Systems for exchange and transport

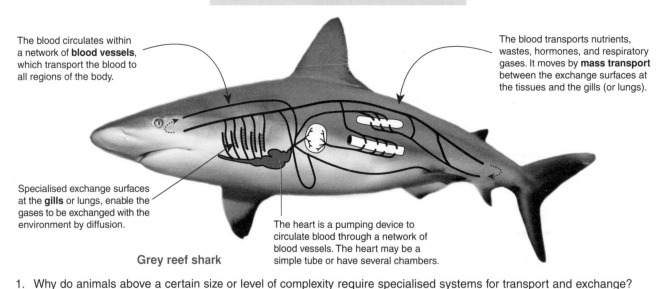

The blood circulates within a network of **blood vessels**, which transport the blood to all regions of the body.

The blood transports nutrients, wastes, hormones, and respiratory gases. It moves by **mass transport** between the exchange surfaces at the tissues and the gills (or lungs).

Specialised exchange surfaces at the **gills** or lungs, enable the gases to be exchanged with the environment by diffusion.

The heart is a pumping device to circulate blood through a network of blood vessels. The heart may be a simple tube or have several chambers.

Grey reef shark

1. Why do animals above a certain size or level of complexity require specialised systems for transport and exchange?

_____

_____

_____

2. (a) How do materials move within the circulatory system of a vertebrate? _____

_____

(b) Contrast this with how materials are transported in a flatworm or single celled eukaryote: _____

_____

_____

(c) Identify two exchange sites in a vertebrate: _____

WEB 185 LINK 186

186 Closed Circulatory Systems

Key Idea: In closed circulatory systems, the blood is contained within blood vessels.

In closed circulatory systems, the blood is contained within vessels and pumped around the body by a heart. Oxygen is transported by the blood and diffuses through capillary walls into the body cells. In large, active animals closed systems efficiently distribute oxygen and nutrients to the body's cells. Closed systems allow the animal to control the distribution of blood flow to different organs and parts of the body by contracting or dilating blood vessels. Vertebrate systems have a pulmonary circuit taking up oxygen and a systemic circuit delivering oxygenated blood to the body.

INVERTEBRATE CLOSED SYSTEMS

Polychaete worm

Wiki: Hans Hillewaert

Earthworm

The closed systems of many annelids (e.g. earthworms) circulate blood through a series of vessels before returning it to the heart. In annelids, the dorsal (upper) and ventral (lower) blood vessels are connected by lateral vessels in every segment (right). The dorsal vessel receives blood from the lateral vessels and carries it towards the head. The ventral vessel carries blood posteriorly and distributes it to the segmental vessels. The dorsal vessel is contractile and is the main method of propelling the blood, but there are also several contractile aortic arches ('hearts') which act as accessory organs for blood propulsion.

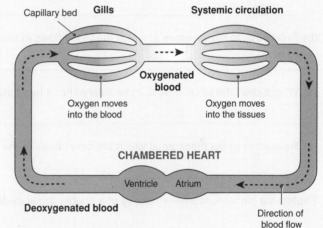

Contractile dorsal blood vessel

Aortic arches

Capillary networks

Tail

Head

Ventral blood vessel

VERTEBRATE CLOSED SYSTEMS

Rays

Bony fish

Sharks

Closed, single circuit systems

In closed circulation systems, the blood is contained within vessels and is returned to the heart after every circulation of the body. Exchanges between the blood and the fluids bathing the cells occurs by diffusion across capillaries. In single circuit systems, typical of fish, the blood goes directly from the gills to the body. The blood loses pressure at the gills and flows at low pressure around the body.

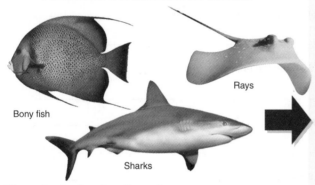

Capillary bed   Gills   Systemic circulation

Oxygenated blood

Oxygen moves into the blood

Oxygen moves into the tissues

CHAMBERED HEART

Ventricle   Atrium

Deoxygenated blood

Direction of blood flow

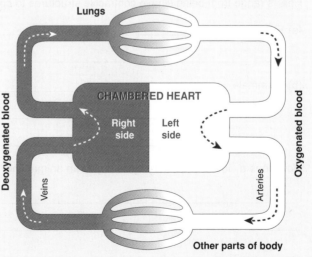

Amphibians

Reptiles

Birds

Mammals

Closed, double circuit systems

Double circulation systems occur in all vertebrates other than fish. The blood is pumped through a pulmonary circuit to the lungs, where it is oxygenated. The blood returns to the heart, which pumps the oxygenated blood, through a systemic circuit, to the body. In amphibians and most reptiles, the heart is not completely divided and there is some mixing of oxygenated and deoxygenated blood. In birds and mammals, the heart is fully divided and there is no mixing.

Lungs

CHAMBERED HEART

Deoxygenated blood

Veins

Right side

Left side

Arteries

Oxygenated blood

Other parts of body

Fish heart

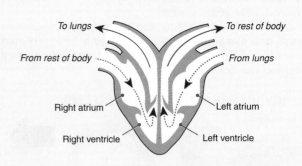

Conus arteriosus — **Ventricle** — **Atrium**

From rest of body

To gills

Sinus venosus

Ventral aorta

Atrioventricular valves — **Sinoatrial valves**

From rest of body

The fish heart is linear, with a sequence of chambers in series. There are two main chambers (atrium and ventricle) as well as an entry (the sinus venosus) and sometimes a smaller exit chamber (the conus). Blood from the body first enters the heart through the sinus venosus, then passes into the atrium and the ventricle. A series of one-way valves between the chambers prevents reverse blood flow. Blood leaving the heart travels to the gills.

Mammalian heart

To lungs **To rest of body**

From rest of body **From lungs**

Right atrium **Left atrium**

Right ventricle **Left ventricle**

In birds and mammals, the heart is fully partitioned into two halves, resulting in four chambers. Blood circulates through two circuits, with no mixing of the two. Oxygenated blood from the lungs is kept separated from the deoxygenated blood returning from the rest of the body.

1. What is the main difference between closed and open systems of circulation? _____

_____

_____

2. (a) Where does the blood flow to immediately after it has passed through the gills in a fish?_____

_____

   (b) Relate this to the pressure at which the blood flows in the systemic circulation: _____

_____

3. (a) Where does the blood flow to immediately after it has passed through the lungs in a mammal? _____

_____

   (b) Relate this to the pressure at which the blood flows in the systemic circulation: _____

_____

4. Explain the higher functional efficiency of a double circuit system, relative to a single circuit system: _____

_____

_____

5. Hearts range from being simple contractile structures to complex chambered organs. Describe basic heart structure in:

   (a) Fish: _____

_____

   (b) Mammals: _____

_____

_____

6. How does a closed circulatory system give an animal finer control over the distribution of blood to tissues and organs?

_____

_____

_____

_____

© 2015 **BIOZONE** International
ISBN: 978-1-927309-25-4
Photocopying Prohibited

187 The Mammalian Transport System

Key Idea: The mammalian circulatory system is double circuit system made up of a pulmonary circuit and a systemic circuit. The blood vessels of the circulatory system form a network of tubes that carry blood away from the heart, transport it to the tissues of the body, and then return it to the heart. The figure below shows a number of the basic circulatory routes. Mammals have a double circulatory system: a **pulmonary** **system**, which carries blood between the heart and lungs, and a **systemic system**, which carries blood between the heart and the rest of the body. The systemic circulation has many subdivisions. Two important subdivisions are the coronary (cardiac) circulation, which supplies the heart muscle, and the hepatic portal circulation, which runs from the gut to the liver.

Schematic overview of the human circulatory system

Deoxygenated blood (coloured blue below) travels to the right side of the heart via the vena cavae. The heart pumps the deoxygenated blood to the lungs where it releases carbon dioxide and receives oxygen. The oxygenated blood (coloured white below) travels via the pulmonary vein back to the heart from where it is pumped to all parts of the body. The **venous system** (figure, left) returns blood from the capillaries to the heart. The **arterial system** (figure right) carries blood from the heart to the capillaries. **Portal systems** carry blood between two capillary beds.

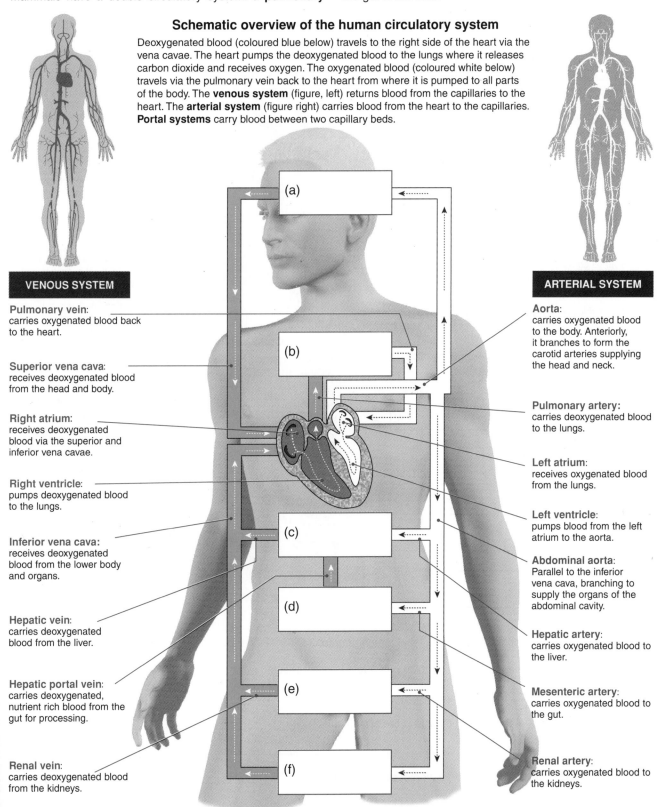

VENOUS SYSTEM

Pulmonary vein:
carries oxygenated blood back to the heart.

Superior vena cava:
receives deoxygenated blood from the head and body.

Right atrium:
receives deoxygenated blood via the superior and inferior vena cavae.

Right ventricle:
pumps deoxygenated blood to the lungs.

Inferior vena cava:
receives deoxygenated blood from the lower body and organs.

Hepatic vein:
carries deoxygenated blood from the liver.

Hepatic portal vein:
carries deoxygenated, nutrient rich blood from the gut for processing.

Renal vein:
carries deoxygenated blood from the kidneys.

ARTERIAL SYSTEM

Aorta:
carries oxygenated blood to the body. Anteriorly, it branches to form the carotid arteries supplying the head and neck.

Pulmonary artery:
carries deoxygenated blood to the lungs.

Left atrium:
receives oxygenated blood from the lungs.

Left ventricle:
pumps blood from the left atrium to the aorta.

Abdominal aorta:
Parallel to the inferior vena cava, branching to supply the organs of the abdominal cavity.

Hepatic artery:
carries oxygenated blood to the liver.

Mesenteric artery:
carries oxygenated blood to the gut.

Renal artery:
carries oxygenated blood to the kidneys.

1. Complete the diagram above by labelling the boxes with the correct organs:
   lungs, liver, head, intestines, genitals/lower body, kidneys.

2. Circle the two blood vessels involved in the pulmonary circuit.

188 Arteries

Key Idea: Arteries are thick-walled blood vessels that carry blood away from the heart to the capillaries within the tissues. In vertebrates, **arteries** are the blood vessels that carry blood away from the heart to the capillaries within the tissues. The large arteries that leave the heart divide into medium-sized (distributing) arteries. Within the tissues and organs, these distributing arteries branch to form **arterioles**, which deliver blood to capillaries. Arterioles lack the thick layers of arteries and consist only of an endothelial layer wrapped by a few smooth muscle fibres at intervals along their length. Blood flow to the tissues is altered by contraction (**vasoconstriction**) or relaxation (**vasodilation**) of the blood vessel walls. Vasoconstriction increases blood pressure whereas vasodilation has the opposite effect.

Arteries

Arteries, regardless of size, can be recognised by their well-defined rounded **lumen** (internal space) and the muscularity of the vessel wall. Arteries have an elastic, stretchy structure that gives them the ability to withstand the high pressure of blood being pumped from the heart. At the same time, they help to maintain pressure by having some contractile ability themselves (a feature of the central muscle layer). Arteries nearer the heart have more elastic tissue, giving greater resistance to the higher blood pressures of the blood leaving the left ventricle. Arteries further from the heart have more muscle to help them maintain blood pressure. Between heartbeats, the arteries undergo elastic recoil and contract. This tends to smooth out the flow of blood through the vessel.

Arteries comprise three main regions (right):

1. A thin inner layer of epithelial cells called the **tunica intima** (endothelium) lines the artery.

2. A thick central layer (the **tunica media**) of elastic tissue and smooth muscle that can both stretch and contract.

3. An outer connective tissue layer (the **tunica externa**) has a lot of elastic tissue.

Structure of an artery

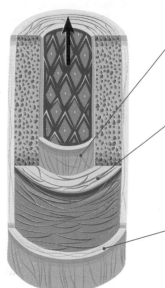

Tunica intima (endothelium)
Thin endothelial layer of squamous epithelium is in contact with the blood. Arrow indicates direction of blood flow.

Tunica media
Thick layer of elastic tissue and smooth muscle tissue allows for both stretch and contraction, maintaining blood flow without loss of pressure.

Tunica externa
Layer of elastic connective tissue (collagen and elastin) anchors the artery to other tissues and allows it to resist overexpansion. Relatively thinner in larger elastic arteries and thicker in muscular, distributing arteries.

Cross section through a large artery

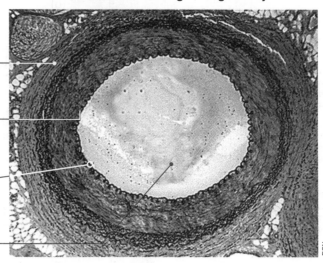

(a)

(b)

(c)

(d)

RCN

1. Using the information above to help you, label the photograph (a)-(d) of the cross section through an artery (above).

2. Why do the walls of arteries need to be thick with a lot of elastic tissue? _____

_____

3. What is the purpose of the smooth muscle in the artery walls? _____

_____

4. How to arteries contribute to the regulation of blood pressure? _____

_____

_____

_____

© 2015 **BIOZONE** International
ISBN:978-1-927309-25-4
Photocopying Prohibited

189 Veins

Key Idea: Veins are blood vessels that return the blood from the tissues to the heart. Veins have a large lumen.

Veins are the blood vessels that return blood to the heart from the tissues. The smallest veins (**venules**) return blood from the capillaries to the veins. Veins and their branches contain about 59% of the blood in the body. The structural differences between veins and arteries are mainly associated with differences in the relative thickness of the vessel layers and the diameter of the lumen (space within the vessel). These, in turn, are related to the vessel's functional role.

Veins

When several capillaries unite, they form small veins called **venules**. The venules collect the blood from capillaries and drain it into **veins**. Veins are made up of the same three layers as arteries but they have less elastic and muscle tissue, a relatively thicker tunica externa, and a larger, less defined **lumen**. The venules closest to the capillaries consist of an **endothelium** and a tunica externa of connective tissue. As the venules approach the veins, they also contain the tunica media characteristic of veins (right). Although veins are less elastic than arteries, they can still expand enough to adapt to changes in the pressure and volume of the blood passing through them. Blood flowing in the veins has lost a lot of pressure because it has passed through the narrow capillary vessels. The low pressure in veins means that many veins, especially those in the limbs, need to have valves to prevent backflow of the blood as it returns to the heart.

Structure of a vein

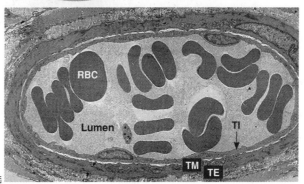

One-way valves
Valves located along the length of veins keep the blood moving towards the heart (prevent back-flow). Arrow indicates direction of blood flow.

Tunica intima (endothelium)
Thin endothelial layer of squamous epithelium lines the vein.

Tunica media
Layer of smooth muscle tissue with collagen fibres (connective tissue). The tunica media is much thinner relative to that of an artery and the smaller venules may lack this layer.

Tunica externa
Layer of connective tissue (mostly collagen) is relatively thicker than in arteries and thicker than the tunica media.

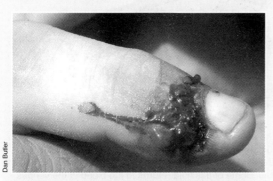

If a vein is cut, as is shown in this severed finger wound, the blood oozes out slowly in an even flow, and usually clots quickly as it leaves. In contrast, arterial blood spurts rapidly and requires pressure to staunch the flow.

Above: TEM of a vein showing red blood cells (RBC) in the lumen, and the tunica intima (TI), tunica media (TM), and tunica externa (TE).

1. Contrast the structure of veins and arteries for each of the following properties:

    (a) Thickness of muscle and elastic tissue: _____

    _____

    (b) Size of the lumen (inside of the vessel): _____

    _____

2. With respect to their functional roles, explain the differences you have described above: _____

    _____

    _____

3. What is the role of the valves in assisting the veins to return blood back to the heart? _____

    _____

4. Why does blood ooze from a venous wound, rather than spurting as it does from an arterial wound?

    _____

    _____

    _____

© 2015 **BIOZONE** International
ISBN: 978-1-927309-25-4
Photocopying Prohibited

190 Capillaries

Key Idea: Capillaries are small, thin-walled vessels that allow the exchange of material between the blood and the tissues. In vertebrates, **capillaries** are very small vessels that connect arterial and venous circulation and allow efficient exchange of nutrients and wastes between the blood and tissues. Capillaries form networks or beds and are abundant where metabolic rates are high. Fluid that leaks out of the capillaries has an essential role in bathing the tissues.

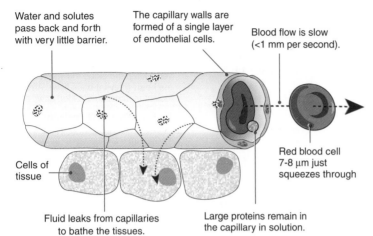

Water and solutes pass back and forth with very little barrier.

The capillary walls are formed of a single layer of endothelial cells.

Blood flow is slow (<1 mm per second).

Red blood cell 7-8 µm just squeezes through

Cells of tissue

Fluid leaks from capillaries to bathe the tissues.

Large proteins remain in the capillary in solution.

Exchanges in capillaries

Blood passes from the arterioles into the capillaries where the exchange of materials between the body cells and the blood takes place. Capillaries are small blood vessels with a diameter of just 4-10 µm. The only tissue present is an **endothelium** of squamous epithelial cells. Capillaries are so numerous that no cell is more than 25 µm from any capillary.

Blood pressure causes fluid to leak from capillaries through small gaps where the endothelial cells join. This fluid bathes the tissues, supplying nutrients and oxygen, and removing wastes (left). The density of capillaries in a tissue is an indication of that tissue's metabolic activity. For example, cardiac muscle relies heavily on oxidative metabolism. It has a high demand for blood flow and is well supplied with capillaries. Smooth muscle is far less active than cardiac muscle, relies more on anaerobic metabolism, and does not require such an extensive blood supply.

Blood, tissue fluid, and lymph

	Blood	Tissue fluid	Lymph
Cells	Erythrocytes, leucocytes, platelets	Some leucocytes	Lymphocytes
Proteins	Hormones and plasma proteins	Some hormones and proteins	None
Glucose	High	None	Low
Amino acids	High	Used by body cells	Low
Oxygen	High	Used by body cells	Low
Carbon dioxide	Low	Produced by body cells	High

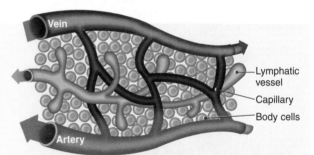

Vein

Lymphatic vessel

Capillary

Body cells

Artery

The pressure at the arterial end of the capillaries forces fluid through gaps between the capillary endothelial cells. The fluid contains nutrients and oxygen and is called tissue fluid. Some of this fluid returns to the blood at the venous end of the capillary bed, but some is drained by lymph vessels to form lymph. Blood transports nutrients, wastes, and respiratory gases to and from the tissues. Tissue fluid facilitates the transport of these between the blood and the tissues. Lymph drains excess tissue fluid and returns it to the general circulation, and it has a role in the immune system.

1. What is the role of capillaries? _____

_____

2. Describe the structure of a capillary, contrasting it with the structure of a vein and an artery:

_____

_____

_____

_____

_____

3. Distinguish between blood, tissue fluid, and lymph: _____

_____

_____

_____

_____

© 2015 **BIOZONE** International
ISBN:978-1-927309-25-4
Photocopying Prohibited

191 Capillary Networks

Key Idea: Capillaries form branching networks where exchanges between the blood and tissues take place.

The flow of blood through a capillary bed is called microcirculation. In most parts of the body, there are two types of vessels in a capillary bed: the true capillaries, where exchanges take place, and a vessel called a vascular shunt, which connects the arteriole and venule at either end of the bed. The shunt diverts blood past the true capillaries when the metabolic demands of the tissue are low. When tissue activity increases, the entire network fills with blood.

1. Describe the structure of a capillary network:

_____

_____

_____

_____

_____

_____

2. Explain the role of the smooth muscle sphincters and the vascular shunt in a capillary network:

_____

_____

_____

_____

_____

_____

3. (a) Describe a situation where the capillary bed would be in the condition labelled **A**:

_____

_____

_____

_____

(b) Describe a situation where the capillary bed would be in the condition labelled **B**:

_____

_____

_____

_____

4. How does a portal venous system differ from other capillary systems?

_____

_____

_____

_____

_____

_____

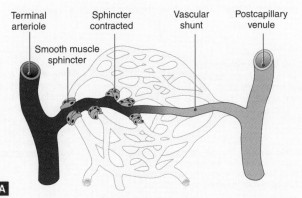

A

When the sphincters contract (close), blood is diverted via the vascular shunt to the postcapillary venule, bypassing the exchange capillaries.

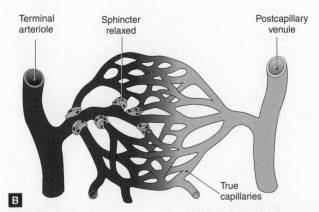

B

When the sphincters are relaxed (open), blood flows through the entire capillary bed allowing exchanges with the cells of the surrounding tissue.

Connecting capillary beds

The role of portal venous systems

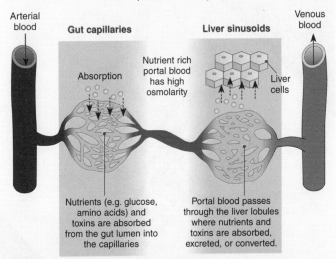

A portal venous system occurs when a capillary bed drains into another capillary bed through veins, without first going through the heart. Portal systems are relatively uncommon. Most capillary beds drain into veins which then drain into the heart, not into another capillary bed. The diagram above depicts the hepatic portal system, which includes both capillary beds and the blood vessels connecting them.

192 The Role and Formation of Tissue Fluid

Key Idea: Tissue fluid is formed by leakage from capillaries. It provides oxygen and nutrients to tissues and removes wastes. The network of capillaries supplying the body's tissues ensures that no cell is far from a supply of nutrients and oxygen. Substances reach the cells through the tissue fluid, moving into and out of the capillaries by diffusion, by cytosis, and through gaps where the membranes are not tightly joined. Specialised capillaries, such as those in the intestine and kidney, where absorption or filtration is important, are relatively more leaky. Fluid moves across the leaky capillary membranes in a direction that depends on the balance between the blood pressure and the oncotic pressure at each end of a capillary bed. Oncotic pressure (also called colloid osmotic pressure) tends to pull water into the capillaries.

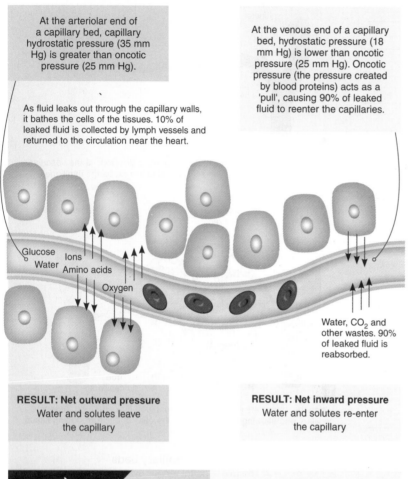

At the arteriolar end of a capillary bed, capillary hydrostatic pressure (35 mm Hg) is greater than oncotic pressure (25 mm Hg).

At the venous end of a capillary bed, hydrostatic pressure (18 mm Hg) is lower than oncotic pressure (25 mm Hg). Oncotic pressure (the pressure created by blood proteins) acts as a 'pull', causing 90% of leaked fluid to reenter the capillaries.

As fluid leaks out through the capillary walls, it bathes the cells of the tissues. 10% of leaked fluid is collected by lymph vessels and returned to the circulation near the heart.

Glucose
Water
Ions
Amino acids
Oxygen

Water, CO$_2$ and other wastes. 90% of leaked fluid is reabsorbed.

RESULT: Net outward pressure
Water and solutes leave the capillary

RESULT: Net inward pressure
Water and solutes re-enter the capillary

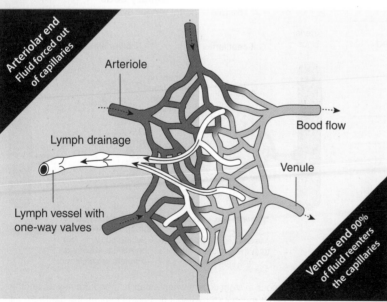

Arteriolar end
Fluid forced out of capillaries

Arteriole

Lymph drainage

Bood flow

Lymph vessel with one-way valves

Venule

Venous end 90% of fluid reenters the capillaries

As described above, not all the fluid reenters the capillaries at the venous end of the capillary bed. This extra fluid is collected by the lymphatic vessels, a network of vessels alongside the blood vessels. Once the fluid enters the lymphatic vessels it is called lymph. Lymph is similar to tissue fluid but has more lymphocytes. The lymphatic vessels drain into the subclavian vein near the heart.

1. What is the purpose of the tissue fluid?

2. Describe the features of capillaries that allow exchanges between the blood and other tissues:

3. Explain how hydrostatic (blood) pressure and solute concentration operate to cause fluid movement at:

(a) The arteriolar end of a capillary bed:

(b) The venous end of a capillary bed:

4. Describe the two ways in which tissue fluid is returned to the general circulation:

(a)

(b)

© 2015 **BIOZONE** International
ISBN:978-1-927309-25-4
Photocopying Prohibited

193 The Human Heart

Key Idea: Humans have a four chambered heart divided into left and right halves. It acts as a double pump.

The heart is the centre of the human cardiovascular system. It is a hollow, muscular organ made up of four chambers (two **atria** and two **ventricles**) that alternately fill and empty of blood, acting as a double pump. The left side (systemic circuit) pumps blood to the body tissues and the right side (pulmonary circuit) pumps blood to the lungs. The heart lies between the lungs, to the left of the midline, and is surrounded by a double layered pericardium of connective tissue, which prevents over distension of the heart and anchors it within the central compartment of the thoracic cavity.

Human heart structure

(sectioned, anterior view)

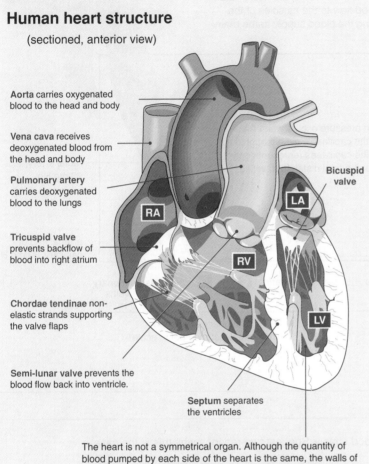

Aorta carries oxygenated blood to the head and body

Vena cava receives deoxygenated blood from the head and body

Pulmonary artery carries deoxygenated blood to the lungs

RA

Tricuspid valve prevents backflow of blood into right atrium

RV

Chordae tendinae non-elastic strands supporting the valve flaps

Semi-lunar valve prevents the blood flow back into ventricle.

Septum separates the ventricles

Bicuspid valve

LA

LV

The heart is not a symmetrical organ. Although the quantity of blood pumped by each side of the heart is the same, the walls of the left ventricle are thicker and more muscular than those of the right ventricle. The difference affects the shape of the ventricular cavities, so the right ventricle is twisted over the left.

Key to abbreviations

RA	Right atrium: receives deoxygenated blood via the anterior and posterior vena cava
RV	Right ventricle: pumps deoxygenated blood to the lungs via the pulmonary artery
LA	Left atrium: receives blood returning to the heart from the lungs via the pulmonary veins
LV	Left ventricle: pumps oxygenated blood to the head and body via the aorta

Top view of a heart in section to show valves

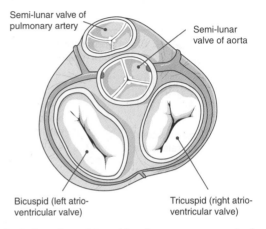

Semi-lunar valve of pulmonary artery

Semi-lunar valve of aorta

Bicuspid (left atrio-ventricular valve)

Tricuspid (right atrio-ventricular valve)

Anterior view of heart to show coronary arteries

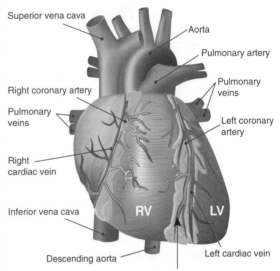

Superior vena cava

Aorta

Pulmonary artery

Right coronary artery

Pulmonary veins

Pulmonary veins

Left coronary artery

Right cardiac vein

Inferior vena cava

RV

LV

Descending aorta

Left cardiac vein

The high oxygen demands of the heart muscle are met by a dense capillary network branching from the coronary arteries. The coronary arteries (left and right) arise from the aorta and spread over the surface of the heart supplying the cardiac muscle with oxygenated blood. The left carries 70% of the coronary blood supply and the right the remaining 30%. Deoxygenated blood is collected by the cardiac veins and returned to the right atrium via a large coronary sinus.

1. In the schematic diagram of the heart, below, label the four chambers and the main vessels entering and leaving them. The arrows indicate the direction of blood flow. Use large coloured circles to mark the position of each of the four valves.

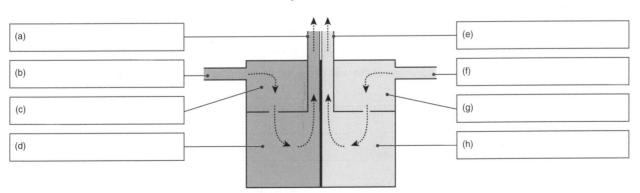

(a)

(b)

(c)

(d)

(e)

(f)

(g)

(h)

LINK **194** LINK **186** WEB **193** KNOW

Pressure changes and the asymmetry of the heart

The heart is not a symmetrical organ. The left ventricle and its associated arteries are thicker and more muscular than the corresponding structures on the right side. This asymmetry is related to the necessary pressure differences between the pulmonary (lung) and systemic (body) circulations (not to the distance over which the blood is pumped *per se*). The graph below shows changes in blood pressure in each of the major blood vessel types in the systemic and pulmonary circuits (the horizontal distance not to scale). The pulmonary circuit must operate at a much lower pressure than the systemic circuit to prevent fluid from accumulating in the alveoli of the lungs. The left side of the heart must develop enough "spare" pressure to enable increased blood flow to the muscles of the body and maintain kidney filtration rates without decreasing the blood supply to the brain.

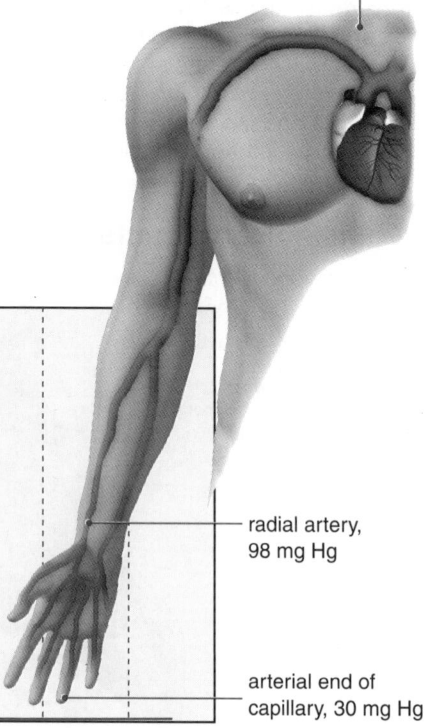

aorta, 100 mg Hg

Blood pressure during contraction (systole)

Blood pressure during relaxation (diastole)

The greatest fall in pressure occurs when the blood moves into the capillaries, even though the distance through the capillaries represents only a tiny proportion of the total distance travelled.

Pressure / mm Hg

120 · 100 · 80 · 60 · 40 · 20 · 0

aorta   arteries   **A**   capillaries   **B**   veins   vena cava   pulmonary arteries   **C**   **D**   venules   pulmonary veins

radial artery, 98 mg Hg

arterial end of capillary, 30 mg Hg

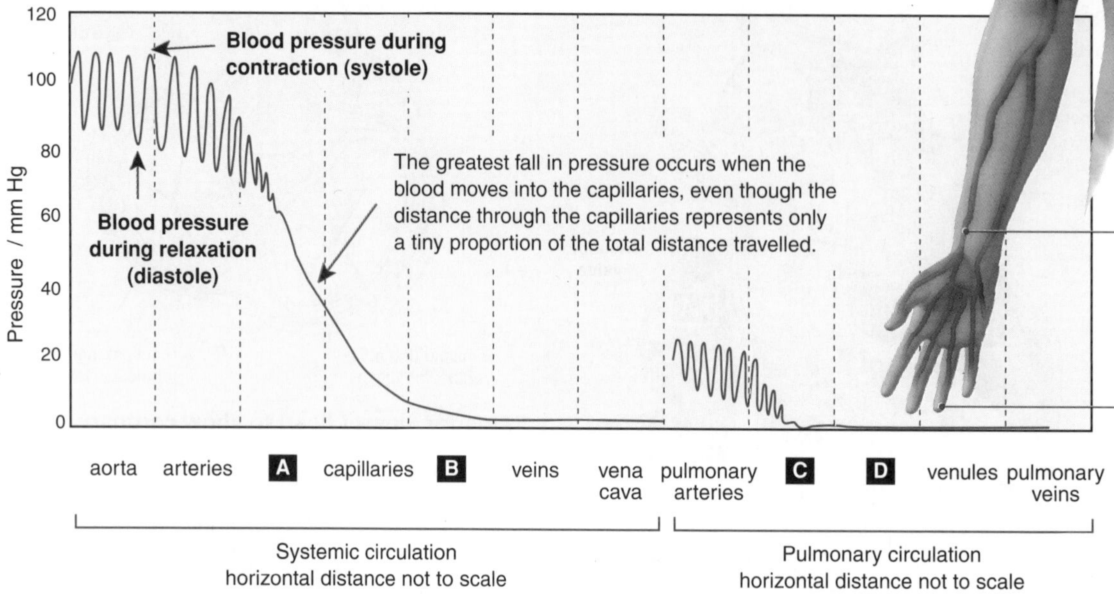

Systemic circulation
horizontal distance not to scale

Pulmonary circulation
horizontal distance not to scale

2. What is the purpose of the valves in the heart? _____

_____

3. The heart is full of blood, yet it requires its own blood supply. Suggest two reasons why this is the case:

(a) _____

(b) _____

4. Predict the effect on the heart if blood flow through a coronary artery is restricted or blocked: _____

_____

_____

5. Identify the vessels corresponding to the letters **A-D** on the graph above:

A: _____   B: _____   C: _____   D: _____

6. (a) Why must the pulmonary circuit operate at a lower pressure than the systemic system? _____

_____

_____

(b) Relate this to differences in the thickness of the wall of the left and right ventricles of the heart: _____

_____

_____

7. What are you recording when you take a pulse? _____

_____

194 Dissecting a Mammalian Heart

Key Idea: Dissecting a sheep's heart allows hands-on exploration of a mammalian heart.

The dissection of a sheep's heart is a common practical activity and allows hands-on exploration of the appearance and structure of a mammalian heart. A diagram of a heart is an idealised representation of an organ that may look quite different in reality. You must learn to transfer what you know from a diagram to the interpretation of the real organ.

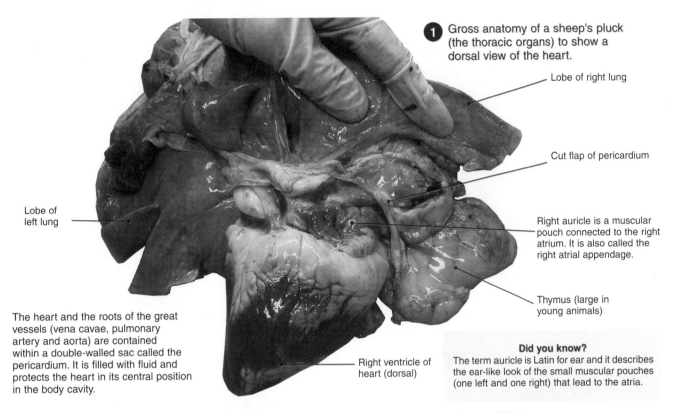

1 Gross anatomy of a sheep's pluck (the thoracic organs) to show a dorsal view of the heart.

Lobe of right lung

Cut flap of pericardium

Lobe of left lung

Right auricle is a muscular pouch connected to the right atrium. It is also called the right atrial appendage.

Thymus (large in young animals)

The heart and the roots of the great vessels (vena cavae, pulmonary artery and aorta) are contained within a double-walled sac called the pericardium. It is filled with fluid and protects the heart in its central position in the body cavity.

Right ventricle of heart (dorsal)

Did you know?
The term auricle is Latin for ear and it describes the ear-like look of the small muscular pouches (one left and one right) that lead to the atria.

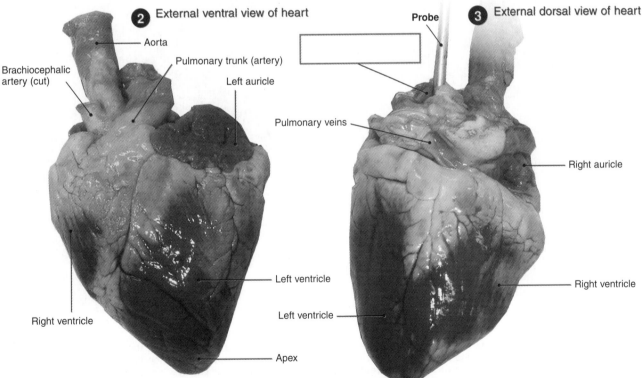

2 External ventral view of heart

Aorta

Brachiocephalic artery (cut)

Pulmonary trunk (artery)

Left auricle

Right ventricle

Left ventricle

Apex

Probe

3 External dorsal view of heart

Pulmonary veins

Right auricle

Left ventricle

Right ventricle

Note the main surface features of an isolated heart. The narrow pointed end forms the **apex** of the heart, while the wider end, where the blood vessels enter is the **base**. The ventral surface of the heart (above) is identified by a groove, the **interventricular sulcus**, which marks the division between the left and right ventricles.

1. Use coloured lines to indicate the interventricular sulcus and the base of the heart. Label the coronary arteries.

On the dorsal surface of the heart, above, locate the large thin-walled **vena cavae** and **pulmonary veins**. You may be able to distinguish between the anterior and posterior vessels. On the right side of the dorsal surface (as you look at the heart) at the base of the heart is the **right atrium**, with the **right ventricle** below it.

2. On this photograph, label the vessel indicated by the probe.

WEB
194 PRAC

4 Dorsal view of heart

5 Shallow section, ventral view of heart

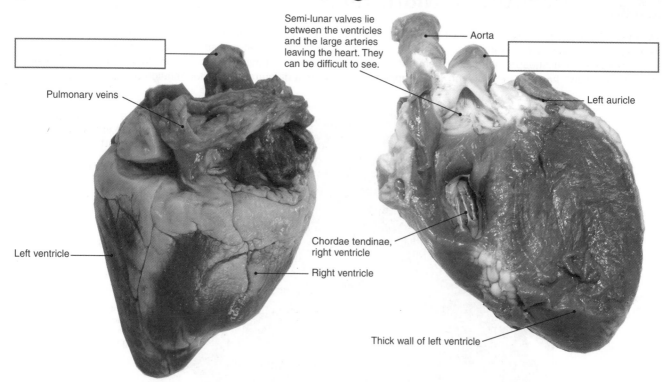

Semi-lunar valves lie between the ventricles and the large arteries leaving the heart. They can be difficult to see.

Aorta

Pulmonary veins

Left auricle

Left ventricle

Chordae tendinae, right ventricle

Right ventricle

Thick wall of left ventricle

3. On this **dorsal view**, label the vessel indicated. Palpate the heart and feel the difference in the thickness of the left and right ventricle walls.

4. This photograph shows a shallow section to expose the right ventricle. Label the vessel in the box indicated.

6 Frontal sections of heart to show chambers

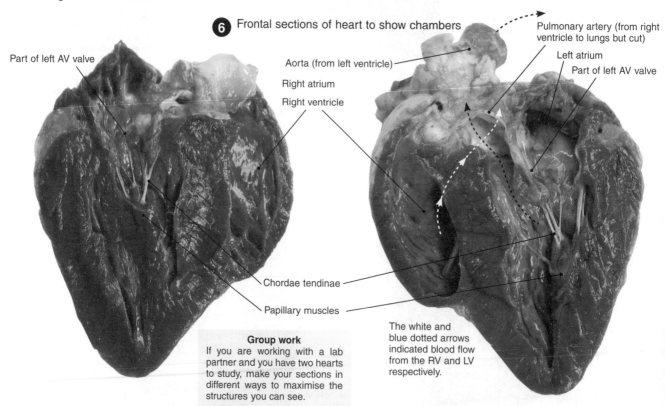

Part of left AV valve

Pulmonary artery (from right ventricle to lungs but cut)

Aorta (from left ventricle)

Left atrium

Right atrium

Part of left AV valve

Right ventricle

Chordae tendinae

Papillary muscles

Group work
If you are working with a lab partner and you have two hearts to study, make your sections in different ways to maximise the structures you can see.

The white and blue dotted arrows indicated blood flow from the RV and LV respectively.

If the heart is sectioned and the two halves opened, the valves of the heart can be seen. Each side of the heart has a one-way valve between the atrium and the ventricle known as the **atrioventricular valve**. They close during ventricular contraction to prevent back flow of the blood into the lower pressure atria.

The atrioventricular (AV) valves of the two sides of the heart are similar in structure except that the right AV valve has three cusps (tricuspid) while the left atrioventricular valve has two cusps (bicuspid or mitral valve). Connective tissue (**chordae tendineae**) run from the cusps to **papillary muscles** on the ventricular wall.

5. Judging by their position and structure, what do you suppose is the function of the chordae tendinae?

_____

_____

6. What feature shown here most clearly distinguishes the left and right ventricles?.

_____

_____

195 The Cardiac Cycle

Key Idea: The cardiac cycle refers to the sequence of events of a heartbeat and involves three main stages: atrial systole, ventricular systole, and complete cardiac diastole.

The heart pumps with alternate contractions (**systole**) and relaxations (**diastole**). Heartbeat occurs in a cycle involving three stages: atrial systole, ventricular systole, and complete cardiac diastole. Pressure changes in the heart's chambers generated by the cycle of contraction and relaxation are responsible for blood movement and cause the heart valves to open and close, preventing backflow of blood. The heartbeat occurs in response to electrical impulses, which can be recorded as a trace called an electrocardiogram.

The cardiac cycle

The **pulse** results from the rhythmic expansion of the arteries as the blood spurts from the left ventricle. Pulse rate therefore corresponds to heart rate.

Stage 1: Atrial contraction and ventricular filling
The ventricles relax and blood flows into them from the atria. Note that 70% of the blood from the atria flows passively into the ventricles. It is during the last third of ventricular filling that the atria contract.

Stage 2: Ventricular contraction
The atria relax, the ventricles contract, and blood is pumped from the ventricles into the aorta and the pulmonary artery. The start of ventricular contraction coincides with the first heart sound.

Stage 3: (not shown) There is a short period of atrial and ventricular relaxation. Semilunar valves (**SLV**) close to prevent backflow into the ventricles (see diagram, left). The cycle begins again. For a heart beating at 75 beats per minute, one cardiac cycle lasts about 0.8 seconds.

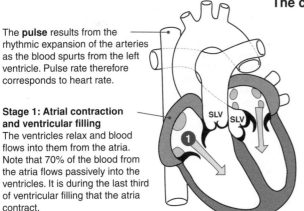

Heart during ventricular filling

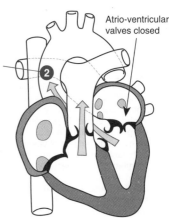
Atrio-ventricular valves closed

Heart during ventricular contraction

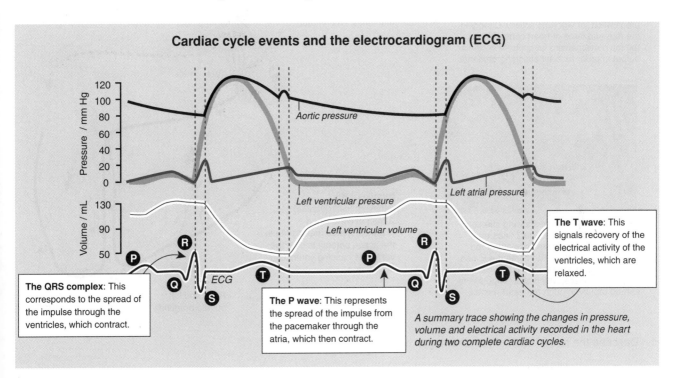

Cardiac cycle events and the electrocardiogram (ECG)

A summary trace showing the changes in pressure, volume and electrical activity recorded in the heart during two complete cardiac cycles.

The QRS complex: This corresponds to the spread of the impulse through the ventricles, which contract.

The P wave: This represents the spread of the impulse from the pacemaker through the atria, which then contract.

The T wave: This signals recovery of the electrical activity of the ventricles, which are relaxed.

1. On the ECG trace above:

   (a) When is the aortic pressure highest? _____

   (b) Which electrical event immediately precedes the increase in ventricular pressure? _____

   (c) What is happening when the pressure of the left ventricle is lowest? _____

2. Suggest the physiological reason for the period of electrical recovery experienced each cycle (the T wave): _____

3. Using the letters indicated, mark the points on trace above corresponding to each of the following:

   (a) E: Ejection of blood from the ventricle

   (b) BVC: Closing of the bicuspid valve

   (c) FV: Filling of the ventricle

   (d) BVO: Opening of the bicuspid valve

LINK 196 | WEB 195 | **KNOW**

196 Control of Heart Activity

Key Idea: Heartbeat is initiated by the sinoatrial node which acts as a pacemaker by setting the basic heart rhythm.
The heartbeat is myogenic, meaning it originates within the cardiac muscle itself. The heartbeat is regulated by a conduction system consisting of the pacemaker (**sinoatrial** node) and a specialised conduction system of Purkyne tissue. The pacemaker sets the basic heart rhythm, but this rate can be influenced by hormones and by the cardiovascular control centre. Changing the rate and force of heart contraction is the main mechanism for controlling cardiac output.

Generation of the heartbeat

The basic rhythmic heartbeat is **myogenic**. The nodal cells (SAN and atrioventricular node) spontaneously generate rhythmic action potentials without neural stimulation. The normal resting rate of self-excitation of the SAN is about 50 beats per minute. The amount of blood ejected from the left ventricle per minute is called the **cardiac output**. It is determined by the **stroke volume** (the volume of blood ejected with each contraction) and the **heart rate** (number of heart beats per minute).

Cardiac muscle responds to stretching by contracting more strongly. The greater the blood volume entering the ventricle, the greater the force of contraction. This relationship is important in regulating stroke volume in response to demand.
The hormone **adrenaline** also influences cardiac output, increasing heart rate in preparation for vigorous activity. Changing the rate and force of heart contraction is the main mechanism for controlling cardiac output in order to meet changing demands.

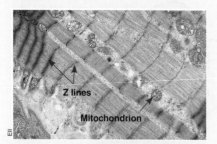

Z lines

Mitochondrion

TEM of cardiac muscle showing striations in a fibre (muscle cell). The Z lines that delineate the contractile units of the rod-like units of the fibre. The fibres are joined by specialised electrical junctions called Intercalated discs, which allow impulses to spread rapidly through the heart muscle.

Sinoatrial node (SAN) is also called the **pacemaker**. It is a small mass of specialised muscle cells on the wall of the right atrium, near the entry point of the superior vena cava. The pacemaker initiates the cardiac cycle, spontaneously generating **action potentials** that cause the atria to contract. The SAN sets the basic heart rate, but this rate is influenced by hormones, such as adrenaline (epinephrine) and impulses from the autonomic nervous system.

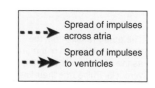

Spread of impulses across atria

Spread of impulses to ventricles

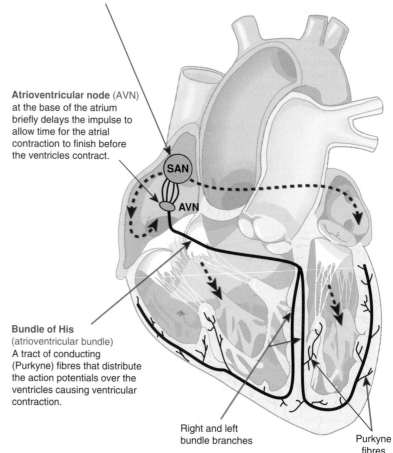

Atrioventricular node (AVN) at the base of the atrium briefly delays the impulse to allow time for the atrial contraction to finish before the ventricles contract.

SAN

AVN

Bundle of His (atrioventricular bundle)
A tract of conducting (Purkyne) fibres that distribute the action potentials over the ventricles causing ventricular contraction.

Right and left bundle branches

Purkyne fibres

1. Describe the role of each of the following in heart activity:

   (a) The sinoatrial node: _____

   (b) The atrioventricular node: _____

   (c) The bundle of His: _____

   (d) Intercalated discs: _____

2. What is the significance of delaying the impulse at the AVN? _____

   _____

3. What is the advantage of the physiological response of cardiac muscle to stretching? _____

   _____

4. The heart-beat is intrinsic. Why is it important to be able to influence the basic rhythm via the central nervous system?

   _____

© 2015 **BIOZONE** International
ISBN:978-1-927309-25-4
Photocopying Prohibited

197 Recording Changes in Heart Rate

Key Idea: Breathing rate and heart rate both increase during exercise to meet the body's increased metabolic demands. During exercise, the body's metabolic rate increases and the demand for oxygen increases. Oxygen is required for cellular respiration and ATP production. Increasing the rate of breathing delivers more oxygen to working tissues and enables them to make the ATP they need to keep working. An increased breathing rate also increases the rate at which carbon dioxide is expelled from the body. Heart rate also increases so blood can be moved around the body more quickly. This allows for faster delivery of oxygen and removal of carbon dioxide.

In this practical, you will work in groups of three to see how exercise affects breathing and heart rate. Choose one person to carry out the exercise and one person each to record heart rate and breathing rate.
Heart rate (beats per minute) is obtained by measuring the pulse (right) for 15 seconds and multiplying by four.
Breathing rate (breaths per minute) is measured by counting the number of breaths taken in 15 seconds
and multiplying it by four.
CAUTION: The person exercising should have no known pre-existing heart or respiratory conditions.

Measuring the carotid pulse

Gently press your index and middle fingers, not your thumb, against the carotid artery in the neck (just under the jaw) or the radial artery (on the wrist just under the thumb) until you feel a pulse.

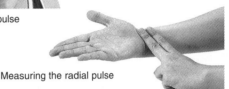
Measuring the radial pulse

Procedure

Resting measurements
Have the person carrying out the exercise sit down on a chair for 5 minutes. They should try not to move. After 5 minutes of sitting, measure their heart rate and breathing rate. Record the resting data on the table (right).

Exercising measurements
Choose an exercise to perform. Some examples include step ups onto a chair, skipping rope, jumping jacks, and running in place.
Begin the exercise, and take measurements after 1, 2, 3, and 4 minutes of exercise. The person exercising should stop just long enough for the measurements to be taken. Record the results in the table.

Post exercise measurements
After the exercise period has finished, have the exerciser sit down in a chair. Take their measurements 1 and 5 minutes after finishing the exercise. Record the results on the table.

	Heart rate / beats minute^{-1}	Breathing rate / breaths minute^{-1}
Resting		
1 minute		
2 minutes		
3 minutes		
4 minutes		
1 minute after		
5 minutes after		

1. (a) Graph your results on separate piece of paper. You will need to use one axis for heart rate and another for breathing rate. When you have finished answering the questions below, attach it to this page.

   (b) Analyse your graph and describe what happened to heart rate and breathing rate **during exercise**: _____

   _____

   _____

   _____

   _____

2. (a) Describe what happened to heart rate and breathing rate **after exercise**: _____

   _____

   _____

   (b) Why did this change occur? _____

   _____

PRAC

198 Review of the Human Heart

Key Idea: The human heart comprises four chambers, which act as a double pump. Its contraction is myogenic, but can be influenced by other factors.

This activity summarises features of heart structure and function. Use it as a self-test, but see the earlier activities in this chapter if you need help.

1. On the diagram below, label the identified components of heart structure and intrinsic control (**a-n**).

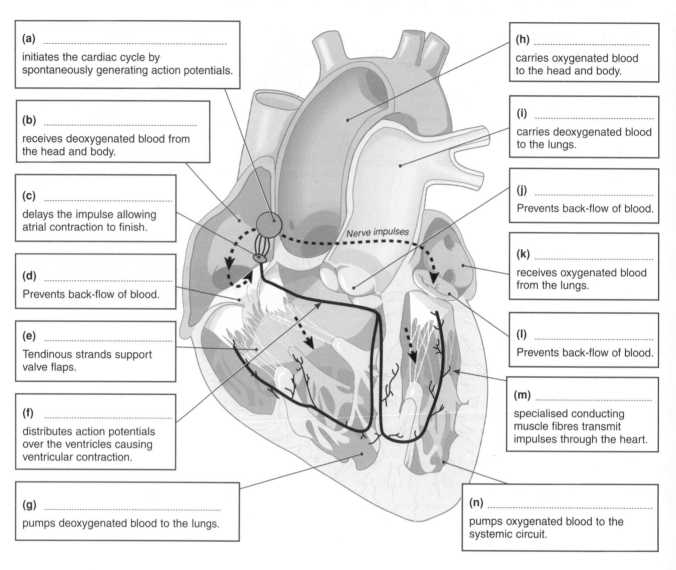

(a) _____
initiates the cardiac cycle by spontaneously generating action potentials.

(b) _____
receives deoxygenated blood from the head and body.

(c) _____
delays the impulse allowing atrial contraction to finish.

(d) _____
Prevents back-flow of blood.

(e) _____
Tendinous strands support valve flaps.

(f) _____
distributes action potentials over the ventricles causing ventricular contraction.

(g) _____
pumps deoxygenated blood to the lungs.

(h) _____
carries oxygenated blood to the head and body.

(i) _____
carries deoxygenated blood to the lungs.

(j) _____
Prevents back-flow of blood.

(k) _____
receives oxygenated blood from the lungs.

(l) _____
Prevents back-flow of blood.

(m) _____
specialised conducting muscle fibres transmit impulses through the heart.

(n) _____
pumps oxygenated blood to the systemic circuit.

Nerve impulses

2. An **ECG** is the result of different impulses produced at each phase of the **cardiac cycle** (the sequence of events in a heartbeat). For each electrical event indicated in the ECG below, describe the corresponding event in the cardiac cycle:

A _____
The spread of the impulse from the pacemaker (sinoatrial node) through the atria.

B _____
The spread of the impulse through the ventricles.

C _____
Recovery of the electrical activity of the ventricles.

Electrical activity in the heart

3. (a) On the trace above, mark the region where the ventricular pressure is highest.

   (b) What is happening to the ventricular volume at this time? _____

   _____

 © 2015 **BIOZONE** International
ISBN: 978-1-927309-25-4
Photocopying Prohibited

199 Blood

Key Idea: Blood is a liquid tissue that performs many important functions in the body.

Blood is a complex liquid tissue comprising cellular components suspended in plasma. It makes up about 8% of body weight. If a blood sample is taken, the cells can be separated from the plasma by centrifugation. The cells (formed elements) settle as a dense red pellet below the transparent, straw-coloured **plasma**. Blood performs many functions. It transports nutrients, respiratory gases, hormones, and wastes and has a role in thermoregulation through the distribution of heat. Blood also defends against infection and its ability to clot protects against blood loss. The examination of blood is also useful in diagnosing disease. The cellular components of blood are normally present in particular specified ratios. A change in the morphology, type, or proportion of different blood cells can therefore be used to indicate a specific disorder, or an acute or chronic infection (see the next page).

Non-cellular blood components

The non-cellular blood components form the plasma. Plasma is a watery matrix of ions and proteins and makes up 50-60% of the total blood volume.

Water

The main constituent of blood and lymph.
Role: Transports dissolved substances. Provides body cells with water. Distributes heat and has a central role in thermoregulation. Regulation of water content helps to regulate blood pressure and volume.

Mineral ions

Sodium, bicarbonate, magnesium, potassium, calcium, chloride.
Role: Osmotic balance, pH buffering, and regulation of membrane permeability. They also have a variety of other functions, e.g. Ca^{2+} is involved in blood clotting.

Plasma proteins

7-9% of the plasma volume.
Serum albumin
Role: Osmotic balance and pH buffering, Ca^{2+} transport.
Fibrinogen and prothrombin
Role: Take part in blood clotting.
Immunoglobulins
Role: Antibodies involved in the immune response.
α-globulins
Role: Bind/transport hormones, lipids, fat soluble vitamins.
β-globulins
Role: Bind/transport iron, cholesterol, fat soluble vitamins.
Enzymes
Role: Take part in and regulate metabolic activities.

Substances transported by non-cellular components

Products of digestion
Examples: sugars, fatty acids, glycerol, and amino acids.
Excretory products
Example: urea
Hormones and vitamins
Examples: insulin, sex hormones, vitamins A and B_{12}.
Importance: These substances occur at varying levels in the blood. They are transported to and from the cells dissolved in the plasma or bound to plasma proteins.

Cellular blood components

The cellular components of the blood (also called the formed elements) float in the plasma and make up 40-50% of the total blood volume.

Erythrocytes (red blood cells or RBCs)

5-6 million per mm^3 blood; 38-48% of total blood volume.
Role: RBCs transport oxygen (O_2) and a small amount of carbon dioxide (CO_2). The oxygen is carried bound to haemoglobin (Hb) in the cells. Each Hb molecule can bind four molecules of oxygen.

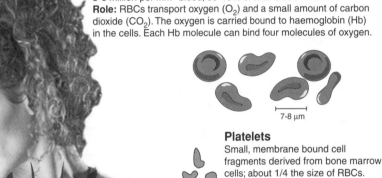

7-8 μm

Platelets

Small, membrane bound cell fragments derived from bone marrow cells; about 1/4 the size of RBCs. 0.25 million per mm^3 blood.

2 μm
Role: To start the blood clotting process by adhering to the damaged endothelium of blood vessels and releasing chemicals to activate clotting proteins.

Leucocytes (white blood cells)

5-10 000 per mm^3 blood
2-3% of total blood volume.
Role: Involved in internal defence.
There are several types of white blood cells:

Lymphocytes
T and B cells.
24% of the white cell count.
Role: Antibody production and cell mediated immunity (targeted response against pathogens).

Neutrophils
Phagocytes.
70% of the white cell count.
Role: Engulf foreign material, such as bacteria.

Eosinophils
Rare leucocytes; normally 1.5% of the white cell count.
Role: Mediate allergic responses such as hayfever and asthma.

Monocytes
Make up about 10% of all leucocytes in the body.
Role: Respond to inflammation signals and replenish macrophages. Increase in response to chronic infection or autoimmune disease.

LINK
200 KNOW

The examination of blood

Different types of microscopy give different information about blood. A SEM (right) shows the detailed external morphology of the blood cells. A fixed smear of a blood sample viewed with a light microscope (far right) can be used to identify the different blood cell types present, and their ratio to each other. Determining the types and proportions of different white blood cells in blood is called a differential white blood cell count. Elevated counts of particular cell types indicate allergy or infection.

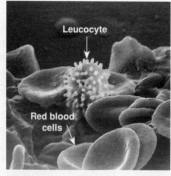
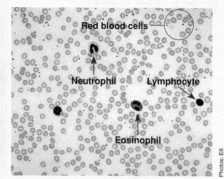

SEM of red blood cells and a leucocytes. **Light microscope** view of a fixed blood smear.

1. For each of the following blood functions, identify the component (or components) of the blood responsible and state how the function is carried out (the mode of action). The first one is done for you:

   (a) **Temperature regulation.** *Blood component:* Water component of the plasma

   Mode of action: Water absorbs heat and dissipates it from sites of production (e.g. organs)

   (b) **Protection against disease.** *Blood component:* _____

   Mode of action: _____

   (c) **Communication between cells, tissues, and organs.** *Blood component:* _____

   Mode of action: _____

   (d) **Oxygen transport.** *Blood component:* _____

   Mode of action: _____

   (e) **CO₂ transport.** *Blood components:* _____

   Mode of action: _____

   (f) **Buffer against pH changes.** *Blood components:* _____

   Mode of action: _____

   (g) **Nutrient supply.** *Blood component:* _____

   Mode of action: _____

   (h) **Tissue repair.** *Blood components:* _____

   Mode of action: _____

   (i) **Transport of hormones, lipids, and fat soluble vitamins.** *Blood component:* _____

   Mode of action: _____

2. Identify a feature that distinguishes red and white blood cells: _____

3. Explain two physiological advantages of red blood cell structure (lacking nucleus and mitochondria):

   (a) _____

   (b) _____

4. Suggest what each of the following results from a differential white blood cell count would suggest:

   (a) Elevated levels of eosinophils (above the normal range): _____

   (b) Elevated levels of neutrophils (above the normal range): _____

   (c) Elevated levels of monocytes (above the normal range): _____

   (d) Elevated levels of lymphocytes (above the normal range): _____

200 Blood Clotting

Key Idea: Blood clotting restricts blood loss from a torn blood vessel, and prevents pathogens entering the wound.

Blood has a role in the body's defence against infection. Tearing or puncturing of a blood vessel initiates **blood clotting** through a cascade effect involving platelets, clotting factors, and plasma proteins (below). Clotting quickly seals off the tear, preventing blood loss and the invasion of bacteria into the site. Clot formation is triggered by the release of clotting factors from the damaged cells at the site of the damage. A hardened clot forms a scab, which acts to prevent further blood loss and acts as a mechanical barrier to the entry of pathogens.

Blood clotting pathway

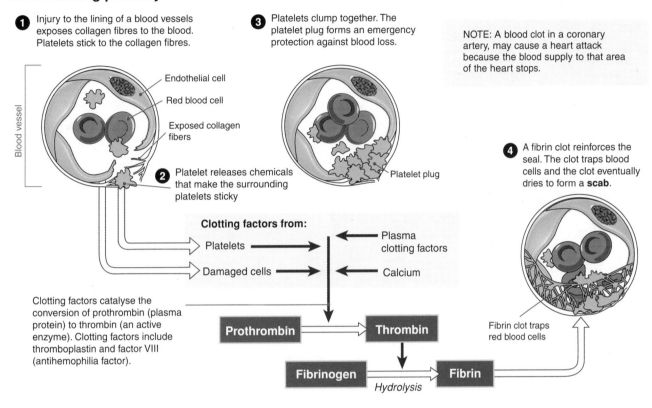

1 Injury to the lining of a blood vessels exposes collagen fibres to the blood. Platelets stick to the collagen fibres.

3 Platelets clump together. The platelet plug forms an emergency protection against blood loss.

NOTE: A blood clot in a coronary artery, may cause a heart attack because the blood supply to that area of the heart stops.

Blood vessel

Endothelial cell

Red blood cell

Exposed collagen fibers

2 Platelet releases chemicals that make the surrounding platelets sticky

Platelet plug

4 A fibrin clot reinforces the seal. The clot traps blood cells and the clot eventually dries to form a **scab**.

Clotting factors from:

Platelets → ← Plasma clotting factors

Damaged cells → ← Calcium

Clotting factors catalyse the conversion of prothrombin (plasma protein) to thrombin (an active enzyme). Clotting factors include thromboplastin and factor VIII (antihemophilia factor).

Fibrin clot traps red blood cells

Prothrombin ⟹ **Thrombin**

Fibrinogen ⟹ **Fibrin**
Hydrolysis

1. What role does blood clotting have in internal defence? _____

_____

2. Explain the role of each of the following in the sequence of events leading to a blood clot:

   (a) Injury: _____

   _____

   (b) Release of chemicals from platelets: _____

   _____

   (c) Clumping of platelets at the wound site: _____

   _____

   (d) Formation of a fibrin clot: _____

   _____

3. (a) What is the role of clotting factors in the blood in formation of the clot? _____

   _____

   (b) Why are these clotting factors not normally present in the plasma? _____

   _____

LINK   WEB
199 **200**   KNOW

201 Atherosclerosis

Key Idea: Atherosclerosis is a disease of the arteries caused by atheromas (fatty deposits) on the inner arterial walls.

An atheroma is made up of cells (mostly macrophages) or cell debris, with associated fatty acids, cholesterol, calcium, and varying amounts of fibrous connective tissue. The accumulation of fat and plaques causes the lining of the arteries to degenerate. Atheromas weaken the arterial walls

and eventually restrict blood flow through the arteries, increasing the risk of **aneurysm** (swelling of the artery wall) and **thrombosis** (blood clots). Complications arising as a result of atherosclerosis include heart attacks, strokes, and gangrene. A typical progression for the formation of an atheroma is illustrated below.

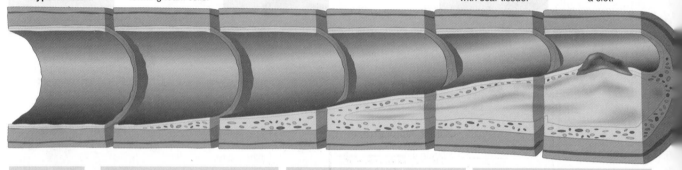

Initial lesion	**Fatty streak**	**Intermediate lesion**	**Atheroma**	**Fibroatheroma**	**Complicated plaque**
Atherosclerosis is triggered by damage to an artery wall caused by blood borne chemicals or persistent **hypertension**.	Low density lipoproteins (LDLs) accumulate beneath the endothelial cells. Macrophages follow and absorb them, forming foam cells.	Foam cells accumulate forming greasy yellow lesions called atherosclerotic plaques.	A core of extracellular lipids under a cap of fibrous tissue forms.	Lipid core and fibrous layers. Accumulated smooth muscle cells die. Fibres deteriorate and are replaced with scar tissue.	Calcification of plaque. Arterial wall may ulcerate. Hypertension may worsen. Plaque may break away causing a clot.

Earliest onset	From first decade		From third decade		From fourth decade	
Growth mechanism	Growth mainly by lipid accumulation				Smooth muscle/ collagen increase	Thrombosis, haematoma
Clinical correlation	Clinically silent			Clinically silent or overt		

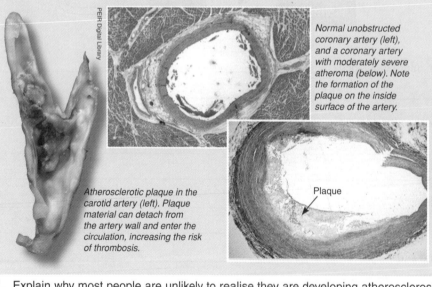

Normal unobstructed coronary artery (left), and a coronary artery with moderately severe atheroma (below). Note the formation of the plaque on the inside surface of the artery.

PEIR Digital Library

Plaque

Atherosclerotic plaque in the carotid artery (left). Plaque material can detach from the artery wall and enter the circulation, increasing the risk of thrombosis.

Recent studies indicate that most heart attacks are caused by the body's **inflammatory response** to a plaque. The inflammatory process causes young, soft, cholesterol-rich plaques to rupture and break into pieces. If these block blood vessels they can cause lethal heart attacks, even in previously healthy people.

Aorta opened lengthwise (above), with extensive atherosclerotic lesions (arrowed).

1. Explain why most people are unlikely to realise they are developing atherosclerosis until serious complications arise:

   _____

   _____

2. Explain how an atherosclerotic plaque changes over time: _____

   _____

   _____

3. Describe some of the consequences of developing atherosclerosis: _____

   _____

© 2015 **BIOZONE** International
ISBN:978-1-927309-25-4
Photocopying Prohibited

WEB
LINK
LINK
201 202 203

202 CVD Risk Factors

Key Idea: CVD risk factors are those factors that may increase the chances of developing cardiovascular disease. CVD risk factors increase the likelihood of a person developing CVD. Controllable risk factors can be modified by lifestyle changes, whereas uncontrollable risk factors, such as age, cannot be modified. A person with more risk factors has a greater likelihood of developing CVD, although total risk can minimised by reducing the number of controllable risk factors. Major controllable risk factors are smoking and the ratio of LDL:HDL cholesterol in the blood. About 13% of deaths from CVD are attributable to smoking. Smoking also acts synergistically with other risk factors to increase their impact.

Cholesterol and CVD

Cholesterol is transported in the blood within complex spherical particles called **lipoproteins**. One form (high density lipoprotein or HDL) helps remove cholesterol from the blood by transporting it to the liver. The other form (low density lipoprotein or LDL) deposits cholesterol on to the walls of blood vessels. Abnormally high concentrations of LDL and lower concentrations of HDL are strongly associated with the development of atheroma. It is the **LDL:HDL ratio**, rather than total cholesterol itself, that provides the best indicator of risk for developing cardiovascular disease, and the risk profile is different for men and women (see below).

Ratio of LDL to HDL		
Risk	**Men**	**Women**
Very low (half mean risk)	1.0	1.5
Mean risk	3.6	3.2
Moderate risk (2X mean risk)	6.3	5.0
High (3X mean risk)	8.0	6.1

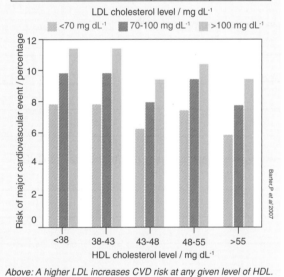

Barter.P et al 2007

Above: A higher LDL increases CVD risk at any given level of HDL.

Smoking and CVD

Smoking is a significant risk factor for the development of all types of cardiovascular disease. The nicotine in cigarette smoke is a stimulant and increases both blood pressure and heart rate, constricting arteries and making the heart work harder. It also causes the body to mobilise fat stores, increasing the risk of **atheromas** (fatty plaques in the arteries). Constriction and blockage of the arteries by plaques increases the risk of stroke and myocardial infarction.

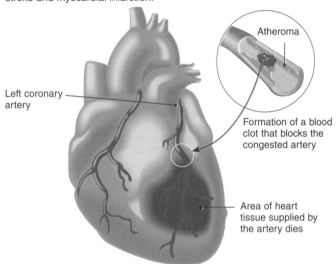

Atheroma

Left coronary artery

Formation of a blood clot that blocks the congested artery

Area of heart tissue supplied by the artery dies

Relative risk of myocardial infarction (heart attack) by current tobacco exposure

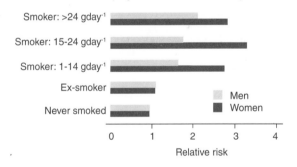

Obesity and CVD

Obesity has been clearly linked to various types of CVD, including coronary heart disease (CHD) as well as diabetes and hypertension. Excessive body weight puts an increased strain on the heart, which leads to increased blood pressure and enlargement of the heart.

The prevalence of obesity is increasing in the UK, despite there also being a general increase in levels of physical activity and healthier eating. For example, between 1980 and 1998 the prevalence of obesity in UK women more than doubled from 8% to 21%. A large cross-sectional study of UK women (left) showed that predicted 10 year risk of CHD (based on a number of measured indicators) was about the same for women with a body mass index (BMI) less than 20 but increased progressively after that (left).

Predicted 10 year CHD risk / percentage

| No. of subjects | 706 | 2390 | 3593 | 2977 | 1883 | 1055 | 1290 |

Predicted 10 year CHD risk / percentage: <5, 5-, 10-, ≥15

Data: European Heart Journal (2001) **22**, 46-55 "Body mass index and metabolic risk factors for coronary heart disease in women."

LINK 203 LINK 201 KNOW

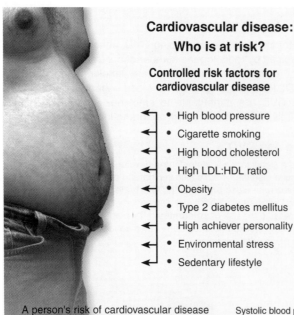

Cardiovascular disease:
Who is at risk?

Controlled risk factors for cardiovascular disease

* High blood pressure
* Cigarette smoking
* High blood cholesterol
* High LDL:HDL ratio
* Obesity
* Type 2 diabetes mellitus
* High achiever personality
* Environmental stress
* Sedentary lifestyle

A person's risk of cardiovascular disease increases markedly with an increase in the number of risk factors. This is particularly the case for smoking, because smoking acts synergistically with other risk factors, particularly high blood pressure and high blood lipids. This means that any given risk factor has a proportionately greater effect in a smoker than in a non-smoker.

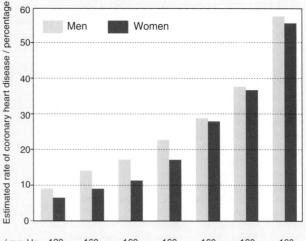

Estimated coronary heart disease rate according to various combinations of risk factors over 10 years (source: International Diabetes Foundation, 2001)

Systolic blood pressure / mm Hg	120	160	160	160	160	160	160
Cholesterol / mg 100 cm⁻³	220	220	259	259	259	259	259
HDL cholesterol / mg 100 cm⁻³	50	50	50	35	35	35	35
Diabetes	–	–	–	–	+	+	+
Cigarette smoking	–	–	–	–	–	+	+
Enlargement of left ventricle	–	–	–	–	–	–	+

Risk factors

1. (a) Distinguish between controllable and uncontrollable risk factors in the development of CVD: _____

   _____

   (b) Suggest why some of the controllable risk factors often occur together: _____

   _____

   _____

   (c) Evaluate the evidence supporting the observation that patients with several risk factors are at higher risk of CVD:

   _____

   _____

   _____

   _____

2. (a) Explain the link between high LDL:HDL ratio and the risk of cardiovascular disease: _____

   _____

   _____

   _____

   (b) Explain why this ratio is more important to medical practitioners than total blood cholesterol *per se*: _____

   _____

   _____

3. (a) Describe the evidence for a link between obesity and risk of CHD as shown by the study of UK women (previous):

   _____

   _____

   (b) What is one strength of this study: _____

© 2015 **BIOZONE** International
ISBN: 978-1-927309-25-4
Photocopying Prohibited

203 Reducing the Risk

Key Idea: Non-smokers, physically active people, and those who consume adequate amounts of fruit and vegetables are less likely to develop cardiovascular disease.

Physically active people and those that don't smoke are less likely to develop CVD. For adults, aerobic activity lasting at least thirty minutes, five time a week is required for maximum benefit. Children should be physically active for at least one hour a day, five times a week. In developed countries, over 20% of all heart disease and 10% of strokes are directly linked to physical inactivity. Eating at least five portions of fruit and vegetables a day is also important for decreasing the risk of CVD. Despite the increases in public education programmes, there has been little improvement in people's overall eating habits in the UK. Only 13% of men and 15% of women consume five or more portions of fruits or vegetables a day.

Controlling risk factors

Fig 1: Effect of exercise on CHD risk in women

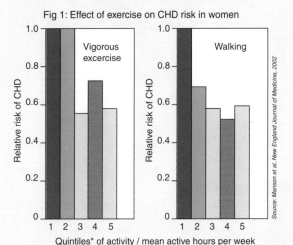

Quintiles* of activity / mean active hours per week
* quintiles = five equally numerous subsets

Source: Manson et al, New England Journal of Medicine, 2002

Fig 2: Relative risk of death from CHD associated with fruit and vegetable intake.

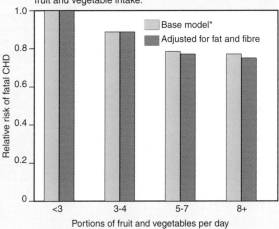

Portions of fruit and vegetables per day

*Base model adjusts for covariates such as smoking and alcohol intake. Fat/fibre model adjusts further for intake of fat and fibre. Source: Marmot, M. European Heart Journal, 2011

Fig. 3: Smoking and CHD statistics, England

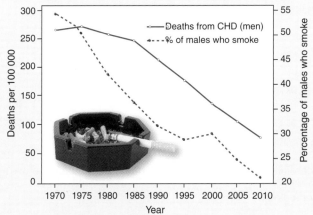

Year

Source: British Heart Foundation Statistics 2008

1. What evidence is there to suggest that exercise reduces the risk of CHD?

_____

_____

_____

_____

2. (a) What evidence is there to support public health recommendations to eat more fruit and vegetables?

_____

_____

_____

_____

(b) What is the approximate percentage reduction in risk for someone eating 8+ portions of fruit and vegetables daily relative to someone eating fewer than 3 portions?

_____

3. (a) Describe the general trend for deaths from heart disease in males since 1970 (fig. 3):

_____

_____

_____

(b) Describe the trend for cigarette smoking during this time:

_____

_____

_____

_____

(c) Can you say from these data alone that smoking causes CHD? Explain your answer:

_____

_____

_____

_____

© 2015 **BIOZONE** International
ISBN: 978-1-927309-25-4
Photocopying Prohibited

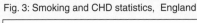

LINK | WEB
19 | **203** | KNOW

204 Myoglobin and Haemoglobin

Key Idea: Myoglobin and haemoglobin have similar properties and perform related, but different, tasks in the body. Haemoglobin transports oxygen in the blood, whereas myoglobin enables oxygen to be stored in the muscle.

Myoglobin and haemoglobin are vertebrate respiratory pigments, globular proteins that bind oxygen. Haemoglobin is carried in red blood cells. It binds oxygen in the blood vessels of the lungs and transports it to the tissues. In muscle tissue, myoglobin, which has a higher affinity for oxygen, takes oxygen from haemoglobin and acts as an oxygen store.

Four haem groups

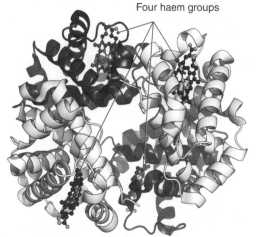

Haemoglobin (tetrameric or four chains)

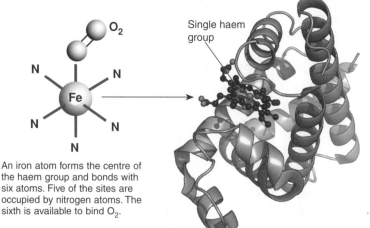

O_2

Single haem group

An iron atom forms the centre of the haem group and bonds with six atoms. Five of the sites are occupied by nitrogen atoms. The sixth is available to bind O_2.

Myoglobin (monomeric or single chain)

Haemoglobin

Oxygen is virtually insoluble in water (< 0.0001 mol dm^{-3}). Without a molecule to transport it in the blood, we would only get about 1% of the oxygen we need. The molecule used to transport oxygen is **haemoglobin** (Hb). It is found in the red blood cells and there is about 150 g dm^{-3} of it in the blood. Hb increases the solubility of oxygen to 0.01 mol dm^{-3}. Hb transports oxygen from the lungs to the muscles and other tissues. It consists of four polypeptide chains, two α-chains and two β-chains, each of which binds one oxygen molecule. It binds oxygen readily when the oxygen concentration is high but releases it when oxygen tensions fall. **Fetal Hb** has a greater affinity for oxygen than adult Hb, allowing the fetus to gain oxygen from the mother's blood. Fetal Hb differs from adult Hb in that it has two γ-chains instead of two β-chains

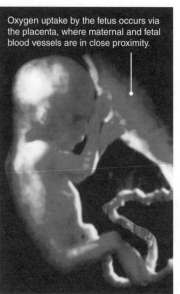

Oxygen uptake by the fetus occurs via the placenta, where maternal and fetal blood vessels are in close proximity.

Myoglobin

Myoglobin (Mb) is found in the muscles and does not readily circulate in the blood. It has a very high affinity for oxygen so oxygen will be transferred from Hb in the blood to Mb in the muscle. Mb keeps oxygen bound even at low oxygen tensions, so it acts as an oxygen store, providing oxygen to the muscles only when supply from Hb is not meeting demands (e.g. after holding breath for a long time or high intensity exercise). Diving mammals, such as dolphins and whales, need to store a lot of oxygen for long dives. Their muscles packed with up to ten times more Mb than is found in human muscles. This allows marine mammals such as sperm whales to store enough oxygen to dive for up to 90 minutes.

Gabriel Barathieu

1. How is myoglobin structurally different from haemoglobin? _____

_____

_____

2. Explain why deep diving mammals have very high concentrations of myoglobin in the muscles: _____

_____

_____

3. What is the difference between oxygen solubility in water and oxygen solubility in blood containing haemoglobin?

_____

4. (a) On the molecular diagram of haemoglobin, above, circle the haem groups:

   (b) Study the haem groups in haemoglobin and myoglobin carefully. They are oxygenated / deoxygenated (delete one)

5. What is the structural difference between adult and fetal haemoglobin? _____

_____

© 2015 **BIOZONE** International
ISBN:978-1-927309-25-4
Photocopying Prohibited

205 Gas Transport in Humans

Key Idea: The transport of respiratory gases is the role of the blood. The oxygen-binding behaviour of haemoglobin in the blood ensures efficient delivery of oxygen to the tissues. The transport of respiratory gases to and from the tissues is the role of the blood. Carbon dioxide is carried mainly as bicarbonate, whereas oxygen is transported bound to the respiratory pigment **haemoglobin** inside the red blood cells. In the muscles, the oxygen from haemoglobin is transferred to and retained by **myoglobin**. The oxygen binding behaviour of haemoglobin and myoglobin at different oxygen tensions provides a dynamic system that facilitates the loading and unloading of oxygen in response to the body's needs.

Gas exchange and transport

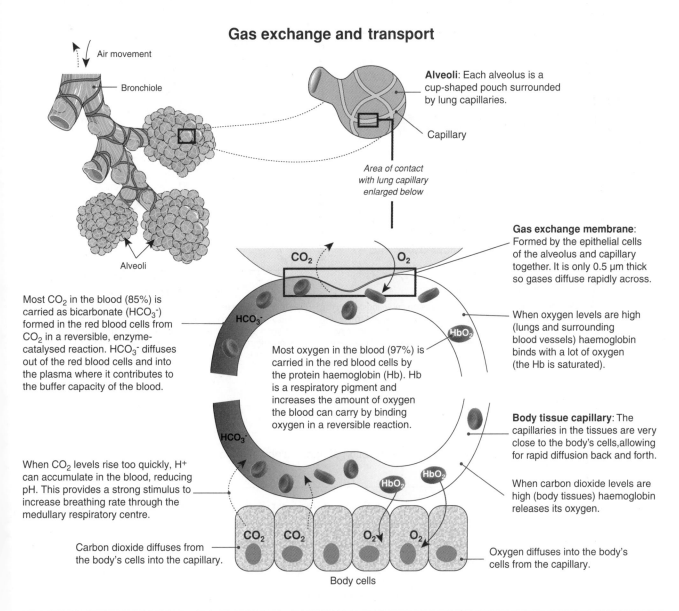

Air movement

Bronchiole

Alveoli: Each alveolus is a cup-shaped pouch surrounded by lung capillaries.

Capillary

Area of contact with lung capillary enlarged below

Alveoli

Gas exchange membrane: Formed by the epithelial cells of the alveolus and capillary together. It is only 0.5 μm thick so gases diffuse rapidly across.

CO_2 O_2

Most CO_2 in the blood (85%) is carried as bicarbonate (HCO_3^-) formed in the red blood cells from CO_2 in a reversible, enzyme-catalysed reaction. HCO_3^- diffuses out of the red blood cells and into the plasma where it contributes to the buffer capacity of the blood.

HCO_3^-

Most oxygen in the blood (97%) is carried in the red blood cells by the protein haemoglobin (Hb). Hb is a respiratory pigment and increases the amount of oxygen the blood can carry by binding oxygen in a reversible reaction.

HbO_2

When oxygen levels are high (lungs and surrounding blood vessels) haemoglobin binds with a lot of oxygen (the Hb is saturated).

HCO_3^-

Body tissue capillary: The capillaries in the tissues are very close to the body's cells, allowing for rapid diffusion back and forth.

HbO_2

HbO_2

When carbon dioxide levels are high (body tissues) haemoglobin releases its oxygen.

When CO_2 levels rise too quickly, H^+ can accumulate in the blood, reducing pH. This provides a strong stimulus to increase breathing rate through the medullary respiratory centre.

CO_2 CO_2 O_2 O_2

Carbon dioxide diffuses from the body's cells into the capillary.

Oxygen diffuses into the body's cells from the capillary.

Body cells

Transport of carbon dioxide in the blood

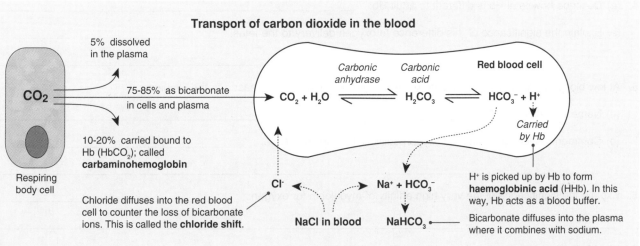

5% dissolved in the plasma

CO_2

75-85% as bicarbonate in cells and plasma

10-20% carried bound to Hb ($HbCO_2$); called **carbaminohemoglobin**

Respiring body cell

Chloride diffuses into the red blood cell to counter the loss of bicarbonate ions. This is called the **chloride shift**.

Carbonic anhydrase   *Carbonic acid*   **Red blood cell**

$CO_2 + H_2O \rightleftharpoons H_2CO_3 \rightleftharpoons HCO_3^- + H^+$

Carried by Hb

Cl^- $Na^+ + HCO_3^-$

NaCl in blood $NaHCO_3$

H^+ is picked up by Hb to form **haemoglobinic acid** (HHb). In this way, Hb acts as a blood buffer.

Bicarbonate diffuses into the plasma where it combines with sodium.

Oxygen does not easily dissolve in blood, but is carried in chemical combination with haemoglobin (Hb) in red blood cells. The most important factor determining how much oxygen is carried by Hb is the level of oxygen in the blood. The greater the oxygen tension, the more oxygen will combine with Hb. This relationship can be illustrated with an oxyhaemoglobin dissociation curve as shown below (Fig. 1). In the lung capillaries, (high O_2), a lot of oxygen is picked up and bound by Hb. In the tissues, (low O_2), oxygen is released. In skeletal muscle, myoglobin picks up oxygen from haemoglobin and therefore serves as an oxygen store when oxygen tensions begin to fall. The release of oxygen is enhanced by the **Bohr effect** (Fig. 2).

Respiratory pigments and the transport of oxygen

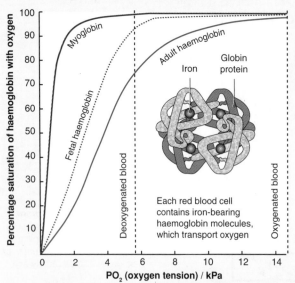

Fig.1: Dissociation curves for haemoglobin and myoglobin at normal body temperature for fetal and adult human blood.

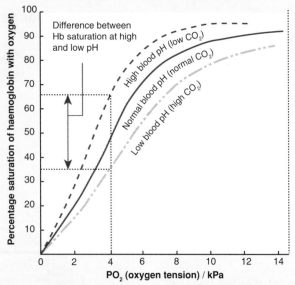

Fig.2: Oxyhaemoglobin dissociation curves for human blood at normal body temperature at different blood pH.

The sigmoidal shape of the oxyhaemoglobin dissociation curve indicates Hb's property of **cooperative binding**; the more oxygen that is bound to Hb, the easier it is for more oxygen to bind. Fetal Hb has a high affinity for oxygen and carries 20-30% more than maternal Hb. Myoglobin in skeletal muscle has a very high affinity for oxygen and will take up oxygen from Hb in the blood.

As pH increases (lower CO_2), more oxygen combines with Hb. As the blood pH decreases (higher CO_2), Hb binds less oxygen and releases more to the tissues (the **Bohr effect**). The difference between Hb saturation at high and low pH represents the amount of oxygen released to the tissues.

1. (a) Identify two regions in the body where oxygen levels are very high: _____

   (b) Identify two regions where carbon dioxide levels are very high: _____

2. Explain the significance of the **reversible binding** reaction of haemoglobin (Hb) to oxygen: _____

   _____

3. (a) Haemoglobin saturation is affected by the oxygen level in the blood. Describe the nature of this relationship:

   _____

   (b) Comment on the significance of this relationship to oxygen delivery to the tissues: _____

   _____

4. (a) Describe how fetal Hb is different to adult Hb: _____

   (b) Explain the significance of this difference to oxygen delivery to the fetus: _____

   _____

5. At low blood pH, less oxygen is bound by haemoglobin and more is released to the tissues:

   (a) Name this effect: _____

   (b) Comment on its significance to oxygen delivery to respiring tissue: _____

   _____

6. Explain the significance of the very high affinity of myoglobin for oxygen: _____

   _____

7. Identify the two main contributors to the buffer capacity of the blood: _____

206 Plant Systems

Key Idea: The plant body is made up of two main connected systems: the root system and the shoot system.

The body of a flowering plant is composed of two distinct, but connected systems. Below the ground, the **root system** anchors the plant and absorbs water and nutrients from the soil. Above ground, the **shoot system** comprises the leaves and stems. The leaves produce sugars by photosynthesis, and the stems provide support for the leaves and reproductive structures and link the roots to the leaves. All plants rely to some extent on turgor pressure to support the tissues. For primitive plants, such as mosses and liverworts, which are small and low-growing, this turgor is sufficient to support the plant body. In vascular plants, which grow to a larger size, the vascular tissues (xylem and phloem) of the shoot and root systems have an important role in supporting the plant and moving materials around the plant body.

Shoot system

The above-ground parts of the plant: including the **leaves** (including buds, flowers, and fruit (or cones) if present) and **stems**.

Leaves

- ► Manufacture food via photosynthesis.
- ► Exchange gases with the environment.
- ► Store food and water.

Stems

- ► Transport water and nutrients between roots and leaves.
- ► Support and hold up the leaves, flowers and fruit.
- ► Produce new tissue for photosynthesis and support.
- ► Store food and water.

Root system

The below-ground parts of the plant, including the roots and root hairs.

Roots

- ► Anchor the plant in the soil
- ► Absorb and transport minerals and water
- ► Store food
- ► Produce hormones
- ► Produce new tissue for anchorage and absorption.

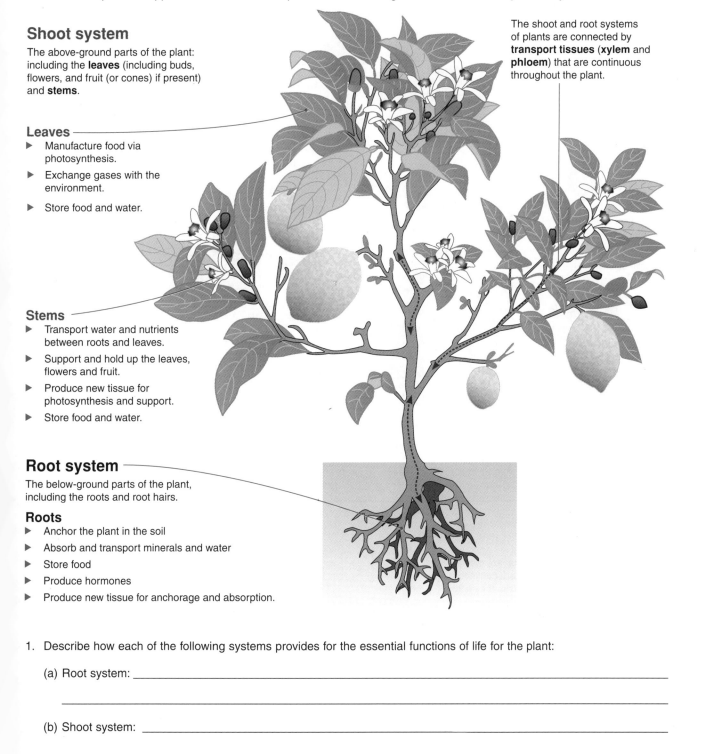

The shoot and root systems of plants are connected by **transport tissues** (**xylem** and **phloem**) that are continuous throughout the plant.

1. Describe how each of the following systems provides for the essential functions of life for the plant:

    (a) Root system: _____

    _____

    (b) Shoot system: _____

    _____

2. In the following list of plant functions, circle in blue the functions that are shared by the root and shoot system, circle in red those unique to the shoot system, and circle in black those unique to the root system:

    Photosynthesis, transport, absorption, anchorage, storage, sexual reproduction, growth

207 Vascular Tissue in Plants

Key Idea: The xylem and phloem form the vascular tissue that moves fluids and minerals about the plant.

The vascular tissues (**xylem** and **phloem**) link all parts of the plant so that water, minerals, and manufactured food can be transported between different regions of the plant. The xylem and phloem are found together in vascular bundles. In dicotyledonous plants (below) the vascular bundles are located in a ring towards the outer edge of the stem. In monocotyledonous plants, the bundles are scattered randomly throughout the stem. The xylem transports water and minerals from the roots to the leaves, while the phloem transports sugars through the plant to where they are needed.

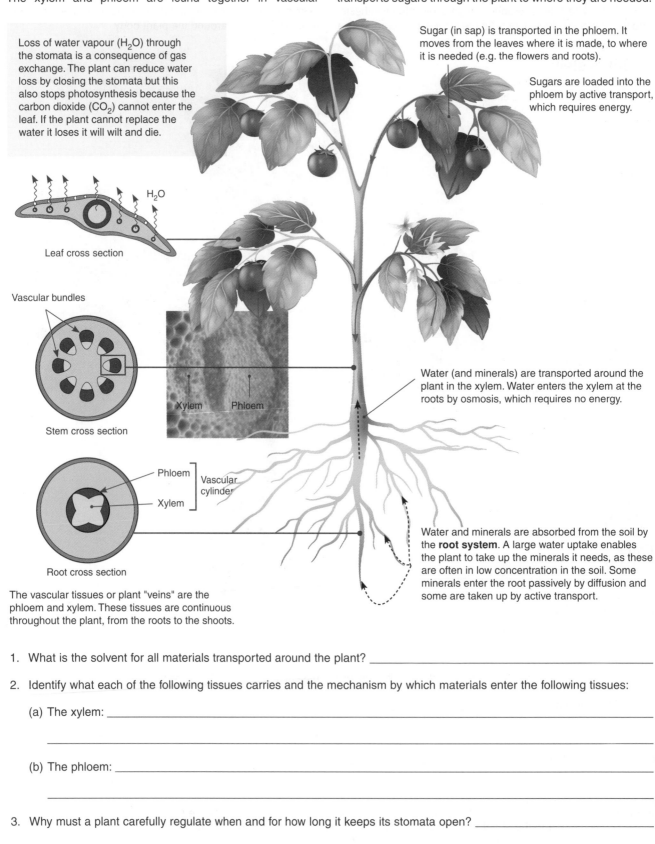

Loss of water vapour (H_2O) through the stomata is a consequence of gas exchange. The plant can reduce water loss by closing the stomata but this also stops photosynthesis because the carbon dioxide (CO_2) cannot enter the leaf. If the plant cannot replace the water it loses it will wilt and die.

Sugar (in sap) is transported in the phloem. It moves from the leaves where it is made, to where it is needed (e.g. the flowers and roots).

Sugars are loaded into the phloem by active transport, which requires energy.

H_2O

Leaf cross section

Vascular bundles

Xylem   Phloem

Stem cross section

Phloem ⎤ Vascular
Xylem ⎦ cylinder

Root cross section

Water (and minerals) are transported around the plant in the xylem. Water enters the xylem at the roots by osmosis, which requires no energy.

Water and minerals are absorbed from the soil by the **root system**. A large water uptake enables the plant to take up the minerals it needs, as these are often in low concentration in the soil. Some minerals enter the root passively by diffusion and some are taken up by active transport.

The vascular tissues or plant "veins" are the phloem and xylem. These tissues are continuous throughout the plant, from the roots to the shoots.

1. What is the solvent for all materials transported around the plant? _____

2. Identify what each of the following tissues carries and the mechanism by which materials enter the following tissues:

   (a) The xylem: _____

   _____

   (b) The phloem: _____

   _____

3. Why must a plant carefully regulate when and for how long it keeps its stomata open? _____

   _____

   _____

© 2015 **BIOZONE** International
ISBN:978-1-927309-25-4
Photocopying Prohibited

208 Xylem

Key Idea: The xylem is involved in water and mineral transport in vascular plants.

Xylem is the principal water conducting tissue in vascular plants. It is also involved in conducting dissolved minerals, in food storage, and in supporting the plant body. As in animals, tissues in plants are groupings of different cell types that work together for a common function. In angiosperms, it is composed of five cell types: tracheids, vessels, xylem parenchyma, sclereids (short sclerenchyma cells), and fibres. The tracheids and vessel elements form the bulk of the tissue. They are heavily strengthened and are the conducting cells of the xylem. Parenchyma cells are involved in storage, while fibres and sclereids provide support. When mature, xylem is dead.

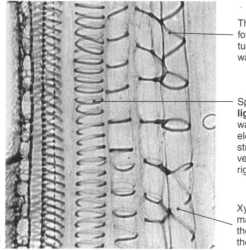

The cells of the xylem form a continuous tube through which water is conducted.

Spiral thickening of **lignin** around the walls of the vessel elements give extra strength allowing the vessels to remain rigid and upright.

Xylem is dead when mature. Note how the cells have lost their cytoplasm.

The structure of xylem tissue

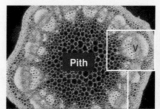

This cross section through a young stem of *Helianthus* (sunflower) shows the central pith, surrounded by a peripheral ring of vascular bundles (V). Note the xylem vessels with their thick walls.

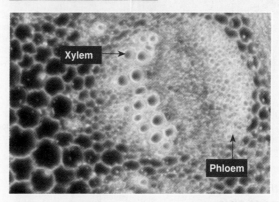

Vessel element

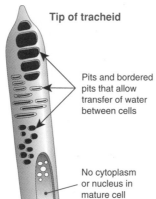

Secondary walls are laid down and lignified to add strength

The end walls are perforated to allow rapid water transport

Tip of tracheid

Pits and bordered pits that allow transfer of water between cells

No cytoplasm or nucleus in mature cell

Vessel elements and tracheids are the two conducting cell types in xylem. Tracheids are long, tapering hollow cells. Water passes from one tracheid to another through thin regions in the wall called **pits**. Vessel elements have pits, but the end walls are also perforated and water flows unimpeded through the stacked elements.

Mature xylem is dead

Mature xylem is dead. Its primary function is to conduct water from the roots to the leaves. This is a passive process, so there is no need for plasma membranes or transport proteins. Xylem that no longer transports water accumulates compounds such as gum and resin and is known as heartwood. In this form it is an important structural part of a mature tree.

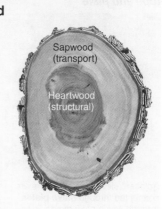

Sapwood (transport)

Heartwood (structural)

1. (a) What is the function of **xylem**? _____

_____

(b) How can xylem be dead when mature and still carry out its function? _____

_____

2. Identify four main cell types in xylem and explain their role in the tissue:

(a) _____

(b) _____

(c) _____

(d) _____

3. Draw the structure of primary xylem from the larger image of a stem section above. Staple it to this page:

© 2015 **BIOZONE** International
ISBN: 978-1-927309-25-4
Photocopying Prohibited

LINK 210 WEB 208 **KNOW**

209 Phloem

Key Idea: Phloem is the principal food (sugar) conducting tissue in vascular plants, transporting dissolved sugars around the plant.

Like xylem, **phloem** is a complex tissue, comprising a variable number of cell types. The bulk of phloem tissue comprises the **sieve tubes** (sieve tube members and sieve cells) and their companion cells. The sieve tubes are the principal conducting cells in phloem and are closely associated with the **companion cells** (modified parenchyma cells) with which they share a mutually dependent relationship. Other parenchyma cells, concerned with storage, occur in phloem, and strengthening fibres and sclereids (short sclerenchyma cells) may also be present. Unlike xylem, phloem is alive when mature.

LS through a sieve tube end plate

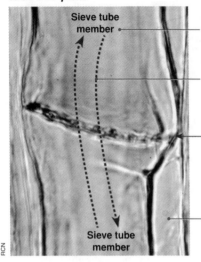

The sieve tube members lose most of their organelles but are still alive when mature

Sugar solution flows in both directions

Sieve tube end plate
Tiny holes (arrowed in the photograph below) perforate the sieve tube elements allowing the sugar solution to pass through.

Companion cell: a cell adjacent to the sieve tube member, responsible for keeping it alive

TS through a sieve tube end plate

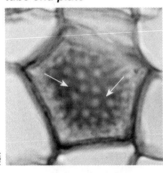

Adjacent sieve tube members are connected through **sieve plates** through which phloem sap flows.

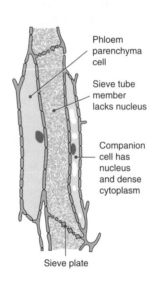

Phloem parenchyma cell

Sieve tube member lacks nucleus

Companion cell has nucleus and dense cytoplasm

Sieve plate

The structure of phloem tissue

Phloem is alive at maturity and functions in the transport of sugars and minerals around the plant. Like xylem, it forms part of the structural vascular tissue of plants.

Fibres are associated with phloem as they are in xylem. Here they are seen in cross section where you can see the extremely thick cell walls and the way the fibres are clustered in groups. See the previous page for a view of fibres in longitudinal section.

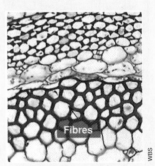

Fibres

In this cross section through a buttercup root, the smaller companion cells can be seen lying alongside the sieve tube members. It is the sieve tube members that, end on end, produce the **sieve tubes**. They are the conducting tissue of phloem.

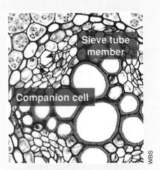

Sieve tube member

Companion cell

In this longitudinal section of a buttercup root, each sieve tube member has a thin **companion cell** associated with it. Companion cells retain their nucleus and control the metabolism of the sieve tube member next to them. They also have a role in the loading and unloading of sugar into the phloem.

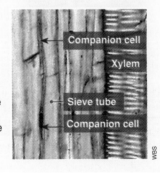

Companion cell

Xylem

Sieve tube

Companion cell

1. Describe the function of **phloem**: _____

_____

2. Mature phloem is a live tissue, whereas xylem (the water transporting tissue) is dead when mature. Why is it necessary for phloem to be alive to be functional, whereas xylem can function as a dead tissue?

_____

_____

_____

3. Describe two roles of the companion cell in phloem: _____

_____

_____

KNOW

WEB
209

LINK
210

© 2015 **BIOZONE** International
ISBN:978-1-927309-25-4
Photocopying Prohibited

210 Identifying Xylem and Phloem

Key Idea: The vascular tissue in dicots can be identified by its appearance in sections viewed with a light microscope. The structure of the vascular tissue in dicotyledons (dicots) has a very regular arrangement with the xylem and phloem found close together. In the stem, the vascular tissue is distributed in a regular fashion near the outer edge of the stem. In the roots, the vascular tissue is found near the centre of the root.

Dicot stem structure

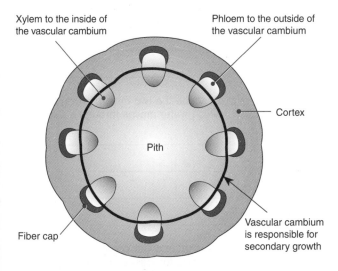

Xylem to the inside of the vascular cambium

Phloem to the outside of the vascular cambium

Cortex

Pith

Fiber cap

Vascular cambium is responsible for secondary growth

Dicot root structure

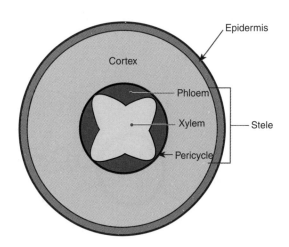

Epidermis

Cortex

Phloem

Xylem

Stele

Pericycle

In dicots, the vascular bundles (xylem and phloem) are arranged in an orderly fashion around the stem. Each vascular bundle contains **xylem** (to the inside) and **phloem** (to the outside). Between the phloem and the xylem is the **vascular cambium**. This is a layer of cells that divide to produce the thickening of the stem.

In a dicot root, the vascular tissue, (xylem and phloem) forms a central cylinder through the root called the stele. The large cortex is made up of parenchyma (packing) cells, which store starch and other substances. Air spaces between the cells are essential for aeration of the root tissue, which is non-photosynthetic.

1. In the micrograph below of a dicot stem identify the phloem (P) and xylem (X) tissue:

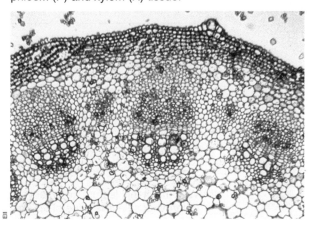

2. In the micrograph below of a dicot root identify the phloem (P) and xylem (X) tissue:

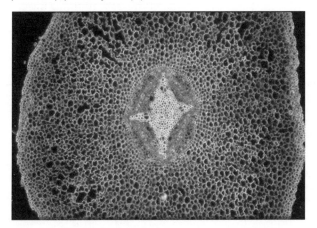

3. In the diagram below identify the labels A - F

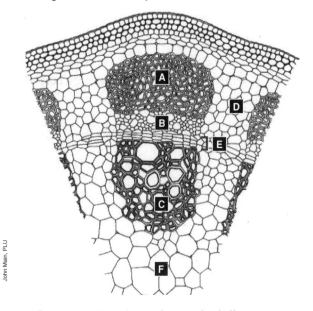

John Main, PLU

Cross section through a typical dicot stem

A. _____

B. _____

C. _____

D. _____

E. _____

F. _____

211 Uptake at the Root

Key Idea: Water uptake by the root is a passive process. Mineral uptake can be passive or active.

Plants need to take up water and minerals constantly. They must compensate for the continuous loss of water from the leaves and provide the materials the plant needs to make food. The uptake of water and minerals is mostly restricted to the younger, most recently formed cells of the roots and the root hairs. Water uptake occurs by osmosis, whereas mineral ions enter the root by diffusion and active transport. Pathways for water movements through the plant are outlined below.

Water and mineral uptake by roots

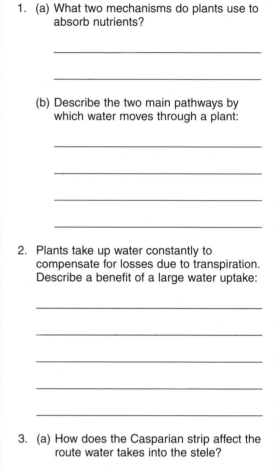

Root hairs have a thin cuticle, so water enters the root easily

Cortex cells of root

Epidermal cell

Xylem

Stele (vascular cylinder). The outer layer of the stele, the pericycle, is next to the endodermis.

Root hair

Water moves by osmosis

Schematic cross-section through a dicot root

The endodermis is the central, innermost layer of the cortex. It is a single layer of cells with a waterproof band of suberin, called the **Casparian strip**, which encircles each cell.

Root hairs are extensions of the root epidermal cells and provide a large surface area for absorbing water and nutrients.

Paths for water movement through the plant

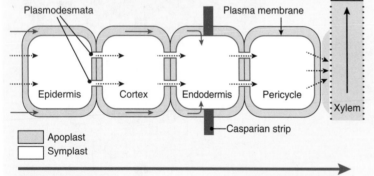

Plasmodesmata

Plasma membrane

Epidermis   Cortex   Endodermis   Pericycle

Xylem

Casparian strip

☐ Apoplast
☐ Symplast

Higher water potential
May be due to fully turgid cells, higher wall pressure, or lower concentration of dissolved substances

Lower water potential
May be due to less turgid cells, lower wall pressure, or higher concentration of dissolved substances

The uptake of water through the roots occurs by osmosis, i.e. the diffusion of water from a higher (less negative) to a lower (more negative) water potential. Most water travels through the **apoplast**, i.e. the spaces within the cellulose cell walls, the water-filled spaces of dead cells, and the hollow tubes of xylem vessels. A smaller amount moves through the **symplast** (the cytoplasm of cells). A very small amount travels through the plant vacuoles.

Some dissolved mineral ions enter the root passively with water. Minerals that are in very low concentration in the soil are taken up by active transport. At the waterproof Casparian strip, water and dissolved minerals must pass into the symplast, so the flow of materials into the stele can be regulated.

1. (a) What two mechanisms do plants use to absorb nutrients?

_____

_____

(b) Describe the two main pathways by which water moves through a plant:

_____

_____

_____

_____

2. Plants take up water constantly to compensate for losses due to transpiration. Describe a benefit of a large water uptake:

_____

_____

_____

_____

_____

3. (a) How does the Casparian strip affect the route water takes into the stele?

_____

_____

_____

_____

(b) Why might this feature be an advantage in terms of selective mineral uptake?

_____

_____

_____

_____

_____

_____

_____

_____

_____

_____

_____

212 Transpiration

Key Idea: Water moves through the xylem primarily as a result of evaporation from the leaves and the cohesive and adhesive properties of water molecules.

Plants lose water all the time through their stomata as a consequence of gas exchange. Approximately 99% of the water a plant absorbs from the soil is lost by evaporation from the leaves and stem. This loss is called **transpiration** and the flow of water through the plant is called the **transpiration**

stream. Plants rely on a gradient in water potential (ψ) from the roots to the air to move water through their cells. Water flows passively from soil to air along a gradient of decreasing water potential. The gradient is the driving force for the movement of water up a plant. Transpiration has benefits to the plant because evaporative water loss is cooling and the transpiration stream helps the plant to take up minerals. Factors contributing to water movement are described below.

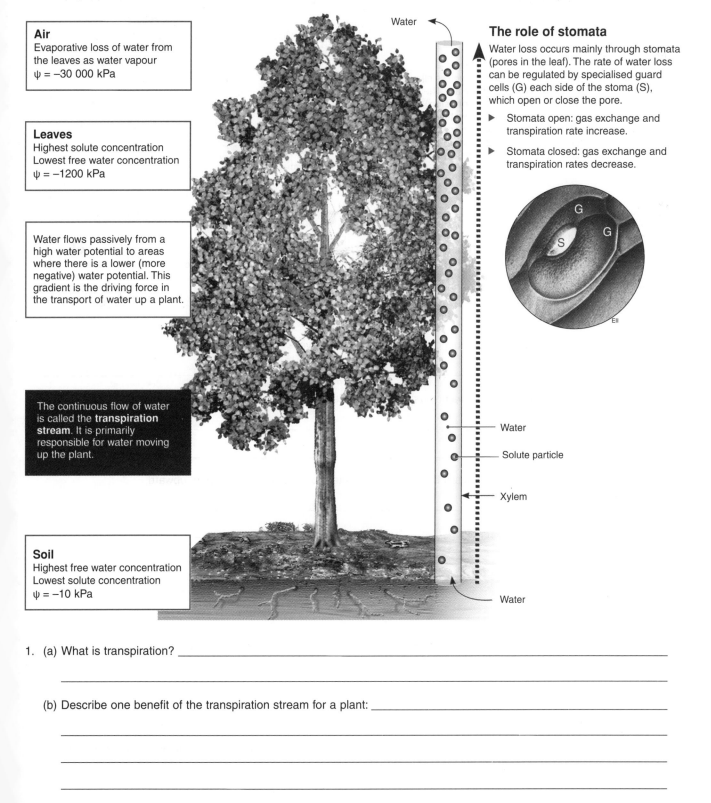

Air
Evaporative loss of water from the leaves as water vapour
ψ = −30 000 kPa

Leaves
Highest solute concentration
Lowest free water concentration
ψ = −1200 kPa

Water flows passively from a high water potential to areas where there is a lower (more negative) water potential. This gradient is the driving force in the transport of water up a plant.

The continuous flow of water is called the **transpiration stream**. It is primarily responsible for water moving up the plant.

Soil
Highest free water concentration
Lowest solute concentration
ψ = −10 kPa

The role of stomata
Water loss occurs mainly through stomata (pores in the leaf). The rate of water loss can be regulated by specialised guard cells (G) each side of the stoma (S), which open or close the pore.

▶ Stomata open: gas exchange and transpiration rate increase.

▶ Stomata closed: gas exchange and transpiration rates decrease.

Water
Solute particle
Xylem
Water
Water

1. (a) What is transpiration? _____

(b) Describe one benefit of the transpiration stream for a plant: _____

2. Why is transpiration an inevitable consequence of gas exchange? _____

LINK 213 WEB 212 **KNOW**

Processes involved in moving water through the xylem

1 **Transpiration pull**
Water is lost from the air spaces by evaporation through stomata and is replaced by water from the mesophyll cells. The constant loss of water to the air (and production of sugars) creates a lower (more negative) water potential in the leaves than in the cells further from the evaporation site. Water is pulled through the plant down a **decreasing gradient in water potential**.

2 **Cohesion-tension**
The transpiration pull is assisted by the special **cohesive** properties of water. Water molecules cling together as they are pulled through the plant. They also **adhere** to the walls of the xylem (**adhesion**). This creates one **unbroken column of water** through the plant. The upward pull on the cohesive sap creates a tension (a negative pressure). This helps water uptake and movement up the plant.

3 **Root pressure**
Water entering the stele from the soil creates a **root pressure**; a weak 'push' effect for the water's upward movement through the plant. Root pressure can force water droplets from some small plants under certain conditions (**guttation**), but generally it plays a minor part in the ascent of water.

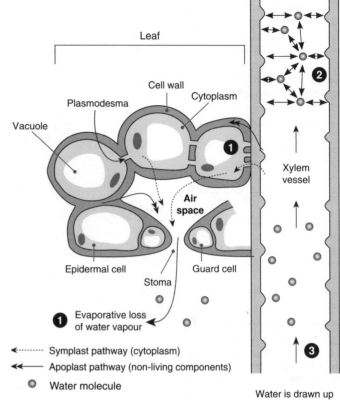

Leaf

Cell wall
Cytoplasm
Plasmodesma
Vacuole
Xylem vessel
Air space
Epidermal cell
Guard cell
Stoma

1 Evaporative loss of water vapour

- - - - - ◄ Symplast pathway (cytoplasm)
◄◄ Apoplast pathway (non-living components)
◎ Water molecule

Water is drawn up the plant xylem

3. How does the plant regulate the amount of water lost from the leaves? _____
_____

4. (a) What would happen if too much water was lost from the leaves? _____
_____

(b) When might this happen? _____

5. Describe the three processes that assist the transport of water from the roots of the plant upward:

(a) _____
_____
_____

(b) _____
_____
_____

(c) _____
_____
_____

6. The maximum height water can move up the xylem by cohesion-tension alone is about 10 m. How then does water move up the height of a 40 m tall tree?

_____
_____
_____

© 2015 **BIOZONE** International
ISBN: 978-1-927309-25-4
Photocopying Prohibited

213 Investigating Plant Transpiration

Key Idea: The relationship between the rate of transpiration and the environment can be investigated using a potometer. This activity describes a typical experiment to investigate the effect of different environmental conditions on transpiration rate using a potometer. You will present and analyse the results provided.

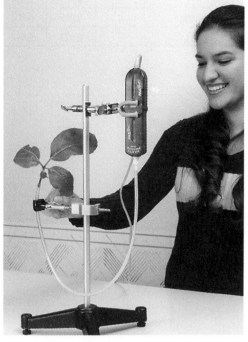

The potometer

A potometer is a simple instrument for investigating transpiration rate (water loss per unit time). The equipment is simple to use and easy to obtain. A basic potometer, such as the one shown right, can easily be moved around so that transpiration rate can be measured under different environmental conditions.

Some physical conditions investigated are:

- Humidity or vapour pressure (high or low)
- Temperature (high or low)
- Air movement (still or windy)
- Light level (high or low)
- Water supply

It is also possible to compare the transpiration rates of plants with different adaptations e.g. comparing transpiration rates in plants with rolled leaves vs rates in plants with broad leaves. If possible, experiments like these should be conducted simultaneously using replicate equipment. If conducted sequentially, care should be taken to keep the environmental conditions the same for all plants used.

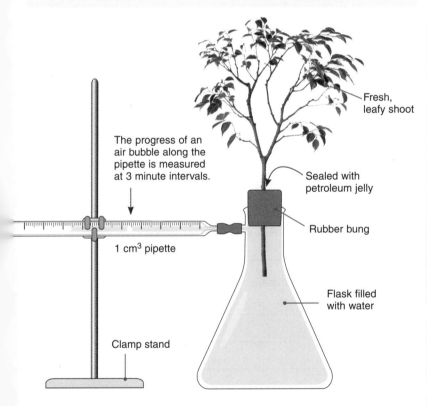

The progress of an air bubble along the pipette is measured at 3 minute intervals.

Fresh, leafy shoot

Sealed with petroleum jelly

Rubber bung

1 cm³ pipette

Flask filled with water

Clamp stand

The aim

To investigate the effect of environmental conditions on the transpiration rate of plants.

Background

Plants lose water all the time by evaporation from the leaves and stem. This loss, mostly through pores in the leaf surfaces, is called **transpiration**. Despite the adaptations of plants to reduce water loss (e.g. waxy leaf cuticle), 99% of the water a plant absorbs from the soil is lost by evaporation. Environmental conditions affect transpiration rate by increasing or decreasing the gradient for diffusion of water molecules between the plant and its external environment.

Hypothesis

All the plants will lose water, but the greatest losses will be in hot or windy conditions.

The apparatus

This experiment investigated the influence of environmental conditions on plant transpiration rate. The experiment examined four conditions: room conditions (ambient), wind, bright light, and high humidity. After setting up the potometer, the apparatus was equilibrated for 10 minutes, and then the position of the air bubble in the pipette was recorded. This is the time 0 reading. The plant was then exposed to one of the environmental conditions. Students recorded the location of the air bubble every three minutes over a 30 minute period. The potometer readings for each environmental condition are presented in Table 1 (next page).

A class was divided into four groups to study how four different environmental conditions (ambient, wind, bright light, and high humidity) affected transpiration rate. A **potometer** was used to measure transpiration rate (water loss per unit time). A basic potometer, such as the one shown left, can easily be moved around so that transpiration rate can be measured under different environmental conditions.

Table 1. Potometer readings in cm³ water loss

Treatment \ Time / min	0	3	6	9	12	15	18	21	24	27	30
Ambient	0	0.002	0.005	0.008	0.012	0.017	0.022	0.028	0.032	0.036	0.042
Wind	0	0.025	0.054	0.088	0.112	0.142	0.175	0.208	0.246	0.283	0.325
High humidity	0	0.002	0.004	0.006	0.008	0.011	0.014	0.018	0.019	0.021	0.024
Bright light	0	0.021	0.042	0.070	0.091	0.112	0.141	0.158	0.183	0.218	0.239

1. (a) Plot the potometer data from Table 1 on the grid provided:

   (b) Identify the independent variable: _____

2. (a) Identify the control: _____

   (b) Explain the purpose of including an experimental control in an experiment: _____

   _____

   _____

   (c) Which factors increased water loss? _____

   (d) How does each environmental factor influence water loss? _____

   _____

   _____

   (e) Explain why the plant lost less water in humid conditions: _____

   _____

   _____

© 2015 **BIOZONE** International
ISBN: 978-1-927309-25-4
Photocopying Prohibited

214 Translocation

Key Idea: Phloem transports the organic products of photosynthesis (sugars) through the plant in an active, energy-requiring process called translocation.

In angiosperms, the sugar moves through the sieve-tube members, which are arranged end-to-end and perforated with sieve plates. Apart from water, phloem sap comprises mainly sucrose. It may also contain minerals, hormones, and amino acids, in transit around the plant. Movement of sap in the phloem is from a **source** (a plant organ where sugar is made or mobilised) to a **sink** (a plant organ where sugar is stored or used). Loading sucrose into the phloem at a source involves energy expenditure; it is slowed or stopped by high temperatures or respiratory inhibitors. In some plants, unloading the sucrose at the sinks also requires energy, although in others, diffusion alone is sufficient to move sucrose from the phloem into the cells of the sink organ.

Phloem transport

Phloem sap moves from source to sink at rates as great as 100 m h^{-1}, which is too fast to be accounted for by cytoplasmic streaming. The most acceptable model for phloem movement is the **mass flow hypothesis** (also know as the pressure flow hypothesis). Phloem sap moves by bulk flow, which creates a pressure (hence the term "pressure-flow"). The key elements in this model are outlined below and right. For simplicity, the cells that lie between the source (and sink) cells and the phloem sieve-tube have been omitted.

❶ Loading sugar into the phloem from a source (e.g. leaf cell) increases the solute concentration (decreases the water potential, ψ) inside the sieve-tube cells. This causes the sieve-tubes to take up water from the surrounding tissues by osmosis.

❷ The water uptake creates a hydrostatic pressure that forces the sap to move along the tube, just as pressure pushes water through a hose.

❸ The pressure gradient in the sieve tube is reinforced by the active unloading of sugar and consequent loss of water by osmosis at the sink (e.g. root cell).

❹ Xylem recycles the water from sink to source.

Measuring phloem flow
Aphids can act as natural phloem probes to measure phloem flow. The sucking mouthparts (stylet) of the insect penetrates the phloem sieve-tube cell. While the aphid feeds, it can be severed from its stylet, which remains in place and continues to exude sap. Using different aphids, the rate of flow of this sap can be measured at different locations on the plant.

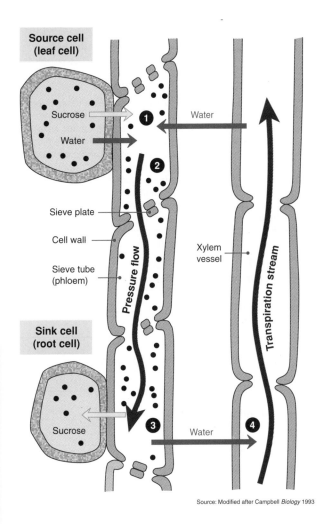

Source: Modified after Campbell *Biology* 1993

1. (a) From what you know about osmosis, explain why water follows the sugar as it moves through the phloem:

_____

_____

_____

_____

(b) What is meant by '**source to sink**' flow in phloem transport?_____

_____

_____

2. Why does a plant need to move food around, particularly from the leaves to other regions? _____

_____

_____

LINK WEB
172 214 **KNOW**

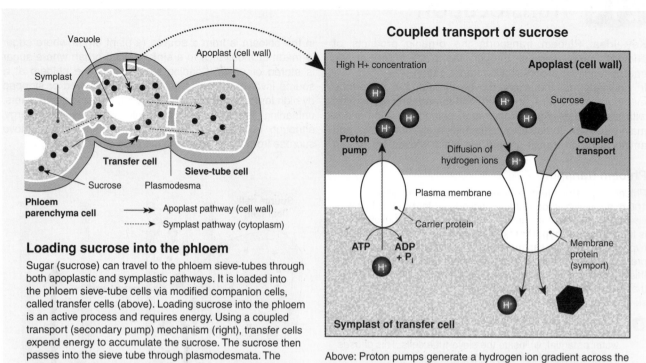

Loading sucrose into the phloem

Sugar (sucrose) can travel to the phloem sieve-tubes through both apoplastic and symplastic pathways. It is loaded into the phloem sieve-tube cells via modified companion cells, called transfer cells (above). Loading sucrose into the phloem is an active process and requires energy. Using a coupled transport (secondary pump) mechanism (right), transfer cells expend energy to accumulate the sucrose. The sucrose then passes into the sieve tube through plasmodesmata. The transfer cells have wall ingrowths that increase surface area for the transport of solutes. Using this mechanism, some plants can accumulate sucrose in the phloem to 2-3 times the concentration in the mesophyll.

Above: Proton pumps generate a hydrogen ion gradient across the membrane of the transfer cell. This process requires expenditure of energy. The gradient is then used to drive the transport of sucrose, by coupling the sucrose transport to the diffusion of hydrogen ions back into the cell.

3. In your own words, describe what is meant by the following:

(a) Translocation: _____

_____

(b) Pressure-flow movement of phloem: _____

_____

(c) Coupled transport of sucrose: _____

_____

4. Briefly explain how sucrose is transported into the phloem: _____

_____

_____

5. Explain the role of the companion (transfer) cell in the loading of sucrose into the phloem: _____

_____

_____

_____

6. (a) What does the flow of phloem sap from a severed aphid stylet indicate?_____

_____

(b) Where would you expect the flow rate to be greatest and why? _____

_____

(c) Why do you think aphid stylets are particularly useful for studying the rate of flow in phloem? _____

_____

_____

215 Experimental Evidence for Plant Transport

Key Idea: The mass flow hypothesis is supported by experiments involving ringing and autoradiographs.
The transport of materials including sugars through the phloem has been established by a number of experiments which include using radioactively labelled atoms and severing the phloem tissue by ring barking a plant.

Ringing

A classic experiment in studying the flow of phloem sap is the removal of a ring of bark from the plant along with the underlying phloem. The experiment is described below:

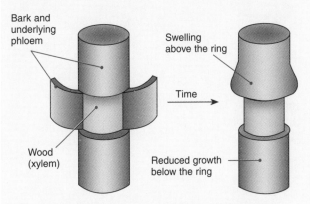

Bark and underlying phloem

Swelling above the ring

Time

Wood (xylem)

Reduced growth below the ring

Sap (from the phloem) oozes out of the wound above the ring showing the phloem is under pressure. Growth continues above the ring but is impeded below it, and leaves are unaffected, showing phloem originates in the leaves and moves down the plant.

Tracers

The radioactive carbon isotope ^{14}C has been used to investigate the site of sugar manufacture and transport. ^{14}C labelled CO_2 was supplied to one leaf of a plant for 20 minutes (left box). The plant was then used to make an autoradiograph on X-ray film and the location of ^{14}C noted (right box).

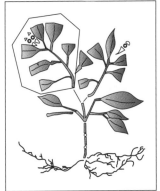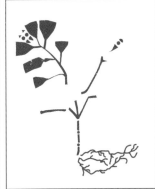

The autoradiograph shows evidence for translocation. Sugars are manufactured in the leaves and transported throughout the plant, including the stem roots, and fruit.

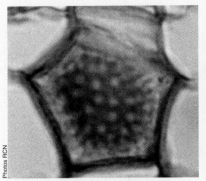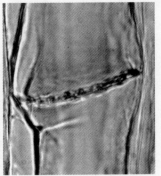

Photos RCN

Phloem sieve plate in TS and LS. The sieve plate is an apparent barrier to mass flow.

Mass flow hypothesis doesn't explain everything

Flow of material through the phloem appears to be bidirectional, and sugars and amino acids move at different rates (mass flow cannot account for the transport of substances in different directions or at different rates). In addition, sieve plates in the phloem represent a barrier (a mechanical resistance) to flow, yet they have not been lost during plant evolution.

1. What does the ringing experiment show about the phloem and the material in it? _____

_____

_____

2. What does the autoradiograph show about the movement of sugars? _____

_____

_____

3. Why does the apparent bi-directional flow in the phloem provide a case against the mass flow hypothesis?

_____

_____

4. Suggest why the presence of the sieve plate is often cited as evidence against the mass flow hypothesis:

_____

_____

LINK
214 WEB
215 KNOW

216 Chapter Review

Summarise what you know about this topic under the headings provided. You can draw diagrams or mind maps, or write short notes. Use the images and hints to help you and refer back to the introduction to check the points covered:

Cell transport mechanisms
HINT: Explain passive and active transport.

Surface area: volume
HINT: The SA: V ratio in relation to cell size.

Gas exchange
HINT: Adaptations for gas exchange in mammals, fish and insects.

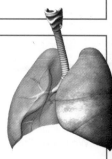

REVISE

Circulation
HINT: Structure of blood vessels and double circulatory system. Heart structure and function. The structure and roles of blood.

Transfer of material between the blood and cells
HINT: Explain how respiratory gases are transported in the blood and the role of haemoglobin.

Transfer of material between the blood and cells
HINT: The formation and role of tissue fluid..

Transport in plants
HINT: Transport tissues in plants and the mechanisms of water and solute transport..

217 KEY TERMS: Did You Get It?

1. (a) What type of blood vessel transports blood away from the heart? _____

   (b) What type of blood vessel transports blood to the heart? _____

   (c) What type of blood vessel enables exchanges between the blood and tissues? _____

2. (a) What is the name given to the contraction phase of the cardiac cycle? _____

   (b) What is the name given to the relaxation phase of the cardiac cycle? _____

3. (a) What does the image (right) show: _____

   (b) Circle the QRS complex.

   (c) Circle the region corresponding to lowest ventricular pressure.

   (d) Ventricular volume at this time is increasing/decreasing (delete one)

4. (a) What is the name given to the loss of water vapour from plant leaves and stems? _____

   (b) What plant tissue is involved in this process? _____

   (c) Is this tissue alive or dead? _____

   (d) Does this process require energy? _____

5. (a) What does the image (right) show: _____

   (b) In what tissue would you find it? _____

   (c) Is this tissue alive or dead? _____

   (d) What transport process is it associated with? _____

   (e) What is being moved in this process? _____

RCN

6. Test your vocabulary by matching each term to its definition, as identified by its preceding letter code.

alveoli	A	A sigmoidal curve describing the oxygen-binding behaviour of haemoglobin at different oxygen tensions.
countercurrent exchange	B	A substance carried in blood that is able to bind oxygen for transport to cells. Examples include haemoglobin and haemocyanin.
gas exchange	C	The exterior opening of the tracheae in arthropods.
gills	D	Pores in the epidermis of a leaf through which gases enter and leave the leaf tissue
haemoglobin	E	The exchange of oxygen and carbon dioxide across the respiratory membrane.
lungs	F	The respiratory organs of most aquatic animals (although not aquatic mammals).
oxyhaemoglobin dissociation curve	G	Any gas that takes part in the respiratory process (usually just oxygen or carbon dioxide).
respiratory gas	H	The complex system in insects and some other arthropods comprising tubes that open to the outside and extend through the body to deliver oxygen directly to the tissues.
respiratory pigment	I	A term describing exchanges between gases in fluids and/or air in which the fluids flow in opposite directions so that diffusion gradients are maintained between the two media.
spiracles	J	Internal gas exchange structures found in air breathing vertebrates.
stomata	K	The act of moving air or water across the gas exchange surface.
tracheal system	L	Microscopic structures in the lungs of air-breathing vertebrates that form the terminus of the bronchioles. The site of gas exchange.
ventilation	M	A large iron-containing protein that transports oxygen in the blood of vertebrates.

© 2015 **BIOZONE** International
ISBN: 978-1-927309-25-4
Photocopying Prohibited

TEST

Command Terms

Questions come in a variety of forms. Whether you are studying for an exam or writing an essay, it is important to understand exactly what the question is asking. A question has two parts to it: one part of the question will provide you with information, the second part of the question will provide you with instructions as to how to answer the question. Following these instructions is most important. Often students in examinations know the material but fail to follow instructions and do not answer the question appropriately. Examiners often use certain key words to introduce questions. Look out for them and be clear as to what they mean. Below is a description of terms commonly used when asking questions in biology.

Commonly used terms in biology

The following terms are frequently used when asking questions in examinations and assessments. Students should have a clear understanding of each of the following terms and use this understanding to answer questions appropriately.

Account for: Provide a satisfactory explanation or reason for an observation.

Analyse: Interpret data to reach stated conclusions.

Annotate: Add **brief** notes to a diagram, drawing or graph.

Apply: Use an idea, equation, principle, theory, or law in a new situation.

Appreciate: To understand the meaning or relevance of a particular situation.

Calculate: Find an answer using mathematical methods. Show the working unless instructed not to.

Compare: Give an account of similarities and differences between two or more items, referring to both (or all) of them throughout. Comparisons can be given using a table. Comparisons generally ask for similarities more than differences (see contrast).

Construct: Represent or develop in graphical form.

Contrast: Show differences. Set in opposition.

Deduce: Reach a conclusion from information given.

Define: Give the precise meaning of a word or phrase as concisely as possible.

Derive: Manipulate a mathematical equation to give a new equation or result.

Describe: Give a detailed account, including all the relevant information.

Design: Produce a plan, object, simulation or model.

Determine: Find the only possible answer.

Discuss: Give an account including, where possible, a range of arguments, assessments of the relative importance of various factors, or comparison of alternative hypotheses.

Distinguish: Give the difference(s) between two or more different items.

Draw: Represent by means of pencil lines. Add labels unless told not to do so.

Estimate: Find an approximate value for an unknown quantity, based on the information provided and application of scientific knowledge.

Evaluate: Assess the implications and limitations.

Explain: Give a clear account including causes, reasons, or mechanisms.

Identify: Find an answer from a number of possibilities.

Illustrate: Give concrete examples. Explain clearly by using comparisons or examples.

Interpret: Comment upon, give examples, describe relationships. Describe, then evaluate.

List: Give a sequence of names or other brief answers with no elaboration. Each one should be clearly distinguishable from the others.

Measure: Find a value for a quantity.

Outline: Give a brief account or summary. Include essential information only.

Predict: Give an expected result.

Solve: Obtain an answer using algebraic and/or numerical methods.

State: Give a specific name, value, or other answer. No supporting argument or calculation is necessary.

Suggest: Propose a hypothesis or other possible explanation.

Summarise: Give a brief, condensed account. Include conclusions and avoid unnecessary details.

In conclusion

Students should familiarise themselves with this list of terms and, where necessary throughout the course, they should refer back to them when answering questions. The list of terms mentioned above is not exhaustive and students should compare this list with past examination papers / essays etc. and add any new terms (and their meaning) to the list above. The aim is to become familiar with interpreting the question and answering it appropriately.

Image credits

The writing team would like to thank the following people and organisations who have kindly provided photographs or illustrations for this edition:

• PASCO for their photographs of probeware • Kristian Peters for the image of the chloroplasts in leaves • Wadsworth Centre (NYSDH) for the photo of the cell undergoing cytokinesis • Waikato Hospital for the images of the karyographs • Liam Nolan for his photographic and text contributions to the activity on the genetic biodiversity of Antarctic springtails • Leo Sanchez for the photo of the Taylor Valley. • UC Berkeley Electron Microscope Lab for the image of *Methanococcus jannaschii* • Aptychus, Flickr for use of the photograph of the Tamil girl • Rita Willaert, Flickr, for the photograph of the Nuba woman • The late Stephen Moore for his photos of aquatic invertebrates • Dept. of Natural Resources, Illinois, for the photograph of the threatened prairie chicken • Kimberley Mallady for the hedgerow • D. Eason (DOC) for the photo of the takahe chick • Louisa Howard and Chuck Daghlian, Dartmouth College for the freeze fracture image of the cell membrane • Dan Butler for the photo of the cut finger • PEIR Digital Library for the cross sectional photos of arteries • John Main for the cross section through the dicot stem • Princeton University, Office of Communications, Denise Applewhite for the press photograph of Peter and Rosemary Grant •

We also acknowledge the photographers who have made images available through **Wikimedia Commons** under Creative Commons Licences 2.0, 2.5, 3.0, or 4.0: • FontanaCG • Rufino Uribe • J. Miquel, D. Vilavella, Z.widerski, V. V. Shimalov and J. Torres • Professor Dr. habil. Uwe Kils • Dr Graham Beards • Jeffery M. Vinocur • CDC: Dr Lucille K. Georg • JPbarrass • Edwin S • Matthias Zepper • Ernie • Meyer A, PLoS Biology • Yathin S Krishnappa • Thomas Breuer • Ron Pastorino • Tony Wills • Laitche • JM Garg • Mbz1 • Bruce Marlin • Lorax • Onno Zweers • Aviceda • UtahCamera • Alan & Elaine Wilson • AKA • Dirk Bayer • Bruce on Flickr • C Johnson-Walker • Piet Spaans • Honza Beran • Keith Hulburt and Paul Zarucki • Micheal Apel • Simon Carey • Cymothoa exigua • Bjorn Schulz • M. Betley • Zephyris • Nephron • Hans Hillewaert • Gabriel Barathieu • USDA • Sbj1976 • The High Fin Sperm Whale • Dave Pape • Yathin S Krishnappa • Danielle Schwarz • Didier Descouens

Contributors identified by coded credits:

BF: Brian Finerran (University of Canterbury), **CDC**: Centers for Disease Control and Prevention, Atlanta, USA, **DC**: Dartmouth College **DH**: Don Horne, **EII**: Education Interactive Imaging, **GW**: Graham Walker, **JDG**: John Green (University of Waikato), **KP**: Kent Pryor, **MEI**: Maungatautari Ecological Island Trust **NASA**: National Aeronautics and Space Administration, **NIAID**: National Institute of Allergy and Infectious Diseases, **NIH**: National Institute of Health, **NOAA**: National Oceanic and Atmospheric Administration, **RA**: Richard Allan, **RCN**: Ralph Cocklin, **TG**: Tracey Greenwood, **WBS**: Warwick Silvester (University of Waikato), **WMU**: Waikato Microscope Unit.

Image libraries:

We also acknowledge our use of royalty-free images, purchased by BIOZONE International Ltd from the following sources: **Corel** Corporation from various titles in their Professional Photos CD-ROM collection; **Dollar Photo Club**, dollarphotoclub. com; **istock photos**, istockphoto.com; **IMSI** (International Microcomputer Software Inc.) images from IMSI's MasterClips® and MasterPhotosTM Collection, 1895 Francisco Blvd. East, San Rafael, CA 94901-5506, USA; ©1996 **Digital Stock**, Medicine and Health Care collection; ©**Hemera** Technologies Inc, 1997-2001; © 2005 JupiterImages Corporation www.clipart.com; ©1994., ©**Digital Vision**; Gazelle Technologies Inc.; ©1994-1996 **Education Interactive Imaging** (UK), **PhotoDisc®**, Inc. USA, www.photodisc.com. We also acknowledge the following clipart providers: TechPool Studios, for their clipart collection of human anatomy: Copyright ©1994, TechPool Studios Corp. USA (some of these images have been modified); Totem Graphics, for clipart; Corel Corporation, for vector art from the Corel MEGAGALLERY collection.

Index